HIPPOCRENE
AMERICA'S SOUTH

WITHDRAWN

Other Books by Tom Weil

A Clearing in the Jungle

A Balance of Power

Last at the Fair: A Book of Travel

America's Heartland: A Travel Guide to the Back Roads of Illinois, Indiana, Iowa and Missouri

America's South: A Travel Guide to the Eleven Southern States

The Cemetery Book: Graveyards, Catacombs and Other Travel Haunts Around the World

The Mississippi River: Nature, Culture and Travel Sites Along the "Mighty Mississip"

America's Heartland: A Travel Guide to the Back Roads of Illinois, Indiana, Iowa, Missouri and Kansas (2nd edition)

to

AMERICA'S SOUTH:

The Atlantic States

The States of Virginia, North Carolina,
South Carolina, Georgia and Florida

TOM WEIL

HIPPOCRENE BOOKS
New York

For Jan and Hedy Gout of Amsterdam, Josette d'Amely Melodia of Rome, and Heinz Mortl of Wiesbaden, with my thanks for friendship and hospitality over many years.

This guide is based on *America's South*, published in 1990 by Hippocrene Books. *America's South: The Atlantic States* covers the five coastal states and includes an extensive new chapter on the Civil War sites. A second volume, *America's South: The Gulf and Mississippi States* will also include a guide on Civil War sites.

Photos courtesy of the Virginia Division of Tourism, North Carolina Division of Travel and Tourism, South Carolina Department of Tourism, Charleston Convention and Travel Bureau, Georgia Department of Tourism, Florida Division of Tourism

For information, address:
Hippocrene Books, Inc.
171 Madison Ave.
New York, NY 10016

Library of Congress Cataloging-in-Publication Data
Weil, Tom.
   Hippocrene U.S.A guide to America's South : the states of
   Virginia, North Carolina, South Carolina Georgia, and
   Florida / Tom Weil.
     p. cm.
   Includes index.
   ISBN 0-7818-0139-7 :
   1. South Atlantic States--Guidebooks. I. Title.
  F207.3.W394 1993
  917.504'43--dc20   93-19741
                 CIP

Contents

Maps

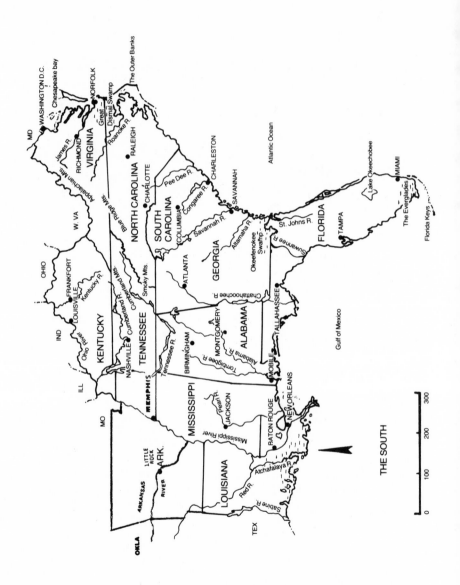

THE SOUTH

Introduction to First Edition

A Welcome to the Reader

This book is a guide to the eleven Southern states. Although *America's South* serves as a complete guide to the entire region, including the cities and the better-known places, the book emphasizes the area's back-road, off-the-beaten-track attractions—the pleasant villages, scenic rural areas, picturesque corners of the countryside, unusual historical enclaves and other such places that typify the small-town old-time South. Many of these sights are delightful; some of them the traveler will find unusual; while a few present a certain eccentricity that recalls the caution voiced by Robert Beverley in his 1705 *The History and Present State of Virginia*, the first comprehensive work on the South's leading state in the early days:

> 'Tis agreed that travelers are of all men the most suspected of insincerity. This does not only hold in their private conversations, but likewise in the grand tours and travels with which

they pester the public and break the bookseller. There are no books (the legends of the saints always excepted) so stuffed with poetical stories as voyages, and the more distant the countries lie which they pretend to describe, the greater the license those privileged authors take in imposing upon the world.

My reason for "imposing upon the world" and "pestering" the public—but, hopefully, not breaking the bookseller—with *America's South* arises from my belief that back-road roamings in the United States provide one of the most delightful travel experiences available anywhere. This book will guide you to the region's unusual and little-known areas, places filled with the flavor and feel of the South where you can gather your own collection of "poetical stories," as Beverley put it, about this historically rich and colorful region of America.

The book presents a series of itineraries. Although all arrangements of guidebooks are arbitrary—apart from the alphabetic, favored by some guides, which lacks all coherence except the purely mechanical—I have tried to devise routings with a certain geographic logic to them, itineraries that make sense and which are convenient to follow. Of course, rarely, if ever, does the traveler follow on the road a path identical to the one on the printed page. So as you wander off the suggested routes, both the index and the section headings will help you locate material on the places you visit. Those headings provide a general idea of the cities included, but the text also contains many other attractions located between those cities not listed at the beginning of each section. Areas such as the Natchez Trace, Cumberland Gap, the Great Dismal Swamp and others that spread across more than one state are usually covered in the chapters on each state whose territory they occupy.

Although it's impossible to include every worthwhile attraction in a region as vast as the South, and equally impossible to know the interests of any particular reader, I've tried to mention at least in passing virtually all of the places that "the unbiased traveler seeking information," as Mark Twain described the ideal tourist, might enjoy. This diverse and comprehensive compilation of sights includes a complete range of subjects so that readers or roamers who favor culture, history, the arts, the outdoors, scenery, food, wineries, recreation, museums, factory tours, festivals, water sports, ethnic enclaves and any number of other interests will find those topics covered.

America's South, however, features those back-road, out-of-the-way and lesser-known attractions—often so difficult to ferret out—that afford unexpected delights and unusual experiences. The text attempts to steer travelers to corners of the South which, in my view, the visitor will find especially colorful, interesting, historic or otherwise rewarding, and I have devoted relatively more space to those less obvious but no less alluring places. Even the city sections usually include some of the offbeat attractions. My presumption, and hope, is that the independent and resourceful traveler will, once introduced to a particular place, by inquiry and exploration find there additional attractions too numerous to list in the text. Whole books could be and have been written about any one of the sights included in *America's South.* So please realize that once you arrive at a certain place, it most likely offers attractions in addition to those mentioned in the text. On the theory that any traveler interested in back-road off-the-beaten-track attractions savors in his soul a certain sense of adventure, I've included bed and breakfast establishments, places that lack the predictability of the chain motels but which offer the delights of individualized and personalized accommodations. Also mentioned are inns and hotels of historic interest or which boast an especially attractive setting or ambiance, as well as restaurants that serve typical regional food or, like the hotels, offer interesting or historic features.

The narrative also includes unusual or typical festivals, fairs and similar such celebrations. These are mentioned not only so the traveler might attend such festive events but also to indicate what a community finds worth commemorating, a facet of a locality that suggests the area's flavor. This conforms with my intention to present to the reader not only the South's attractions but also its ambiance. With a view to that end, I have laced the narrative with a scattering of anecdotes, quotations, historical references, minibiographies of colorful characters and other such vignettes that suggest something of the South's flavor, culture and background. This added dimension hopefully makes *America's South* suitable not only for the sightseer but also for the armchair traveler who wants to read about the region.

Frequent references in the text to sights listed on the National Register of Historic Places (referred to in the book as the National Register) arise because Register listing, although not infallible, seems to me to indicate the probable merit of an attraction. Criteria for Register designation include "significance in American history, architecture, archaeology, engineering, and culture" of places

> that possess integrity of location, design, setting, materials, workmanship, feeling, association, and: A. are associated with events that have made a significant contribution to the broad patterns of our history; or B. are associated with the lives of significant persons in our past; or C. embody the distinctive characteristics of a type, period, or method of construction; represent the work of a master; possess high artistic values; or represent a significant and distinguishable entity whose components may lack individual distinction; or D. have yielded, or may be likely to yield, information important in prehistory or history.

The inclusion of Historic Register references and brief historical comments, it is hoped, will enrich the travel experience by integrating place and time: the text puts into the context of the past the sight you see. As for the past, many places in the South boast that they are the "oldest" or "first" of their kind and I have recorded such claims even though localities elsewhere in the region may put forth the same boast of antiquity or longevity, a competition I leave to the different claimants to sort out.

America's South is a companion volume to *America's Heartland,* a guide to and evocation of the Middle West, also published by Hippocrene. In the course of my travels to collect material for these two books, which cover nearly one third of the states, both the remarkable openness of the American people and the fascinating variety offered by the United States have greatly impressed me. Those who complain that the country has become standardized and homogeneous need only leave the interstates and the airports to roam the inner states and back roads, where travelers will find an extraordinary mix of cultures, ethnic groups, religions, societies, customs, attitudes, sights and traditions as interesting as anywhere in the world.

For me, and I hope for you as well, there is something alluring about starting not only a trip but also a travel book. Anticipation sharpens the senses and whets one's appetite for the world that lies before us, either on the road or on the printed page. In 1857 Sir Richard Burton, the greatest traveler of modern times, wrote:

> The gladdest moment in human life methinks is the departure on a distant journey. Shaking off with one mighty effort the fetters of habit, the leaden weight of routine, the cloak of many cares, the slavery of home, man feels once more happy. The blood flows with the fast circulation of childhood. Excitement lends unwonted freedom to the muscle, and the sudden sense

of freedom adds a cubit to the mental stature. . . . A journey, in fact, appeals to the imagination, to memory, to hope—the sister Graces of our mortal being.

So I welcome you to *America's South*—both the book and the region—with the wish that your hopes, memory and imagination will all be filled and fulfilled by that historic, colorful and often eccentric corner of the country.

Travel in America's South

The American South has always exerted a fascination for outsiders as well as Southerners. From the very earliest days of the continent's exploration, the region attracted travelers. The first extended expedition through the North American interior included much of the South when Hernando de Soto and his six hundred soldiers trekked across an area comprising some three hundred and fifty thousand square miles starting in western Florida, where the adventurers landed in October 1539. From there the Spaniards proceeded to the Blue Ridge Mountains, then southwest across Alabama to the Mobile Bay area, on to Mississippi and over to Arkansas. So began organized tours through the South. Soon additional groups—not quite yet on a Cook's Tour or an American Express jaunt—traveled from Europe to visit the region, and before long the French, the Spanish and the English each established in the South their first North American colonies. From 1861 to 1865 a number of Northerners—not exactly tourists—journeyed through all parts of Dixie, a veritable invasion of Yankees, and about a century later, not far from where de Soto departed on the first group travel excursion through the region, Walt Disney colonized a corner of Florida, an outpost that stimulated a new invasion of visitors into the South.

The entire South is a theme park of sorts. If the region didn't exist, someone would have to invent it. Because the South does exist, many observers have tried to reinvent it. Library shelves—and perhaps readers—groan under weighty tomes about the fabled region, books that examine, analyze, interpret and misinterpret the area. What other American region could supply such fertile ground for all the legends and lore, speculations, studies, introspections, inspections and dissections, factions and fictions—not to mention novels and other fiction—that stem from the South? And what other corner of the country affords the traveler such a colorful array of people and traditions—white and blue collar, blue bloods and redskins and red-neck types, blacks and the blues, the Blue Ridge Mountains, Kentucky's Bluegrass country and Alabama's Black Belt region, the Navy's Blue Angels and the Army's Green Berets, the Green and the Red rivers, a Greeneville and Greenvilles, Greensboros and Greenwoods, Baton Rouge, oranges and lemons, yellow fever memorials, white columns and white cotton, an Auburn University and a Scarlett O'Hara plus many other hues across the South's spectrum? Such familiar staples as cotton fields and columned antebellum plantation houses typify the image of the region most outsiders hold. Travelers to the South carry with them mental baggage heavy with accumulated perceptions, myths even, that seem to define the area, one of Faulknerian complexity—so the mythology goes—permeated with a not yet *Gone with the Wind* romanticism, a land garnished with moss-draped oaks, irrigated with mint juleps, embellished with those stately mansions and oozing with antebellum charm.

As America's most self-conscious region, the South seemingly likes to cultivate its myriad mythologies—the soil there nurtures myths as readily as it does cotton or tobacco—just as outsiders apparently enjoy being beguiled by them. Familiarity breeds content, making it comforting to view the South through Scarlett-colored glasses. When the Hachette publishing house in Paris wanted to define the region for French readers it issued a book entitled *Le Sud au temps de Scarlett*— "The South of the Scarlett Era." *Gone with the Wind*'s Scarlett O'Hara, the forward affirms, symbolizes the South much as Don Quixote does Spain, a comparison the region's first tourists, the Spaniard de Soto and his men, might not appreciate. Americans as well as foreigners tend to see the South in those myth-laden antebellum terms. "The average American thinks of the old South as a unit," says the evocatively named Thomas Jefferson Wertenbaker in *The Old South*. "To him the region below the Mason and Dixon Line was a land of wealthy planters who built stately mansions, filled their broad acres with the labor of scores of slaves, [and] lived luxuriously." This quintessential image of the South conforms with the 1823 description by John A. Quitman, later Mississippi governor, of daily life in the great houses of Natchez: "Mint juleps in the morning are sent to our rooms, and then follows a delightful breakfast in the open veranda. We hunt, ride, fish, pay morning visits, play chess, read or lounge until dinner, which is served at two p.m. in great variety." These strenuous exertions demanded an afternoon nap, after which "the tea table is always set before sunset, and then, until bedtime, we stroll, sing, play whist, or croquet. It is an indolent, yet charming life, and one quits thinking and takes to dreaming." This sort of dreamy routine at least one latter-day observer described as *The Lazy South,* the title of David Bertelson's study of Southern attitudes toward work—an X-rated four letter word in the region, he claims.

Back in those lazy days long before Martin Luther King, cotton was king and blacks the monarch's vassals. The South, so myth had it, enjoyed in those days an idyllic existence. "Plenty was the rule; want was a stranger to the humblest. Life was prolonged by the feeblest exertion," maintained W. Brewer in his 1872 history of Alabama. "Her citizens were hospitable, her officials were faithful, her slaves contented and happy." So seemed the South in the antebellum era, a time doomed to end but destined to survive in the region's mythology. An early precursor of future frictions occurred in April 1830 when—to President Andrew Jackson's Jefferson Day dinner toast, "Our Federal Union—it must be preserved!"—Vice-president John C. Calhoun of South Carolina tellingly replied, "The Union—next to our liberty, the most dear!" This succinct response, which cost Calhoun Jackson's support for the 1836 Presidential nomination, speaks volumes about the attitudes of the two antagonists, as does the Civil War battlefield colloquy between the Confederate trooper who shouted across the lines to a Union soldier, "Why don't you come over to our side? We're fighting for honor and you're only fighting for money," to which the Yankee retorted, "Well, I reckon each of us is fighting for what we need the most."

Tourist bureaus in the South can thank the Civil War for creating throughout the region a countless number of attractions—museums, monuments, mementos, memorials, and even myths, all of which travelers in the Southern states will find in abundance. You could muster an entire army with all the soldiers' statues that stand in courthouse squares in Dixie. To this day the War Between the States, as Southerners call the conflict, survives as one of the regions overriding myths. Who in the North, or elsewhere, ever thinks about the war? In the South, however, the conflict which so split families, the nation and even the South itself serves, ironically, as a kind of unifying force, a historical trauma and drama whose impact still lingers in the former Confederate states.

These archetypical elements—the columned mansions, a *Gone with the Wind*ism, the laid-back and perhaps even lazy way of life, the war's lingering influence—and others have all contributed to the South's image and to the mythology that the region remains a land apart, different in its essence from other areas of the nation. "Myths about slavery, plantations, poor whites, Secession, the Civil War, Reconstruction, black-white relations and a host of other topics envelop the South," notes Grady McWhiney in *Southerners and Other Americans.* "One of the great myths of American history is that when the Civil War began Southerners were fundamentally different from the Northerners." As the visitor to the South will learn in the course of his travels, the myths—the antebellum atmosphere and all the rest—are true in the sense that they define certain aspects of the South. But those myths, viewed alone, present a false image of the area, for they reflect only a small portion of the South's culture and thus fall far short of defining the Southern states as they are today. As for differences, the South, to be sure, is different, but so in their own way are the Middle West, New England, the cowboy West and other American regions, each of which boasts its own distinctive characteristics. Although the South likes to fancy itself as a distinct sort of place—an area defined by its seemingly unique quirks, eccentricities, grotesqueries, folklore, legends and mythologies—taken as a whole today's South, much as it might like to be different, "is really just another region," as Edmund Fawcett and Tony Thomas conclude in *The American Condition.*

It is the South's remarkable and unexpected variety, rather than its unique traits as represented by the myths, which characterizes the region. Although the South, like any section of the nation, does in some ways offer a different and distinctive flavor, the area contains many attractions which visitors might not expect to find in that part of the country. A traveler who spends any length of time in the Southern states may well be surprised at the wide range of sights there. Much of the South, in fact, seems quite un-South-like. Even the old South didn't always operate true to its conventional image. Before the Civil War, to take just one example, Virginia opposed secession, North Carolina never officially seceded but only repealed its 1789 legislation authorizing it to join the Union, and Kentucky never seceded at all. All this is just not Southern-like behavior. As for today's South, it may well be the nation's most varied region, for Dixie boasts examples of features found elsewhere, along with many attractions unique to the Southern states. This combination of home-grown and outside characteristics lends the area its variety and a richness travelers will find appealing.

The South's geographical variety—its characteristics typical of other regions—includes elements more commonly associated with the North, the East and the West. As Fletcher M. Green asserts in *The Role of the Yankee in the Old South,* Northern influences and institutions abound in the South, phenomena which belie "the myth that the people of the Northern and Southern states constituted two distinct and irreconcilable social and cultural groups." Around the South a traveler will encounter such New England-like attributes as covered bridges, ski resorts (in North Carolina, Tennessee and Kentucky), colonial architecture, Elizabethan-era gardens and accents and a British burial ground (all in North Carolina), Revolutionary War monuments and battlefields, fishing villages, Atheneum-like cultural societies (Charleston and Louisville boast such institutions), and a Boston Route 128-type high-tech enclave at North Carolina's Research Triangle Park. Middle Western touches in the South include such Wrights and wrongs as structures built by Illinois' Frank Lloyd Wright (in Frankfort, Kentucky and many in Lakeland, Florida) and monuments to Ohio's Orville and Wilbur Wright and a bank (in Russellville, Kentucky) robbed by Missourian Jesse James's gang, while Missourian Mark Twain's ancestral town (in Tennessee) and Abe Lincoln of Illinois's birthplace (in Kentucky) recall those two figures associated with mid-America.

In the nineteenth century the South was the West, the American frontier. Wild West traces still survive there with any number of exhibits, memorials, houses and historic sites that recall Daniel Boone, Davy Crockett, George Rogers Clark, Jim Bowie and other such pioneers. Rodeos and buffalo herds bring Western touches to two Southern states (Florida and Kentucky), South Carolina's town of Cowpens recalls where America's first wranglers tended cattle herds, and, to go with the cowboys, Indians still reside in their own settlements in North Carolina (Cherokee), South Carolina (Catawba), Mississippi (Choctaw) and Florida (Miccosukee and Seminole). On view in North Carolina and Georgia are mines where the nation's earliest gold deposits surfaced there in the South, not in the mineral-rich West, and in Louisiana and Arkansas gushes oil, a commodity more commonly associated with the Southwest. Heavy industry, a far cry from the cotton-dominated plantation culture, operates at Birmingham's steel factories and at shipbuilding facilities in Mississippi and Virginia, while in the Washington, D.C. area, a corner of Virginia so permeated with outsiders a Southern atmosphere barely survives, functions the government industry, including the Pentagon and other installations of the once-hated Federals.

One of the South's most pronounced traits, the drawl, sounds forth less and less, giving way to the crisp tones of the SUPPY—Southern-based Urban Professional, Probably Yankee. During the Carter years drawl-tongued Southerners observed how nice it was to have a person in the

White House who didn't speak with an accent. Thanks, or no thanks, to modernization some Southern cities resemble those glossy high-rise high-energy places common elsewhere around the land, light–years away from John Quitman's slow-paced, or no-paced, Natchez way of life. "When I asked a Columbia, South Carolina, banker what he wanted his city to become," recounts John Syelton Reed in an essay in *The American South: Portrait of a Culture,* edited by Louis D. Rubin, "he expressed his admiration for Charlotte. Charlotte, meanwhile, wants to look like Atlanta; and Atlanta, it seems, wants to look like Tokyo." If Atlanta resembles Tokyo, then the new South even includes a touch of the Far East as well as the Northeast, Wild West, Middle West and other regions.

In addition to the South's variety of place—those attractions reminiscent of other regions' cultures—a varied temporal mix exists in Dixie. The Southern states encompass areas of different eras, places that reflect the region's stages of development. Still today survive primeval lands—or waters—such as the Everglades and the Great Dismal Swamp, which contain corners believed never yet explored. Here exists the true "deep" South—places hidden deep in the countryside and in time preserved in their pristine pre-exploration state. Indian settlements recall the days before the palefaces arrived, while at Bradenton, Florida, a National Historical Site commemorates where Hernando de Soto landed in the New World in 1539. Dozens of re-created or restored colonial and pioneer settlements—like Virginia's Jamestown and Williamsburg, Fort Boonesborough in Kentucky and many others—recall the region's early days. In addition to those reconstructions the South offers any number of original settlements which, tiered in time, trace the area's evolution. These include eighteenth-century showplaces like Charleston and Savannah and the lesser known Old Maryland Settlement in Mississippi, remote villages founded during and reminiscent of the earliest pioneer days, once frontier but now back-tier towns that seem to have strayed into the wrong century, isolated Appalachian enclaves of another era, self-contained cultures like the Melungeons in Tennessee and the Cajuns (not connected with the Louisiana culture of that name) near Mobile who live a hundred years behind the times, and a wide variety of other attractions that exist contemporaneously but which originated in and represent different epochs. Those time capsules range from prehistory through the colonial, pioneer, Revolutionary and Civil War eras—preserved pockets of the past—and up to the present day and even tomorrow, with such modernisms and (for the South) newfangled phenomena as Republicans, the Wal-Mart (of Arkansas) retailing revolution, Miami's state of the art social problems, up–to–the–minute Japanese factories and the General Motors futuristic Saturn plant in Tennessee, Saturn and other planetary probes at Cape Canaveral and other NASA bases which send rockets to the stars, other sorts of stars of the universe at the brand new high-tech 1990s Universal Studios in Florida, and Disney's EPCOT "community of tomorrow." With this wide range of past and present, a temporal spectrum, the South's entire history coexists simultaneously: In the Southern states you can travel in time as well as place.

So deeply ingrained in the nation's consciousness has the South's traditional antebellum image become, travelers may not expect such a wide variety of attractions—geographical, featuring those which recall other regions, and temporal, with those that represent all the area's eras. Perhaps only in the Southern states can the visitor find such a rich mix of cultural variety and historical continuity. Along with this breadth of tone and time goes a depth rooted in the familiar, including both family and locale—a deep attachment, among Southerners, to place. A sense of place is one of the South's most characteristic traits. In an article on "Place and Time:

The Southern Writer's Inheritance," the *Times Literary Supplement* of London commented: "If one thing stands out in all these writers, all quite different from another, it is that each feels passionately about place. And not merely in the historical and prideful meaning of the word, but in the sensory meaning, the breathing world of sight and smell and sound."

The much commented on agricultural orientation of the South reflects this deeply rooted sense of place. Unlike the North, where plants meant factories, in the South plants stemmed from the land and produced foods, not goods. Walt Whitman's poem on the region, "O Magnet-South," sings the praise of "the cotton plant! the growing fields of rice, sugar, hemp!" So central was cotton to the South's economy, and the very fabric of the region, that back in 1861 Mississippi used the commodity—a kind of white gold—to back paper money, a development which prompted a plantation owner (as quoted in *Confederate Mississippi,* by John K. Bettersworth) to comment that such notes were "safer than that of the Bank of England, which is based on credit, while this is based on a staple commodity indispensable to the commerce of all Christendom." The Founding Fathers, in their day, seemed happily married to Mother Earth. So attached was Patrick Henry to his Virginia plantation that in the 1790s he turned down offers to serve as U.S. senator, Secretary of State, U.S. Supreme Court Chief Justice, and Ambassador to France. In 1794 Thomas Jefferson wrote John Adams: "No occupation is so delightful to me as the culture of the earth," while George Washington, as Philip Alexander Bruce notes in *The Virginia Plutarch,* was constantly drawn back to Mount Vernon for "his interest in the operations of his plantation; the allurement of his own fields, forests, and streams; the excitement of the fox hunt."

This sense of place, along with the South's strong interest in kin and clan—the familiar and the family—perhaps explains why the region boasts hundreds of show houses, family homesteads that recall the generations which, each in its time, occupied the property, as well as dozens of pageants, shows and theatrical presentations which dramatize a locale's characters and history. Homey houses, filled with family furnishings and portraits, and stage plays filled with local dramas and people, seem to evidence the South's orientation toward place and personalities. What Thomas D. Clark wrote about families in his native state, in *Agrarian Kentucky,* describes much of the South: "For most Kentuckians their history is translated into the personal terms of revered ancestors, political and military heroes, self-sacrificing pioneers, unforgivable family enemies, and uninhibited scoundrels who have furnished them moments of vicarious enjoyment." Southern clans—and even the racists chose to organize themselves into a Klan—remain tied by a web of associations, memories, domestic dramas and family lore, connections that link generations as well as contemporaries. Still common in the region are family reunions such as the one described by Ben Robertson in *Red Hills and Cotton:* "During the morning we would sit in the shade of the trees and Cousin Unity and our Great-Aunt Narcissa and Cousin Ella would begin at the beginning of time, long before the Revolution, and trace the kinfolks from then until the moment of that reunion. They would tell us who had married whom, who had gone where, and what had happened."

Of course, as Jefferson once wrote: "The earth belongs always to the living generation. . . . The dead have no rights. They are nothing; and nothing cannot own something. . . . This corporeal globe, and everything upon it, belongs to its present corporeal inhabitants during their generation." But in the South the past—with its vanished but remembered generations, history-filled show homes, lingering Civil War memories, age-old oak trees and ever growing family trees— somehow seems more of a presence than elsewhere. A tonality of time suffuses the South, along with a sense of place and family. The irresistibly human account (in *Bluegrass Craftsman*) of Ebenezer Stedman, returning to his Kentucky home one autumn afternoon after spending the summer of 1822 in Ohio, preserves a moment in past time, an evocation of place and family that seems to summarize some of the south's underlying traits:

> Jest at this Moment . . . he put his hand on the Gate To open & the next few Steps to nock on the Dore & then to hear once more the voice of Dear Mother. I Rap. Then i hear, "Who is thare?" That is Mother. I Speak. She new my Voice. But didn't She get up quick & the Dor open quick & Didnt She have me in hur arms quick.

A traveler's journey through the Southern states will, in time, hopefully afford the visitor a feel for the land's texture—its sense of place and past, the ties of kin and clan, the stereotypical antebellum attractions interwoven with varied elements reminiscent of other regions and with varied places from all eras, for such are some of the characteristics which typify the eleven states that comprise America's South.

I

The Old South

1. Virginia

Virginia is one of the least Southern of the states covered in this book. More moderate than its confederates in the Confederacy, Virginia opposed secession and finally left the Union only after war broke out with the shelling of Fort Sumter, South Carolina, on April 14, 1861. Referring to itself as a South Atlantic state, Virginia lacks that moss-draped antebellum atmosphere typical elsewhere in Dixie. As Jean Gottmann observes in *Virginia in Our Century,* "Virginia is not, and probably never was, a completely 'Southern' area." And in *Virginia: A Bicentennial History,* Louis D. Rubin, Jr. noted: "By the 1940s and 1950s Virginia had become less and less a Southern community, so far as its patterns of life, its economy, even its percentage of black population were concerned. Its ties with the Deep South were more historical and emotional than economic and political."

The state began as England's first permanent colony in America, with George Percy noting in the log book as his ship approached the Atlantic coast on April 26, 1607: "About foure a clock in the morning we descried the land of Virginia." For some years the colony evolved as a New World England, and as late as the 1850s English novelist William Makepeace Thackeray saw the state, as portrayed in his *The Virginians,* as a simpler version of England. Hard times dogged the early Jamestown settlers, finally reduced to cannibalism, with John Smith, who headed the colony for a time, commenting in his 1624 *Generall Historie of Virginia* about one woman devoured by her husband: "Whether she was better roasted, boyled, or carbonado'd, I know not." In 1622

Indians massacred a third of the colony's twelve hundred settlers, but it managed to survive and soon started earning a livelihood by exporting to the mother country tobacco, so prominent a part of the culture that the product "became the standard of value, and supplied, in part at least, the place of a circulating medium of the precious metals," as William Henry Foote wrote in *Sketches of Virginia*. When the first single women arrived at Jamestown in 1619 bachelors claimed them at a hundred and twenty pounds of the best Virginia leaf.

Indians later provoked the first stirrings of home-rule longings when, in April 1676, a young man named Nathaniel Bacon became the leader of a group seeking vengeance against marauding redskins. Bacon organized a private army that challenged the authority of the governor, Sir William Berkeley, forcing the royal representative to flee. Bacon's Rebellion, as the affair is called, soon collapsed, but the events of 1676 foreshadowed those of 1776. In the early eighteenth century tobacco prices rose and Virginia enjoyed the golden age of the plantation way of life, but that gilded existence began to lose its glitter in 1765 when the hated Stamp Tax was passed. The measure crystalized anti-royalist feeling, with Patrick Henry orating against the tax in the House of Burgesses by declaring, "If this be treason, make the most of it." A decade later Henry averred, "Give me liberty or give me death," and in mid-1776 the Earl of Dunmore, the colony's governor, left the territory, Henry became the new governor and a hundred and sixty-nine years of English domination over Virginia came to an end. Until British forces arrived in the Hampton Roads area (Norfolk–Newport News–Portsmouth) in 1779, Virginia for the most part escaped Revolutionary War campaigns, although it was there, at Yorktown, where the conflict ended with Cornwallis's surrender on October 19, 1781.

After the Revolution Virginia emerged as the largest and

most populous of the thirteen original states, with one-fifth of the nation's inhabitants. Virginians took the lead in replacing the loose Articles of Confederation with a Constitution that would bring about a stronger central government. In the early years Virginia gave to the nation Washington, Jefferson, Madison and Monroe, while later four other natives became president, and out of the state's original territory were carved Illinois, Indiana, Kentucky, Michigan, Minnesota, Ohio, West Virginia and Wisconsin. These eight chief executives and eight territorial offspring have given Virginia the nicknames "Mother of Presidents" and "Mother of States." British Prime Minister William Gladstone once observed: "Virginia produced more contemporary great men than any other piece of real estate on earth, Greece and Rome not excepted."

Soon racial problems surfaced in the state. In August 1831 Nat Turner, a rather mystical figure born not far from the birthplace of Dred Scott, another famous slave, led a rebellion in which fifty-seven whites were murdered. Turner hung for his insurrection, as did John Brown in 1859, captured by Virginia's Colonel Robert E. Lee after Brown's daring raid on the federal arsenal at Harpers Ferry, then in Virginia. Lincoln asked Lee to command the Union army, but even though the officer opposed slavery he opted to return to Virginia "and share the misery of my native state." In contrast to the Revolutionary War, the Civil War brought heavy fighting to Virginia, with fully 60 percent of the conflict unfolding on the state's soil. The war thus ravaged Virginia, which lost a good part of its antebellum wealth when more than three hundred and fifty thousand slaves were freed. In November 1989 the grandson of two of them became in Virginia the nation's first elected black governor. The war shattered not only the state's economy but also dislocated its social structure. "The introduction of the African slave system was the most important single factor in the evolution

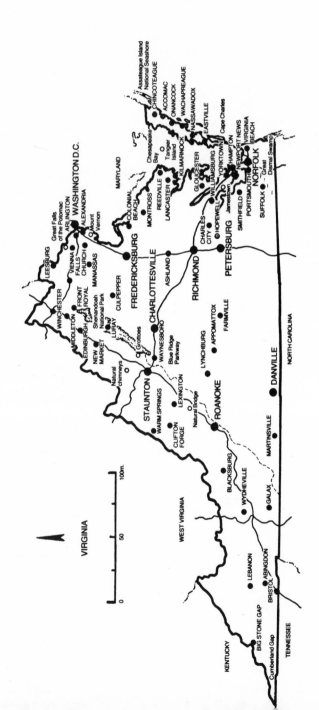

of the Virginia aristocracy," observed Louis B. Wright in *The First Gentlemen of Virginia*. Now slavery had ceased, but resentments and nostalgia for the old way of life lingered. Richmond native James Branch Cabell wrote bitingly in *Let Me Lie* how "we were taught always to look backward, toward the glories of which we had been dispossessed at Appomattox. And to each one of us it seemed unjust that he, the defrauded heir to a peerage in the Old South, should have to work for a living."

It took another war—World War I—to bring prosperity to the state, and by now Virginia's economy is a fairly well balanced combination of agriculture, industry and services, the latter including tourism and activities of the federal government, which has a greater impact on Virginia relative to its size than any other states except Alaska and Hawaii. Fully three-quarters of the residents in Fairfax County, largest of the Washington suburbs—where a quarter of all Virginians now live—come from another state or country. Tourism thrives, thanks to the rich range of colonial and Civil War history, architecture, back road attractions, natural features, museums, wineries and old towns that make Virginia one of the South's most varied states.

Eastern Virginia

Alexandria, Arlington and the Washington, D.C. Area—Leesburg, Middleburg and Fredericksburg—The Northern Neck—Williamsburg—Norfolk, Virginia Beach—The Eastern Shore—Petersburg—The James River Plantations—Richmond

Virginia, known as "The Mother of Presidents," is also the daughter of England and the sister of other Southern states. From the area's very earliest days an English way of life permeated the colony. As Philip Alexander Bruce noted in *Social Life in Virginia in the Seventeenth Century,* "the most remarkable general feature of that life was its close resemblance to the social life of England in the same age." In 1908 appeared a book entitled *Virginia Heraldica,* a compilation of "Virginia Gentry Entitled to Coat Armor." It's hard to imagine such a listing being published for such other Southern states as Arkansas, Kentucky or Florida. In the eastern part of the state, called the Tidewater region, stand stately homes, old-time churches and taverns, English-ish Williamsburg and other remnants of the motherland that so influenced Virginia. Through the center of the state spreads the farm-filled Piedmont area, a low rolling plateau land reminiscent of terrain found in such sister Southern states as Kentucky and middle Tennessee, while toward the west runs the Shenandoah Valley, the Allegheny and Blue Ridge mountains and extensive forests, a hilly region offering attractive landscapes, picturesque villages and a back country culture quite different from that toward the coast.

Such towns as Alexandria and Arlington belong as much to Washington, D.C., as to Virginia, for both settlements serve as suburbs of the capital. Alexandria boasts such historic attractions as Robert E. Lee's boyhood home (Feb. 1–Dec. 15 M–Sat., 10–4, Sun. 12–4, adm.); 1752 Carlyle House (Tu.–Sat. 10–5, Sun. 12–5, adm.); 1773 Christ Church (M.–Sat. 9–5, Sun. 2–4:30, free), the nation's first Episcopal church; Gadsby's Tavern Museum (Tu.–Sat. 10–5, Sun. 1–5, adm.); the George Washington Masonic National Memorial (9–5, free), featuring one of the largest displays in existence of Washington memorabilia; the 1785 Lee-Fendall House (Tu.–Sat. 10–4, Sun. 12–4, adm.), once occupied by the famous "Lees of Virginia," one of the state's renowned clans, and last owned privately by labor leader John L. Lewis; and the Apothecary Shop Museum (M.–Sat. 10–4, free). The

Fort Ward Museum and Historic Site (Tu.–Sat. 9–5, Sun. 12–5, free) recalls the one hundred and sixty-two installations, known as the Defenses of Washington, that guarded the nation's capital—at least capital of half the nation— during the Civil War, while another former military facility, an old torpedo factory, now houses some two hundred arts and crafts shops (10–5, free). River Farm in Alexandria (M.–F. 8:30–5, Sat. and Sun. 10–4, free) serves as headquarters of the American Horticulture Society, with display and test gardens and a "ha-ha" wall, an eighteenth-century era barrier that contained grazing cattle while affording open views of the property's vistas. Just down the road is the Collingwood Library and Museum on Americanism (open daily except Tu., free) featuring a special genealogy section. The Little House in Alexandria (703-548-9654 or 548-8675) offers bed and breakfast accommodations. At Arlington, adjacent to Alexandria, you'll find the famous National Cemetery, whose centerpiece is the impeccably restored 1817 Arlington House (April–Sept. 9:30–6; Oct.–March 9:30–4, free), occupied for thirty years by Robert E. Lee. In 1824 the Marquis de Lafayette described the panorama from the mansion across the Potomac River to Washington as the "finest view in the world." Arlington also boasts the Pentagon, perhaps the world's only Defense Ministry which offers tours: America's open society at its most open.

Off to the west of the metropolitan area a number of attractions dot the Fairfax County countryside, among them Evans Farm Inn (12–9) at McLean, as much a museum as an eatery, so crammed is the restaurant with old-time tools, utensils and furnishings; Wolf Trap Farm, a popular center for the performing arts (703-255-1900); Great Falls Park (7–dusk, adm.), perched by the Potomac where in the eighteenth century a company headed by George Washington built one of the nation's first canals; Colvin Run Mill Historic Site (mid-March–Dec. W.–M. 11–5, adm.), a rustic enclave featuring a restored early nineteenth-century mill; the A. Smith Bowman Distillery (open for tours) at Sunset Hills near Reston, supposedly the nation's oldest such family-owned facility; and at Chantilly, Sully Plantation (mid-March–Dec. W.–M. 11–5, adm.), built in 1794 by Richard Bland Lee, Robert E. Lee's uncle and the area's first U.S. Congressman.

Farther west, in Loudoun County, thirty-five miles from Washington, lies the town of Leesburg, near which rise such show places as Oatlands (March–late Dec. M.–Sat. 10–5, Sun. 1–5, adm.), an 1803 country estate owned from 1897 to 1903 by Stilson Hutchins, founder of *The Washington Post,* and Morven Park (Memorial Day–Labor Day Tu.–Sat. 10–5, Sun. 1–5, adm.), a twelve-hundred-acre estate where two Virginia governors once lived, with the Carriage Museum and the Museum of Hounds and Hunting. Farther north lies Waterford—site of the state's oldest crafts fair, established in 1944—a beguiling village, listed in its entirety on the National Register, virtually unchanged from when Quakers settled there on the banks of Catoctin Creek in 1733. Quakers still dominate the peaceful and pleasant village of Lincoln, west of Leesburg. In Leesburg—near which is the site of the country's smallest National Cemetery, at the Ball's Bluff Civil War battlefield—the Loudoun Museum (M.–Sat. 10–5, Sun. 1–5, free) traces the history of the county, whose slow-paced rural areas typify the motto of Lord Loudoun himself: "I byde my time." Leesburg hosts the Sheep Dog Trial and British Festival, a mid-May event (703-777-3174) featuring a typical 1930s English village fair. Loudoun and adjoining Fauquier County serve as the center of Virginia's hunt country, a verdant corner of the state with large estates and horse farms demarked by stone walls and split-rail fences. The Work Horse Museum at Paenian Springs (April–Oct. W. 9–5 or by appointment: 703-338-6290, adm.) contains displays of tack and farming implements, while Upperville—whose

Piedmont Hunt, which dates from 1840, is supposedly the nation's oldest such event—hosts in late May the annual Stable Tour, featuring visits to breeding establishments. "Stable" well describes the lovely region, little changed from the old days. Middleburg, another "horsey" town, presents a picture out of the past, with 1728 Red Fox Inn on Washington Street, built by a first cousin of George Washington, still serving meals. Middleburg offers bed and breakfast at Welbourne (703-687-3201), a c. 1775 house on a six-hundred-acre farm, while Piedmont Vineyards (summer 10–5, winter W.–Sun. 12–4, free) and the fifty-five-acre Meredyth Vineyards (10–4, free), one of the state's largest wineries, offer tours and tastings.

Toward the south lies Manassas, scene of two major Civil War encounters, the conflict's first significant battle in 1861 and the bloodier engagement a year later which opened the way for Robert E. Lee's first invasion of the North, all recalled at the Manassas National Battlefield Park (summer 8:30–6, winter 9–5, adm.). The combatants fought to control the train network in the area, site of the world's first military railroad, built by the Confederates in the winter of 1861. Around the town of Manassas, whose City Museum (10–5, free) traces much local history, stand a scattering of old buildings, among them the 1825 Liberia plantation house; Annaburg, now a nursing home, once the summer residence of beer baron Robert Portner; the 1906 Connor Opera House; the 1914 Old Town Hall; and the mid-eighteenth-century Katie Hooe House, remnant of the railroad hamlet of Tudor Hall which became the town of Manassas. Sleepy Warrenton, off to the west, also offers some old architecture, with venerable houses and other structures lining such streets as Main and Culpeper, while elsewhere stand the Old Court House, adapted from previous versions, in the first of which (1791) John Marshall, later U.S. Supreme Court Chief Justice, received his license to practice law; the old Warren Green

Hotel, fronted by a handsome two-story arcade; the 1808 Old Gaol, which now houses a museum; and the California Building, constructed by two-time Virginia governor William "Extra Billy" Smith, so called for stationing extra horses along the Washington to Atlanta stage route he owned. Fourteen miles south of Warrenton near Bealeton soars the Flying Circus Air Show (May–Oct. Sun. 2:30, adm.), with barnstorming daredevil pilots maneuvering antique "flying machines."

Back to the east near the Potomac lies Occoquan, an art colony that started up in 1977 in the basement of an old funeral home, now appropriately known as the Undertaking Artist's Co-op. Packed into the tiny town's four-block area, listed on the National Register, are a number of historic houses and old commercial buildings that now contain shops and galleries and, at 1758 Rockledge (703-690-3377), a bed and breakfast establishment. At nearby Woodbridge Leesylvania State Park, opened in 1989, is the site of the house where "Light Horse Harry" Lee, father of Robert E. Lee, was born. Other historical attractions abound in the area, among them 1774 Pohick Church, listed on the National Register, designed by George Washington; the U.S. Army Engineer Museum (W.–Sun., free) at Fort Belvoir; nearby Woodlawn (9:30–4:30, adm.) an estate given by Washington to his nephew, who commissioned the splendid 1805 Georgian mansion that now embellishes the plantation, and the adjacent Pope-Leighey House (9:30–4:30, adm.), designed by Frank Lloyd Wright; Washington's Grist Mill State Park (for hours, call 703-339-7265), a reconstruction of the mill the famous man designed and built in the early 1770s; and the ultra-famous Mount Vernon (Nov.-Feb., 9–4; March–Oct., 9–5, adm.), which needs no introduction. On Mason Neck, the tiny peninsula to the south, stands lesser known Gunston Hall (9:30–5, adm.), built in 1755 by George Mason, father of the Bill of Rights and a drafter of the Con-

stitution, while near Dale City, farther south, you'll find
Potomac Mills, no rustic corner of Virginia but a shopping
complex claimed to the be world's largest outlet mall, with
nearly two hundred stores. At Dumfries, the Weems-Bott
Museum (April–Oct. M.–Sat. 10–5, Sun. 2–5; Nov.–Mar.,
Mon.–Sat. 10–4, Sun. 1–4, free) contains displays relating
to Washington housed in the bookstore owned by Parson
Weems, whose famous biography of the president created
the "I cannot tell a lie" legend about the cherry tree young
George supposedly felled. Nearby Quantico is the nation's
only town completely surrounded by a military base, the
Marine Corps facility which includes the Air-Ground Museum (April 1–late Nov., Tu.–Sun. 10–5, free), featuring
displays on the history of the Corps' plane-troop team
techniques, developed in 1913 as the world's first such military combination.

At Falmouth, just outside historic Fredericksburg to the
south, is the Gari Melchers Memorial Gallery (April–Sept.
M.–Sat. 10–5, Sun. 1–5; Oct.–March M.–Sat. 10–4, Sun.
1–4, adm.), former home and studio of the artist installed
at antique-filled Belmont, listed on the National Register,
an eighteenth-century estate overlooking the Rappahannock
River. Fredericksburg's forty-block National Historic District includes more than three hundred and fifty eighteenth-
and nineteenth-century buildings, among them such George
Washington-connected places as the Masonic Museum
(April–Oct. M.–Sat. 9–5, Sun. 1–4; Nov.–March M.–Sat.
9–4, Sun. 1–4, adm.), where he was initiated into the order
in 1752; Kenmore (March–Nov., 9–5; Dec.–Feb., 10–4,
adm.), the Georgian-style home with exquisite plaster work,
where Washington's sister Betty lived; the Mary Washington
House (March–Oct., 9–5; Jan.–Feb. and Nov.–Dec., 9–4,
adm.), purchased by the president for his mother; and Rising
Sun Tavern (March–Nov., 9–5; Dec.–Feb., 9–4, adm.), a
hotbed of Revolutionary sentiment in colonial times, built

in 1760 by Charles, George's youngest brother, where you'll find such treasures as a desk supposedly owned by Thomas Jefferson and over-sized checkers made from a whale's backbone. Another local presidential attraction is the James Monroe Museum and Library (9–5, adm.), with such exhibits as the desk on which the chief executive signed the Monroe Doctrine in 1823.

Yesteryear survives at the Hugh Mercer Apothecary Shop (March–Nov., 10–5; Dec.–Feb., 10–4, adm.), which gives an idea of an early eighteenth-century medical office, and at the new (1989) bank museum, with displays of gold-dust weighing pans and other such artifacts from the early days of banking. Scattered around the Fredericksburg area are four Civil War battlefields that form a National Military Park (9–5, free) which recalls the nation's bloodiest fighting, with some hundred thousand men killed or wounded. Sights at the park include the house where "Stonewall" Jackson died, mortally wounded by the mistaken fire of his own troops. Bed and breakfast accommodations at Fredericksburg include La Vista Plantation (703-898-8444) and the Richard Johnston Inn (703-899-7606), while the Kenmore Inn (703-371-7622) also offers a delightful place to stay. At Bowling Green, to the south, you'll find bed and breakfast at the Old Mansion (804-633-5781).

Off to the east of Fredericksburg stretches the so called Northern Neck, a peninsula between the Potomac and Rappahannock rivers, here not mere streams but wide estuaries. From Tappahannock sails a cruise boat (May–Oct., 10 a.m., adm., for reservations: 804-333-4656) along the Rappahannock, with one of the stops at Ingleside Plantation, listed on the National Register, the state's first winery (M–Sat., 10–5; Sun. 12–5) to produce champagne. Across the "Neck" you'll find such other sights as the George Washington Birthplace National Monument (9–5, adm.), a colonial era farm that recreates the environment where the boy, born in 1732, lived until age three and a half and again as a teenager. A few miles east stands Stratford Hall (9–4:30, adm.), a boxy brick building constructed in the late 1730s by Thomas Lee, home of the two Lee brothers who signed the Declaration of Independence and birthplace (in 1807) of Robert E. Lee, the Southern general who became the clan's most famous member. Sixteen hundred of the plantation's original acres survive still today as a farm, one of the nation's oldest continuing agricultural operations. On the way to the bridge at the "Neck's" southeast corner you'll pass by Lively, near which Mary Ball, Washington's mother, was born at Epping Forest. Farther on stands beautifully restored Christ Church (9–5, free), considered by some the nation's best preserved colonial church. Robert "King" Carter, agent for the proprietor of the Northern Neck, Lord Halifax, as well as treasurer and acting governor of the colony and speaker of the House of Burgesses, built the church between 1730 and 1734 to house the graves of his parents. Carter, buried in an ornate tomb outside the sanctuary, fathered fifteen children who, in turn, produced descendants that included eight Virginia governors, two U.S. presidents (the Harrisons), Robert E. Lee and other notables.

On the other side of the Rappahannock River you'll come to Urbanna, whose Old Court House recalls the town's founding in the late seventeenth century by the House of Burgesses as site of the county court, complete with such necessary enhancements as a ducking stool and stocks. Pirates threatened the settlement in the early years, with two buccaneers being hanged at Urbanna in 1719. Other old buildings include the restored Tobacco Warehouse, now the town library, believed to be the only such surviving colonial era facility, the Old Tavern, and the Customs House. The first weekend in November Urbanna celebrates the annual Oyster Festival, featuring shucking competition, a gathering of ships, music and other festive events. In 1974 the legislature adopted the oyster as Virginia's "State Shell." Off to the east by Chesapeake Bay stretches tiny Mathews County, the state's smallest, with the 1805 New Point Comfort Lighthouse, listed on the National Register; the handsome courthouse at Mathews, in continuous use since 1792; and Poplar Grove, birthplace of Captain Sally Tompkins, the only female Confederate Army officer, an estate that includes a tide-operated grist mill that supposedly ground grain for Washington's Continental Army. From Cricket Hill, overlooking Gwynn's Island to the north, Continental troops on July 9, 1776 chased from American soil Lord Dunsmore, the last of Virginia's royal governors, an event recalled at the National Historic Landmark at the site. In adjacent Gloucester County, home of John Buckner, who in 1689 brought the first printing press into the colony, was born Walter Reed, conqueror of yellow fever. In the seventeenth and eighteenth centuries the region served as a tobacco-producing area, an era recalled by the many old plantation homes and private estates that still survive. Around the courthouse green in the town of Gloucester stand some early buildings, while the Virginia Institute of Marine Science at Gloucester Point houses aquatic exhibits (M.–F., 10–4, free).

Just across the York River lies Yorktown, whose visitor center (8:30–5:30, free), in the Colonial National Historic Park at the battlefield where General Cornwallis surrendered to the Americans on October 19, 1781, contains Revolutionary War exhibits. Negotiations for the surrender—during which the British band played "The World Turn'd Upside Down"—took place at the Moore House (mid-June–Labor Day, 10–5; mid-April–mid-June and Labor Day–Oct., Sat. and Sun. 1–5, free), while the Nelson House (mid-June–Labor Day, 11–4:30, free) recalls Thomas Nelson, Jr., signer of the Declaration of Independence and wartime governor of Virginia. The Yorktown Victory Center (9–5; to 7, June 15–Aug. 15, adm.) is a kind of theme park that chronicles events of the Revolution from the Boston Tea Party to the surrender. At nearby Fort Eustis the U.S. Army Transportation Museum (9–4:30, free) traces the history of military transport over the last two centuries, with trains, trucks, aircraft and even a "flying saucer" on display. The Colonial Parkway, lined with interpretive markers, winds its way for twenty-three scenic miles from Yorktown to Williamsburg to Jamestown, but you'll need to leave the Parkway to visit Busch Gardens (10–10, adm.), with an "Old Country" theme featuring England, France, Germany and Italy, and Carter's Grove Plantation (March–Nov., 9–5, adm.), a 1755 Georgian-style manor house.

At the turn of the century Williamsburg lay dilapidated and neglected, a crumbling remnant of the days when it served as Virginia's capital from 1699 to 1780. In 1902 Episcopal minister William A. R. Goodwin arrived in town to serve at Bruton Parish Church, which he proceeded to restore with the help of contributions from such luminaries as J. P. Morgan, Teddy Roosevelt and even King Edward VII, apparently holding no grudge against the former royal colony that so vexed his predecessors. When Goodwin, later addressing a Phi Beta Kappa convention in New York, told of Williamsburg's sorry state John D. Rockefeller, Jr., happened to be in the audience, and the financier soon took an interest in restoring the historical settlement. Over sixty years of revitalization, some five hundred buildings have been restored or reconstructed, including eighty-eight original structures, and ninety acres of gardens replanted. Goodwin, who inspired this massive undertaking, died in 1939 and reposes beneath the aisle of the Bruton Parish Church, which originally brought him to Williamsburg. With its photogenic colonial and colonial-style structures, peopled with craftsmen and attendants in period dress, Williamsburg presents a picture out of the past, but in a way it seems to be a picture much retouched. Unlike such architecturally rich

Southern settlements as Natchez, Mississippi, or Charleston, South Carolina, vibrant, living cities with an organic connection to time and place, Williamsburg appears rather like a cross between a theme park and an exclusive residential suburb. As Marshall W. Fishwick suggested in *Virginia: A New Look at the Old Dominion,* the town is "*too* restored. The ever-fresh paint and unlimited expenditures have turned the mellow old town into a glossy movie set."

Apart from the famous government buildings, colonial homes, craft shops and taverns, Williamsburg also offers such museums as Bassett Hall (10–5, adm.), where Mr. and Mrs. John D. Rockefeller, Jr., lived in the mid-1930s during the main restoration period; the Abby Aldrich Rockefeller Folk Art Center (reopened spring 1991); the Winthrop Rockefeller Archeological Museum for Martin's Hundred (opened fall 1990), with findings salvaged from a plantation, now known as Carter's Grove, destroyed by Indians in 1622; the Dewitt Wallace Decorative Arts Gallery (10–6, W. to 8, adm.); and the Public Hospital of 1773 (10–6, W. to 8, adm.), a reconstruction of an early mental institution. The College of William and Mary, where presidents-to-be Jefferson, Monroe and Tyler studied, boasts the nation's oldest academic facility, the 1695 building designed by Christopher Wren, England's most renowned architect, and the town's first major structure to be restored by Rockefeller. In July and August the college hosts the Virginia Shakespeare Festival (for information: 804-253-4377). More than a dozen bed and breakfast places and an equal number of guest houses provide comfortable noncommercial accommodations in Williamsburg. Less expensive bed and breakfast establishments include the Cedars (804-229-3591), Fox Grape (804-229-6914), Governor's Trace (804-229-7552) and Hite's (804-229-4814), while among the lower-priced guest homes are Barnes (804-229-6250), Carter's (804-229-1117), Goswick-Whittaker (804-229-3920), Hollands (804-229-6321), Johnson's (804-229-3909), Lewis (804-229-6116), Ran (804-229-1675) and Thompson (804-229-3455).

Not far south of Williamsburg lies Jamestown Island, site of the first permanent English settlement (1607) in the United States, a colony recreated at the Jamestown Festival Park (9–5; to 7, June 15–Aug. 15, adm.), while exhibits at the National Historic Site visitor center (8:30–4:30, extended hours from spring to fall, adm.) recall the settlement's early days. After much rivalry among the first settlers John Smith, a soldier of fortune, finally emerged as leader of the new colony. Although a rough-hewn adventurer, Smith won the praise of at least one of his colleagues, Thomas Carleton, who wrote of him: "I never knew a Warrior yet, but thee / From wine, Tobacco, debts, dice, oaths, so free." Smith survived death at the hands of the Indians when, as he wrote in his 1624 *Generall Historie,* just as the redskins prepared "with their clubs, to beate out his brains, Pocahontas the king's dearest daughter when no intreaty could prevaile, got his head in her armes, and laid her owne upon his to save him from death." Later severely wounded, Smith returned to England in October 1609, leaving "my wyfe, to whom I have given all," referring to his beloved Virginia, not to Pocahontas, wife of John Rolfe who introduced commercially grown tobacco into Virginia. Just across the James River, traversed by a toll ferry from Jamestown to Scotland (June 1–Sep. 15, daily every half hour; Sept. 16–May 31, slightly less frequent), lies Smith's Fort Plantation (third week of April–Sept., Tu.–Sat. 10–5; Sun. 1–5, adm.), built in the mid-eighteenth century on property owned by Thomas Rolfe, son of John Rolfe and Pocahontas. In mid-July the annual Pork, Peanut and Pine Festival takes place at nearby Chippokes Plantation State Park (for information: 804-294-3625), which comprises an agricultural property with boundaries unchanged since 1619 and farmed continuously since then. Nearby stands Bacon's Castle, the oldest documented brick house in British North America. To switch from Bacon to ham, S. Wallace Edwards & Sons in Surry offers tours which show you how the firm turns out its Virginia hams (for tour reservations: 804-294-3121), while at nearby Smithfield four meat-packing plants confection the famous Smithfield hams from peanut-fed porkers pampered on area farms. The town boasts St. Luke's (9:30–5, free), the nation's oldest surviving English-built church (1632) and the only existing original Gothic-style sanctuary, a solid brick building with a simple yet impressive dark wood and white wall interior. Farther south stretches the Great Dismal Swamp National Wildlife Refuge, remnant of the once two thousand square-mile bog that covered the border area between Virginia and North Carolina. In 1763 George Washington himself set up the Dismal Swamp Land Company, which undertook draining and logging operations. Over the years farmers reclaimed land for crops and foresters cut trees, until the swamp seemed on the verge of disappearing. But in the 1970s the Department of the Interior acquired some hundred and sixty-five square miles of wetland, now home to three hundred or so black bears, two hundred species of birds, and other wildlife, some visible on boardwalk paths through the area (dawn to dusk, free).

Just beyond the swamp's northern edge cluster a group of cities around Hampton Roads, the world's largest natural harbor, along which spreads the Norfolk Naval Shipyard, the largest on earth—or on water. In the waters of Hampton Roads clashed the ironclad craft "Monitor" and "Merrimac" in a famous Civil War encounter. Harbour Tours runs boat excursions around the port area (June 1–Labor Day, departs Norfolk M.–F., 10, 12, 2, 4; departs Portsmouth fifteen minutes later; Sat. and Sun, 12, 2 and 4; rest of the year daily at 12 and 2). For landlubbers Portsmouth offers Portside, a well-preserved area filled with antique houses where the town began in 1752. Museums in or near the old town include the Naval Shipyard Museum, the Virginia Sports Hall of Fame, and the Light Ship Museum (all three open Tu.–Sat., 10–5; Sun. 1–5, free), the latter installed in the "Charles." From Portsmouth's Portside you can reach Norfolk's glossy shop- and restaurant-crammed Waterside area on a ferry, modern-day successor to the skiff *Adam Thoroughgood* used in the 1630s to carry passengers at a charge of one bale of hay. These days only dough—no hay—is accepted on the ferry. The Adam Thoroughgood House (Tu.–Sat., 10–5; Sun., 12–5, adm.) at Virginia Beach, among the nation's oldest brick dwellings (1636), is one of the three area showplaces managed by Norfolk's Chrysler Museum (Tu.–Sat., 10–4; Sun. 1–4, adm.), which houses a well-regarded art collection as well as major glass and photo collections. The other two houses, both in Norfolk, are Moses Myers, with many original family furnishings, and Willoughby-Baylor, occupied by family members up until 1890 (both houses: April–Dec., Tu.–Sat., 10–5, Sun., 12–5; Jan.–March, Tu.–Sat., 12–5, adm.). Other Norfolk sights include St. Paul's, built in 1739—as the raised brick date on the facade indicates—and sole survivor of the 1776 British bombardment of the city, an attack recalled by the cannonball lodged in the sanctuary's southeastern wall; the Hunter House Victorian Museum (April–Dec., W.–Sat., 10–4; Sun., 12–4, adm.); the Hermitage Foundation Museum (M–Sat., 10–5; Sun., 1–5, free), with a collection of art objects featuring Oriental works; the Douglas MacArthur Memorial (M.–Sat., 10–5; Sun., 11–5, free), four buildings that contain displays, archives and memorabilia—including the famous corncob pipe the general favored—relating to MacArthur's life and career; and the Norfolk Naval Base, the world's largest navy facility, which offers bus tours (9–2:30, free; for information: 804-444-2163). From Waterside in downtown Norfolk departs the sailing ship "American Rover," while its sister ship "Virginia Rover" sails from nearby

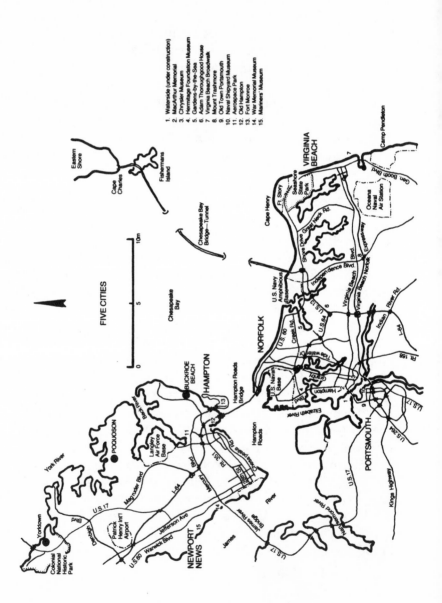

1. Waterside (under construction)
2. MacArthur Memorial
3. Chrysler Museum
4. Hermitage Foundation Museum
5. Gardens-by-the-Sea
6. Adam Thoroughgood House
7. Virginia Beach Broadwalk
8. Mount Trashmore
9. Old Town Portsmouth
10. Naval Shipyard Museum
11. Aerospace Park
12. Old Hampton
13. Fort Monroe
14. War Memorial Museum
15. Mariners Museum

FIVE CITIES

Hampton, both craft cruising area waters on sightseeing tours (Sat. before Memorial Day–Labor Day, from Norfolk, 11 and 6:30; from Hampton, 2 and 6).

From downtown Hampton—which claims to be the nation's oldest continuous English-speaking settlement—you can also catch a cruise boat to Fort Wool, a fifteen-acre man-made island used by Yankees to bombard Norfolk. Hampton boasts St. John's, a congregation founded along with the town in 1610 and now America's oldest English parish in continuous service (the present church dates from 1728; M.–F., 9–3; Sat., 9–12, free). Memories of pre-English residents in the area survive at the Kecoughtan Indian Village Syms-Eaton Museum (M.–F., 10–4; Sat. and Sun., 10–5, free); displays at NASA's Langley Research Center visitor center (M.–Sat., 8:30–4:30, free), with exhibits on the history of flight and space exploration, evoke more modern times; and at Hampton University, founded in 1868 to educate freedmen, among whom was Virginia's Booker T. Washington, the student- and faculty-built Academy Building, one of the campus's six National Register-listed sites, houses the University Museum (Sept.–May, M.–F., 8–5; Sat. and Sun., 12–4, free) featuring a collection of African art and ethnic items. At nearby Fort Monroe—the largest stone fort ever built in the United States (1834) and the nation's only moat-encircled installation still used by the Army—the Casemate Museum (10:30–5, free) includes the cell which held Confederate president Jefferson Davis after the Civil War, displays relating to Robert E. Lee and Edgar Allen Poe, both stationed at the fort, and weapons, uniforms and other martial items. The forty-nine thousand-pound "Lincoln Gun" that overlooks the parade field recalls the time when the base served as the country's first artillery school, established in 1824. Outside the moat rises a milepost from which the Chesapeake and Ohio Railroad measured distances west to Cincinnati, six hundred and sixty-five miles away, while near the fort stands the Chamberlin (804-723-6511), an old-fashioned boxy brick hotel out of the 1920s whose restaurant's name, The Great Gatsby, recalls the era. Hampton also offers bed and breakfast accommodations at River House (804-723-7847) and Squirrel Hotel (804-723-7462). Bed and Breakfast of Tidewater (804-627-1983) can make reservations for you at other establishments in the region.

Adjacent to Hampton is Newport News—named for two "Sirs": Christopher Newport and William Newce—home of the world's biggest commercial shipbuilder, Virginia's largest private employer. Harbor Cruise (804-245-1533) takes you past the huge Newport News shipyard and other Hampton Roads sights, while the Mariners' Museum (M.–Sat., 9–5, Sun., 12–5, adm.) contains displays of nautical items and, in a new wing opened September 1989, exhibits on the Chesapeake Bay area. Newport News—which in the fall of 1991 was connected with Suffolk by a four-lane interstate highway resting on the ocean floor—also boasts the Virginia Living Museum (mid-June–Labor Day, M.–Sat., 9–6, Sun., 10–6; post Labor Day–mid-June, M.–Sat., 9–5, Sun., 1–5, every Th. evening year round 7–9, adm.), with natural history exhibits, animals and a planetarium, and the War Memorial Museum of Virginia (M.–Sat., 9–5, Sun., 1–5, adm.) featuring more than fifty thousand artifacts that trace American military history.

Back to the east, along the Atlantic coast, sprawls Virginia Beach, primarily a resort area but with a scattering of attractions hidden away among the motels, stores and night spots. At Fort Story, where the Atlantic and the Chesapeake Bay meet, stands the Old Cape Henry Lighthouse, built in 1791 as, in effect, the nation's first public works project, promoted by George Washington. The lovely octagonal tower (Memorial Day–Oct., 10–5, adm.)—built of stone from the same quarry used to supply materials for the U.S. Capitol, the

White House and Mount Vernon—served until a more modern lighthouse replaced the structure in 1881. Nearby stands a cross marking the site where the Jamestown colonists first arrived in the New World, April 26, 1607. Another seaside memorial is the Norwegian Lady statue, put there to commemorate the 1891 wreck of the Norwegian bark "Dictator" off the shores of Virginia Beach, a tragedy recalled in a display at the nearby Maritime Historical Museum (Memorial Day–Sept., M.–Sat., 10–9, Sun., 12–5; Oct.–Memorial Day, Tu.–Sat., 10–5, Sun., 12–5, adm.), with a collection of nautical artifacts installed in a former Coast Guard station, while the Virginia Marine Science Museum (June–Aug., M.–Sat., 9–9, Sun., 9–5; Sept.–May, 9–5 every day, adm.) offers exhibits on the natural history of the sea.

Somewhat more ethereal or surreal are the attractions at "A.R.E.," the Association for Research and Enlightenment (June–Aug., M.–Sat., 9–10, Sun., 1–10; Sept.–May, M.–Sat., 9–5:30, Sun., 1–6, free), devoted to the psychic work of Edgar Cayce (from Hopkinsville, Kentucky: see the third section of that chapter), known for his more than fourteen thousand "readings" (discourses on various topics), extrasensory skills and other parapsychological talents. A.R.E. includes areas devoted to ESP, holistic healing and—come prepared to meditate—both a Meditation Room and a Meditation Garden. Also on the spiritual side of things is the Christian Broadcasting Network Center (M.–F., 8:30–5, free), with tours of the CBN complex, while more mundane Mount Trashmore takes its name from compacted layers of soil and garbage transmuted into a park. Old dwellings include the above-mentioned Adam Thoroughgood House and the c. 1725 Lynnhaven House (Tu.–Sun., 12–4, adm.). For a true change-of-pace, Motorworld (Memorial Day–Labor Day, 10–nighttime; weekends only, spring and fall, adm.) offers two-thirds size race cars you can rev up to compete in the local version of the Grand Prix, here better described as the Petit Prix. Toward the south edge of the urban area lies Sandbridge Beach, a somewhat less frenetic corner of town along the sea, while down the coast you'll find the even more unspoiled and pristine Back Bay National Wildlife Refuge and the False Cape State Park, reached by hiking or biking along a six-mile trail leading you to marshlands, dunes, maritime forests and other natural features.

From Virginia Beach it's convenient to cross the seventeen-mile-long Chesapeake Bay Bridge-Tunnel to gain access to the otherwise hard-to-reach Eastern Shore, that long narrow stretch of Virginia land which dangles below Maryland. Hamlets named Oyster, a fishing and seafood village, and Birds Nest suggest the shore's natural ambiance, while to the far north Temperanceville, called Crossroads until 1824, recalls the era when four landowners sold terrain there with the provision that no whiskey be purveyed on the sites. In 1603 a landing party led by a nephew of Sir Walter Raleigh reached the Eastern Shore, the first known visit to Virginia by Europeans, and five years later from nearby Jamestown arrived a group commanded by Captain John Smith, who gave his name to Smith Island where the Cape Charles Light-house stands. Cape Charles—with the Shore's only Chesapeake Bay public beach, along which stretches a mile-long boardwalk—began as a railroad town in 1884, and still today it serves as headquarters of the Eastern Shore line, which operates a twenty-six-mile rail-barge ferry link across the Bay to Norfolk. Bed and breakfast places in Cape Charles include Henrietta's Cottage (804-331-4133), Nottingham Ridge (804-331-1010), Pickett's Harbor (804-331-2212) and Seagate (804-331-2206).

North of Cape Charles lies Eastville, where the Northampton County Courthouse holds the nation's oldest continuous civic records, dating from 1632. The first entry—"the Minister complains about not having rec'd his tythes of Tobacco"—seems timeless. By the 1731 courthouse stands the Debtor's Prison, complete with a whipping post. At Wachapreague, farther north, the Burton House (804-787-4560) offers bed and breakfast, and at nearby Painter the Accomack Vineyard offers tours (Tu.–Sun., 12–4), while in Accomac itself (the town's name omits the final "k") Perdue Farms receives visitors at its plant which processes more than three hundred thousand chickens daily (for information: 804-787-2700). Accomack County once bore the name Greenbackville for the new paper money the U.S. issued in 1861. The backs of these Demand Notes—the nation's first currency backed by the government's full faith and credit rather than gold or silver—were printed in green ink. In nearby Onancock Kerr Place (March–Dec., 10–4, free), a 1779 brick mansion, houses the Eastern Shore Historical Society. From Onancock (as well as Reedville on the mainland) depart ships for Tangier Island, an excursion you arrange at the same ticket window in Onancock's 1842 Hopkins & Bro. store where passengers bought steamboat tickets a century ago. Tangier, a soft-shell crab center, survives as a car-less corner of Virginia, a delightful enclave of the past where locals speak with the vague trace of an Elizabethan-era accent. So isolated remained the island for years that as recently as the 1930s three-quarters of the residents had a total of only nine last names, with nearly one-quarter called Crockett. One of Tangier's most delightful places to eat or stay, or both, is Chesapeake House (open April 15–Oct. 15, 804-891-2331). On another island, Wallops, at the northeastern corner of the Eastern Shore, NASA operates a visitor center (late June–early Sept., 10–4, off-season, Th.–Mon., 10–4, free) with exhibits on the history and future of flight. At Wallops, one of the world's oldest launch facilities—the first rocket burst into action there, appropriately enough, on July 4, 1945—operates a space research lab, NASA's balloon program and a satellite tracking station. You'll find more earthbound adventures at nearby

Chincoteague—"beautiful land across the water," in Indian language—best known for the annual pony round-up the last Wednesday and Thursday of July, an event held since 1924 to finance the island's volunteer fire company. Supposedly descendants of mustangs who swam ashore from a wrecked Spanish galleon three centuries ago, the ponies roam free on nearby Assateague Island at the Chincoteague National Wildlife Refuge (for tours: 804-336-5593 or 336-5511) until, once a year, the firemen cull the herd and then swim the animals across the channel where they're sold at auction. At the Chincoteague Miniature Pony Farm (Memorial Day–Labor Day, 10–9, off-season, 12–5, adm.) the ponies pose and perform, while a museum there includes the original "Misty," the herd's most famous member, stuffed and mounted. Local museums emphasize the island's hunting and fishing: the Oyster Museum (Memorial Day–Labor Day, 10–5, adm.), focusing on shellfish farming and the seafood industry, and the Waterfowl Museum (Memorial Day–Labor Day, 10–5; offseason, weekends only, adm.), with displays of boats, traps and decoys. At Easter Chincoteague hosts the annual decoy carving and duck head painting festival.

Returning now to the Hampton Roads area, nearby off to the west you'll find Petersburg and Richmond, the state capital, two river cities envisioned by Colonel William Byrd II, one of the famous Virginia Byrds, who on September 19, 1733 noted in his diary: "When we got home we laid the foundations of two large cities, one [on the James River], to be called Richmond, and the other at the falls of the Appomattox River, to be named Petersburg. . . . Thus we did not build castles only, but also cities in the air." Exhibits at the Siege Museum in Petersburg (M.–Sat., 9–5, Sun., 12:30–5, adm.), installed in the well-proportioned Greek Revival-style Exchange Building, recall the ten-month siege, the longest of any American city, which brought the town to its knees. Within a week after the siege ended Lee surren-

dered at Appomattox. Reminders of the campaign survive
at Petersburg National Battlefield (June–Aug., 8–7, Sept.–
May, 8–5, adm. to visitor center), including a huge crater
carved by the explosion of four tons of gunpowder touched
off by a Union regiment of Pennsylvania coal miners who
used their skills to tunnel beneath Confederate territory. At
Fort Lee more military memories linger in the U.S. Army
Quartermaster Museum (Tu.–F., 10–5, Sat. and Sun., 11-5,
free), with displays of old supplies and equipment and a collection of antique uniforms. You'll also find at Petersburg
the sibilantly abbreviated USSSA—the United States Slo-
pitch Softball Association (M.–F., 9–4, Sat., 11-4, Sun., 1–4,
adm.), with one of those odd-ball, off-beat museums that
lend travel around the nation its delight and which so enrich
the fabric of Americana. A twenty-minute movie in the Hall
of Champions introduces you to the titans of softball, while
photos, hats, bats and balls touch other bases of the game.
Relics of yesteryear in Petersburg include the Old Blandford
Church (9–5, adm.), a 1735 sanctuary embellished with
fifteen Tiffany windows; 1817 Farmers Bank (M.–Sat.,
10:30–4, Sun., 1–4, adm.), with displays relating to early
banking; the 1816 Trapezium House (M.–Sat., 10:30–4,
Sun., 1–4, adm.), which bachelor Charles O'Hara built with
no right angles, supposedly to leave no corners where ghosts
or evil spirits could hide; and 1823 Centre Hill Mansion
(M.–Sat., 10–4, Sun., 12:30–4, adm.), with finely confec-
tioned wood and plaster work, where Union forces headquartered after the siege and where Gore Vidal's *Lincoln*
was filmed. High Street Inn (804-733-0505) at Petersburg
offers bed and breakfast.

At the confluence of the James and the Appomattox rivers
not far from Petersburg perches Hopewell, named in 1635
by Captain Francis Eppes for the ship that had brought him
to Virginia. That year Eppes acquired a huge tract of land
on which still stands Appomattox Manor (8:30–4:30, free),

which remained in the family for three hundred and forty years. In 1864 General Ulysses S. Grant set up Union headquarters in a primitive T-shaped cabin on the mansion's front lawn from where he directed the siege of Petersburg. President Lincoln twice came to City Point, as the area is called, to visit Grant. At that time City Point functioned as the world's busiest port, with Union supplies and troops funnelling through Hopewell. Around City Point stand many old houses, and on Pecan Avenue rises what's supposedly the nation's oldest (c. 1675) and largest pecan tree. At the corner of Appomattox Street and Randolph Road, site of the present-day John Randolph Hospital, once stood Cawsons, a mansion where Randolph, orator, U.S. Senator and Ambassador to Russia, was born in 1773. This historic plot of ground is believed to have been the first privately owned property in America (c. 1613). Down the road by the river lies Weston Manor (open by appointment: 804-458-2206), a restored 1735 plantation house, listed on the National Register, supposedly built as a wedding present for a member of the Eppes family.

Along the banks of the James River near Hopewell stands a series of historic and architecturally rich plantations. On the south side of the James is Flowerdew Hundred Plantation (April–Nov., Tu.–Sun., 10–5, adm.), named for a property in Norfolk, England. Flowerdew is for the most part an archaeological site where excavations started in 1971 have unearthed artifacts—many displayed in the museum—dating from 9000 B.C. to the Civil War era. A rather cumbersome looking windmill reproduces an eighteenth-century version of the device. On the north side of the James River you'll find more complete plantation properties, among them such outstanding treasures as Shirley (9–5, adm.), owned since 1723 by nine generations of Carters, one of them Robert E. Lee's mother; 1726 Berkeley (8–5, adm.), site of the first official Thanksgiving (1619), birthplace of President William

Henry Harrison, the place where America's first bourbon
(an honor also claimed by Kentucky) was distilled (1622)
and where the bugle tune "Taps" was composed (1862) while
Union forces, visited by President Lincoln, encamped on
the property; Westover (gardens only, 9–6, adm.), a magnificent Georgian mansion built about 1730 by Richmond
and Petersburg founder William Byrd II, buried on the estate; Evelynton (by appointment only: 804-829-5068 or
829-5075), owned by the same family since 1847 when purchased by Edmund Ruffin, Jr., whose agronomist father fired
the first shot of the Civil War at Fort Sumter and wrote
a nearly five-hundred-page best-seller with the catchy title
Essay on Calcareous Manures; and Sherwood Forest (grounds
9–5, adm., mansion by appointment: 804-829-5377), the nation's largest frame house (three hundred feet), owned by
two U.S. presidents, John Tyler and William Henry Harrison. Touring these estates it's perhaps tempting to suppose
that the landed gentry who owned the properties lived idle
carefree existences, the gentlemen genteel idlers, the ladies
paragons of Southern belle-ism. But the plantations functioned not as showplaces but as businesses, those that survived being diligently run. As Thomas Nelson Page put it
in *Social Life in Old Virginia Before the War:* "It has been
assumed by the outside world that our people lived a life
of idleness and ease, a kind of hammock-swung, 'sherbet-
sipping' existence, fanned by slaves, and served on bended
knees . . . but any master who had a successfully conducted
plantation was sure to have given it his personal supervision
with an unremitting attention which would not have failed
to secure success in any other calling. If this was true of
the master, it was much more so of the mistress."

Tobacco, cotton and other products yielded by the James
River estates' fertile soil—perhaps enriched by Edmund
Ruffin, Sr.'s, "calcareous manures"—were sent upstream to
Richmond, which started in 1610 as a trading post. The

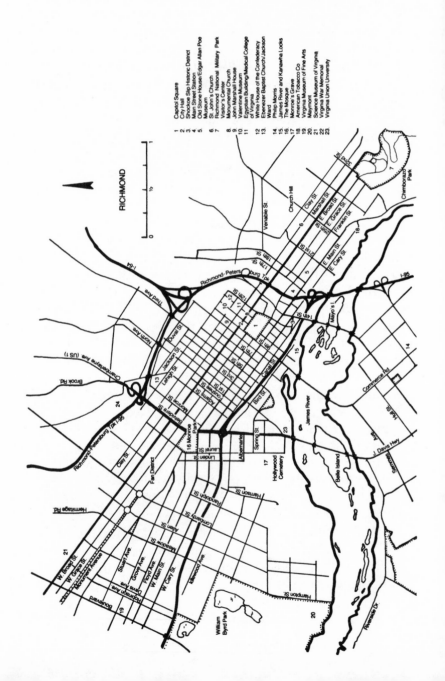

RICHMOND

1   Capitol Square
2   City Hall
3   Shockoe Slip Historic District
4   Main Street Station
5   Old Stone House/Edgar Allan Poe
    Museum
6   St. John's Church
7   Richmond National Military Park
    Visitor's Center
8   Monumental Church
9   John Marshall House
10 Valentine Museum
11 Egyptian Building/Medical College
    of Virginia
12 White House of the Confederacy
13 Ebenezer Baptist Church/Jackson
    Ward
14 Philip Morris
15 James River and Kanawha Locks
16 The Mosque
17 Monroe's Grave
18 American Tobacco Co
19 Virginia Museum of Fine Arts
20 Maymont
21 Science Museum of Virginia
22 Virginia War Memorial
23 Virginia Union University

town itself began in 1737 on land given by William Byrd II, and in 1780 the seat of government moved there from Williamsburg. Richmond today remains rich in remnants of the past. The Virginia State Capitol (M.–Sat., 9–5, Sun., 1–5, free), designed by Thomas Jefferson in 1785 and housing Houdon's famous marble statue of Washington modeled from life, stands in a pleasant parklike enclave which also includes the 1813 governor's mansion, the nation's oldest such dwelling. Within walking distance of the capitol in downtown Richmond you'll find a number of other attractions of historic or cultural interest, among them St. Paul's, embellished with Tiffany windows, where in April 1865 Jefferson Davis received word that Federal troops were about to invade the city; Shockoe Slip, an old commercial area where Richmond began, now revitalized, the cobblestone streets filled with shops and restaurants, including the Tobacco Company, an eatery installed in an 1870s tobacco warehouse; the nearby Kanawha Canal Locks, remnants of the nation's first canal system; a Money Museum located in the Federal Reserve Bank, a modernistic building by the James; the Edgar Allan Poe Museum (Tu.–Sat., 10–4, Sun. and M., 1:30–4, adm.), five buildings—including the 1736 Old Stone House, the original city's most venerable structure—with displays on the author's life and writing career; the Valentine Museum (M.–Sat., 10–5, Sun., 1–5, adm.), covering the history and life of Richmond; the Museum and White House of the Confederacy (M.–Sat., 10–5, Sun., 1–5, adm.), said to contain the largest collection of Confederate memorabilia in existence; the 1790 John Marshall House (Tu.–Sat., 10–5, Sun., 1–5, adm.), with displays on the life and career of the Secretary of State and U.S. Supreme Court Chief Justice; the Old City Hall (1885), across from which atop the new City Hall a Skydeck offers a view over downtown Richmond; the 1845 Egyptian Building, used by the College of Medicine, the main Southern center for the education of physicians during the Civil War; 1814 Monumental Church, designed by South Carolina's Robert Mills, America's first native-born professional architect, who also designed the Washington Monument.

In the house at 1 West Main Street, corner of Foushee, lived for fifty-eight years Pulitzer Prize-winning author Ellen Glasgow, who wrote there all but one of her twenty novels—a saga based on Virginia's social history between the 1890s and the 1940s depicting the rise of the state's middle class and the decline of a rural way of life. In the Jackson Ward corner of town, a National Historic District at the edge of downtown, lived such famous black Richmond residents as dancer Bill "Bojangles" Robinson, commemorated by a statue, and Maggie Walker, daughter of a former slave, whose life as founder of a bank and advocate of black women's rights is recalled at the Walker National Historic Site (Th.–Sun., 9–5, free) installed in her restored house. Farther afield around Richmond you'll find such areas as Bon Air, a turn-of-the-century summer resort whose big Victorian-style houses, laden with "gingerbread" trim, survive, and The Fan, with galleries and shops in century-old restored townhouses, named for its streets that fan out toward the west and are bordered by Monument Avenue, a one and a third-mile long tree-lined thoroughfare embellished with handsome houses and statues of Southern leaders, some—including Jefferson Davis and J. E. B. Stuart—buried at Richmond's Hollywood Cemetery, as are Presidents James Monroe and John Tyler. You'll find at the American Historical Foundation Museum (M.–F.) personal artifacts of Confederate general Stuart, as well as the nation's largest collection of military knives and bayonets, while other area museums include the Science Museum of Virginia (M.–Th., 11:30–5; F.–Sun., 11:30–8, adm.), the Virginia Museum of

Fine Arts (Tu.–Sat., 11–5; Sun., 1–5, free), the Virginia Aviation Museum (Tu.–Sat., 10–4; Sun. 12–4 April–Sept., 1–5,
Oct.–March, adm.) and the Virginia (her name, not the
state's) Randolph Museum (M., W., F., Sat., 1–4; Sun., 3–5,
free), commemorating the black educator who founded Virginia's vocational curriculum. Out on East Broad are the
Richmond National Battlefield Park (visitor center 9–5, free,
park open daylight hours), recalling the defense of the city
against Generals McClellan in 1862 and Grant in 1865—"On
to Richmond" became the rallying cry of Union forces—and
1741 St. John's, the still-active church where Patrick Henry
delivered his "Give me liberty or give me death" speech
on March 23, 1775 to an audience which included Washington and Jefferson. Jefferson grew up at Tuckahoe Plantation
(open by appointment: 804-784-5736 or 784-3493), west of
Richmond, a working farm with a distinctive "H"-shaped
house (c. 1712) and also a schoolhouse attended by young
Tom. Other area showhouses include Agecroft Hall (Tu.–
Sat., 10–4; Sun., 2–5, adm.), a Tudor era manor house trans-
planted from England to Richmond; Maymont (grounds
open April–Oct., 10–7; Nov.–March, 10–5, hours vary for
house: 804-358-7166, free), an opulently furnished century-
old mansion set in a hundred acres of gardens; and Wilton
(Tu.–Sat., 10–4:30; Sun—except July—1:30–4:30, adm.), an
antique-filled 1753 Georgian-style dwelling visited by such
luminaries as Washington, Jefferson and Lafayette and now
headquarters of the Colonial Dames of America's Virginia
branch. For a look at the product which has so enhanced
the Richmond economy for many years, you might want
to tour the Philip Morris Manufacturing Center (M.–F., 9–4,
free) installed in an ultra-modern complex on the south side
of town (the firm's factories at Concord, North Carolina,
and Louisville, Kentucky, also take visitors), while for a
different perspective on the area the "Anabel Lee" (804-

222-5700), an old-style steamer, cruises the James River. The Catlin-Abbott House (804-780-3746) in Richmond offers bed and breakfast, while Bensonhouse (804-648-7560) serves as a bed and breakfast booking agency for Richmond, Williamsburg and some other areas around Virginia.

To complete your tour of eastern Virginia, the area north of Richmond offers a few attractions of interest. At Ashland you'll find Randolph-Macon College, novelist Pearl Buck's alma mater, with the delightful 1872 Washington and Franklin Hall, laden with thick borders above the windows and a wood-fringed half-circle embellishment atop the facade. Farther north lies Kings Dominion, a king-sized theme park (for schedules: 804-876-5000) featuring eleven live shows, rides on land, water and through the air, and other attractions. At Hanover, to the east, stands the 1723 Hanover Tavern, listed on the National Register, where British General Cornwallis headquartered for eighteen days, supposedly departing without paying his bill. At the tavern you can dine in one of the five candlelit eating rooms and also attend performances (W.–Sat., 804-537-5333) at what is claimed to be America's oldest dinner theater. Tavern owner John Shelton's daughter Sarah married Patrick Henry, who lived at the place for three years. At the still-used 1735 courthouse across the road Henry argued the famous "Parsons' Cause" case, attacking the powers of the English king to govern Virginia's internal affairs. During Henry's most active political years he lived at Scotchtown (April–Oct., M.–F., 10–4:30; Sun., 1:30–4:30, adm.), northwest of Ashland. In 1771 Henry moved to the estate—on which stands his law office where, no doubt, he composed many of his stirring ovations—and five years later he became Virginia's governor. This brought to an end Virginia's hundred and sixty-nine years as an English colony. Ahead lay revolution, and the birth of a nation.

Central Virginia

*Winchester—Front Royal—East of the Skyline Drive to
Charlottesville—West of the Skyline Drive via the
Shenandoah Valley, Harrisonburg, Staunton and Lexington
to Lynchburg—Danville—Martinsville*

Central Virginia (described in this section) and western
Virginia (covered in the next section) differ from the eastern
part of the state. As Marshall W. Fishwick noted in *Virginia:
A New Look at the Old Dominion:* "Each region has its own
ecology, each town its local variations. Tidewater emphasizes
colonialism, English ways, and Georgian building. Piedmont
favors antebellum days, the Virginia Dynasty [planter-
politicians such as Jefferson and Monroe], and Greek Revival
architecture. The Scotch-Irish and Germans in the Valley
have their own historical patterns, family farms, and con-
victions. Southwestern Virginia stresses log-cabin culture,
mountain ballads, and new industries."

At the northern edge of central Virginia lies Winchester,
hometown of Virginia's latter-day Byrd clan, or flock, which
began with Tom, Dick and Harry. At age fifteen, Harry
took over his father's nearly bankrupt *Evening Star* in Winchester in 1902 and saved the floundering newspaper. Later,
along with brother Tom, Harry became one of the world's
biggest apple growers, and in 1915 he began his political
career with election to the state senate. In 1926 Byrd took
office as governor, then in 1933 he started the first of six
terms as U.S. Senator, serving until 1965 when his son,
Harry F. Byrd, Jr., succeeded him. Richard, meanwhile,
gained fame as a polar explorer. In addition to the famous
Byrds who once perched in Winchester—also hometown of
writer Willa Cather, who at a young age moved with her
family to Nebraska—other historical figures lived in the city.

In 1748 sixteen-year-old George Washington worked as a surveyor in the area, and ten years later the citizens of Frederick County elected him to serve in the House of Burgesses, his first political office. Washington's Office Museum (April–Oct., 9–5, adm.), a small log building he used as his headquarters in 1755–56 while serving in the Virginia Militia, recalls the great man's presence in Winchester, while the Gothic Revival-style dwelling now the "Stonewall" Jackson Headquarters Museum (April–Oct., 9–5, adm.) housed that Civil War Confederate general during the winter of 1861–62. Other sights in Winchester—which in early May for more than sixty years has hosted the annual Shenandoah Apple Blossom Festival—include Abram's Delight (April–Oct., 9–5, adm.), believed the town's oldest house (1754); the Frederick County Courthouse, a beautifully proportioned 1840 Greek Revival-style structure; and the Handley Library and Archives, with an extensive collection of genealogical records. The Henkel-Harris Company, which produces replicas of George and Martha Washington's Mount Vernon china and furniture, offers tours of the workshop (703-667-4900), while the Winchester Winery (W.–Sun., 10–5) also receives visitors.

Scattered around rustic Clarke County you'll find remote old churches and their graveyards, apple orchards, backcountry roads and other evidences of the simple life. Near Pine Grove an isolated monastery turns out delicious bread, much appreciated by area residents; at Berryville, Coiner's Department Store still uses an old-fashioned system of overhead pulleys and cables to send payments to the office; Millwood boasts an old-time country store as well as the 1782 Burnwell-Morgan Mill (May–Oct., W.–M., 9:30–4:30), listed on the National Register, which functioned until 1953; and at Boyce the River House (703-837-1476) offers bed and breakfast, while Blue Ridge Reservation Service at Berryville (703-955-1246) can book you at other bed and breakfast

places. Off to the west at Middletown you'll find Belle Grove
Plantation (mid-March–mid-Nov., M.–Sat., 10–4; Sun.,
1–5, adm.), designed by Thomas Jefferson for Major Isaac
Hite, Jr., brother-in-law of James Madison, who in 1794
honeymooned there with his wife, Dolley. Century-and-a-
half-old St. Thomas Church in Middletown, listed on the
National Register, is a miniature version of York Cathedral
in England. Wayside Inn, established in 1797 as a stagecoach
way-station, still takes overnight guests (703-869-1797) and
serves colonial-style meals featuring such dishes as peanut
soup, spoon bread and huntsmen's pie in seven dining areas,
one of them, the President's Room, filled with memorabilia
of the nation's chief executives. Bed and breakfast is available
in Middletown at a Victorian-era house (703-869-4115 before 9 a.m. and after 6 p.m.), while the Wayside Theatre
(703-869-1776) offers plays during the summer. At nearby
Strasburg—around which swirled Civil War battles, recalled
at the local museum (May–Oct., 10–4, adm.) installed in
the old Southern Railway depot—Tumbling Run (703-465-
4403) also offers bed and breakfast. The museum also
contains displays of the once popular locally made pottery, an industry which functioned in the area from 1833
to 1908 and which gave Strasburg and Maurertown to the
south the nicknames Pot Town and Jug Town. It was in
this area where an enterprising woman named Charlotte
Hillman dropped a tollgate in front of the entire army of
Civil War general Sheridan who humored her by paying
for himself and his staff, suggesting she collect the rest of
the toll from the U.S. government. Hillman counted the
soldiers as they filed past, tallied the total and after the
war submitted a bill to the Federal authorities, who paid
her.

   Near Strasburg lies Front Royal, called Helltown before
the Revolutionary War for the boisterous behavior of its residents. The new name originated when a drill sergeant took

to commanding troops to "front the royal oak," a giant tree
in the public square. The Warren Rifles Confederate Museum
(April 15–Nov. 1, M.–Sat., 9–5; Sun., 12–5, free) contains
Civil War exhibits, while at Skyline Caverns (March–Oct.,
8–7; Nov.–Feb., 9–5, adm.) a miniature train takes you
through part of the natural formations, and at nearby Hume
Oasis Vineyard offers tours (10–4). At Front Royal—where
you'll find bed and breakfast at Constant Spring Inn (703-
635-7010)—begins the one hundred and five-mile long Skyline Drive which takes you south through Shenandoah
National Park and then connects with the Blue Ridge Parkway that continues for four hundred and seventy miles on
down through North Carolina, linking Shenandoah and
Great Smoky Mountain National parks. Along Skyline
Drive, which offers a never-ending series of panoramas,
you'll find campgrounds (for information: 703-999-2266),
lodges, lookout points and "waysides" with shops and provisions. Places to stay include log cottages at Lewis Mountain
(mid-May–Oct., 703-999-2255); Skyland Lodge (April–
Nov., 703-999-2211), established in 1894 and located at the
Drive's highest point; and Big Meadows Lodge (mid-May–
Oct., 703-999-2221), situated on a high plateau overlooking
the Shenandoah Valley. Through the park also runs part of
the Appalachian Trail. If you opt not to take Skyline Drive
south from Front Royal you can continue toward the south
through the Shenandoah Valley (a route covered below) west
of the Drive or follow an itinerary (which starts in the next
paragraph) through the countryside east of the Drive down
to Charlottesville, which lies not far from Skyline's southern
entrance or exit.

At Markham, off to the east of Front Royal, which in
early June hosts the annual Virginia Wineries Festival, the
Naked Mountain Vineyard and Winery (March–Dec., W.,
Th., F., 12–5; Sat. and Sun., 10–5) perches on the east slope
of the Blue Ridge with a lovely view onto the countryside,

while down at Flint Hill you'll find the Farfelu Vineyard (hours by appointment: 703-364-2930), established in 1967 as one of Virginia's first wineries, as well as 1812 Caledonia Farm (703-675-3693), a working farm that takes bed and breakfast guests. Other bed and breakfast places in the area include Conyers House (703-987-8025) in the country, Meadowood (703-547-3851) at Slate Mills, Four and Twenty Blackbirds at Amissville (703-937-5885) and, in the village of Washington—laid out in 1749 by Washington himself and the first of twenty-eight American towns named for him— the Foster-Harris House (703-675-3757), Gay Street Inn (703-675-3410), Heritage House (703-675-3207 or 675-3738) and Mayes House (703-675-3410). Beyond Sperryville, which offers a scattering of antique shops, lies Syria where the Graves Mountain Lodge complex (703-923-4231) offers cottages, cabins, houses, motels, a lodge, family-style meals and the old-fashioned Syria Mercantile general store, while Rose River Vineyards at Syria offers tours (April–Nov., F.–M., 10–5). Not far from nearby Banco—where Olive Mill Inn (703-923-4664), named after Madison County's last mill open to the public, takes bed and breakfast guests—Herbert Hoover established his "Summer White House."

Around Culpeper, whose Fountain Hall (703-825-8200) offers bed and breakfast, operate a few wineries, among them Prince Michel (10–5), the state's largest at a hundred and ten acres, featuring a wine museum; Dominion Wine Cellars, brand name for the Virginia Winery Cooperative (Tu.–Sat., 10–6; Sun., 12–6), which processes grapes from some twenty vineyards; and Rapidan River (10–5), specializing in German-type wines. At Brandy Station, east of Culpeper, occurred in 1863 the largest cavalry battle in U.S. history, while farther east, where route 3 crosses the Rapidan River, Virginia governor Alexander Spotswood built his home, known as the "Enchanted Castle" (now being excavated; for visiting information: 703-399-1043) for its formidable and elaborate appearance. From here in 1716 Spotswood led his famous expedition over the Blue Ridge into the Shenandoah Valley to claim for King George I the trans-mountain territory, an area the governor described in his account of the trek as "World's End." John Fontaine, one of the adventurers (to each of whom Spotswood gave a gem-studded golden horseshoe, thus establishing Virginia's Knights of the Golden Horseshoe) noted in his diary that the expedition's "abundant provisions" included an ample supply of "wine, brandy, stout, two kinds of rum, champagne, cherry punch, cider, etc.," that "etc." no doubt referring to such lesser supplies as food, weapons, equipment and the like.

In Madison you'll find the 1790 Arcade Building and the 1829 courthouse, while just north of town stands 1740 Hebron Church, the nation's oldest Lutheran church in continuous use, and nearby is the Misty Mountain Winery (tours by appointment: 703-923-4738). On highway 622 off route 15 north of Madison Mills, down toward Orange, nestles the Woodberry Forest School, a college-prep school which boasts the National Register-listed "The Residence," designed by Thomas Jefferson and built in 1793 for James Madison's brother. Madison memories abound in the area. In Orange the James Madison Museum (March–Nov., M.–F., 10–12, 1–5; Sat., and Sun., 1–4; Dec.–Feb., M.–F., 10–12, 1–4, adm.) recalls the nation's fourth president, with such personal items as his books, correspondence and furnishings from nearby Montpelier (10–4, adm.), a lovely twenty-seven hundred-acre estate with one hundred and thirty-eight buildings including the fifty-five-room mansion where Madison grew up and lived in later life. After his second term ended in 1817 he and his wife, Dolley, whom Madison met in 1794 through an introduction by Aaron Burr, retired to Montpelier, where the former president (he died in 1836) is buried. In 1901 members of the du Pont family acquired the estate, operating it as a private hunt country residence until 1984, and only since 1987 has the property been opened to the public. In June 1989 the National Trust, which took title to Montpelier in 1984, held a convocation to consider how the historic property should be restored and managed.

In the town of Orange you'll also find the 1858 courthouse, listed on the National Register, with archives dating back to 1734, including the wills of Madison and Governor Spotswood, and 1834 St. Thomas Church, also Register-listed, the only surviving example of church architecture reflecting the design of Thomas Jefferson. For bed and breakfast at Orange you can choose from the Shadows (703-672-5057), Willow Grove (703-672-5982), the Hidden Inn (703-672-3625) and National Register-listed Mayhurst (703-672-5597), a rather odd looking pile with fanciful embellishments. Route 231 down to Gordonsville—Sleepy Hollow on that road offers bed and breakfast (703-832-5555)—is a lovely winding way bordered by attractive farms and houses. Along Main Street in Gordonsville—where the old (1860) Exchange Hotel (Tu.–Sat., 10–4, adm.), a train-stop hostelry, served as a hospital during the Civil War—stand attractive Victorian-era structures. At Barboursville off to the west, near Montebello, thought to be the birthplace of Zachary Taylor, you'll find the Barboursville Vineyards (tours, Sat., 10–4; tastings, M.–Sat., 10–4), located at Governor James Barbour's former plantation, its Thomas Jefferson-designed mansion, destroyed by fire in 1884, still in ruins. Off to the east, near Mineral, the Virginia Power Company operates the North Anna Nuclear Information Center (M.–F., 9–4; Sun., 12–5, free), with displays on the commercial nuclear power industry.

Some of the historic sights mentioned in the previous paragraph lie along the so-called Constitution Route, a road which passes by or near many Revolutionary and Civil War era attractions. This route goes through Charlottesville, where such historic places abound. Near the city lies the most famous of those sights—Jefferson's Monticello (March–Oct., 8–5; Nov.–Feb., 9–4:30, adm.) which, like Washington's Mount Vernon, needs no introduction. So well preserved and homey is Monticello that a modern-day visitor finds little difficulty imagining Jefferson's presence there as described by John Edwards Caldwell, who recalled his 1808 visit to "Monticello and its philosophic owner" in *A Tour Through Part of Virginia:*

> Until breakfast, which is early, he is employed in writing, after that he generally visits his work-shops, labourers, & c. and then, until 12 o'clock, he is engaged in his study, either in drawing, writing or reading; he then rides over his plantation, returns at two, dresses for dinner, and joins his company; he retires from table soon after the cloth is removed, and spends the evening in walking about, reading the papers, and in conversation with such guests as may be with him. His disposition is truly amiable, easy of access, quick and ready in the dispatch of business.

Near Monticello stands Michie Tavern (9–5, adm.), moved there in 1927 from a site some seventeen miles northwest where in 1784 the Michie family opened the inn on a stage-coach route. The establishment, which remained in the family until 1910, now serves as a museum, but meals are available (11:30–3) at a converted two-century-old former slave house on the property called "The Ordinary." The ground floor of 1797 Meadow Run Grist Mill there houses an old-time general store, while the upstairs area contains the Virginia Wine Museum (free). It was Jefferson himself—believing that a civilized nation should consume wine, a more moderate beverage than hard liquor—who started the wine industry in Virginia by bringing Filippo Mazzei to the area from Italy before the Revolution. During Prohibition the vineyards were destroyed but in 1974 began the area's first recent plantings, at La Abra Farm (M.–Sat., 11–5; Sun., 12–5) in Lovingston, south of Charlottesville, and now some forty wineries operate in the state, with about ten in the Monticello Viticultural Area, including La Abra; Barboursville (described in the previous paragraph) and Burnley at Barboursville (March–Dec., W.–Sun., 11–5); Autumn Hill (tours by appointment: 804-985-3081) at Stanardsville; Bacchanal (May–Oct., Sat. and Sun., 10–4) at Afton; Chermont (Tu.–Sat., 1–5) at Esmont; and, in Charlottesville, Montdomaine (May–Oct., W.–Sun., 10–4, Nov.–April by appointment: 804-971-8947), Oakencroft (April–Dec., M.–F., 9–4; Sat. and Sun., 11–5; Jan.–March by appointment: 804-295-8175) and Simeon (by appointment only: 804-977-0800). In early October the Boar's Head Inn at Charlottesville hosts the annual Monticello Wine Festival. Before proceeding to Charlottesville it's worth visiting Ash Lawn (March–Oct., 9–6; Nov.–Feb., 10–5, adm.), two and a half miles from Monticello, to which James Monroe and his wife Elizabeth moved in 1799 to be near his friend, Thomas Jefferson. On a clear day, from the porch of the house—which contains Monroe memorabilia and possessions—one can see nearby Monticello. It was perhaps at a tavern like Michie's where in the early nineteenth century Madison, Jefferson and Monroe, three Founding Fathers (by then grandfathers) and ex-presidents who retired in Virginia's Piedmont area, gathered to chat about matters of state and about future prospects of the young nation those old men helped to establish.

Around Court Square in Charlottesville stand some old buildings, while west of downtown spreads the University of Virginia campus, whose nucleus—the famous "academical village" featuring the classical-style Rotunda—Jefferson designed. In 1976 the American Institute of Architects voted his design the most outstanding achievement in American architecture. At the university you can visit the room occupied by Edgar Allan Poe, who enrolled in 1826, the second session of the then new institution. In the oddly named *The Virginia Plutarch* Philip Alexander Bruce described Poe there as "a magnetic and not a sympathetic figure; rarely seeking company, though not averse to it; but under all circumstances, at heart and in mind, solitary even when surrounded by companions of congenial tastes and similar pursuits." On Main Street east of the university stands a memorial to explorers Meriwether Lewis and William Clark, local residents whom Jefferson chose to lead the famous expedition up the Missouri River in 1804. Guesthouses (804-979-7264, M.–F., 12–5) represents bed and breakfast establishments in the Charlottesville area and the Piedmont, while bed and breakfast inns in town include Clifton (804-971-1800), Silver Thatch (804-978-4686), 200 South Street (804-979-0200) and National Register-listed Woodstock Hall (804-293-8977). Also Register-listed is High Meadows (804-286-2218), a bed and breakfast house at Scottsville—another there is Chester (804-286-3960)—south of Charlottesville where you'll find some nineteenth-century architecture and a local museum installed in a former church.

James River Runners (804-286-2338) at Hattons Ferry near Scottsville provides canoes and equipment for trips on the James River. Trillium House (804-325-9126) at Nellysford off to the west is a relatively new (1983) but tastefully mounted country inn located at Wintergreen, a nearby eleven thousand-acre four-season resort (800-325-2200) in the Blue Ridge Mountains which in the winter offers skiing. To the south, at Lovingston, stands the attractive 1809 courthouse of heavily forested Nelson County—trees cover three-quarters of its area—while to the north at tiny Afton cluster a group of antique and craft shops. Afton once served as the nation's largest apple shipping point, the fruit being sent out by trains that used a tunnel designed in the 1840s by Claudius Crozet, Napoleon's engineer, a hand-dug construction through the Blue Ridge that took eight years to complete. In the heights above Afton perches Swannanoa (summer, 8–6; winter 9–5, adm.), a marble mansion that houses archives, information and mementos relating to the cosmic philosophical and religious teachings of Walter and Lao Russell. At nearby Waynesboro you'll find a museum and sales gallery devoted to the works of P. Buckley Moss, a folk-style painter.

Returning now to the Winchester-Front Royal area where this itinerary to places east of Skyline Drive began, here's a suggested route that will take you south through the Shenandoah Valley west of the Drive and to nearby areas. "Shenandoah" is a poem of a word, and even more poetic is its supposed meaning in Indian language—"daughter of the stars." For reasons not known, most of the Indian tribes departed from the area in the early 1600s, and a century later Scotch-Irish and German settlers from Pennsylvania began drifting into The Valley, as Virginians call Shenandoah. Inns, wineries, antique shops, Civil and Revolutionary War memories, apple orchards and corners where history lingers fill The Valley, nearly two hundred miles long and ten to twenty miles wide. Unfortunately, in recent years gypsy moths have infested the northern part of Shenandoah. At Woodstock, a town whose chartering by the House of Burgesses in 1761 George Washington sponsored, you'll find the 1792 courthouse, built from a design by Thomas Jefferson, the Massanutten Military Academy, the national headquarters of Sigma Sigma Sigma sorority, and the Woodstock Museum (May–Sept., Th., F., Sat., 10–4, free). On the crest of Massanutten Mountain four miles from town stands an observation tower affording splendid views of the valley and the river's seven bends there.

The third weekend in June Woodstock—where the Inn at Narrow Passage (703-459-8000) takes bed and breakfast guests—celebrates its annual Court Days, featuring re-creations of historical cases, meals and turn-of-the-century customs. Back in 1776 local pastor Peter Muhlenberg preached a dramatic call to arms, shouting, "There's a time to pray and a time to fight" as he organized on the spot the 8th Virginia Regiment and then marched the unit from the Woodstock church into the Revolutionary War. At Edinburg, where Mary's Country Inn (703-984-8286) offers bed and breakfast, nestles Shenandoah Vineyards (10–6), The Valley's first winery. Farther on, south of Mt. Jackson, location of the Widow Kip's (703-477-2400) Bed and Breakfast house, stands Meems Bottom Bridge, longest, at some two hundred feet, of Virginia's seven surviving covered bridges. On Halloween 1976 vandals burned the 1893 span, later reconstructed from the original timbers and reopened to traffic. The Tuttle & Spice 1880 General Store (April–Oct., 9–9; Nov.–March, 9–6, free) in Mt. Jackson houses old fixtures and artifacts, while the town's Confederate cemetery is Virginia's sole graveyard where only Southern soldiers, and no Yankees, repose. Nearby lies Camp Roosevelt, the nation's first Civilian Conservation Corps facility. Off to the west, beyond Shenandoah Caverns (June 16–Labor Day, 9–6:15; shorter hours in winter, adm.), one of The Valley's half dozen or so commercial caves, lies Basye with the Bryce Resort (703-856-8150), a large complex that features skiing in the winter. At nearby Orkney Springs the lovely pre-Civil War Orkney Springs Hotel, listed on the National Register, hosts the Shenandoah Valley Music Festival in July, August and September (for information: 703-459-3396).

At New Market, south of Mt. Jackson, clashed Union General Franz Sigel with General John C. Breckinridge, former U.S. vice-president, in a bloody battle that included two hundred and forty-seven cadets from the Virginia Military Institute at Lexington to the south. As Breckinridge commanded into battle the youngsters, some only fifteen years old, he muttered, "Order them up, and God forgive

me for the order." Ten of the cadets died and forty-seven
fell wounded as the Confederates pushed the Yankees back
north. Virginia Military Institute administers the New Market Museum (9–5, adm.), known as the Hall of Valor, whose
exhibits recall the battle. New Market also boasts another
museum with a rather unusual theme—Bedrooms of America (March–April and Sept.–Dec., 9–5; June–Aug., 9–9,
adm.), eleven period rooms outfitted with bedroom furniture from the late seventeenth-century William and Mary
period up to the Art Deco style of the 1930s. Being curator
of the bedroom museum must be one of the most restful
jobs in America. Near New Market you'll find another
of The Valley's cave attractions, Endless Caverns (June
15–Labor Day, 9–7; to 6, spring and fall, adm.), while to
the east are Luray Caverns (June–Labor Day, 9–7; to 6, spring
and fall, adm.), whose pride and joy is a "Stalacpipe" organ
that uses stalactite formations as tone sources. At Luray
stands the restored Massanutten one-room school, used from
1875 to 1937, and also the Guilford Ridge Vineyard (May–
mid-Nov. tours by appointment: 703-778-3853).

Shenandoah River Outfitters (703-743-4159) at Luray rents
canoes and equipment for excursions on the Shenandoah,
"a short and friendly river to have so rich a history," observes
Julia Davis in *The Shenandoah.* So mild-mannered is the waterway that T. S. Eliot could well have been referring to
the stream in his poem "Virginia," which describes a slow
or even never-moving river that sits between still hills.
The Mimslyn (703-743-5105) at Luray is an elegant resort,
while bed and breakfast places include Boxwood Hill
(703-743-3550), Boxwood Place (703-743-4748), Grey House
Inn (703-743-3200), Ruffner House (703-743-7855), Shenandoah Countryside (703-743-6434), River Roost (703-
743-3467) and Spring House (703-743-4701), and down
at Stanley to the south lies Jordan Hollow Farm Inn
(703-778-2209 or 778-2285), a restored colonial-era horse

farm converted into a country inn. At McGaheysville farther south Shenandoah Valley Farm (703-289-5402), a working farm which raises Black Angus cattle, also takes overnight guests, and nearby is the Massanutten resort and ski complex (703-289-9441).

West of McGaheysville, back in The Valley, lies Harrisonburg where the Warren-Sipe Museum (April–early Oct., Tu.–Sat., 10–4, donation) houses a computer-controlled twelve-foot relief map that graphically portrays with lights the 1862 Valley Campaign led by Thomas J. "Stonewall" Jackson, a professor from Lexington who outmaneuvered sixty thousand Union troops with fewer than a third as many men. Also in Harrisonburg—where yellow fever pioneer Walter Reed spent part of his youth—is the Mennonite Visitor Center (M.–F., 8–4, free) with art, books and displays relating to the area's Mennonite culture. At Harrisonburg—where Kingsway (703-867-9696) offers bed and breakfast—two factory tours take you inside the food industry: Shenandoah Pride Dairy (703-434-7328), a cooperative which processes milk supplied by more than three hundred farmers, and Rocco Enterprises, a chicken processing plant. The Pumpkin House (703-434-6963) at nearby Mt. Crawford not only takes bed and breakfast guests but also lets them buy the antiques that outfit the place. Just beyond Dayton—where the Cromer-Trumbo House (April–early Oct., Tu., W., F., Sat., 10–4, free) contains area archives, exhibits and genealogical records—lies Bridgewater where the Revel B. Pritchett Museum (Tu., Th., 2–4, free) at Bridgewater College houses an eclectic assemblage of historic artifacts, including rare books, glassware, weapons and more than six thousand other objects. Nearby bristle the Natural Chimneys (9–dark, adm.), one hundred and twenty-foot-high limestone formations whose castle-like appearance inspired the Jousting Tournament, first held in 1821, supposedly the nation's oldest continuous sporting event, which takes place annually on the third Sunday in August.

Down at Staunton, which in 1908 devised the city manager form of government, survive a large group of old buildings. In one, a Greek Revival-style townhouse (9–5, to 6 in summer; Dec.–Feb., closed Sun., adm.), Woodrow Wilson first saw the light of day. "A man's rootage is more important than his leafage," the president once remarked, and here in the manse occupied by his father, Presbyterian minister Joseph Wilson, began Woodrow's roots. In areas like Gospel Hill, North End and Newtown around town remain such relics of yesteryear as Victorian-era warehouses at the Wharf Historic District; stately Stuart House (1791), with a delicately designed wooden gate out front; the Oaks, sporting an angular addition built in 1888 by cartographer Jed Hotchkiss, whose Civil War maps the Library of Congress now owns; and the Victorian and Greek Revival-style buildings on the Mary Baldwin College campus. In the restored downtown commercial district a c. 1903 bank building houses a museum of banking history (M.–F., 9–12, free); the fanciful 1920 Temple House of Israel seems a transplant from some exotic Eastern land; and the 1901 courthouse is the latest to serve Augusta County which, when established in 1738, extended to the Mississippi River, five states eventually being carved out of the territory. Out at Gypsy Hill Park, near which the Statler Brothers Museum (tours, M.-F. at 2, free) commemorates the singing group, the 'Stonewall Brigade Band," supposedly the nation's oldest continuously performing band, presents concerts every summer on Monday evenings at 7. The new (fall 1988) Museum of American Frontier culture (9-5, adm.) consists of four farmsteads representing the nationalities of The Valley's early settlers—Irish, American, German (completed fall 1989) and English (completed fall 1990). A delightful restau-

rant in town is White Star Mill, installed in the cellar of
an old flour mill, while inns at Staunton include Frederick House (703-885-4220), Belle Grae (703-886-5151) and
Thornrose (703-885-7026), and at Churchville twelve miles
west the Buckhorn Inn (703-337-6900) offers meals as well
as accommodations. The following two paragraphs present
an itinerary for the region west of Shenandoah Valley; the
Valley tour continues in the paragraph following those.

Beyond Churchville, highway 250 takes you across
Cowpasture and Bullpasture rivers and on out to Highland
County, one of Virginia's least populated and most scenic
areas, a region with the highest elevation of any county east
of the Mississippi. Around the Monterey area centers the
county's maple sugar country, which comes to life the third
and fourth weekends of March with the annual Maple Festival, featuring displays, visits to the sugar camps, and such
maple sugar treats as syrup and candy. In Monterey the Highland Inn (703-468-2143) takes bed and breakfast guests. On
the eastern edge of McDowell stretches the battlefield where
"Stonewall" Jackson fought the first skirmish of his famous
Valley Campaign. To the south lies aptly named Bath
County, a hot spring and spa area, much of it covered by
million-acre George Washington National forest. For information on the many camping and recreational facilities of
the forest, which spreads across the western Virginia landscape: 703-433-2491. Sixteen miles north of Hot Springs rise
Mad Sheep Mountain, where the animals used to graze on
"loco weed," and Mad Tom Mountain, named for a slave
who went crazy after getting lost in the area around 1800.

Nearby, west of the highway, nestles Hidden Valley, a
campground in a verdant valley where the 1850 Warwick
Museum, listed on the National Register, stands. All around
the county bubble and flow springs, many with water "very
Clear and Warmer than new Milk," wrote a 1750 visitor
to the area. Baths are available at Bolar Springs, Warm

Springs and Hot Springs. Gristmill Square at Warm Springs offers meals and lodging, while at Hot Springs you'll find accommodations at the famous Homestead (800-336-5771; in Virginia, 800-542-5734), and at the less renowned but attractive Vine Cottage Inn (703-839-2422) and Cascades Inn (703-839-5355). Hot Springs became fashionable a century ago when J. P. Morgan floated a bond issue in 1891 to finance a railroad syndicate that owned spas in the area. In the evocatively titled *The Springs of Virginia: Life, Love and Death at the Waters 1775–1900* Perceval Reniers recalls the first days of prominence: "Seven private cars of seven railroad magnates were on the siding at one time. Six Harvard men, also all at once, took everybody's breath away. . . . Railroad money had passed a miracle. The ancient Hot, so long shunned by the pleasure bent, had been transformed into a stylish spa." From the last week in June through the first week in September the Garth Newel Music Center (703-839-5018) in Hot Springs hosts chamber music concerts. Around the county you'll encounter such sights as the world's largest pumped storage dam, operated by Virginia Power at Mountain Grove, and the Guild Factory, a silk-screening operation installed in the one-time company store of a lumber firm at Bacova. Falling Spring, to the south toward Covington, plunges two hundred feet into a gorge, a sight that greatly impressed Thomas Jefferson. Off U.S. highway 60 between Callaghan and Covington arches the one hundred-foot long 1835 Humpback Bridge, supposedly the only wooden covered bridge of its type in the nation.

From this side trip to the western edge of the state you can return to the Shenandoah Valley and Lexington to see some sights back to the east. If, instead, you proceed south from Staunton, rather than—as covered in the previous two paragraphs—detouring west to drive through Highland and Bath Counties, you'll come to Steele's Tavern where a replica of the first reaper (April–Oct., 8–6, free) recalls local resident Cyrus McCormick, who in 1831 tried out the new device he'd just invented on a grainfield in the area. Walnut Grove, the McCormick farm, remains little-changed from that era, with the old farmhouse and the inventor's log and stone blacksmith shop still standing. After McCormick invented the reaper he had to invent the reaper business, so he moved to the agricultural heartland to establish a factory in Chicago, the forerunner of International Harvester. On the original McCormick farm at Steele's Tavern stands the Osceola Mill Country Inn (703-377-MILL), installed in restored structures that once served as mill facilities on Marl Creek. Magnus House, the 1873 miller's residence, and the mill store have been converted into delightful places to stay, as is Irish Gap Inn (804-922-7701) over by the Blue Ridge Parkway.

To the south lies Lexington, a pleasant town with a nineteenth-century feel to it. Next to each other spread the campuses of Washington and Lee University and Virginia Military Institute, founded in 1839, one of the nation's two remaining state-supported military colleges (the other is The Citadel in Charleston, South Carolina). Every Friday at 4:15 a parade takes place on the V.M.I. campus, a National Historic District which includes two museums: the V.M.I. Museum (M.–Sat., 9–5; Sun., 2–5, free), with old uniforms, military artifacts, items from the school's history and a scale model of a cadet's room; and the George C. Marshall Museum (April–Oct., M.–Sat., 9–5; Sun., 2- 5; Nov.–March, to 4, free), which traces the life and career of the 1901 graduate who became Army Chief of Staff and Secretary of State. At Washington and Lee, which still receives dividends from stock George Washington gave to the school, stands the Lee Chapel and Museum (April–Oct., M.–Sat., 9–5; Sun., 2–5; Nov.–March, M.–Sat., 9–4; Sun., 2–5, free), with Lee's tomb, office and belongings, as well as a statue of Lee and a Peale portrait of Washington. Back before the Civil War

Thomas J. "Stonewall" Jackson taught at Washington and Lee, which he left to lead troops in the conflict. Memories of the Southern military leader survive at the 1842 Jackson House (M.–Sat., 9–4:30; Sun., 1–4:30, adm.), furnished with many of his belongings, and in Memorial Cemetery where a statue of Jackson, binoculars in one hand and sword in the other, stands. Over the summer two theater companies perform at Lexington: Henry Street Playhouse (703-463-8637) in an 1856 theater in the Historic District, and Theater at the Kiln (703-463-7088), an outdoor facility at a nineteenth-century lime kiln.

Lexington is a good place to see one of the state's Lawyer's Rows, found in many courthouse towns, which recall the high prestige lawyers in Virginia enjoyed in the early days. Such attorneys as Jefferson, Madison, Patrick Henry and U.S. Supreme Court Chief Justice John Marshall lent the profession standing and made a town's Lawyer's Row a social and political center. The prominence of politicians and lawyers in Virginia has, according to at least one observer, given them more prestige than intellectual types: "The pervasive tone of Virginia's thought for generations has been anti-intellectual," maintains Marshall W. Fishwick in *Virginia: A New Look at the Old Dominion.* "Poets, thinkers, logicians have never been admired like the soldier, politician, or preacher." Bed and breakfast choices in Lexington include the 1789 Alexander-Withrow House and the 1809 Mc-Campbell Inn, across the street from each other on Main Street, and 1850 Maple Hall, a country house six miles north of town (for reservations at these three inns: 703-463-2044), while adjacent to the Virginia Horse Center—a four-hundred-acre facility for auctions, shows and other equine activities—is Fassifern (703-463-1013).

South of Lexington lies Natural Bridge (7–dusk, adm.), one of those landscape features so often commercialized in the U.S. into tourist attractions. Helped by the formation's romantic history—Jefferson bought the bridge from George III for twenty shillings (about $2.40) and in 1803 built there a family cabin, and Washington carved his initials (still visible) on the structure when surveying it for Lord Halifax—the rock arch has been turned into a tourist attraction, complete with hotel, wax museum and "The Drama of Creation" sound and light show.

From Natural Bridge it's convenient to leave Shenandoah Valley and head southeast to Lynchburg to begin your visit to south-central Virginia. Historic and cultural attractions abound in Lynchburg, founded by Quaker John Lynch, while his less pacifist brother Charles opted to fight in the Revolution. The Lynchburg Museum (1–4, adm.), installed in the mid-nineteenth-century courthouse, houses exhibits on the town's history, while the past also survives at such places as the 1798 South River Meeting House (Sun.–F., 9–3, free), where Quakers such as the Lynchs gathered; the Joseph Nichols Tavern (dinner-theater presentations: 804-845-6153) in the 1815 Western Hotel; the Confederate Cemetery and Pest House Medical Museum; the c. 1791 Miller-Clayton House, where Thomas Jefferson ventured to taste a "love apple" (tomato), then thought to be poisonous. Also, the "Point of Honor" (1–4, adm.), with unusual octagonal corner sections, a mansion built about 1815 by Patrick Henry's physician and so named for duels fought on the property's lawn; the Anne Spencer House (by appointment: 804-846-0517), home of the black poet; the Maier Museum of Art (Tu.–Sun., 1–5, by appointment in July and August: 804-846-7392, ext. 362, free) featuring a collection of nineteenth- and twentieth-century American paintings; Fort Early, where Confederate General Jubal A. Early repulsed Union General Hunter, whose staff included two future U.S. presidents, Rutherford B. Hayes and William McKinley; and 1806 Poplar Forest (varying hours while under restoration; for schedule: 804-525-1806, adm.), an octagonal brick home designed by Jefferson and used by him to escape the non-stop stream of visitors at Monticello.

At Lynchburg in 1979 began the Moral Majority movement led by Jerry Falwell, who preaches at Thomas Road Baptist Church, one of the city's more than one hundred and twenty churches, and who operates Liberty University in town. For bed and breakfast in Lynchburg there are Lamplighter (804-384-1635), Micajah-Davis House Inn (804-846-5622) and Sojourners (804-384-1655). Near Bedford just to the west, Elmo's Rest (703-586-3707) is a horse, cattle and fruit farm that takes overnight guests. The farm nestles at the foot of the Peaks of Otter, a scenic area with a lodge and restaurant (703-586-1081; in Virginia, 800-542-5927) where a trail takes you up distinctively shaped Sharp Top, thought incorrectly by Jefferson to be the state's tallest mountain, from which was taken a stone as Virginia's contribution to the Washington Monument in 1852. Bedford boasts Lions, Moose, Woodmen, Odd Fellows, cats, and dogs, but the Elks reign supreme there as the town claims the National Home of the Fraternal Order of Elks, a facility for retired members. In the countryside near Bedford you'll find Holy Land U.S.A. ("never closed," free), a four-hundred-acre replica of *the* Holy Land, while also in the area once stood the homestead of John M. Clemens, who moved his family on to Kentucky and Tennessee before finally settling in Missouri where he fathered a fellow who became known as Mark Twain. In *Pudd'nhead Wilson,* Twain wrote of Judge Driscoll, believed to be modeled after John Clemens: "In Missouri a recognized superiority attached to any person who hailed from Old Virginia."

Off to the east and southeast of Lynchburg lies a scattering of attractions. To the east beyond Concord—where Stonewall Vineyards offers tours and tasting (April–Dec., Tu.–Sat., 1–5)—you'll find Appomattox, made famous as the place where the Civil War, 60 percent of which was fought in Virginia, came to an end. Appomattox Court House National Historic Park (spring and summer, 9–5:30; fall and winter, 8:30–5, adm.) comprises a village restored to its 1860s appearance with twenty-seven structures, including the McLean House where the surrender took place; Meeks General Store; Surrender Triangle where on April 12, 1865, the Confederates stacked their arms; and 1819 Clover Hill Tavern, the oldest village building. More history survives down at Red Hill (April–Oct., 9–5; Nov.–March, 9–4, adm.), an attractive reconstruction and restoration of Patrick Henry's last house, law office and outbuildings where a museum traces the life and times of the famous orator and politician, who reposes on the property (he died in 1799) beneath a stone inscribed: "His fame his best epitaph." Near Gladys (south for 3.3 miles on 761 from U.S. 501, then right for 1.5 miles on 705) to the northwest stands 1878 Marysville Covered Bridge, the state's second oldest such span, while off to the northwest lies Sailor's Creek Battlefield Historical Park, site of the Civil War's last major encounter in which the Confederates suffered a major defeat on April 6, 1865, seventy-two hours before the surrender at Appomattox. According to legend the area's records at Amelia, the county seat—named for George II's daughter—survived the Civil War when Union General George Custer, of Little Big Horn fame, posted a guard with the order that the archives were to be preserved.

To the south lies Blackstone, the metropolis of Nottoway County with thirty-eight hundred people. "Blacks & whites" originally designated the pre-Revolutionary War village, the name stemming from two rival taverns, Schwarz (German for "black") and Whites, that stood at the intersection of three stagecoach roads. In 1885 locals adopted the name Blackstone, after the famous British jurist. Victorian-era storefronts and old lampposts embellish the town, which boasts the Doll House Museum (Tu.–F., 10–12, 1–4; Sat.

and Sun., 2–5, adm.), a collection of more than three thousand dolls and accessories. At Lawrenceville to the south stand such old churches as St. Paul's and St. Andrew's, while the town's St. Paul's College, founded in 1888, occupies an attractive campus. Kennon House, on route 626 by Lake Gaston, serves Southern-style meals in a 1792 dwelling that remained in the same family until 1962. Another old house survives at National Register-listed Prestwould (May–Sept., M.–Sat., 12:30–4:30; Sun., 1:30–4:30; Oct., weekends only, adm.), just north of Clarksville, a handsome stone structure built between 1790 and 1795 by Sir Peyton Skipwith, an American-born baronet. On the property survive many outbuildings, including an octagonal cottage. At Clarksville operates the state's oldest continuous tobacco market, with auctions (open to the public) from July through November. To the north at Chase City bloom the MacCallum More Gardens (open by appointment: 804-372-4184 or 372-4213), with thousands of boxwood, dogwood and flowers as well as statues from around the world. Off to the west in Halifax County—at the bottom of which the border town of Virgilina takes its name from the first letters of "Virginia" and the last letters of "Carolina"—South Boston offers a historical museum (Th. and F., 9–4; Sun., 2–4:30) with area artifacts, including tobacco industry memorabilia, and also the Speedway where stockcar racers compete. On the fourth Wednesday of July nearby Tuberville celebrates the annual Cantaloupe Festival.

Not far west lies Danville, center of Virginia's tobacco industry. Since the state's early days tobacco has played a leading role in Virginia's economy and culture. Not long after the colony's founding in 1607 John Rolfe grew a leaf that yielded a smoke more mellow than the rather bitter variety of tobacco the Indians cultivated. In 1604 James I had complained in *A Counterblaste to Tobacco* how the leaf was "loathsome to the eye, hateful to the nose, harmful to the brain . . . dangerous to the lungs," but, nonetheless, in 1617 the "George" sailed for England carrying twenty thousand pounds of the royally scorned plant, the first of many shipments of Virginia leaf, and by 1636 so dominant had tobacco become that Charles I complained "how little that colony hath advanced in Staple commodities fit for their own subsistence and clothing." In *The Planters of Colonial Virginia* Thomas J. Wertenbaker summarizes the pervasive influence of the plant on Virginia: "Tobacco was the chief factor in bringing final and complete failure to the attempts to produce useful raw materials, it was largely instrumental in molding the social classes and the political structure of the colony, it was almost entirely responsible for the system of labor, it even exerted a powerful influence upon religion and morals."

At Danville originated the auction method of selling tobacco, a system started in 1858 to replace the previous practice of selling the crop in large barrels (hogsheads) that prevented buyers from inspecting the entire lot. From mid-August to early November, Monday through Thursday, auctions—featuring auctioneers chanting at four hundred words a minute—take place in Danville's eight tobacco warehouses. For schedules you can call (804-799-5149 or 797-9437) the Tobacco-Textile Museum (M.-F., 10-4; Sat. and Sun., 2-4, adm.), where splendid displays recall both the area's tobacco culture and agriculture and the textile industry, begun in 1882. Exhibits include a model of the Dan River Schoolfield plant, said to be the world's largest single-unit textile mill. Cobbled streets around the museum run through the city's old-time tobacco district, which flourished after the Civil War, while along eight blocks on Main Street extends Millionaire's Row, listed on the National Register, lined with Victorian-era mansions. The former Sutherlin House on Main, now the Danville Museum of Fine Arts and History (Tu.-F., 10–5; Sun., 2–5, free), housed the Confederacy's final full cabinet meeting in April 1865, thus giving the residence the name "the Last Confederate Capitol." At 117 Broad Street still stands the cottage (now a privately owned attached duplex) where Nancy Witcher, later Lady Astor, the British House of Commons' first woman member, was born. Her sister Irene, who married artist Charles Dana Gibson, inspired the famous "Gibson Girl" look.

North of Danville you'll find scattered around Pittsylvania County, at nearly a thousand square miles Virginia's largest, some out-of-the-way relics of the area's old days. Chatham survives as a photogenic town, once named Competition for the controversy over where to locate the courthouse, built in 1853 and listed on the National Register. Among the notables portrayed in paintings there is one Stanhope S. Hurt, featured in Ripley's "Believe It or Not" for longevity in office: sixty-two years as court clerk. Opposite the courthouse stands the Town Hall, with the County Museum (May–Oct., Sun. 2–5) housed upstairs, while out back is the National Register-listed 1813 clerk's office. Sims-Mitchell House in Chatham takes bed and breakfast guests (804-432-0595). At Gretna to the north remains the c. 1750 restored Yates Tavern (May–Oct., Sun., 2–5), and at Callands to the west stands the restored 1773 courthouse and jail, while in the hamlets of Tomahawk, Mt. Airy, Cedar Forest and Stoney Mill you'll find operating water mills. West of Danville lies Martinsville, home of the Virginia Museum of Natural History (M.–Sat., 10–5; Sun., 1–5, adm.) and seat of Henry County, named after Patrick Henry, which boasts such claimed superlatives as the world's largest textile nylon plant, knit outerwear manufacturer, grandfather clock maker, wood furniture plant and upholstery factory, and the nation's largest mirror, sweatshirt and table producers.

At Ferrum to the north the Blue Ridge Farm Museum (June–Aug., Sat., 10–5; Sun., 1–5, adm.) presents the history and culture of early settlements in the nearby hill country, featuring an 1800-era German farmstead showing the way of life followed by settlers from the German parts of Pennsylvania. In late October Ferrum College hosts the Blue Ridge Folklife Festival (703-365-4415), Virginia's largest such event, with crafts, music and traditional food. Beyond Rocky Mount, where the Chateau Naturel Vineyard offers tours (703-483-0758), lie Smith Mountain Lake, a recreational area formed by a dam built across the Roanoke River in 1966 (The Manor at Taylor's Store [703-721-3951] in the hamlet of Wirtz offers bed and breakfast) and the Booker T. Washington National Monument (8:30–5, adm.). Reconstructed farm buildings and the Jack-O-Lantern Trail around the two-hundred-acre property take you back to the time when Washington, born there in 1856, grew up on the tobacco farm. In 1861 farm owner James Burroughs entered Booker's name on an inventory list, valuing the boy at $400. In his autobiography *Up From Slavery,* Washington, who left the farm in 1865 at age nine, recalled, "I was not large enough to be of much service, still I was occupied most of the time in cleaning the yards, carrying water to the men in the fields, or going to the mill." After struggling to get an education, Washington founded Tuskegee Institute in Alabama and in time became the nation's leading black educator. Such were the beginnings of Virginia's "other" famous Washington.

Western Virginia

Roanoke—Blacksburg—Galax—Abingdon—Bristol— Norton—Big Stone Gap—Cumberland Gap

Western Virginia has always remained rather remote from the mainstream events that transpired in the central and eastern parts of the state. In the early nineteenth century western

Virginia, less slave-intensive than and more distant from the centers of power and commerce to the east, complained that the area was under-represented in the state legislature at far-off Richmond. The region even tried to get the capital moved west of the Blue Ridge, with complaints out of the west finally becoming so vocal the state called a constitutional convention in October 1829 at Richmond, an event people from miles around attended in order to see "the last gathering of the giants," so called as Madison, Monroe and U.S. Supreme Court Justice John Marshall participated in the conclave. Although Virginia before the Civil War remained moderate in its views, refusing even to send delegates to the meeting of seceding states in Montgomery, Alabama, on April 17, 1861, three days after the war began at Fort Sumter, the state finally seceded, only to lose the Union-sympathizing western region—nearly a third of Virginia with more than three hundred thousand people—when that area seceded from Virginia in 1863 to become the new state of West Virginia.

In at least one respect Roanoke typifies the west, for it began quite late in the state's history, growing from a village called Big Lick, with four hundred people in 1881, to a railroad boom town with twenty-five thousand inhabitants ten years later. Roanoke's rail-driven economy also epitomized the lessened post-Civil War importance of the landed gentry, a class once dominant in eastern Virginia, and the rise of businessmen, industrialists, financiers and railroad entrepreneurs. As Jean Gottmann notes in *Virginia in Our Century:* "The planter element that had played so powerful a role in antebellum Virginia politics was no longer a major factor in the state's political life. . . . Landed wealth, which had previously constituted a sufficient economic foundation for most Virginians, no longer sufficed." Roanoke's Virginia Museum of Transportation (M.–Sat., 10–5; Sun., 12–5, adm.), housed in a restored Norfolk Southern freight station, contains a large collection of rail equipment and artifacts, from engines to cabooses, that recalls the time more than a century ago when the Norfolk and Western and Shenandoah Valley lines established shops in the town, touching off its growth. The city's other museums all cluster in a restored 1914 warehouse called Center in the Square, by the lively open-air Farmers Market, where you'll find the Roanoke Museum of Fine Arts (Tu.–Th. and Sat., 10–5; F., 10–8; Sun., 1–5, adm.), the Roanoke Valley History Museum (Tu.–Sat., 10–5; Sun. 1–5, adm.), and the Science Museum of Western Virginia (Tu.–Th. and Sat., 10–5; F., 10–8; Sun., 1–5, adm.), as well as Mill Mountain Theatre (703-342-5730). From atop Mill Mountain, where a one-hundred-foot tall electric star shines over the city at night, you can gain a wide panorama over Roanoke. The Country Inn (703-366-1987) takes bed and breakfast guests, while the Hotel Roanoke (800-336-9684, in Virginia, 800-542-5898), a Tudor-style pile dating from the town's early railroad days (1882), offers luxury accommodations in the center of town. North of Roanoke lies the village of Fincastle (population, 450), once center of government for a vast area that included Kentucky and much of West Virginia, Ohio, Indiana and Illinois. At the town, listed on the National Register, survive antique churches, houses and government buildings that recall Fincastle's days of glory. Near Salem, the town adjacent to Roanoke, the Bloom Winery (M.–Sat., 10–6; Sun., 1–5), one of the state's smallest, occupying only three hillside acres, features fruit wines made from dandelions, roses, elderberries, strawberries, raspberries and even grapes. You know you're in Virginia's wild west if you visit Salem the second week of January when the town hosts the Stampede Rodeo.

Before heading west out of Roanoke, you may want to follow the Blue Ridge Parkway south, which will take you alongside Floyd County, one of Virginia's most rustic areas.

No interstate highway, airport, railroad or McDonald's intervenes to spoil the rural atmosphere of the county, in all of which glows only one stoplight. At Floyd, the largest settlement, with less than five hundred souls, Cockram's General Store hosts a folksy free jamboree every Friday night, while the County Records shop in town claims to be the world's largest distributor of bluegrass music. During the month before Christmas Brookfield Plantation, one of the area's many Christmas tree farms, presents wreath-making demonstrations. At Buffalo Mountain stands one of the six stone churches built in the 1920s and '30s by Reverend Bob Childress, who defused many of the family feuds that then tormented the area, while down near Meadows of Dan stands Mabry Mill (June–Aug., 8–7; May, Sept., Oct., 8–6, free), a relic which still grinds cornmeal and buckwheat flour. The nearby Chateau Morrisette Winery (M.–Sat., 10–5; Sun., 12–5) offers tours, and Brookfield Inn (800-443-TREE or 703-763-3363) on route 8 between Floyd and Christiansburg takes bed and breakfast guests. Near Woolwine, east of the Blue Ridge Parkway, remain two of Virginia's seven surviving covered bridges, both spanning the Smith River: forty-eight-foot Jack's Creek (on route 615) and eighty-foot Bob White (off route 869 via 816). To the south lies the Reynolds Homestead (Tu.–F., 10–4; March–Nov., Sat. and Sun., 1–5, adm.), a restored 1850 Georgian mansion where tobacco magnate R. J. Reynolds and the father of the founders of Reynolds Metals were born.

Off to the west beyond Fancy Gap, named by an early traveler who found a passage through the hills more convenient than the Good Spur Road then in use, lies Galax—a region settled by Quakers and named for the galax evergreen plant native to the area—where the Old Fiddler's Convention, supposedly the world's largest and oldest (1935) such event, attracts thousands of on-lookers and on-listeners the second weekend of August. In Galax the Jeff Matthews Memorial Museum (Th. and F., 1–5; Sat., 11–4; Sun., 1–4, free—and worth it), contains a themeless but rather endearingly confused collection featuring dozens of different types of items, a veritable granny's attic of objects—knives, old newspapers, stuffed animals, African artifacts, a carved elephant tusk musical instrument and other such miscellany. In Galax, Hanes Knitwear offers a textile mill tour and at nearby Independence you can visit the Nautilus factory that turns out the well-known exercise equipment, while up at Hillsville you'll find bed and breakfast rooms at Tipton House (703-728-2351).

The itinerary west from Roanoke takes you to Blacksburg, home of Virginia Polytechnic Institute and State University, the state's largest school of higher education (22,000 students), whose campus surrounds Smithfield Plantation (April 1–Nov. 1, W., Sat., Sun., 1–5, adm.), a 1772 house where two Virginia governors were born and where a third lived. Near Newport—where the Newport House (703-961-2480) takes bed and breakfast guests—stand two covered bridges over Sinking Creek, one a seventy-foot affair (by route 601 via highway 42 north of town), the other (by route 700 just north of U.S. 460) a fifty-five-foot span bright with barn-red paint. Nearby forty-two-hundred-foot high Bald Knob Mountain overlooks Mountain Lake, one of only two major natural lakes in Virginia, where the attractive Mountain Lake Hotel resort (800-346-3334 or 703-626-7121), tucked away in an isolated corner of the state, offers in the winter cross-country skiing and horse-drawn sleigh rides. Newbern, to the south, survives as an early nineteenth-century village which served as Pulaski County seat from 1839 to 1893. Twenty or so original buildings in Old Newbern, listed on the National Register, line the hamlet's only street, which follows the path of the Wilderness Road that took thousands of pioneers westward. The Wilderness Road Regional Museum (W.–Sun., 2–5, adm.), in part installed in the 1810 house of town founder Adam Hance, recalls the heyday of Newbern, named after Bern, Switzerland, by the early Swiss settlers. After Newbern's courthouse burned in 1893 the county seat moved to Pulaski, then truly a tank town called Martin's Tank, with a water tower that supplied passing trains. Along and near Main Street in Pulaski stand century-old buildings that comprise the National Register-listed Historic District.

At Wytheville stands the 1823 Rock House, a handsome grey limestone dwelling now a museum (May–Oct., Sat. and Sun., 2–4:30, adm.) featuring furniture brought there from Pennsylvania by the town's first resident physician, while the adjacent Thomas J. Boyd Museum (May–Oct., Sat. and Sun., 2–4:30, adm.) contains area artifacts and memorabilia. In Wytheville was born Edith Bolling (wife of Woodrow Wilson) whose father, a judge, delayed court for an hour because of his daughter's arrival. Southeast of town rises the early-1800s Shot Tower (Memorial Day–Labor Day, 10–6; April 1–Memorial Day and Labor Day–Nov. 1, Sat. and Sun., 9–5, adm.), one of three remaining in the U.S., used to make shot for firearms of the frontiersmen and settlers; while to the northwest a chair lift will carry you to the Big Walker Lookout, which affords a panoramic view over the Appalachians. Farther west lies Hungry Mother State Park, the evocative name arising when the child of a pioneer woman captured by a Shawnee raiding party whined about his "hungry mother." To the south, in a section of the Jefferson National Forest, rises Mt. Rogers, at 5,729 feet the tallest point in Virginia. Up at Tazewell displays at the Crab Orchard Museum of Pioneer Park (Tu.–Sat., 10–5; April–Nov., Sun., 2–5, adm.), with ten old log and stone buildings, depict the history of southwestern Virginia. Grundy to the west, home of Mountain Mission School with a well-known choir, is the only incorporated town in the coal-mining country of Buchanan County,

where the Jewell Company operates the world's largest cok-
ing facility, with more than two hundred ovens. Farther west,
on the Kentucky–Virginia border, lies Breaks Interstate Park,
through which runs the Russell Fork River that has carved
the five-mile-long sixteen-hundred-foot deep "Grand Canyon of the South," the largest canyon east of the Mississippi.
Rhododendron Lodge, perched on the canyon rim, affords
attractive views of the area.

Down toward the southern edge of the state at Abingdon
the Barter Theatre (703-628-3991) presents stage shows from
April to October. Such players as Gregory Peck, Ernest
Borgnine, Patricia Neal and Hume Cronyn trained at the
Barter, supposedly the nation's oldest professional resident
theater (1933), so named for the first patrons who bartered
products, trading "ham for *Hamlet*," to attend productions.
At the end of the first season, relates an account of the early
days, "the company cleared $4.35 in cash, two barrels of
jelly, and a collective weight gain of over three hundred
pounds." Five miles north of Abingdon—which in late July
and early August celebrates the Virginia Highlands Festival—
stands rustic White's Mill, a century-and-a-half-old facility listed on the National Register. Summerfield Inn
(703-628-5905) at Abingdon offers bed and breakfast, and
you'll also find accommodations at the Martha Washington
Inn (703-628-3161, in Virginia 800-533-1014), built in 1832
as a private residence and later used until 1932 to house
a college. At nearby Bristol, which spreads across the
Virginia–Tennessee state line, a marker on State Street indicates the boundary, while an electric sign with a split personality boasts, "Bristol Va Tenn A Good Place To Live." A
colorful mural in town proclaims Bristol as the birthplace
of country music. At Maces Spring, up on route 614 three
miles east of Hiltons, the Carter Family Memorial (museum,
Sat., 5–7, adm.; show, Sat., 7:30 p.m.) recalls the early days
of country and bluegrass music. Between 1927 and 1942

A. P. Carter, his wife Sara and her cousin Maybelle recorded three hundred songs—music once described as "haunting, mournful and beautiful as the Appalachians from which it came"—with some still played at the Saturday night hoedown held in the Carter Family Fold, a huge music shed that also houses the annual festival that runs for a week starting the first weekend in August.

Big Stone Gap to the north lies in the middle of coal country. From highway 23 and route 68 you can view the Westmoreland Coal Company transloader that processes some five million tons of coal a year, while the Meador Coal Museum (Th., F., Sat., 10–5; Sun., 1–4, free) features mining artifacts and equipment. In September the town pays homage to "king coal" with a Coal Appreciation Week. The Southwest Virginia Museum Historical State Park (Memorial Day weekend–Labor Day, 9–5; March–Memorial Day and post-Labor Day–Dec., Tu.–Sat., 9–5, adm. charged during summer months) features displays on the area's late nineteenth-century years, an era described in *The Trail of the Lonesome Pine* by John Fox, Jr., recalled at the museum (June–Labor Day, Tu.–Sun., 2–5, adm.) installed in the author's residence. A gift shop with local arts and crafts now occupies the house of June Tolliver, heroine of the novel, dramatized at the Tolliver Playhouse (late June–late Aug., 8:30 p.m.). From the High Knob observation tower spread vistas into North Carolina, Tennessee, Kentucky and West Virginia as well as Virginia, while at Natural Tunnel State Park the Early Historical Railroad Museum features old-time trains. West of Big Stone Gap, at the far western edge of Virginia, lies the more famous Gap—Cumberland. Here Virginia narrows down to its final point, far from the handsome houses, spacious plantations, colonial culture, Revolutionary and Civil War battlefields and haunts of Washington, Jefferson, Monroe and Madison. Here the state looks westward, beyond the mountains to a new world, one that promised land and a new way of life to the pioneers who ventured across the Cumberland Gap to brave the frontier. As early as 1787 Jefferson predicted in *Notes on the State of Virginia* that "The Missisipi [sic] will be one of the principal channels of future commerce for the country westward of the Alleghaney [sic]." Twelve years before, Daniel Boone and his followers blazed the Wilderness Road through the Gap, and between 1775 and the early 1800s an estimated two hundred thousand pioneers traveled through the pass to the west, a migration recalled at the visitor center in Cumberland Gap National Historical Park (mid-June–Sept., 8–6; Oct.–mid-June, 8–5, free). Here at the very end of Virginia ended one era and began another as the nation established by the state's native sons, the Founding Fathers, expanded into the West to fulfill its destiny, and here one can fairly hear the faint echoes of those early Virginians as they left home for the unknown, singing: "Oh, Shenandoah, I hear you call me. Away, you rolling river! Oh, Shenandoah I'm goin' to leave you. Away, away I'm bound to go, Across the wide Missouri."

Virginia Practical Information

The Virginia Division of Tourism is at Suite 500, 202 North Ninth Street, Richmond, VA 23219, 804-786-2051. The state also operates a tourist office at 11 Rockefeller Plaza, New York, NY 10020, 212-245-3080. The Virginia Travel Council, which promotes tourism in the state, is at 7415 Brook Road, Richmond, VA 23227, 804-266-0444.

For information on the state parks and historic areas: 804-786-1712. For accommodations at state park facilities: 804-490-3939. For information on the state's more than forty wineries: Virginia Wine Growers Advisory Board, Box

1163, Richmond, VA 23209, 804-786-0481. For information on historic sites: Association for the Preservation of Virginia Antiquities, 2300 East Grace Street, Richmond, VA 23223, 804-648-1889.

Virginia operates ten highway information centers. To the east: on U.S. 13 at New Church, on Interstate 95 at Fredericksburg, on I-66 at Manassas, and on I-81 at Clear Brook. To the west: on I-64 at Covington, on I-81 at Bristol, on I-77 at Lambsburg, and I-77 at Rocky Gap. To the south: on I-85 at Bracey and on I-95 at Skippers. At the Bell Tower in Capitol Square in Richmond is a state information office, and at Williamsburg is a Virginia Attractions Desk.

Phone numbers at tourist offices of popular destinations include: Alexandria, 703-549-0205; Charlottesville, 804-293-6789; Fredericksburg, 703-373-1776; Lexington, 703-463-3777; Norfolk, 804-441-5266; Petersburg, 804-733-2400; Richmond, 804-358-5511; Shenandoah Valley, 703-740-3132; Virginia Beach, 800-446-8038; Williamsburg, 804-253-0192.

Bed and breakfast booking agencies in Virginia include: Guesthouses Bed and Breakfast, Box 5737, Charlottesville, VA 22905, 804-979-7264 (for the Piedmont area); Blue Ridge Bed and Breakfast Reservation Service in Berryville, 703-955-1246; Bed and Breakfast of Tidewater, Box 3343, Norfolk, VA 23514, 804-627-1983 (the Hampton Roads and the Eastern Shore areas); Bensonhouse, 2036 Monument Avenue, Richmond, VA 23220, 804-648-7560 (for Richmond, Williamsburg and some other areas); and Shenandoah Valley Bed and Breakfast Reservations, Broadway, VA 22815, 703-896-9702 (4–11 p.m.).

2. North Carolina

North Carolina has always been a little different from its sister states in the South and, for that matter, from many other areas of the Union. Because no Atlantic coast deep-water port offered early-day immigrants easy access to North Carolina, it was American pioneers from Virginia, Pennsylvania and other nearby regions who populated the area, with the result that North Carolina has always had the nation's lowest percentage of foreign-born population. Of independent temperament, North Carolina was the next to last colony to join the Union, for the populace feared domination by a strong central government, and the last of the Southern states to leave the Union. But North Carolina furnished 125,000 troops to the Confederate cause, more than any other state, fully one-sixth of the South's total forces. More progressive than some of its Southern peers, North Carolina founded the nation's first state university (in 1795) and in more recent times elected the country's first female Supreme Court chief justice (1974) and established America's first publicly funded state art collection, zoo, symphony and specialized state-supported schools, one for gifted science and mathematics scholars, another for performing arts students.

North Carolina began in 1587 when an expedition promoted by Sir Walter Raleigh established a colony on Roanoke Island along the Atlantic coast. This settlement soon became "the lost colony," as its members somehow dispersed and disappeared—a mystery of history to this day still unsolved—and it wasn't until the early 1650s when settlers from Virginia began to cross into the Albemarle, the northern region of the territory Charles I granted to his attorney

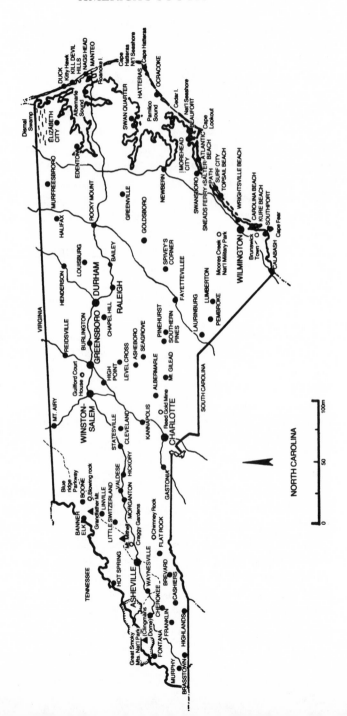

general, Sir Robert Heath, in 1629. To the south of the Albemarle, eventually North Carolina, lay Craven, which in 1670
began to evolve into South Carolina, an area first distin-
guished from its neighbor when Governor Edward Hyde's
commissioning papers referred in 1712 to a territory "that
lyes North and East of Cape Fear called North Carolina."
In 1722 Edenton, on the coast, began to serve as the first
official center of government, and in 1729 the area became
a royal colony when George II acquired it from the Lords
Proprietors. Scottish Highlanders and Germans as well as
Scotch-Irish—a group that produced such leaders as Daniel
Boone and U.S. presidents Jackson, Polk and Andrew
Johnson—migrated to the territory, whose forests supported
a thriving "naval stores" industry, with North Carolina supplying half of England's tar, turpentine and pitch prior to
the Revolution.

Residents of the colony rallied early to the Revolutionary
cause, fighting the 1771 Battle of Alamance, sometimes
called the first military encounter of the Revolution, which
pitted royal governor Tryon against the "Regulators," a re-
bellious group of citizens who wanted to regulate their own
affairs. On the North Carolina flag appear the dates of two
later antiroyalist events—the April 12, 1776 Halifax Resolves,
the first formal resolution passed by a colony supporting
independence, and the May 20, 1775, Mecklenburg pre-
Jefferson Declaration of Independence, disputed for its lack
of contemporary documentation but no less appreciated for
that. Late in the war Yankee General Nathanael Greene lured
the British into the state and in March 1781 at Guilford
Courthouse in Greensboro inflicted decisive losses on the
forces of Cornwallis, whose feelings were supposedly hurt
when Greene didn't think the Englishman's army worth pur-
suing after it withdrew. Although the Cherokee Indians
fought alongside the British during the Revolution, after
the war the Americans allowed some of them to retain land

in the state, which now claims the largest concentration of Native Americans east of the Mississippi, some 45,000, more than any states except Arizona, California, New Mexico and Oklahoma.

During the Civil War North Carolina remained a moderate state, never officially seceding but on May 20, 1861, simply repealing the 1789 legislation by which the state had joined the Union. But North Carolina served the Confederacy as a provider of manpower—losing more than any other Confederate state: 11,000 killed, 24,000 dead of disease, 30,000 wounded. The state was also a key supply center, with ships bypassing the Northern blockade and entering the South at Wilmington, protected by nearby Fort Fisher. When the fort finally fell in January 1865 Wilmington, the last major port supplying Confederate General Robert E. Lee, closed, so severing the South's lifeline. Union General William Tecumseh Sherman, fresh from his triumphant march through Georgia and then South Carolina, entered the state on March 8, 1865 and by April 18 the Southerners in the region surrendered to him.

The war brought North Carolina not only ruin but also the beginnings of a new and eventually highly lucrative industry when Union soldiers discovered the area's mellow tobacco, a crop said to be worth more to the state than "all the wheat in Kansas, or all the pigs in Iowa, or all the cotton in Mississippi." In the last part of the nineteenth century the tobacco business grew like a weed, and during the same era there developed the furniture and textile trades, two of the state's other leading industries. North Carolina these days is an especially well-balanced state both economically and culturally. Although heavily forested—trees cover 60 percent of the thirty-one million acres, and one-fifth of the labor force works in furniture, paper and other forestry-related jobs—North Carolina enjoys a mixture of commerce, agriculture, light industry and technology, the latter two

dominant in the pioneering Research Triangle Park established in the Raleigh-Durham area to tap resources of nearby
Duke, North Carolina and North Carolina State Universities.

Within the five-hundred-mile-wide state that extends farther west than Cleveland, Ohio rise more than fifty peaks
over 6,000 feet, including the East's highest mountain, Mt.
Mitchell at 6,684 feet, the nation's largest expanse of inland
waters, and the longest network of state highways in the
country. Small farms and moderately sized cities characterize
North Carolina, dominated by no one metropolis and boasting a dispersed, countrified but up-to-date way of life
thought by some observers to represent what a twenty-first
century society might look like: decentralized but intercon-
nected low-density urban centers, human-scale-sized cities
with the nearby areas offering a small town or rural, but
not farm-oriented, way of life. Visitors to North Carolina
will find such pleasant small towns and moderately sized
cities scattered across the state's attractive wooded, hilly
landscapes and along the flat, well-watered Atlantic coast—
diversified settlements, scenes and scenery offering a wide
range of cultural, historic and natural attractions.

Eastern North Carolina

*The Outer Banks—Edenton, Windsor and Bath to New
Bern—Murfreesboro, Tarboro and Goldsboro to New
Bern—New Bern—Beaufort—Wilmington*

Water dominates the eastern region of North Carolina.
Inlets, bays, swamps, sounds and salt-water marshes wet
the area with 3,000 miles of tidal shoreline and with the
nation's largest expanse of inland waters, more than two

million acres. Unique to the coastal plain are dozens of elliptically shaped lakes, origin unknown, called "Carolina Bays." But the region's most distinctive and best-known feature is the chain, or thread, of long narrow islands off the coast known as the Outer Banks, low sand ridges formed when the sea stabilized after the Great Ice Age ended some 10,000 years ago. Although nautical sights—old lighthouses, shipwrecks, fishing villages, watery vistas—predominate along the Outer Banks, the area's most evocative attraction is the Wright Brothers National Memorial at Kill Devil Hills, where human flight began.

Back in 1900 Mrs. W. J. Tage, postmaster at Kitty Hawk, near Kill Devil Hills, received an inquiry about the area's topography from two Dayton, Ohio, brothers named Orville and Wilbur Wright who planned to come to the Outer Banks to conduct some "scientific kite-flying experiments." Wilbur commented, laconically but prophetically, "It is my belief that flight is possible." Exhibits at the Memorial vividly recreate those turn-of-the-century times when the Wright brothers launched the world's first flight. This twelve-second effort covered only one hundred and twenty feet, but three other attempts the same day spanned longer distances. By two reconstructed shed-like buildings—a hangar and a bunkhouse used as living quarters and as a workshop—stands a granite boulder with a plaque that reads: "From a 60-foot wooden track laid on these sands Orville Wright rose into the wind on the morning of December 17, 1903." The museum at the site contains well-mounted exhibits that document and describe the great feat, while atop nearby Kill Devil Hill, where the Wrights conducted many of their glider experiments, rises a granite pylon, similar to those used to mark air-race courses, bearing busts of Orville and Wilbur. Just below stretches the "First Flight Airstrip," where Kitty Hawk Aero Tours (919-441-4460) offers scenic excursions over the Outer Banks through the same skies where man first learned to fly, while the First Flight Society (Box 1903, Kitty Hawk, NC 27949), a nonprofit group established in 1926, promotes awareness of the history of flight, which had its start there on the lonely wind-swept dunes at Kill Devil Hills. So breezy is this sea-surrounded strip of land that kites and gliders fill the air above the dunes, which supposedly offer soft landings. Kitty Hawk Kites at Nags Head offers hang-gliding equipment and lessons (for information: 919-441-4124). At Jockey's Ridge State Park in Nags Head rises a 138-foot dune, Jockey's Ridge, the highest on the Atlantic or Gulf coasts, and the town also boasts the Rear View Mirror Museum (11–8, adm.) featuring a collection of more than sixty antique and classic cars as well as a library with books on automobile restoration.

The unusual names of the Outer Banks settlements in the area encapsulate some of the local history. Some area historians believe that Kitty Hawk, so designated in 1738, originated from the Indian expression "killy honk," referring to goose hunting the redskins practiced there. In *The Outer Banks of North Carolina*, David Stick relates that "Kill Devil" perhaps stemmed from the time a ship went aground there while carrying a cargo of rough rum of a type William Byrd of Virginia described in 1728 as "so bad and unwholesome, that it is not improperly call'd 'Kill-Devil'." As for Nags Head, Stick recounts that in the old days a nag with a lantern would be paraded along the beach to create what seemed a ship-like motion that lured vessels toward what they supposed was a sea route but which grounded the boats so locals could plunder the stranded craft. Up to the far north at Corolla stands one of the Outer Banks five beacons, the 1874 Currituck Beach Lighthouse, its natural red brick contrasting with the others, all painted. At Duck, about halfway up to Corolla, the Army Corps of Engineers operates a research pier where you'll find sea-related displays (June 1–mid-Aug., M.–F., tours at 10 a.m., free), while the Sanderling

Inn (919-261-4111) in the village offers a pleasant place to stay, as does Ye Olde Cherokee Inn (919-441-6127) at Kill Devil Hills, where Figurehead (919-441-6929) takes bed and breakfast guests.

Just west of the evocatively named hamlet of Whalebone perches Roanoke Island, afloat between the Outer Banks and the mainland—or mainwater, for fully two-thirds of Dare County's 1,300 square miles consists of water. On the island began England's settlement of the New World, a colony promoted in 1585 by Sir Walter Raleigh, helped with publicity generated by Manteo and Wanchese, two Indians taken to London as curiosities from the Carolina coast the year before. Encounters with area Indians back then brought to the English language such new words as hickory, persimmon, hominy, raccoon, hurricane, canoe, moccasin and tomahawk. When Sir Francis Drake called in at Roanoke Island on June 1, 1586, most of the colonists took the opportunity to return to England, but in the spring of 1587 Raleigh sent 120 new settlers to the outpost, including the Indian Manteo, baptized in the New World's first Protestant baptismal service, and created Lord of Roanoke, the first American peer. On 18 August that year Eleanor Dare, daughter of Governor John White, delivered a baby girl christened Virginia, the first white—and White—child born on the continent. A week later Governor White sailed for England where the famous encounter between the British fleet and the Spanish armada delayed his return to Roanoke for three years. On arriving there in 1590 White found the village abandoned, the settlers vanished and the word "Croatoan"—Indian for "Hatteras"—carved on a tree. Between 1590 and 1607 Raleigh made several attempts to locate the colonists but no trace of the settlers was ever found, and the English outpost in the New World became known as the "Lost Colony of Roanoke," adjudged by Hugh T. Lefler and William S. Powell in *Colonial North Carolina* as American history's greatest mystery: "The fate of the Lost Colony of Roanoke has probably been the subject of more speculation than almost any other event in American history." Displays at the Fort Raleigh National Historic Site on Roanoke Island recall the ill-fated colony. A sickle recovered from a ditch at the supposed site of the lost "cittie" is believed to be the oldest English-made implement yet found in America. At the adjacent outdoor theater *The Lost Colony* (early June–late Aug., 8:30 p.m. M.–Sat., 919-473-3414) by Pulitzer Prize-winning author and North Carolina native Paul Green depicts the settlement's story. The nearby Elizabethan Gardens (9–5, to 8 before performances of *The Lost Colony,* closed Dec.–Jan., Sat. and Sun., adm.) contains plantings and statuary, while not far away is the Thomas Hariot Nature Trail, named for the settler whose book *Brief and True Report of the New Found Land of Virginia,* illustrated with splendid watercolors by Governor John White, presents a remarkably complete picture of the vanished colony and culture. Along the trail appear excerpts from the work, such as: "There is an herb which is . . . called by the inhabitants Uppowoc . . . . The Spaniardes generally call it Tobacco"—a brief extract that speaks volumes in light of the plant's later importance to the region. Moored just off the shore at Manteo, the island's main town, is the "Elizabeth II," a state historic site (April–Oct., 10–6; Nov.–March, Tu.–Sun., 1–4, adm.), a sixteenth-century-style sailing ship typical of the vessels that transported Sir Walter Raleigh's colonists to the New World between 1584 and 1587.

The state also runs the North Carolina Aquarium (M.–Sat., 9–5; Sun., 1–5, free) at Manteo, one of three such facilities along the Carolina coast, with the others at Atlantic Beach and at Kure Beach to the south. A micro-brewery at the Weeping Radish Restaurant turns out German-type beer, and the adjacent Christmas Shop houses more than thirty rooms of gift items, while the Manteo Booksellers

store occupies homey quarters with easy chairs and oil paint-
ings. For accommodations in Manteo the Tranquil House
Inn (919-473-1404), perched on the waterfront opposite the
"Elizabeth II," is true to its name, while the Scarborough
Inn (919-473-3979) and Booth's Guest House (919-473-3696)
also offer pleasant rooms, as does Pugh's Bed and Breakfast
(919-473-5466) at nearby Wanchese, named after one of those
Indians Raleigh used to promote his colony in London.

Back at the Outer Banks on the south end of Bodie Island
stands another lighthouse (visitor center, May–Sept., free),
completed in 1872, while along the inner side of Hatteras
Island just south of Oregon Inlet stretches bird-filled Pea
Island National Wildlife Refuge. Federal and state preserves
and enclaves comprise fully three-quarters of the Outer
Banks' 17,000 acres, leaving only a small area for private
development. Cape Hatteras National Seashore, the nation's
first such preserve, extends for seventy miles along the Outer
Banks, from Nags Head to Ocracoke Island. At the village
of Rodanthe the original 1874 Chicamacomico Lifesaving
Station contains exhibits on rescues and in the summer offers
reenactments of lifesaving techniques featuring drills with
old equipment. Farther south lies the "Laura A. Barnes,"
high and dry on the shore after encountering a "nor'easter"
in June 1921. One of the last sailing ships in an era dominated
by engine-powered craft, the boat ran aground while sailing
from New York to Georgetown, South Carolina, one of
the more than six hundred ships—including the iron-clad
"Monitor" of Civil War fame—that fell victim over the years
to the hidden sand ridges called Diamond Shoals, to the
vicissitudes of the ocean winds, and to the turbulent waters
where the northbound Gulf Stream encounters the colder
waters of the Labrador Current, hazards that brought about
the ominous name for the area there off the Outer Banks:
"Graveyard of the Atlantic." Once-proud "Laura" now lies
forlorn and disintegrating, her great wooden beams weath-

ered and splintered, the grounded hulk sprawled on the sand
like the skeleton of some giant sea beast. Overhead squawk
sea birds, while just beyond the dunes the rolling, roaring
waves—lively waters from the deadly Graveyard—bring
tongues of foam onto the unspoiled sand beach. All these
elements—the wreck, the sea, the birds, the sky—combine
to make this corner of North Carolina one of the state's
most enchanting places.

Farther south rises thick-striped black and white Cape
Hatteras Lighthouse, at two hundred and eight feet the nation's tallest. Built in 1870, the structure survives as one
of the country's 850 lighthouses—450 of them still in
operation—legacies of the two-century-old legislation which
on August 7, 1789, in the ninth bill passed by the first Congress, established the U.S. Lighthouse Service, merged in
1939 into the Coast Guard. In 1990 the U.S. Postal Service
issued a stamp commemorating the Hatteras lighthouse.
Hatteras's powerful 1972 lighting mechanism, whose warning beam has signaled to sailors as far as fifty-one miles
out at sea, recalls George Bernard Shaw's comment that
lighthouses, which serve solely to guide unknown sailors
to a safe haven, are the most altruistic structures built by
man. (Connoisseurs of architectural altruism can get information on the structures from the Lighthouse Preservation
Society, P.O. Box 736, Rockport, MA 01966, 508-281-6336.)
Although the Hatteras lighthouse is closed to visitors, the
former keeper's quarters there houses a display and bookstore. A lighthouse would seem to be a rather permanent
feature of the landscape, or seascape, but one of these days
the structure may stand in a different place. Because of erosion, only two hundred feet of sand now separate the tower
from the Atlantic's churning waters, so in June 1989 the
National Park Service proposed moving the 2,800-ton building half a mile inland. At Frisco, a few miles down the road,
the Native American Museum contains Indian artifacts,

while the nearby town of Hatteras hosts for a week in mid-
June the annual Blue Marlin Tournament (919-986-2454).

A free car ferry (April 15–Oct., about every forty minutes
to 11 p.m.; Nov.–April 15, every hour on the hour) will
carry you from Hatteras to adjacent Ocracoke Island, an
isolated strip of land where pirates once lurked. One of
history's most famous buccaneers, Blackbeard, met his end
at Ocracoke. Professing to abandon his cutthroat escapades,
Blackbeard, born Edward Teach, settled in 1718 in Bath on
the North Carolina coast not far from Ocracoke. When
Teach married a planter's teenage daughter, none other than
North Carolina Governor Charles Eden, who had granted
the pirate a pardon, performed the service. The former renegade seemingly settled into domesticity, but rumors soon
surfaced that Teach—who, as Blackbeard, wore a huge coal-
black beard covering his entire face that lent him a fearsome
appearance—planned to establish a pirate's nest on Ocracoke.
When the British navy ship "Ranger" arrived at the island
in November 1718, Blackbeard and his men boarded the
vessel and proceeded to engage the crew in hand-to-hand
combat. Finally cornering the outlaw, "Ranger" commander
Lieutenant Robert Maynard pointed a pistol at the pirate,
whereupon Blackbeard swung his cutlass aloft. Just as he
prepared to slash Maynard a seaman stabbed Blackbeard
from behind in the neck and throat and the sword feebly
fell, only grazing the lieutenant's knuckles. Like an enraged
bull tormented by a matador, Blackbeard fought on, blood
pouring from his neck. Suddenly he fell dead; Blackbeard's
days of piracy were over. But not his presence at festive
occasions, for according to local legend the buccaneer's skull
was made into a punch bowl.

Ocracoke these days is more peaceful than when pirates
infested the area. At the village of Ocracoke, the laid-back
island's only settlement—population, 660—stands the bright
white 1823 lighthouse, the oldest such operating facility on

the Atlantic coast. You'll also find there a British cemetery, complete with the Union Jack flapping in the breeze, where repose four English sailors washed ashore on May 14, 1942, after a German submarine sank the H.M.S. *Bedfordshire*. Seven miles north of town resides a herd of ponies, believed descendants of animals brought to the island in the early days by Spaniards or by one of Sir Walter Raleigh's expeditions. Inns and bed and breakfast places on the island include Crews (919-928-7011), Lighthouse Keepers (919-928-1821), Oscar's (919-928-1311), Scarborough (919-928-4271), the Island Inn (919-928-4351) and Ships Timbers (919-928-6141), built with lumber from the "Ida Lawrence," grounded on Ocracoke in 1902. Ferries from the island take you in about two and a half hours across Pamlico Sound, where dolphins cavort and pelicans perch on sandbars, either to Cedar Island (April 15–Oct., to or from Ocracoke, 7, 9:30, 12, 3, 6, 8:30; Nov.–April 14, from Ocracoke, 10, 4; from Cedar 7, 1; for reservations from Ocracoke: 919-928-3841, from Cedar: 919-225-3551), or to Swan Quarter (year-round from Ocracoke, 6:30, 12:30; from Swan Quarter, 9:30, 4; for reservations from Ocracoke: 919-928-3841, from Swan Quarter: 919-926-1111).

Returning to the northern corner of the state, the coastal and inland route in eastern North Carolina will take you to some of the state's most historic towns. U.S. highway 17 south from Virginia parallels the twenty-two-mile long Dismal Swamp Canal, which bisects the forty-mile long marshland once exploited by George Washington, who in the 1760s formed a company called "The Adventurers for Draining the Great Dismal Swamp." The new (1989) visitor center, north of South Mills, serves both boat and automobile traffic along the Canal, listed on the National Register and the nation's oldest such man-made waterway, chartered in 1787 by the Virginia legislature. Like the Everglades in Florida, the swamp remains even in this day and age impenetrable in many places, unseen by the eye and untouched by the hand of man, although loggers cull parts of the area for trees cut into lumber at a sawmill on U.S. 158. At Elizabeth City the Museum of the Albemarle recalls the history of one of North Carolina's earliest areas, while in the thirty-block Historic District, listed on the National Register, survive the town's eighteenth- and nineteenth-century structures, including the state's largest group of antebellum commercial buildings. The peeling barn-red wooden structure at the corner of Main Street and U.S. 17 houses Clayton Sawyer's music store, featuring hand-crafted banjos, guitars and other instruments offered for sale, or for strumming, in an old-fashioned down-home atmosphere. From Elizabeth City's U.S. Coast Guard base, which includes what is supposedly the world's largest aircraft repair and supply center, sail ships that track icebergs in the North Atlantic for the International Ice Patrol. In the early days around the Albemarle area arose two factions, one supporting the Lords Proprietors, to whom Charles II had given land along the coast south down to Florida, and the Populists, led by John Culpepper who in 1677 led an uprising called Culpepper's Rebellion, believed the first revolt against the English crown in America. River City Bed and Breakfast (919-338-3337) offers accommodations in Elizabeth City, while Bed and Breakfast in the Albemarle (919-792-4584) operates a reservation service for the region. The little town of Old Trap in adjacent Camden County took its designation from a local tavern where men idled their time away, prompting their wives to ask the postal service to name the settlement for the too popular hangout.

Over at Hertford to the west survive such old buildings as the 1849 Gothic Revival-style Holy Trinity Church, the c. 1851 Quaker-sponsored Temperance Hall (later converted into a residence, 116 North Front Street), the c. 1775 Skinner-Whedbee House, believed the town's oldest dwelling, and the c. 1825 Perquimans ("land of beautiful women") County Courthouse, partly built by Masons in exchange for the use of a second-floor room where the group still meets. The residence-like building houses North Carolina's oldest public records, including the state's first known land deed, a document recording a settler's 1661 purchase of property from an Indian chief. Not long after that transfer, in May 1672, Hertford hosted North Carolina's first organized religious service, recalled by a marker at the corner of Church and McCraney Streets, while in 1793 a woman named Sarah Decrow became the town's postmaster, supposedly the first woman in the United States to hold such a position after adoption of the Constitution. Hertford's unusual S-shaped bridge, successor to the 1798 float span, is supposedly the only structure of its kind in existence. Three miles from town stands the restored c. 1685 Newbold-White House (April–Dec., Tu.–Sat., 10–4:30; Sun., 1:30–4:30, adm.), the state's oldest brick dwelling, listed on the National Register, seat of North Carolina's government in the late seventeenth century and site of Quaker religious services held in 1672 by George Fox, founder of the Society of Friends.

More early history haunts nearby Edenton, an attractively preserved colonial-era town—the colony's capital for twenty years—filled with old architecture, including the 1725 Corbin residence (Tu.–Sat., 10–4:30; Sun., 2–5, adm.), topped by an octagonal cupola, whose original first-story woodwork now resides at the Brooklyn Museum; the c. 1773 National Register-listed Iredell House (Tu.–Sat., 10–4:30; Sun., 2–5, adm.), occupied by U.S. Supreme Court Justice James Iredell and by his son, a governor of North Carolina; and the beautifully proportioned 1767 brick Chowan County Courthouse, set on the village green that stretches out to the water. At the cemetery of Register-listed 1760 St. Paul's Church, which houses a congregation established in 1701, reposes the body of Governor Charles Eden, for whom Edenton was named. Supposedly in cahoots with Blackbeard, Eden pardoned the pirate, thus enabling him to remain free to continue his escapades. Before and during the Revolutionary War Edenton served as a hotbed of Patriot activity. On October 25, 1774, ten months after the Boston Tea Party, fifty-one area women gathered at what some historians consider the nation's first political conclave organized by females—an event recalled by the teapot-shaped marker on the town green—to support the tea-tossing and shunning New Englanders, resolving: "We the ladys of Edenton do hereby solemnly engage not to conform to that pernicious practice of drinking tea . . . from England." Instead, the women sipped a raspberry-leaf brew and munched Penelope Barker Tea Cakes, named for the presiding officer and on occasion still made in Edenton, as follows:

1 quart flour	2 cups brown sugar
3/4 cup butter/lard mixture	1 tablespoon water
1 teaspoon soda	1/2 teaspoon salt
3 eggs	

Beat eggs, and sugar and soda dissolved in water. Mix flour, butter and lard, add to other mixture. Roll and cut. Bake in hot oven.

Places to stay in Edenton include Trestle House Bed and Breakfast (919-482-2282), located on a private lake and built from abandoned redwood timbers which once formed a train trestle, Jason House Inn (919-482-3400), and The Lords Proprietors' Inn (919-482-3641), with seventeen antique-furnished rooms installed in three adjacent restored houses, among them Pack House, with the town's largest front porch.

At Windsor, off to the west, you'll find 1839 St. Thomas Episcopal Church as well as such dwellings as Rosefield, acquired in 1729 by John Gray whose descendants still own the property and whose grandson, William Blount, Tennessee territorial governor and U.S. senator, was born there, and National Register-listed Hope Plantation (March–Dec., 23, M.–Sat., 10–4; Sun. 2–5, adm.), the elegant and impeccably restored c. 1803 Federal-style house of David Stone, two-term North Carolina governor and U.S. senator. Nearby stands the Register-listed King-Bazemore House (same hours as Hope), a simpler structure built in 1763 by a planter and cooper. At nearby Hamilton, Fort Branch (April–Nov., 10:30–4:30; Sun., 1:30–4:30) survives as a Southern outpost overlooking the Roanoke River. After the Confederate surrender in April 1865 Southern troops abandoned the fort, dumping into the river the base's eleven cannons. In May of that year the U.S. Navy recovered three cannons, and as late as 1972 a trio of antique hunters from Alabama retrieved another three, which North Carolina impounded after obtaining a restraining order to prevent the Alabamans from removing the weapons. In 1977 workers raised four more cannons, leaving one yet to be found. Earlier martial encounters occurred in the Fort Branch area when a group of Roanoke Island colonists sailed up the river to Rainbow Banks looking for copper and gold mines but, instead, finding the hostile Tuscarora Indians who sent down on the intruders a "volley of their arrows," the first recorded attack by Indians on white men. Later, in 1711, the fierce Tuscarora—whose word for "yes," the exclamation "uh-huh," the English adopted to signify assent—began a war against the settlers, who two years later finally defeated the Indians. Forests abound in Martin County, including stands of cypress—one, eleven feet in diameter, is thought to be 2,000 years old—in the lowlands flanking the Roanoke River. The Martin County Lumber Company in Everetts furnished planks used in the famous Atlantic City boardwalk, while the Dennis-Simmons Lumber Mill outside Jamesville, the area's largest firm until Weyerhaeuser Paper Company arrived, produced cypress shingles used to reroof Mount Vernon. The forest has reclaimed Dymond City, settled in 1870 by Quakers who founded the area's first railroad, from Jamesville to Washington, named the J and W but affectionately called the Jiggle and Wiggle because of the line's springy swampland roadbed.

Off to the east stretches a ragged-edged water-soaked peninsula filled with lakes and surrounded by sounds. At Plymouth, Weyerhaeuser operates a plant (tours by reservation: 919-793-8162) located on the site of an Indian town, which makes pulp, paper and paperboard. In the mid-nineteenth century Plymouth served as a leading shipping port for wood products, especially staves sent to the West Indies to make barrels in which rum and molasses were exported to the United States. During the Civil War the armored Confederate ship "Albemarle" managed to float over chains strung by Federal forces across the Roanoke River to protect the city, which the Southerners proceeded to capture, but in October 1864 Union troops finally sank the boat, removing it as a threat, and retook the town. At nearby Roper an early settler started a mill that functioned from 1702 to 1921, perhaps the state's longest-operated business, ceasing only when a band of farmers, angry because water behind the mill's dam backed up over their fields, destroyed the installation. Next to Lake Phelps—by which First Colony Farms, North Carolina's largest farming firm, operates an experimental program to harvest peat for use as fuel—stands Somerset Place (April–Oct., M.–Sat., 9–5; Sun., 1–5; Nov.–March, Tu.–Sat., 10–4; Sun., 1–4, free), a splendid old plantation established in the 1780s by Joseph Collins, an Englishman who formed a company to exploit "the Great Alegator Dismal," as the area was once called. Grist- and sawmills, corn and then rice enriched the family, which developed Somerset Place into one of the state's largest plantations, one of only four in North Carolina that owned more than three hundred slaves. After the Civil War the property passed out of the family's hands and in 1939 the state acquired the spread, where restoration began in 1951.

Adjacent Pettigrew State Park recalls the early Pettigrew clan, also area plantation owners, whose descendant General Thomas J. Pettigrew led the Confederate charge at Gettysburg. In the Pettigrew Cemetery near Lake Phelps repose three generations of the family. Columbia, Tyrrell County seat since 1800, nestles along the picturesque Scuppernong River, explored in 1680 by Edenton settlers who termed the territory a "Heart's Delight." Hyde County to the south boasts Lake Mattamuskeet, North Carolina's largest natural lake, a popular fishing and hunting area by which, in Fairfield on the north shore, stands Mattamuskeet Inn (day: 919-926-3021, evening: 919-926-4851). The large former pumping station on the edge of the water recalls the failed 1913 effort of a company to drain the lake and establish there a farm settlement named New Holland. Near Lake Landing stands the "Ink Bottle" House, an octagonal mid-nineteenth-century dwelling topped by an eight-sided chimney, while down at Swan Quarter, site of some of the nation's first tourist homes, you'll find 1876 Providence Methodist, a rebuilt version of a church "moved by the hand of God" when a storm supposedly transferred the sanctuary from its original site to one a wealthy landowner had refused to donate to the congregation. From Swan Quarter departs the ferry for Ocracoke Island in the Outer Banks.

To the west at Belhaven, where River Forest Manor (919-943-2151) offers pleasant accommodations, the Memorial Museum (1–5, free), installed in the National Register-listed City Hall, contains a collection of historic artifacts. Nearby Bath, North Carolina's oldest city, offers an even richer residue of relics from the area's past. Founded in 1705, the town—once a bustling commercial center and port, with the colony's first shipyard and Andrew Duncan's popular tavern—survives as a quiet backwater that occupies about the same area as it did back in the settlement's heyday. Remnants from the early days include 1790 Van Der Veer House, which features a museum; the 1830 Bonner House, an example of typical early nineteenth-century Carolina architecture; the 1744 Palmer-Marsh House, one of the state's oldest homes, a wooden dwelling with a striking seventeen-foot-wide brick double chimney on its flank; and diminutive St. Thomas Church, the state's oldest (1734) sanctuary. (Hours for these buildings: April–Oct., Tu.–Sat., 9–5; Sun., 1–5; Nov.–March, Tu.–Sat., 10–4; Sun., 1–4, adm. except for St. Thomas.) At Bath still functions Swindell's, a general store installed in a late nineteenth-century brick building, and from mid-June to mid-August the outdoor pirate drama *Blackbeard: Knight of the Black Flag* enlivens the town, where the Bath Guest House (919-923-6811) offers bed and breakfast, as does Pamlico House (919-946-7184) at nearby Washington, once called Forks of Tar River and renamed in 1775 as the nation's first town to so honor the famous man. The 1786 Beaufort County Courthouse and the 1854 Bank of Washington building survive from the old days of the venerable town, incorporated in 1776. Scattered about nearby Greenville are seven structures listed on the National Register, including five houses as well as the 1911 Pitt County Courthouse and the handsome low-rise 1914 Florentine Revival Federal Building, a rare style in the South. Greenville also boasts East Carolina University, the state's third largest, with some 14,000 students, and a Voice of America transmitter that's supposedly the world's most powerful broadcasting station. From the Washington-Greenville area it's convenient to proceed south to New Bern, one of North Carolina's most attractive and historic towns, described below after the inland itinerary that takes you from north to south and also ends in New Bern.

At the northern edge of the state, just south of the Virginia line, lies Murfreesboro whose old houses—some of mellowed and often crumbling brick, others of wood—host much history. On Main Street stands the residence where yellow fever conqueror Walter Reed, who in 1876 married Emilie Lawrence, "the girl across the street," lived as a boy. A few doors west resided U.S. Congressman Jesse Jackson Yeates, grandson of Sarah Boone, frontiersman Daniel Boone's sister. On Sycamore stands the National Register-listed old Hertford Academy building, once part of Chowan College, whose striking 1851 McDowell Columns Building, also listed on the Register, now houses the college's administrative offices. At the Morgan-Myrick House, which bears North Carolina's only example of brick dentil work, lived James Morgan, whose slave Emily, heroine of the 1836 Battle of San Jacinto in Texas, inspired the song "The Yellow Rose of Texas." Next door on Broad Street the old Winborne Law Office houses a collection of country store memorabilia as well as antique lawyer's furniture and books. Just behind stands the William Rea Museum, installed in what's believed to be the state's oldest commercial building, once headquarters of the Ferguson Agriculture Implement Company, builder of the first peanut picker, and which now contains such items as a Gatling gun, the rapid-fire weapon invented in 1862 by Richard Gatling, and woodwork salvaged from the Gatling family plantation, located near Como to the north, where he was born in 1818. The plantation house no longer stands, but a cemetery at the site contains the graves of various Gatlings, including James Henry Gatling, who supposedly constructed and flew a flying machine twenty-five years before the Wright brothers.

Off to the west lies the Roanoke Rapids area, where Lake Gaston, with fishing, boating and water sport facilities, snakes across the landscape to form more than three hundred and fifty miles of shoreline. At Halifax survive two century-old buildings, scenes of historic early political events. The 1840 colonial-style courthouse replaces an early structure where renegade Americans met to pass the "Halifax Resolves" on April 12, 1776, the first official action by an entire colony supporting independence from England, a document incorporated in part the following July Fourth into the Declaration of Independence. North Carolina's flag commemorates the event by including the date "April 12, 1776," while a play called *First for Freedom,* performed at an outdoor theater in Halifax, recreates the event (first two and a half weeks in July, Th.- Sun., 8:15 p.m., 919-583-1776 or 583-7191). A frame house where early political figures drafted the North Carolina constitution, antique taverns and dwellings, the nation's oldest Masonic Lodge in continuous use (1767), former government offices and other venerable structures lend the Historic Halifax enclave, a state historic site (April–Oct., M.–Sat., 9–5; Sun., 1–5; Nov.–March, Tu.–Sat., 10–4; Sun., 1–4, free), an ambiance of yesteryear.

At Littleton off to the west stands 1770 Person's Ordinary, a wooden house that survives as the state's only remaining stagecoach stop, and near Essex to the south reside 2,000 of North Carolina's remaining Indians, the Haliwa-Saponi. While "Saponi" designates the name of an ancient tribe, "Haliwa" is no exotic Indian word but derives from the first letters of Halifax and Warren, the counties where the Indians live. The third weekend of April the tribe presents its annual powwow at the Indian school near Essex; while off to the west a peanut festival takes place at Enfield, where such old houses as Strawberry Hill and Shell Castle, both 1790, and sanctuaries as Eden Whitaker's Chapel, site of the first annual Methodist Conference (1828), survive. Peanut addicts will find the Growers Peanut Food Promotions, a trade group that promotes treats made from the nut, at 109 South Main Street down at Rocky Mount, which also boasts the Tank Theater, a community playhouse; while the town of

Gold Rock just off to the west recalls the nation's first gold rush (a claim also made by Dahlonega, Georgia), which occurred in North Carolina near Charlotte soon after deposits were discovered in 1799. Griffin-Pace (919-459-4746) at nearby Nashville takes bed and breakfast guests.

To the east lies Tarboro, whose forty-five-block residential historic district includes dozens of attractive tree-shaded old houses, while neatly restored commercial structures fill the recently revitalized downtown area, chosen in 1980 by the National Main Street Center as one of thirty small towns across the country to participate in a renewal program. By the train tracks at the edge of the sixteen-acre Town Common, laid out in 1860, survives an old cotton press (c. 1860), and a few blocks away stand the Pender Museum and the Blount-Bridgers House (M.–F., 10–4; Sat. and Sun., 2–4, free). The house was built around 1800 by Thomas Blount, a member of the gifted family that furnished North Carolina and other states with any number of merchants, politicians (a congressman, a senator, two governors of Tennessee), military leaders, accomplished professional people and other over-achievers, many documented in the clan's letters and archives published in the *John Gray Blount Papers,* the title referring to the Washington, North Carolina, native who managed one of the nation's largest mercantile operations. In 1982 "The Grove," as the Blount-Bridgers mansion was originally called, became a museum housing the Matisse-like works of impressionist artist Hobson Pittman, a native of Edgecombe County.

At Tarboro, Little Warren (919-823-1314), with a cozy wrap-around porch and antiques on sale, offers bed and breakfast, as does National Register-listed Pilgrims Rest (919-243-4447), the 1858 residence of the son of T. C. Davis, the state's first printer, taught the trade by no less an expert than Benjamin Franklin himself. The house fronts Nash, claimed by some to be one of the world's ten most beautiful streets. Wilson also boasts old architecture, with an unusually wide variety of styles, including a Spanish mission-type train depot (1924), the Art Deco Municipal Building (1938) and such National Register-listed structures as the classic Wilson County Courthouse (1924), the boxy brick Wilson Theater (c. 1920) and the serenely elegant neo-classic Branch Banking Building (1903), not a branch bank but named for Alpheus Branch and home of the state's oldest bank in continuous operation. Some forty antique and decorative art shops serve to make Wilson a center for collectibles, while the city also claims to be the world's largest tobacco market, with tours of the warehouses available from August through October (for information: 919-237-0165). By Bailey, off to the west of Wilson, the Country Doctor Museum (March–Nov., W. and Sun., 2–5), the nation's only such medical display, features a nineteenth-century apothecary and family physician's office as well as a medicinal garden modeled after a similar one at Padua, Italy, believed to be the world's oldest botanic garden; while to the south, at Kenly, you'll find another unusual collection at the Tobacco Museum of North Carolina (M.–Sat., 9:30–5; Sun., 1–5, adm.), whose exhibits recall the plant's importance to the region. An estimated half of America's nearly billion pound harvest of flue-cured tobacco stems from within fifty miles of the town. The museum offers not only artifacts, equipment, video presentations and historical displays that recall the tobacco culture that remains so deeply rooted in this area of North Carolina, but also seasonal tours of a working farm (July and Aug., M.–Sat., 10–2, adm.) which will introduce you to growing and harvesting methods. Another corner of rural North Carolina remains at the nearby Charles B. Aycock Birthplace (April–Oct., M.–Sat., 9–5; Sun., 1–5; Nov.–March, Tu.–Sat., 10–4; Sun., 1–4, free), a state historic site where a mid-1800s farm house, outbuildings and a one-room schoolhouse preserve the setting where Aycock, elected governor in 1900 on a

platform of expanded public school education, grew up as
the youngest of ten children.

Goldsboro is a good place to taste North Carolina's renowned barbecue, especially savory in this part of the state.
The Goldsboro version of barbecue vies with that around
Lexington, in the central part of North Carolina, for being
the tastiest type of such dish. Scott's Famous Barbecue, at
1201 North William Street in Goldsboro, features meat from
the entire pig rather than just the pork shoulder common
in the center of the state. The establishment, founded in
1917, also offers Brunswick stew—long-simmered meat and
chicken in light tomato sauce with vegetables—as well as
fried chicken livers, especially favored by the locals. A portrait of a huge porker hangs on the wall at Wilber's Barbecue,
on highway 70 east, which also favors entire pigs or hogs
cooked over oak coals. A popular item at both places is
the chopped pork sandwich, while in the central part of
the state sliced meat sandwiches are the order of the day
and hickory wood the fuel of preference. Around Goldsboro,
leaf by jowl with the barbecue eateries, stand cavernous tobacco warehouses, beyond which stretch leafy tobacco fields
dotted with small barns. Henry Weil (919-735-9995) offers
bed and breakfast rooms in Goldsboro.

South of town stretches the Cliffs of the Neuse State Park,
with nature trails and a ninety-foot cliff, carved by the Neuse
River, streaked with bands of sedimentation that exhibit its
geologic history, while off to the west the Bentonville Battleground State Historic Site (April–Oct., M.–Sat., 9–5; Sun.,
1–5; Nov.–March, Tu.–Sat., 10–4; Sun., 1–4, free) includes
terrain where the Confederate Army, led by General Joseph
E. Johnston, mounted its last full-scale offensive action during the Civil War, the largest battle fought in North Carolina
and the only significant attempt to defeat Union General
William Tecumseh Sherman after his "march to the sea"
through Georgia. After a valiant effort from March 19 to

21, 1865, the Southerners withdrew and on April 26 Johnston surrendered to Sherman at Bennett Place near Durham.
Union trenches, a Confederate cemetery, displays in the visitor center and the Harper House, furnished as a field hospital, a function the residence served during the encounter,
recall the battle. The third weekend in June nearby Spivey's
Corner holds the annual National Hollerin' Contest to recall
how in the old days farmers would communicate by shouting
across their fields to one another, and every September
Mount Olive hosts not an olive but a pickle festival, with
pickled people, locals clad to resemble a pickle, a sight better
seen than described—or perhaps vice versa. Down at Clinton, seat of Simpson County, largest of North Carolina's
hundred counties, the Shield House (919-592-2634), a c. 1916
Greek Revival-style dwelling listed on the National Register,
offers bed and breakfast, while the attractive Squire's Vintage
Inn (919-296-1831) at nearby Warsaw also provides a pleasant
place to stay.

At Kenansville, just to the east, survives Liberty Hall (Tu.–
Sat., 10–4; Sun., 2–4, adm.), homestead of the family recalled by the town's name. Descendants of patriarch Thomas
Kenan, who arrived in North Carolina from Ireland in 1730,
served prominently in the state's political and commercial
communities. In the early 1800s Kenan's grandson, Thomas
II, built Liberty Hall, whose motto is "He who enters these
open gates, never comes too early, never leaves too late."
In 1887 his unmarried granddaughter left the property to
her niece, Mary Lily Kenan, who in 1901 married at Liberty
Hall Henry M. Flagler, an original partner of John D. Rockefeller and developer of properties on Florida's east coast (see
the Florida chapter for Flagler's activities in that state). After
Liberty Hall passed out of the Kenan family in 1964 local
citizens established a restoration commission headed by
Thomas S. Kenan III, great-great-great-great-grandson of
the original Thomas, who arrived in America in 1730—a

rare chain of continuity in a restless, transient nation. On the grounds stand the "necessary house" (privy and bathing area) and the hen house, where you'll meet more descendants of early residents—chickens whose ancestors combatted in cockfights, the battling birds known as "Bacon War Horses" for South Carolina's Lord Bacon, who owned unbeatable fighting cocks.

Also at Kenansville still flows the spring unearthed in the 1730s by Barbara Beverette, wife of one of the early settlers, Scotch-Irish Presbyterians who established Grove Church, the oldest of that denomination in North Carolina. The town's Cowan Museum (Tu.–Sat., 10–4; Sun., 2–4, adm.) contains antique tools and utensils, an odd assortment of artifacts and such miscellany as a travel churn, a dog treadmill and a chastity belt, while *The Liberty Cart* (mid-July–late Aug., Th., F., Sat., 8:15 p.m., 919-296-0721) dramatizes the history of eastern North Carolina over a century, ending with the Civil War. Kinston, back to the north, took its name after an earlier war, the Revolution, when zealous patriots dropped the "g" in Kingston, the town's original designation when founded in 1740. Near the city Confederates scuttled the iron-sided "Neuse" in March 1865 to keep the gunboat and ramming vessel out of Union hands. In 1964 workers salvaged the ship's remains, now on display at the Richard Caswell Memorial (April–Oct., M.–Sat., 9–5; Sun., 1–5; Nov.–March, Tu.–Sat., 10–4; Sun., 1–4, free), where a museum recalls the career of the state's first governor, buried in the Caswell family cemetery on the property.

On the Neuse River not far east of Kinston lies New Bern, a photogenic town filled with excellent examples of old colonial and Federal-style structures. So well preserved is old New Bern, which nestles on a spit of land between the Trent and Neuse rivers, that the town seems little changed from a century or more ago. A hundred or so historic houses and other buildings fill the city, a fairly spacious place thanks to John Lawson, who in 1710 laid out the settlement with wide streets and large lots "since in America they do not like to live crowded." New Bern was founded by Swiss and German settlers led by Baron Christoph von Graffenreid, recently (1989) memorialized by a bust next to City Hall, whose facade bears a splendid relief bear, fangs bared and curled red tongue, a symbol of old Bern in Switzerland. Centerpiece of the old architecture in New Bern is the Tryon Palace (M.–Sat., 9:30–4; Sun., 1:30–4, adm.), a splendid remnant of colonial times completed in 1770 as the colony's capitol and Governor William Tryon's official residence, and later North Carolina's capitol. This exceptional building is one of the South's outstanding showplaces. Also part of the Palace complex are the Federal-style Dixon-Stevenson House (late 1820s) and the John Wright Stanly House (1780s), owned by a privateer whose personal navy numbered some fourteen ships, host to George Washington, who pronounced the place "exceedingly good lodgings" when the president stayed there in 1791. In 1990 another attraction opened at Tryon, the newly restored New Bern Academy building, which dates from the early nineteenth century. In the churchyard of the Gothic Revival-style Christ Episcopal Church (M.–F., 9–5; Sat., 9–12, free), which stands in a tree-filled enclave in the middle of town, is a cannon from the British ship "Blessington," captured by one of Stanly's marauding vessels. Another striking church in town is First Presbyterian, completed in 1822, a truly beautiful New England-type sanctuary sporting a graceful five-tiered tower.

At the 1847 Charles Slover House, 201 Johnson Street, lived C. D. Bradham, who at his pharmacy at the corner of Pollock and Middle Streets invented a refreshment he called "Brad's Drink," marketed after 1898 as Pepsi Cola. Displays in town include the Fireman's Museum (Tu.–Sat., 9:30–12, 1–5; Sun., 1–5, adm.), with a collection of early firefighting equipment; Bank of the Arts (M.–F., 10–4; Sat., 10–1, free), an art gallery installed in a c. 1913 bank building; and the c. 1790 Attmore-Oliver House (Tu.–Sat., 1–4:30, adm.), with local historic objects. Bed and breakfast places in New Bern include The Aerie (919-636-5553), New Berne House (919-636-2250), whose furniture includes a brass bed supposedly saved from a burning brothel in 1897, Harmony House Inn (919-636-3810), and King's Arms (919-638-4409). Throughout the year Tryon Palace hosts such events as a decorative arts symposium, colonial-era festival and other special celebrations; for information and schedules: 919-638-1560.

Off toward the east of New Bern lies the sound-side city of Oriental, a New England-type fishing village which bills itself as "Sailing Capital of North Carolina," where you'll find seafood restaurants featuring Neuse River blue crabs in the summer. At Minnesott Beach near "The Point" where, according to tradition, Sir Walter Raleigh first landed in the New World a free ferry crosses the mile-wide river near Cherry Point, location of the marine corps' largest air station and site of the Naval Air Rework Facility, which overhauls and repairs aircraft. Across the landscape around Havelock— in 1857 named for Sir Henry Havelock, hero of the besieged British military garrison at Lucknow in far off India— spreads Croatan National Forest where four rare insectivorous flower species grow, including the Venus Fly Trap. The village of Croatan boasts the delightfully eccentric "Self Kicking Machine," a device you can use to fulfill the vow "I could kick myself for doing that."

The so-called Crystal Coast stretches along the Atlantic Ocean just to the south. Morehead City, the Coast's largest town, operates an ocean port with two modern fumigation chambers and a pair of one hundred and fifteen-ton gantry cranes. The Museum of History (Tu.–Sat., 1–4, free) houses exhibits on the area's past and culture, while the North Carolina Aquarium (M–Sat., 9–5; Sun., 1–5, free) and the Marine Resources Center (M.–F., 9–5; Sat., 10–4; Sun., 1–5, free) on nearby Bogue Banks, the long narrow strip of land just off the coast, contain displays on the sea aspects of the well-watered region. Corners of Carteret County that will give you the salty tangy flavor of the sea include Harkers Island, where craftsmen who speak in an Old English Elizabethan-era dialect use traditional techniques to build distinctive wooden boats redolent with freshly cut cedar, and Cape Lookout National Seashore, accessible by ferry from Harkers Island, an unspoiled natural area with the 1859 Cape Lookout Lighthouse at the southern end. To the far north by Ocracoke Island (reached by a ferry from Cedar Island just off the mainland coast) lies Portsmouth Island, once a thriving port and now uninhabited, the abandoned village there listed on the National Register.

The Crystal Coast's most beguiling town is Beaufort (pro-nounced "BO-furt" by the locals), North Carolina's third oldest settlement, founded by French Huguenots and English sailors in 1709. At the Restoration Area (M.–Sat., 9:30–4:30, adm.) survive seven historic structures spanning the years from 1732 to 1859, among those relics a mid-nineteenth-century apothecary shop, the 1796 courthouse and the antique-filled townhouse of plantation owner Joseph Bell. Around town stand a hundred or so other eighteenth-century dwellings, many painted white with characteristic free-standing chimneys, two-story porches, distinctive roof lines and traces of the West Indies architecture that influenced con-struction in Beaufort. Gnarled live oaks garnish the Old Burial Ground where privateer Otway Burns, naval hero of the War of 1812 and builder in 1818 of North Carolina's first steamboat, the "Prometheus," reposes beneath a gun from his ship the "Snapdragon," while nearby lies—or, rather, stands—a British soldier, for he asked to be buried

Bruton Parish Church, Colonial Williamsburg, Virginia.

Home of George Washington, Mount Vernon, Virginia.

Lighthouse on
Assateague Island,
Virginia.

Booker T. Washington Cabin, Rocky Mount, Virginia.

Virginia Beach, Virginia.

Stalagmites and Stalactites, Luray Caverns, Virginia.

Linn Cove Viaduct, Blue Ridge Parkway, North Carolina.

Village of Ocracoke, Outer Banks, North Carolina.

Tweetsie Railroad, Blowing Rock, North Carolina.

Hang gliding, Nags Head, North Carolina.

Biltmore House, Asheville, North Carolina.

Tryon Palace and Gardens, New Bern, North Carolina.
Oconaluftee Indian Village, Cherokee, North Carolina.

U.S.S. *Yorktown*, Charleston, South Carolina.

Dock Street Theatre, Charleston, South Carolina.

Table Rock Mountain, South Carolina.

Myrtle Beach,
South Carolina.

Joseph Manigault House, Charleston, South Carolina.

Battery at
White Point
Gardens,
Charleston,
South Carolina.

Croquet at Jekyll Island, Georgia.

Underground shopping, Atlanta, Georgia.

A historic home in "most picturesque" Madison, Georgia.

Martin Luther King Center, Atlanta, Georgia.

A big one in the Okefenokee Swamp, Georgia.

Vizcaya, Miami, Florida.

Sugar Mill Gardens, Port Orange, Florida.

Ybor City Cuban
quarter, Tampa, Florida.

Luxury hotels on beach, Miami, Florida.

Thomas Edison Home,
Fort Myers, Florida.

La Leche Shrine, St. Augustine, Florida.

Kennedy Space
Center, Cape
Canaveral, Florida.

upright, saluting the king, as the Englishman didn't want
to recline in foreign soil.

In the early days the town lived from the sea, with docks,
fishermen, whalers and the colony's only shipbuilding industry, and it also almost died from the sea in 1747 when pirates
attacked Beaufort twice and again in 1782 when the British
plundered the settlement in what is believed to have been
the last major landing of the English during the Revolutionary War. The North Carolina Maritime Museum (M.–F.,
9–5; Sat., 10–5; Sun., 2–5, free) contains ship models, wildlife exhibits and maritime artifacts that recall the area's close
connection with the sea, while from the waterfront boardwalk you can view yachts, shrimping trawlers and, on Carrot
Island just offshore, the wild ponies that graze there. In early
May the museum sponsors the annual Traditional Wooden
Boat Show, while in mid-August it presents the Strange
Seafood Exhibition (for information on these events:
919-725-7317). The Harvey Smith Watercraft Center (M.–F.,
9–1, 2–5, free) on Front Street, a wooden boat firm, contains
displays of old-type small craft. Bed and breakfast choices
in Beaufort include the Inlet Inn (919-728-3600), Shot-
gun House (919-728-6248), Beaufort Inn (919-728-2600),
Langdon House (919-728-5499), Captain's Quarters (919-
728-7711) and the Cedars (919-728-7036), which occupies, in part, a c. 1768 residence built by a local shipbuilder.

On the eastern tip of Bogue Banks, just across from Beaufort, stands Fort Macon, a splendid example of a nineteenth-
century fortification. The North Carolina legislature built
earlier outposts there to protect the coast against pirates and
other sea-borne threats, but only 1834 Fort Macon survives.
During the Civil War, Federal forces occupied the fortress,
which saw duty later during the Spanish-American War in
1898 and as recently as World War II. Powder magazines,
living quarters, a hot shot furnace used to heat ammunition

fired at wooden ships and other casemate areas recall the
fort's days of active duty. Beyond Salter Path, founded by
squatters who lose rights to their property if their houses
aren't kept in the family, lies the resort town of Emerald
Isle where the Crepe Myrtle Inn (919-354-4616) offers
bed and breakfast, as does Scottskeep (919-326-1257) at nearby
Swansboro. From Swansboro departs a free fringe-topped
ferry that takes you through the white heron-filled sand
marshes out to Hammocks Beach State Park, an unspoiled
area filled with wildlife where from May through September
the endangered loggerhead sea turtle nests. The waterfront
Crystal Coast Amphitheatre near Swansboro presents the
recently instituted (1988) *Worthy Is The Lamb,* a Passion play
(mid-June–early Sept., Tu.–Sat., 8:30 p.m., 800-662-5960 or
919-393-8373). Along the coast south of the Marine Corps
Camp Lejeune (tours for groups by arrangement), the nation's second largest amphibious warfare training base, lies
the Topsail area, pronounced "Tops'l" and so designated for
the sails that peeked over the dunes, telltale—or tellsail—
signs to passing ships that pirates lurked there in the channels
behind the hills of sand. In 1940 the federal government
took over Topsail, which the Confederates used as a salt
source during the Civil War, and built Camp Davis, an anti-
aircraft training base that opened in April 1941. In the middle
of that year the Navy began a program of testing rockets
and guided missiles, later constructing launching pads and
seven concrete observation towers that still stand to recall
the beginnings of the nation's space research, a project later
moved to Cape Canaveral in Florida. Two years after the
government released the island for civilian use in 1949, de-
scriptively named Surf City started up, and now twenty-six-
mile long Topsail offers beaches, marinas, fishing piers and
other resort facilities. At Scotts Hill to the south, Poplar
Grove (Feb.–Dec., M.–Sat., 9–5; Sun., 12–6, adm. for house
tour, grounds free), listed on the National Register, survives

as a good example of a mid-nineteenth-century plantation. The manor house and outbuildings recall the era when the Foy family, who owned the property from 1795 to 1971, ran a self-supporting agricultural community, specializing in the cultivation of peanuts. The Cultural Arts Center houses craftsmen who demonstrate old techniques for fabricating objects, many on sale at the Scotts Hill Country Store, and the Manor House Restaurant provides meals in a pleasant setting.

Nearby Wilmington retains its old-time air, with many of the city's antique houses embellishing the National Register-listed historic district, whose more than two hundred blocks make it North Carolina's largest such enclave. The city began to prosper as a trading center soon after its founding on the Cape Fear River in 1739. Planters in the river valley exported through the port wood products and so-called "naval stores"—supplies of turpentine, rosin, tar and pitch used in England for sailing ships. Janet Schaw of Edinburgh, Scotland, who in 1775 visited John Rutherford's "fine plantation," noted in her *Journal of a Lady of Quality* the production of these tree-based commodities, so important to North Carolina's early economy: "He makes a great deal of tar and turpentine, but his grand work is a saw-mill, the finest I have ever met with. It cuts three thousand lumbers a day . . . the plantation not only affording lumber, but staves, hoops and ends for barrels and casks for the West Indian trade." From North Carolina's voluminous tar production stemmed the state's nickname, "Tar Heel," which supposedly originated when Carolinians threatened during the Civil War to apply tar to the heels of Confederate troops to make them stick to the line of fire. Although the Southern ranks failed to hold, melting away under Sherman's and Grant's fire, the name did stick to the people from North Carolina. During the Civil War Wilmington continued to thrive as the Confederacy's last

Atlantic coast port to stay open, enabling blockade runners to bring in needed military supplies for Southern fighting forces. Between the mid-nineteenth century and 1910 Wilmington remained the largest city in North Carolina, and today the town survives as a pleasant tree-filled place with a strong ambiance of yesteryear. Around town you'll find such carryovers from the past as the 1770 Burgwin-Wright House (Tu.–Sat., 10–4 adm.), a garden-rich gentleman's townhouse where British General Cornwallis headquartered not long before his surrender at Yorktown; the 1852 antique-filled Zebulon Latimer House (Tu.–Sat., 10–4, adm.); the 1859 Bellamy House, whose beautifully carved facade capitals recall the elaborate capitals at nearby Thalian Hall, a still-used theater that forms the east wing of City Hall; the George R. French and Sons Building (1873), with an ornamental cast-iron facade; and the exotic looking Temple of Israel, the state's oldest synagogue, with onion domes and a horseshoe arch over the door. Two restored old-time commercial enclaves now serve as shopping areas: Chandler's Wharf, with cobblestone streets and what is supposedly the nation's oldest tugboat on display; and the Cotton Exchange, which once housed one of the country's largest cotton exporting companies. Museums in Wilmington include the St. John's Museum of Art (Tu.–Sat., 10–5; Sun., 12–4, free), featuring American works; the New Hanover County Museum (Tu.–Sat., 9–5; Sun., 2–5, free) with displays on the Cape Fear region; the "U.S.S. North Carolina" (8–dusk, adm.), offering a two-hour guided tour through the battleship; and the Railroad Museum (Tu.–Sat., 10–5; Sun., 1–5, free), installed in the boxy brick former office building of the Atlantic Coast Line.

In 1840, six years after incorporation of the city's original train company, the firm's track stretched north from Wilmington to Weldon, one hundred and sixty-one miles, then the world's longest rail line. At the old trainyard operates the new (February 1989) Coast Line Inn (919-763-2800), surrounded by a railroad atmosphere and with a restaurant installed in a renovated train building. At Oakdale Cemetery, a lushly landscaped 1852 burial ground, repose many of the city's leading citizens of yesteryear, while for a view of today's Wilmington you can visit the North Carolina State Port Authority to watch shiploading and unloading operations (by reservation only: 919-763-1621, free). Although a spur of interstate highway 40 heads north out of Wilmington toward Raleigh, the state capital, for the time being the city remains the only port on the East coast not yet linked to the interstate network. On the south side of town Greenfield Gardens (free) offers nature trails and a five-mile lakeside scenic drive, and the sternwheeler "Henrietta II" sails on short day cruises on the Cape Fear River (April–Dec., Tu.- Sun., 2:30 p.m.) as well as two-and-a-half-hour dinner cruises (Tu., F., Sat., 7 p.m.; for reservations: 919-343-1611), while horse-drawn carriage tours of the city are also available (919-251-8889 or 253-4894). Bed and breakfast choices in Wilmington include Five Star Guest House (919-763-7581), the Inn on Orange (919-251-0863), Murchison House (919-343-8580), Anderson Guest House (919-343-8128), Worth House (919-762-8562) and the elegant Graystone (919-762-0358).

Around Wilmington you'll find a few other Cape Fear area attractions. Beyond Airlie Gardens, open only in the spring (8–6, adm.) when the azaleas are in bloom, is Wrightsville Beach, a pleasant resort area where the Edgewater Inn (919-256-2914) takes bed and breakfast guests, while to the north lie Wallace, named for a president of the Wilmington and Weldon Railroad, and Rose Hill—home of what's supposedly the world's largest frying pan, fifteen feet wide with a capacity of two hundred and sixty-five chickens—where you'll find the Dupline Wine Cellars that offers tours and tastings (M.–Sat., 9–5, free).

The Genteel Plantation (919-283-5298), a private hunting preserve near Atkinson, provides accommodations in a restored Civil War era plantation house and nearby, to the south, lies Moores Creek National Battlefield (8–5, to 6 Sat. and Sun. June–Aug.), site of a crucial encounter on February 27, 1776, early in the Revolutionary War. After royal governor Josiah Martin urged Loyalists to suppress the Patriot's "most daring, horrid and unnatural rebellion," troops loyal to the crown assembled at Cross Creek (now Fayetteville). The British planned to cross a bridge at Moores Creek, where the Americans stealthily removed part of the span's floor, then greased the girders, causing enemy soldiers, bagpipes wheezing and swords held aloft, to slip off, while those behind retreated in defeat. This dealt a blow to Britain's "Southern Plan" and prevented the British from gaining control of the South. Displays and a diorama at the visitor center recall the episode, while trails to battlefield sites take you to reconstructed earthworks and other remnants of the fighting. At Lake Waccamaw to the southwest, where Bed and Breakfast at the Lake (919-646-4744) takes overnight guests, the Lake Waccamaw Depot Museum (Tu.–F., 2–5; Sat., 10–12, 2–5; Sun., 2–5, free), installed in a turn of the century depot, contains train memorabilia, old logging equipment and other historic items, while the nearby Green Swamp Nature Preserve teems with wildlife. In early May Chadbourn to the west hosts the annual Strawberry Festival, an event held since the early 1930s, and at Tabor City down on the South Carolina line you'll find bed and breakfast at the Todd House (919-653-3778).

Back on the coast south of Wilmington lie Carolina Beach, where a state park contains a variety of natural areas, and Kure Beach, with a popular fishing pier in the center of town. At Kure Beach you'll find one of the three coastal

North Carolina Aquariums (M.–Sat., 9–5; Sun., 1–5, free) as well as Fort Fisher State Historic Site (April–Oct., M.–Sat., 9–5; Sun., 1–5; Nov.–March, Tu.–Sat., 10–4; Sun., 1–4, free), where a museum and earthwork fortifications recall the outpost's role during the Civil War as protector of the area's shipping lanes for blockade runners who supplied the Confederacy. Fort Fisher finally fell to Federal forces on January 15, 1865, after the largest naval bombardment of the nineteenth century. This severed the South's last supply line and hastened the war's end. The nearby North Carolina Marine Resources Center (M.–Sat., 9–5; Sun., 1–5, free) features exhibits pertaining to the sea's natural history. From Fort Fisher a toll ferry crosses to the mainland (mid-May–Labor Day, every fifty minutes; winter, every hour and forty minutes). On the Cape Fear's west bank south of Wilmington two areas from the past recall earlier eras: live oak-shaded Orton Plantation Gardens (March–Aug., 8–6; Sept.–Nov., 8–5, adm.) at a nineteenth-century rice property where the Orton House (not open to the public), built in 1735 and later embellished with a second story, columns and wings, glistens bright white above the gardens; and Brunswick Town (April–Oct., M.–Sat., 9–5; Sun., 1–5; Nov.–March, Tu.–Sat., 10–4; Sun., 1–4, free), site of both a once-thriving colonial port town established in 1726, and of Fort Anderson, a Confederate outpost. When Spanish privateers invaded the town in 1748 the citizens rallied to seize the intruder's ship, later selling the contents and using the proceeds to build St. Philips, one of North Carolina's oldest churches, now in ruins. In 1765 the people of Brunswick Town rebelled against the Stamp Tax, one of the first outbursts of armed resistance to British rule. When the Revolution broke out the residents fled, and in 1776 the British burned the deserted town. Nearly a century later, in 1862, the Confederates constructed Fort Anderson, which they held until the Union navy bombarded the post on February

19, 1865, a month after the fall of Fort Fisher across the river. Exhibits at the visitor center, including excavated foundations of Brunswick Town buildings, along with earthworks of the fort, recall the area's long history.

Farther south, beyond the Sunny Point Military Ocean Terminal—the nation's first military installation (1955) designed solely for the transfer of ammunition, explosives and other hazardous cargoes from land to sea—lies live oak-garnished Southport, a picturesque fishing village where the movie *Crimes of the Heart* was filmed. The Old Smithfield Burying Ground, established in 1792, provides a peaceful place to linger, while a more electrifying attraction in Southport—the east coast's northernmost subtropical region— is the Carolina Power and Light Company's Brunswick Nuclear Power Plant visitor center (Sept.–May, M.–F., 9–5; June–Aug., M.–F., 9–5; Sat. and Sun., 1–5, free), which contains exhibits on electricity, nuclear power and energy conservation. Southport mounts an especially lively three-day Fourth of July celebration and in December the town presents its "Christmas by the Sea" festivities, featuring a flotilla with lighted vessels on the Cape Fear River. At the mouth of the river in the summer of 1718 an expedition captured Stede Bonnet, a former British army major turned pesky pirate, supposedly induced to take up that profession by his nagging wife.

On Oak Island, where the North Carolina Baptist Assembly gathers, stands a latter-day (1958) lighthouse (M.–Sat., 4- sunset; Sun., 12–sunset, grounds only), while on nearby Bald Head Island rises "Old Baldy," North Carolina's oldest standing lighthouse (1817), which remained in service until 1935. Bald Head, reached from Southport by ferries dubbed "The Revenge," after the ship Bonnet owned, and "The Adventure," Blackbeard's vessel, has been tastefully developed as a secluded resort community modeled after Martha's Vineyard off Cape Cod, with houses for sale and rent (for

information: 919-457-6763, in-state 800-722-6450). In Southport, novelist Robert Ruark's hometown, the Dosher Plantation House (919-457-5554) provides bed and breakfast
accommodations, as does Doe Creek Inn (919-754-6882) at
Shallotte off to the west beyond Bolivia, so named for the
South American country that supplied fertilizer shipped
through the town in the early 1900s. It is perhaps passing
strange to end a tour of eastern North Carolina with Bolivian
fertilizer, but such is one of the many curiosities provided
by back-road, off-the-beaten track travel in America.

Central North Carolina

Raleigh, Durham and Chapel Hill—North of Raleigh:
Warrenton, Henderson, Williamsboro—South of Raleigh:
Smithfield, Fayetteville, Pinehurst—West of Raleigh:
Burlington, Reidsville, Greensboro, High Point,
Winston-Salem, Salisbury, Charlotte

The rum punch at Isaac Hunter's tavern in Wake County
back in the late eighteenth century packed a real punch. So
popular was Hunter's drink that circuit-riding judges and
lawyers, as well as many other characters, shady and colorful, frequented the establishment to imbibe the liquid refreshments there. Back in those days a dispute arose as to where
to locate North Carolina's new state capital. Westward expansion had made New Bern, over on the coast, too far
east to continue as the seat of government. Many towns
vied to attract the new capital, but it was finally decided
at a meeting in 1788 to establish the state house at a site
within ten miles of Hunter's Tavern, not far from the pub's
punchy, potent potion. Years later, however, when the legislature chose the official state beverage it wasn't Hunter's
punch but a somewhat milder drink—milk. In 1792 the state

bought one thousand acres of land from Joel Lane, then surveyor William Christmas laid out four hundred acres in a grid pattern, and later that year the cornerstone of the capital was put in place. So began Raleigh.

As with state capitals everywhere, Raleigh boasts a generous assortment of museums and government-connected attractions. In the center of town rises the original capitol (M.–F., 8–5; Sat., 9–5; Sun., 1–5, free), which houses a replica of the toga-clad George Washington statue carved by Italian sculptor Antonio Canova, commissioned for the job on the advice of Thomas Jefferson (an 1834 fire destroyed the original work). The squat, gray capitol with its low dome contrasts with the slim columns, white hue and modernistic style of the nearby 1963 State Legislative Building (M.–F., 8–5; Sat., 9–5; Sun., 1–5, free), the nation's first structure built exclusively for a state legislature, designed by renowned architect Edward Durrell Stone, who also created the 1983 North Carolina Museum of Art building (Tu.–Sat., 10–5; F. to 9, Sun., 12–5, free), on the west side of town, which houses a well-respected collection of Old Masters and American works, some acquired starting in 1947 with the nation's first state funds appropriated to buy artworks. There are two other official collections near the capitol: the Museum of History (Tu.–Sat., 9–5; Sun., 1–6, free) and the State Museum of Natural Sciences (M–F., 8–5; Sat., 9–5; Sun., 1–5, free), while the Governor's Mansion, completed in 1891 with prison labor, also takes visitors (by appointment: 919-733-3456).

Old houses of interest stand in the Mordecai Historic Park (Tu.–Th., 10–2; Sat. and Sun., 1–4) which includes the modest abode where Andrew Johnson, Lincoln's successor, was born. In the Oakwood Historic District, an 1870s Victorian neighborhood listed on the National Register, Oakwood Inn offers bed and breakfast (919-832-9712), while c. 1760 Wakefield, home of Revolutionary War colonel Joel Lane, whose land the state acquired to establish Raleigh, recalls the city's earliest days. At the western edge of the Oakwood district stretches Oakwood Cemetery, whose permanent residents include six governors and Josephus Daniels, *Raleigh News and Observer* editor and Wilson's secretary of the navy. By Oakwood nestles the small Hebrew Cemetery (1869) and beyond stretches the Confederate Cemetery where Southern troops were buried after federal authorities evicted them from the National Cemetery so Union war dead could be interred there. Across from the capitol stands National Register-listed 1853 Christ Episcopal, a striking Gothic Revival-style church, while a few blocks away, on the northwest corner of Blount and North Streets, grows the Henry Clay Oak, under which the famous politician wrote a letter to the *National Intelligencer* on the Texas situation, declaring in regard to the matter, "I'd rather be right than president," a wish granted to Clay who lost out in competition for the White House to the warmongering James K. Polk, a North Carolina native.

Between Raleigh and nearby Durham lies the innovative sixty-seven hundred-acre Research Triangle Park, where more than fifty firms operate research or high-tech assembly facilities. The largest research center of its kind in the world, Triangle opened in 1960 as a cooperative effort by three nearby leading universities, Duke in Durham, the University of North Carolina at Chapel Hill and Raleigh's North Carolina State. The area that includes these schools now boasts more Ph.D.s per capita than anywhere else in the country. In order to retain the well-wooded park's rural atmosphere, buildings can occupy only up to 15 percent of their lots. Perhaps the park's most striking structure is the Burroughs Wellcome drug company's modernistic research lab, an angular building with boxy sections protruding from the facade. Nearby Durham enjoys a certain alluring atmosphere that makes it seem an eminently livable place. Built on a human scale, the tree-filled tobacco town offers the world-class cultural and educational amenities of Duke University, spread over a pair of campuses connected by two-sectioned shuttle buses–the East Campus, Trinity College until 1924 when tobacco king James Buchanan Duke gave the school forty million dollars, where you'll find the University Museum of Art (Tu.–F., 9–5; Sat., 10–1; Sun., 2–5, free), and the West Campus, the justifiably famous Gothic-style enclave, an ivory tower sort of place, its centerpiece the Chapel (8–5, free) with a bell tower, stone not ivory, modeled after Canterbury Cathedral, and where the Sarah P. Duke Memorial Gardens (8–sunset, free) lie in a pine valley.

Durham also boasts two other lesser-known educational institutions—North Carolina Central, the nation's first state-supported liberal arts college for blacks (1925) and the unique North Carolina School of Science and Mathematics, the country's first residential public high school (1978) for gifted science and math scholars, where nearly five hundred students, who habitually win more National Merit Scholarships than any other U.S. high school, study. Downtown Durham, North Carolina's first major commercial district to be listed on the National Register, is a rather cozy area with many low-rise buildings overshadowed by only a few skyscrapers, among them the glassy, angular Peoples Security Insurance building and the twelve-story North Carolina Mutual edifice (tours, M.–Th., 9:30–11; 2–3:30, free), home of the nation's largest black-managed financial institution, founded in 1898. Brightleaf Square—specialty shops housed in restored brick tobacco warehouses—along with the huge brick Liggett & Myers building, and a chimney and a white water tower bearing red Lucky Strike logos all serve to recall the leading role tobacco has played in the history of Durham, named for Dr. Bartlett Durham who donated a right of way to the North Carolina Railroad in the 1840s after a general store owner had refused to deed land to the line for fear the passing trains would hurt business by frightening his customers' horses.

The tobacco trade got its start after the Civil War. In April 1865 Union General William Tecumseh Sherman, who reached North Carolina after his "march to the sea" across Georgia and his passage through South Carolina, parlayed with Confederate General Joseph E. Johnston, who had failed to stop Sherman at the Battle of Bentonville. When the men met at the Bennett Place (April–Oct., M.–Sat., 9–5; Sun., 1–5; Nov.–March, Tu.–Sat., 10–4; Sun., 1–4, free), now a state historic site just west of Durham, Johnston surrendered to Sherman nearly 90,000 Confederate troops in the Carolinas, Georgia and Florida, the largest number of men yielded in the Civil War at one time. Soldiers of both armies stationed in the area discovered Durham's light-bodied bright leaf tobacco, and when the men returned home after the war they began to request the product. To supply the increased demand, tobacco factory owner John Ruffin Green created at the suggestion of a friend named Julian Shakespeare Carr the Bull Durham brand, so called from the representation of a bull on the jar of Coleman's mustard made in the town's namesake, Durham, England. The trademark, as well as the mustard, soon spread around the country, with the Bull Durham logo painted behind the New York Yankee dugout giving origin to the baseball term "bullpen." In 1865 tobacco farmer Washington Duke left his fields and started to manufacture tobacco products, packed into cloth bags with a hand-lettered yellow tag labeled "Pro Bono Publico" ("for the public good"), Duke's first trademark. Soon Washington and his son James began to peddle the products in eastern North Carolina, and in the 1880s the family's factory installed the Bonsack cigarette machine and began the first mass production of cigarettes, an operation that evolved into the Duke-dominated American Tobacco and the Liggett & Myers companies. By 1904 the Dukes

controlled three-quarters of the nation's tobacco industry,
a near monopoly the U.S. Supreme Court ordered dissolved
in 1911. From these businesses stemmed the fortune James B.
Duke gave to Trinity College in 1924.

The Duke Homestead in Durham (April–Oct., M.–Sat.,
9–5; Sun., 1–5; Nov.–March, Tu.–Sat., 10–4, Sun., 1–4, free)
includes the family's mid-nineteenth-century estate as well
as a tobacco museum and tobacco fields. In and around Durham you'll find such other attractions as the Stagville Preservation Center (M.–F., 9–4), the nation's first state-owned
research facility for the study of historic and archeological
preservation technology, located near Falls Lake, a recreational area formed by the 1981 Falls Dam; the North Carolina
Museum of Life and Science (M.–Sat., 10–5; Sun., 1–5; free),
with exhibits ranging from pre-history to the aerospace era;
West Point on the Eno (Sat. and Sun., 1–5, free), a re-creation
of a mill facility which operated from 1778 to 1942, including
the Hugh Mangum Photography Museum and a restored
1850s farmhouse; and, downtown, the Book Exchange, a
huge emporium whose sign outside proclaims with little
exaggeration "The South's Greatest Bookstore." Arrowhead
Inn (919-477-8430), seven miles north of town, offers bed
and breakfast, while popular local eateries include Bullock's,
with memorable Brunswick stew, the Top Hat Saloon, and
Crook's Corner, featuring such specialties as fried chicken
and red onion potato salad.

Before proceeding to nearby Chapel Hill, third corner of
the central North Carolina educational triangle, you may
want to look in at historic Hillsborough, west of Durham,
where more than one hundred late eighteenth- and early
nineteenth-century structures, a dozen of them listed on the
National Register, lend the town a look of yesteryear. Once
a leading political center, Hillsborough was the hometown
of such politicos as Archibald Murphy, an ardent promoter

of public education in North Carolina, and Thomas Hart Benton, a renowned U.S. Senator from Missouri instrumental in the nation's nineteenth-century westward expansion. At Hillsborough—whose city hall, installed in a former residence, is one of the South's most pleasant government buildings—the Orange County Museum (Tu.–Sun., 1:30–4:30) traces the area's history, some of which haunts the Revolutionary War-era Colonial Inn (919-732-2461), supposedly the nation's oldest continuously operated hostelry, where you'll find Old South-style meals as well as accommodations. South of Hillsborough lies Chapel Hill, home of the nation's first state university, chartered in 1789 and opened six years later (the University of Georgia, chartered four years before the North Carolina institution, began operations in 1801). Among the one hundred and twenty-seven major buildings on the lovely hilly and wooded campus of the university, from which nearly half of North Carolina's governors have graduated, are the nation's two oldest state university structures: National Register-listed Old East (1795), still used as a dormitory, and Person Hall (1797); while 1852 Playmakers Theatre also merits Register listing. In 1918, the year Professor Frederick H. Koch established at the university the soon-famous Carolina Playmakers, a creative writing program, his students included novelist-to-be Thomas Wolfe from Asheville, who wrote for the course a play called *Return of Buck Gavin,* its preface asserting: "The dramatic is not the unusual. It is happening daily in our lives." Displays in Chapel Hill include the North Carolina Botanical Garden (M.–F., 8–5; Sat. and Sun., summer, 10–5; winter, 2–5, free); Morehead Planetarium (12:30–5, 6:30–9:30, Sat., from 10, adm.), the nation's first on a university campus (1949); Ackland Art Museum (for information: 919-966-5736); and Patterson's Mill (M.–Sat., 10–5:30; Sun., 2–5:30), an old country store with tobacco exhibits, along with an antique pharmacy and doctor's office. Along Franklin Street, lined with college hangouts and local commercial establishments, stand such dwellings as Kennette House (524 East Franklin), residence of chemist Charles Herty, who developed the process for producing newsprint from Southern pine; the Kyser House (504), formerly occupied by band leader Kay Kyser, dean not at the state university but of the "Kollege of Musical Knowledge" on the radio show; the university president's house (400); and also the 1848 Gothic Revival-style Chapel of the Cross church, erected by the Reverend William Mercer Green, second academically in the class of 1818 only to James K. Polk, who later became President of the United States. Over on Rosemary (200 East) stands the c. 1853 Old Methodist Church, home of an integrated congregation back before the Civil War, and the Mickle-Mangum-Smith House (315 East), where novelist Betty Smith lived when she wrote *A Tree Grows in Brooklyn.* Local down-home eating places include Dips Country Kitchen, 405 Rosemary; and wooden animal-decorated Crook's Corner, 610 West Franklin; while The Inn at Bingham School (919-563-5583), installed in the National Register-listed headmaster's home at a former prep school eleven miles west of Chapel Hill, takes bed and breakfast visitors. Other bed and breakfast spots include Hillcrest (919-942-2369), Pineview Inn (919-967-7166), and Windy Oaks Farm (919-942-1001), former home of Carolina Playmakers' student made-good Paul Green, a Pulitzer Prize winner.

From the Raleigh area fan out roads that will take you around the central section of North Carolina. North of Wake Forest—where the Southeastern Baptist Theological Seminary occupies the 1834 former campus of Wake Forest College, lured away in 1956 to Winston-Salem by the gift of a large endowment—lies Louisburg, which in mid-August hosts the annual National Whistlers' Convention. East of

Wake Forest is Perry's Mill Pond, a rustic corner of the countryside where a latter-day successor to a mill originally established there in 1778 stands. At Warrenton, northeast of Louisburg, stand such historic buildings as the John White House, where Robert E. Lee stayed in 1870 while visiting his daughter's grave; the house where the Bragg brothers grew up—Thomas, governor from 1855 to 1859, U.S. Congressman John, and Confederate General Braxton after whom Fort Bragg near Fayetteville is named; and Emmanuel Episcopal Church, built in 1822 by the Bragg boys' father, where New York editor and publisher Horace Greeley married in 1836. Traub's Inn (919-257-2727) in Warrenton offers pleasant accommodations, while at nearby Macon grew up contemporary North Carolina novelist Reynolds Price, whose works—most notably the richly wrought *The Surface of the Earth*—present a picture of the state, its culture and people. Four miles north of Vaughan lies Buck Spring, Nathaniel Macon's home, listed on the National Register, residence of the U.S. Senator and Speaker of the House of Representatives, who served in Congress for thirty-seven years. Macon, who died in 1837, requested that dinner and grog be served to the mourners at his funeral and that each friend cast a stone onto his grave, now covered by a large mound of stones. Off to the west lies Henderson, named for the son of Richard Henderson who financed Daniel Boone's western expeditions and who headed the Transylvania Company which negotiated the largest private real estate transaction in American history (see the East Tennessee section of Chapter 9).

At Henderson stands the delightful Fire Station, with a tall slim clock tower, and the "gingerbread" trim-bedecked 1883 Mistletoe Villa. The J. P. Taylor Company in Henderson, a subsidiary of Universal Leaf Tobacco, processes more than eighty million pounds of leaf a year. Henderson Manor (919-492-5064), Pool Rock Plantation (919-492-6399) and

National Register-listed La Grange Plantation Inn (919-438-2421) at the edge of Kerr Lake offer bed and breakfast accommodations. Also by Kerr Lake—a 50,000-acre expanse, formed in 1953 by a dam across the Roanoke River and lined with recreational facilities—stands Ashland, Vance County's oldest house (1740), where Richard Henderson lived. At now sleepy Williamsboro, in 1781 capital of North Carolina, rises 1772 St. John's (June–Oct., Sun., 2–5, free), an attractive white wood sanctuary, the state's third oldest church, after those at Bath and Edenton on the coast, and the oldest of frame construction. In the Williamsboro area lived Varine Howell, wife of Jefferson Davis, and Mary Pinckney Hardy, Douglas MacArthur's mother. Off to the west at Oxford—which claims both Oxford Orphanage, the state's oldest, and Central Orphanage, the state's oldest such facility established for blacks—functions the Tobacco Research Station, an experimental organization with two labs and four hundred acres of tobacco lands.

Back in the Raleigh area, toward the south the 1757 Atkinsons Mill (M.–F., 8–5, free) near Clayton continues in operation; while over at Selma, which the first weekend in October celebrates Railroad Days, Southland Estate Winery receives visitors (M.–Sat., 9–6, free) for tours, including a wine museum, and tastings of some or all eleven wines the firm produces. In August and September, Smithfield, tucked in a bend on the Neuse River, hosts tobacco market tours (M.–Th., 11 a.m.) which leave from Carolina Pottery, a factory outlet shopping center (M.–Sat., 9–9; Sun., 1–6), while the third weekend in April the town holds a Ham 'n' Yam Festival, commemorating the ranking of Johnston County—first in North Carolina in cash receipts of all crops—as the nation's leading sweet potato producer. On Brogden Road to the east of Smithfield—where Eli Olive's (919-934-9823 or 934-0246) offers bed and breakfast—you'll find the childhood home of actress Ava Gardner, who died in January 1990, where the "Barefoot Contessa" first went barefoot. A collection of Gardner memorabilia recalls the star's more than sixty films (July–mid-Aug., Th.–Sun., or by appointment: 919-934-2176). In Coats another unusual museum (open by appointment: 919-934-4763, free) features bells; while nearby Benson celebrates two colorful festivals: Mule Days the last weekend in September and, the fourth weekend in June, gospel singers gather in a grove of stately oak trees for the annual singing convention, a tradition since the early 1920s. At Dunn, just to the south, the General William C. Lee Museum honors the officer who developed the Army's airborne organization, while the nearby Averasboro Battleground recalls the first organized Confederate resistance, on March 16–17, 1865, to General Sherman's march north from Georgia through North Carolina. At Lillington, up the Cape Fear River—where the Pickett Fence Inn (919-893-4382) provides bed and breakfast—stands the lovely little Summerville Presbyterian Church (1811), whose cemetery contains the grave of a mysterious stranger found dead on the sanctuary's steps. Also in the area is the deliciously named Barbecue Presbyterian Church, established in 1757 by the Scottish Highlanders who founded Lillington, birthplace of Pulitzer Prize-winning playwright Paul Green. Before continuing south to Fayetteville you may want to see a few places back toward Raleigh. You'll find pleasant accommodations in Cary, adjacent to the capital city, at the Macfarlane Inn (919-469-3400) and at Fearrington House (919-542-2121) at Pittsboro to the west.

On the banks of nearby B. Everett Jordan Lake, a recreational area, the Carolina Power and Light Harris Visitor Center (May–Oct., M.–F., 9–4; Sun., 1–4, free) in New Hill houses energy displays; while the North Carolina Railroad Museum (April–Oct., 1st Sun. of month, 12–5, excursion trains leave every hour, 1–4) at Bonsal includes a collection of old train cars and engines where the 1904 New Hope

Valley line, called "the Lightnin' Bug Route," originated. Sanford is also an early rail center, named after the local line's chief engineer, as recalled by the 1872 Railroad House, now a historical museum installed in the first train depot agent's residence. To the west stands the House in the Horseshoe (April–Oct., M.–Sat., 9–5; Sun., 1–5; Nov.–March, Tu.–Sat., 10–4; Sun., 1–4, free), so called because the mansion—built as one of the Piedmont area's first plantation "big houses" about 1772 by Phillip Alston, later twice indicted for murder—occupies a horseshoe bend of the Deep River. After Alston left North Carolina in 1790, four-time Governor Benjamin Williams acquired the property, now restored and filled with period furnishings. At Carthage the Tom Jones House (919-947-3044), built in 1880 by a buggy manufacturer, offers bed and breakfast, while at Cameron you'll find a historic district and more than sixty antique dealers, as well as the Sandhills Vineyards and Herb Gardens.

Although a devastating fire in May 1831 destroyed some six hundred structures in Fayetteville, a few buildings survived, among them three National Register-listed properties at Heritage Square (M.–F., 9–3, adm.), including the handsome Sanford House, once the office of North Carolina's first United States bank, and nearby 1789 Register-listed Cool Spring Tavern, the town's oldest dwelling. On the site of the old state capitol, where in 1789 North Carolina ratified the U.S. Constitution, chartered the University of North Carolina and ceded its western lands to form the state of Tennessee, stands the Register-listed 1832 Market House, an angular four-tiered structure of mixed styles. Register-listed old dwellings around town include 1838 Kyle House (M.–F., 8–5, free), now the mayor's office, and the Belden-Horne House (M.–F., 8:30–5, free) with a handsome hand-stenciled floral design ceiling, while among the old churches, also on the Register, are St. John's, with spikey

twin towers; St. Joseph's, featuring Tiffany stained glass;
and First Presbyterian, sporting whale-oil chandeliers (now
electrified) and a sundial that duplicates the one at Sir Walter
Scott's garden in England. The Museum of the Cape Fear
(Tu.–Sat., 10–5; Sun., 1–5) contains history displays on the
southeastern region of the state, while the Museum of Art
(Tu.–F., 10–5; Sat. and Sun., 1–5, free) houses not only paintings but a collection of more than eighty objects from central
and west Africa. As recalled by the Marquis de Lafayette
statue in Cross Creek Park, named for two local streams
that seemed to cross one another and continue on their separate flows, Fayetteville became the nation's first city (1783)
named for the famous Frenchman, so much a Yankeephile
he named his son for George Washington and his daughters
for Carolina and Virginia. In early September the town observes Lafayette Week, while the first weekend in April the
Dogwood Festival celebrates Fayetteville's one hundred thousand dogwood trees. Perhaps the city's greatest claim to fame
is as the site of the first professional home-run hit on March
7, 1914 by "Babe" Ruth, who acquired his nickname in Fayetteville. The Pines Guest Lodge (919-864-7333) in town offers bed and breakfast.

Just west of Fayetteville spreads the huge Fort Bragg and
Pope Air Force Base complex, a veritable city that sprawls
over 121,000 acres and supports half as many people. At
Fort Bragg, established in 1918 as Camp Bragg, are trained
unconventional warfare units—the famous "Green Berets"—
and psychological warfare forces, groups whose history and
operation museums on the base recall: the John F. Kennedy
Special Warfare Museum (Tu.–Sat., 11:30–4, free) with a
collection of unusual weapons; the Hall of Heroes (8–9, free),
commemorating Special Forces Medal of Honor winners;
and the 82nd Airborne Division Museum (Tu.–Sat., 10–4:30;
Sun., 11:30–4, free), whose more than 3,000 artifacts com-

prise the largest collection in the army museum system. For demonstration times of the Golden Knights, free-fall precision parachutists, you can call 919-396-2036.

Southeast of Fayetteville lies Elizabethtown, where local Sallie Salter spied on the English encampment by selling eggs to the troops there, an exploit that led to a patriot victory in August 1781. In the area lie oval-shaped lakes thought to have been formed by a meteor bombardment 100,000 years ago, and at Clarkton is the site of the house of "Whistler's Mother." Off to the west beyond Lumberton lies the town of Pembroke, once referred to as Scuffletown. Lumbee Indians, who some historians believe descend from "the Lost Colony of Roanoke" settlers, comprise the majority of the town's population. In 1909 an Indian group bought ten acres of ground to establish Pembroke State University, one of the only two schools east of the Mississippi to offer a degree in American Indian studies (the other is Northland College in Ashland, Wisconsin). In Old Main on the campus the Native American Resource Center (M.–F., 8–5, free) houses Indian-related items, as does the North Carolina Indian Cultural Center three miles east of town where the redskin epic *Strike at the Wind* is performed in July and August (Th., F., Sat., 8:30; 919-521-2489 from 9–5; box office after 6 on performance nights: 919-521-3112).

Up at Raeford near Fort Bragg the three-day Turkey Festival in September includes the Turkey Olympics, turkey hotdogs and other such gobbler attractions, while off to the west at the larger than hamlet-sized town of Hamlet (9,000 people) the National Railroad Museum (Sat., 10–5; Sun., 1–5, free), installed in the splendid round-cornered Seaboard Line turn-of-the-century depot, contains train models and rail memorabilia. At Ellerbe the Rankin Museum of American Heritage (Tu.–F., 10–4; Sat. and Sun., 2–5, adm.) houses a mixed collection, including natural history, regional history, crafts, pottery and a century-old turpentine still. The nearby Town Creek Indian Mount (April–Oct., M.–Sat., 9–5; Sun., 1–5; Nov.–March, Tu.–Sat., 10–4; Sun., 1–4, free) recalls the Creek settlement that occupied the site more than three centuries ago, and the National Register-listed Malcolm Blue Historical Farm (March–Oct., Sun., 2–5 or by appointment: 919-692-7894 or 692-2959) at Aberdeen back to the east recalls the nineteenth-century rural way of life. Near the farm rises the handsome 1790 Bethesda Church, also listed on the Register, which bears bullet holes from a Civil War battle, and in Aberdeen stands the turn-of-the-century Victorian-style train station, listed on the Register.

Although Pinehurst offers tennis, harness racing, horseback riding, polo at Little River Farm, trap and skeet shooting, and other such diversions, the more than thirty area golf courses—one, called The Pit, carved out of abandoned sand pits, ranks among North Carolina's top ten links—has lent the resort town the slogan "world's most famous birdie sanctuary." The PGA World Golf Hall of Fame (9–5, adm.) contains an extensive collection of golf-related curiosities and artifacts, including supposedly the world's oldest sporting implements, artworks and displays illustrating the game's history and lore; while the James Walker Tuft Archive at Given Memorial Library (M.–F., 9:30–12:30; 2–5, free) traces the history of Pinehurst, which the Boston soda fountain manufacturer founded in 1895 with the assistance of town planner Frederick Law Olmstead, designer of New York's Central Park. The Sir Walter Raleigh Gardens (daylight hours, free) at Sandhills Community College, reproduce a period garden similar to those common in Elizabethan times. The famous Pinehurst Hotel and Country Club (800-334-9560, in-state 800-672-4644) boasts seven golf courses, including the renowned Number 2 designed by Donald Ross, the father of links architecture. Other places to stay include Pine Crest Inn (919-295-6121), Magnolia Inn (919-295-6900), Holly Inn (919-295-2300) and the Manor Inn

(919-295-2700), which also houses Emma's Restaurant, named for hostelry founder Emma C. Bliss; and the Jefferson Inn (919-692-6400) at nearby Southern Pines, where you'll find Weymouth Center (M.–F., 10–12, 2–4, free), listed on the National Register, the pine-surrounded former home of author and publisher James Boyd, and the Boyd Wing of the Southern Pines Library (M.–F., 9–6; Sat., 9–5, free) with the writer's manuscripts and personal library. Nearby Weymouth Woods Sandhills Nature Preserve (natural history museum M.–Sat., 9–7; Sun., 12–5, free), donated to North Carolina in 1963 by Mrs. James Boyd as the first natural area to form part of the state park system, includes a few grains of the million-acre Sandhills region, longleaf pine-filled sandy ridges formed from sediments on terrain once covered by the sea.

From the Raleigh-Durham area the route west leads over to Greensboro, Winston-Salem and other of those characteristic North Carolina cities moderate in size and pleasant in atmosphere scattered across the Piedmont landscape. Thanks to the efforts of an environmental group, the forty-mile long Eno River valley near Durham remains an unspoiled green-belt that forms part of the Eno River State Park. At tiny Mebane, north of which stretches the "Old Belt" tobacco area where the famous bright leaf variety originated, began North Carolina's now-thriving furniture industry when the first factory started to mass produce the product in 1881. That pioneering firm, White Furniture Company, still turns out bedroom and dining room pieces. At nearby Graham the Leftwich House (919-226-5978) takes bed and breakfast guests, as does The Southern General (919-226-9909), filled with antiques and Confederate memorabilia over at Burlington, which began in 1853 as a railroad repair center called Company Shops. After the shops moved to Spencer south of Winston-Salem the town changed its name in the 1880s to Burlington, where in 1923 Burlington Mills started as a small rayon manufacturing company. Some of the area textile firms operate shops at the two outlet malls out by Interstate 85.

The town's Historic District, listed on the National Register, contains houses built during the time Burlington's economy shifted from railroad repair to the textile industry, while the Alamance Museum, also Register-listed, occupies the birthplace of Edwin Michael Holt, who in 1837 established the state's and the South's first plaid-dyeing cotton mill on Alamance Creek. In Burlington's City Park whirls the delightful antique (1910) Dentzel Carousel, populated by a menagerie of forty-six hand-carved wooden animals (Meridian, Mississippi, also boasts a similar merry-go-round), while more than five hundred specimens of real animals fill the McDade Wildlife Museum. To the south lies the Alamance Battleground (April–Oct., M.–Sat., 9–5; Sun., 1–5; Nov.–March, Tu.–Sat.; 10–4, Sun., 1–4, free), where in 1771 a group of rebels called the "Regulators" mounted one of the first armed rebellions against the British crown. At Snow Camp, toward the southern edge of Alamance County, lived the ancestors of author Alex Haley, who discussed the area in his book *Roots. The Sword of Peace* show at Snow Camp (late June–mid-Aug., Th., F., Sat., 8:30 p.m., 919-376-6948) dramatizes the Quaker community's peaceful resistance during the Revolutionary War. Old log buildings, a sorghum cane mill, Quaker meetinghouses and other venerable structures lend Snow Camp a touch of yesteryear, while the Quaker Museum (summer, W.–Sat., 6–8 p.m.) and the Post Office Museum contain exhibits that also recall the old days. Ye Old Country Kitchen at the settlement serves meals (W.–Sun., 11–9; for dinner reservations: 919-376-6991).

North of Burlington lies Yanceyville, which boasts a National Register-listed Historic District with a handsome 1861 courthouse and more than twenty antebellum dwellings, while up at Milton survives a well-preserved commercial district also listed on the Register. The c. 1838 Greek Revival-style plantation manor house Woodside Inn (919-234-8646) at Milton offers both bed and breakfast and a restaurant (Th., 6–9; F. and Sat., 6–9:30; Sun., 11:30–2). Some of the mansion's finely carved woodwork is attributed to Thomas Day, a pre-Civil War free black renowned as a cabinet-maker. At the house a Confederate officer named Dodson Ramseur courted and married (1863) Ellen Richmond, daughter of the plantation owner. While off at war General Ramseur wrote his wife that the memory of her face in the moonlight sustained him through the hard times. The week of their first wedding anniversary the couple's first child was born, just three days before Ramseur was killed at the Battle of Cedar Creek near Winchester, Virginia. On highway 86 between Yanceyville and Prospect Hill, an old stagecoach stop, you'll find White Rock Village, literally North Carolina's smallest town, for it consists of miniature buildings three to four feet high made of white flint rock.

At Reidsville, farther west along the state's northern tier, the twenty-seven-room grey stone Chinqua-Penn mansion (W.–Sat., 10–4; Sun., 1:30–4:30, adm.) houses a disparate collection of artifacts acquired around the world by the estate's owners. Among the trove are replicas of King Tut's throne and Marie Antoinette's powder room at Versailles. Five greenhouses along with a series of gardens embellish the property, named for the dwarf chestnut chinquapin bush. The American Tobacco Company plant at Reidsville offers factory tours (919-349-6261) as does Macfield Texturing (919-342-3361), which texturizes and dyes synthetic yarn, and also the Fieldcrest Mills sheet and bedspread factory (919-627-3000) at Eden. You'll find bed and breakfast places scattered around the area, at Boxley (919-427-0453) in Madison; farther west, in comfortable log cabins at Pilot Knob (919-325-2502) on Pilot Mountain; and, still farther west, at Pine Ridge Inn (919-789-5034) in Mt. Airy, which in early June hosts a bluegrass and old-time fiddler's convention.

Mt. Airy, the hometown of actor Andy Griffith, boasts the world's largest open-faced granite quarry and the rustic 1827 Kapps Mill, while nearby White Plains goes Mt. Airy one better—or two better—as the last resting places, or place, of the original Siamese Twins, Eng and Chang Bunker, buried together in an oversized tin coffin on the Baptist church grounds. Born near Bangkok, Siam (Thailand) on May 11, 1811, the twins attracted the attention of Robert Hunter, a British merchant who brought them to Boston in 1829 where the duo earned a living as exhibits. After a European tour the twins moved to Mt. Airy, cut off their pigtails, became naturalized citizens and began farming. In 1843 they married two sisters, Sarah and Adelaide Yates, who quarrelled so much the women set up separate residences, each of which the twins would occupy half-time. This arrangement in no way inhibited their love life, for Chang and Eng fathered a total of twenty-two children. One evening Chang fell sick but, true to the schedule, they moved to Eng's house. The bitter cold weather did Chang in and the next morning, January 17, 1874, he died, followed a few hours later by his inseparable companion, brother Eng.

Back toward the center of the state, just to the west of Burlington—beyond Sedalia, where the Charlotte Hawkins Brown State Historic Site (April–Oct., M.–Sat., 10–5; Sun., 1–5; Nov.–March, Tu.–Sat., 10–4, Sun., 1–4, free) honors the black woman who established a preparatory school at the site—lies Greensboro, home of three of the world's largest textile companies: Burlington Industries, Cone Mills and Guilford Mills. It is also home of TV newscaster Edward R. Murrow and of First Lady Dolley Madison and author O. Henry, the latter two remembered with exhibits at the Greensboro Historical Museum (Tu.–Sat., 10–5; Sun., 2–5, free), housed in National Register-listed turn-of-the-century church buildings. More local history survives at the Guilford Courthouse National Military Park (summer, 9:30–6; winter, 8:30–5, free), where in 1781 General Nathanael Greene's American troops blunted the advance of Lord Cornwallis, who headquartered at the nearby two-story log Hoskins/ Wyrick House (M.–Sat., 8–5; Sun., 1–5, free) in Tannenbaum Park. Also on the north side of town is the 1753 Old Mill of Guilford (9–7, free), listed on the National Register, which still grinds flour and meal. Back in the center the National Register-listed Blandwood Mansion (M.–F., 11–2; Sun., 2–5, adm.), owned by 1841–45 governor John Motley Morehead, survives as supposedly the nation's oldest Tuscan villa-style structure.

Museums in town include the Weatherspoon Gallery (Tu.–F., 10–5; Sat. and Sun., 2–6) on the University of North Carolina's Greensboro campus, featuring modern art; the African Heritage Museum (M.–F., 9–3) at North Carolina A and T University; and the Natural Science Center (M.– Sat., 9–5; Sun., 1–5, free), with a zoo, planetarium and exhibits. The Register-listed Carolina Theatre, whose sign outside boasts "Showplace of the Carolinas Since 1927," presents performances in the ornate former movie palace, while the nearby Old Greensborough section contains revitalized commercial structures. Two other such recycled areas are State Street Station, shops installed in a pink awning-bedecked 1920s building in McAdoo Heights; and Cotton Mill Square, with stores and a museum in the restored Pomona Cotton Mill; while the Greenwich Inn (919-272-3474) occupies the cozy three-story century-old former Cone Mills home office. Other accommodations include Shady Lawn Inn (919-275-4581), Plaza Manor (919-274-3074), Greenwood Bed and Breakfast (919-274-6350) and College Hill Bed and Breakfast (919-274-6829). Perhaps Greensboro's most unusual business is Replacements, Ltd. (302 Gallimore

Dairy Road, Greensboro, NC 27409, 919-668-2064), the world's largest supplier of discontinued china and crystal patterns, whose 40,000 square-foot warehouse holds objects with more than 20,000 different patterns. It was in Greensboro—which gave the world Vicks Vaporub, invented there—where on February 1, 1960, began the nation's first organized lunch counter sit-in when four students from North Carolina A and T entered the Woolworth store in town. After further attempts to get served at Woolworth's, on July 25 three blacks, store employees, managed to eat at the counter there, and over the summer other Southern cities proceeded to desegregate their eating places. In November 1989 pioneering Greensboro became North Carolina's first city to pass by popular vote a ban on smoking in some public areas, a bold act in a state with 14,000 tobacco farmers and 20,000 people employed in making cigarettes. In Greensboro and nearby towns you'll find some of the renowned North Carolina barbecue eateries, the establishments in this part of the state preparing the delicacy in ways somewhat different than in the eastern region, as typified by cafes in Goldsboro. In Greensboro locals flock to Stamey's Old-Fashioned Barbecue, 2206 High Point Road, while Lexington also boasts some popular places.

At Jamestown, just southwest of Greensboro toward Lexington, survive structures that recall the once-thriving settlement's gold deposits and Quaker culture. The National Register-listed Mendenhall Plantation, established by the son of town founder James Mendenhall, a Pennsylvania Quaker who arrived in the area in the 1760s; a nineteenth-century Society of Friends Meetinghouse; the Register-listed Jamestown and Oakdale Cotton Mill Historic Districts; and the splendid moat-surrounded Gothic-style Castle McCulloch, built in 1832 by gold refinery owner Charles McCulloch and now a restaurant (919-887-4383) and site in mid-May of a medieval festival, all witness the early prominence of the town, home of the famous Jamestown Rifles, a popular weapon in the old days.

High Point took its name in 1859 as the highest place along the state's first east-west railroad, from Goldsboro to Charlotte. Thanks to transportation facilities and the area's thick hardwood forests, High Point developed as a furniture center, an industry that began in 1871 when William Henry Snow moved from Vermont to establish a woodworking operation. Because furniture is one of the few retail products salesmen can't conveniently carry from town to town to sell, the need arose for a centralized place to exhibit the wares, so in 1921 the Southern Furniture Exposition Company opened its showroom facility in High Point. In the first half of the twentieth century the number of North Carolina furniture firms increased from less than fifty to more than three hundred, and by 1939 the state ranked first in the manufacture of wood furniture, with over 60 percent of the nation's production now originating there. Apart from six-week periods encompassing the months of April and October, when thousands of buyers arrive for the Southern Furniture Market, visitors to the city—whose High Point College offers the nation's only degree in home furnishings marketing—can tour the furniture showrooms (groups of fifteen or more, by arrangement only: 919-884-5255, adm.), while the Furniture Library (M.–F., 9–12, 1–5, free) contains 6,000 books which form the world's largest collection of volumes on the history of the industry. Other collections include the High Point Museum (Tu.–Sat., 10–4:30; Sun., 1–4:30, free) and Historical Park (Sat. and Sun., 1–4:30), with displays on the area's history along with the 1786 Haley House, listed on the National Register. The Angela Peterson Doll and Miniature Museum (Tu.–Th. and Sun., 1:30–4:30, free) displays 1,000 antique dolls dating from the 1490s to 1820. In late summer and fall the North Carolina Shakespeare Festival (800-672-6273 or 919-841-6273) stages plays at High Point, where you'll find bed and breakfast at the Premier (919-889-8349). Not satisfied with its laurels as the nation's leading furniture city, High Point also serves as the country's hosiery center, with fourteen major manufacturers turning out nearly a million pairs of socks, hose and other garments every day.

At nearby Thomasville an eighteen-foot high six-times-life Duncan Phyfe dining room chair commemorates the area's furniture industry. A previous slightly smaller model—made of enough pine wood to build one hundred ordinary chairs—deteriorated and was dismantled in 1936, replaced in 1951 by the present version. The nearby early 1870s train depot, listed on the National Register, is supposedly North Carolina's oldest remaining station. Thomasville Furniture Company in town gives tours of its factory and showroom (M.–F., 10 and 2, except April and Oct., free). Furniture and textiles also support nearby Lexington, which boasts such barbecue establishments as Jimmy's, 1703 Cotton Grove Road, and the Lexington Barbecue, 10 Highway 29–70 south, two popular places that feature the central and western North Carolina version of the food. At Lexington, where Lawrence's Bed and Breakfast (704-249-1114) takes overnight guests, stands the 1858 classic revival-style former Davidson County Courthouse.

South of the High Point-Greensboro area lie a few sights you may want to see before proceeding to Winston-Salem. Beyond Level Cross, where the Richard Petty Museum (M.–Sat., 10–4, adm.) houses race-car exhibits, lies Asheboro—the Doctor's Inn there (919-625-4916) offers bed and breakfast accommodations—near which the North Carolina Zoological Park (April–Oct. 15, M.–F., 9–5; Sat. and Sun., 10–6; Oct. 16–March, 9–5, adm.) contains some seven hundred animals in natural habitats, including the African area with an aviary and elephants, gazelles, impalas, rhinos, gorillas and other species you're unlikely to encounter elsewhere in North Carolina. Seagrove to the south preserves the area's two-century-old pottery making tradition, with nearly thirty potters (M.–Sat., 8–5) and the Museum of North Carolina Traditional Pottery. At the village of Biscoe farther south, Anita's (919-673-2722) takes bed and breakfast guests, and off to the west lies heavily-forested Montgomery County where Thomas Alva Edison and Herbert Hoover once came to prospect for gold.

Winston-Salem, like many of the other Piedmont urban areas, presents a clean, open feeling with mostly low-rise architecture on a human scale. A statue downtown depicts young Richard Joshua Reynolds astride his steed and nearby on the eastern edge of the central business district stands the huge Reynolds Tobacco Company complex, new and old buildings spread across the area. In 1875 R. J. Reynolds began producing chewing tobacco not far from the Whitaker Park complex, and in the early 1900s he introduced such brands as Prince Albert pipe tobacco and Camel cigarettes. In 1986 corporate restructurings removed the headquarters of RJR Nabisco from Winston-Salem, but the production facilities remained. At Whittaker Park, one of the world's largest and most modern cigarette manufacturing centers, you can see exhibits on tobacco cultivation and industry memorabilia and also tour the factory (M.–F., 8 a.m.–10 p.m., free), and if you fancy factory visits you can also tour the Stroh Brewery in Winston-Salem (M.–F., 11–4:30, free).

Reynolda House (Tu.–Sat., 9:30–4:30; Sun., 1:30–4:30, adm.), built in 1917 by Reynolds, recalls the tobacco magnate's way of life. Lightened and brightened by a white exterior made open by dozens of window panes and by a light green roof, the handsome dwelling lacks all pretension but exudes a modestly presented sense of comfort and well being. The residence houses a splendid assemblage of American art as well as a collection of family clothing. Other displays at Winston-Salem—which in the mid-1960s futurist

Alvin Toffler predicted would be the "culturopolis of the South"—include the Southeastern Center for Contemporary Art (Tu.–Sat., 10–5; Sun., 2–5, free), known as "Secca," lodged in textile industrialist James G. Hanes's English manor house, across the road from Reynolda; the Nature Science Center (M.–Sat., 10–5; Sun., 1–5, adm.); and the little known Selma Burke Art Gallery (Tu.–F., 12–5, free) in Carolina Hall at Winston-Salem State University, with works by such artists as Romare Bearden, Reginald Marsh and Burke, whose profile of Franklin D. Roosevelt appears on the dime. Downtown you'll find Piedmont Craftsmen (M.–F., 10–6; Sat., 10–5; Sun., 1–5, free), with hand-made artifacts fashioned by regional artists. There is also the Roger L. Stevens Performing Arts Center, opened in 1983 in a refurbished Greek Revival-style 1929 movie and vaude-ville house, a theater for performances by students from the city's North Carolina School of the Arts, the nation's only state-supported residential high school and college for the performing arts, analogue to the state's special science school in Durham.

Historic Bethabara Park (M.–F., 9:30–4:30; Sat. and Sun., 1:30–4:30, free) contains late eighteenth-century buildings that recall the early German Moravian settlers, but the more famous vintage Moravian section is Old Salem (M.–Sat., 9:30–4:30; Sun., 1:30–4:30, adm.), established in 1766. This is a truly magnificent corner of the South and not to be missed. Nine of the more than eighty restored structures built in a wide variety of styles can be visited, among them a bakery, school, tavern and shoemaker's shop. Private homes line the tree-filled enclave where brick sidewalks and lantern-like lights lend touches of yesteryear, and historic Salem College there brings young blood into the old neigh-borhood, which preserves and vividly presents a way of life long vanished elsewhere.

The Museum of Early Southern Decorative Arts (M.–Sat.,

10:30–4:30; Sun., 1:30–4:30, adm.) at Old Salem contains nineteen period rooms and six galleries dedicated to regional decorative arts of the early South, while at the north edge of the area, near the huge teapot marker, nestles the hilly Moravian cemetery, a lovely place to spend a few passing minutes—or eternity. Near Old Salem stands the Brookstown Inn (919-725-1120), a bed and breakfast establishment installed in the 1837 brick building, listed on the National Register, originally occupied by the Salem Cotton Manufacturing Company, the first factory in the South to be lighted by electricity (1880). Other bed and breakfast places include 1912 Lowe-Austin House (919-727-1211), also listed on the Register, and the Colonel Ludlow House (919-777-1887); while at Tanglewood Park (adm.), a recreation area southwest of town, a campground, cottages and the 1859 Manor House mansion (919-766-0591), a restaurant and inn, provide places to stay.

Farther off to the southwest of Winston-Salem lies Mocksville, where Squire and Sarah Boone (parents of famous frontiersman Daniel and supposedly the area's first permanent settlers, arriving about 1750) repose in the still-used Joppa Cemetery. Along both sides of U.S. highway 65 two miles west of Mocksville stretches the farm once owned by Daniel Boone, whose cabin became the kitchen for a farmhouse occupied by Hinton Rowan Helper, author of the widely read *The Impending Crisis of the South,* an 1857 book that inflamed passions by attacking the institution of slavery. At Cooleemee, on highway 64 by the Yadkin River, stands the 1855 Hairston homestead, a plantation residence (Memorial Day–Labor Day, W., Sat., Sun., 3–5, adm.) that vaguely resembles the White House, with the main entrance oddly installed at the angle formed by two wings. Just north of Statesville, originally called Fourth Creek Community, are the remains of Fort Dobbs (April–Oct., M.–Sat., 9–5; Sun., 1–5; Nov.–March, Tu.–Sat., 10–4; Sun., 1–4, free), with artifacts and archeological sites that recall the frontier outpost built in 1756 by the British during their clash with the French over control of North America, a conflict known as the French and Indian War, ended by the 1763 Treaty of Paris that gave the British dominion over the continent.

The center of Salisbury, not far away, encompasses the twenty-three-block West Square Historic District, listed on the National Register, with buildings more than two hundred years old reflecting a variety of styles. Among the venerable structures in or near the District are the c. 1800 Henderson Law Office; the Register-listed former Rowan County Courthouse; the 1907 train depot, known back then as the "finest station between Washington and Atlanta"; the old Post Office (1912); 1828 St. Luke's Episcopal; the heavy-set but somehow delightful red brick and white stone 1892 Presbyterian Church bell tower; the imposing Confederate Monument; and the Civil War-era National Cemetery. During the war the Southerners operated at Salisbury an ill-famed prison whose chief physician was Dr. Josephus Hall, recalled by his lovely 1820 home (Sat. and Sun., 2–5, adm.). Other places open to visitors include the Rowan Museum (Th.–Sun., 2–5, adm.), which occupies an 1819 residence; the Waterworks Visual Arts Center (June–Labor Day., M.–Th., 10–5; F., 10–9; Sept.–June, Tu.–F., 10–5; Sat., 9–4; Sun., 1–4, donation), installed in the town's former waterworks and police station; Grimes Mill (May–mid-Oct., Sat. and Sun., 2–5, adm.), a splendid 1896 brick pile with the original machinery that functioned as recently as 1982; and the Old Stone House (April–Oct., Sat. and Sun., 2–5, adm.), one of the state's earliest stone structures, built in 1766 of native granite. On the brick wall of a downtown building appears a large, finely executed mural depicting Salisbury around the turn of the century. Rowan Oak (704-633-2086) and the 1868 Stewart-Marsh House (704-633-6841) provide bed and breakfast accommodations.

Spencer, adjacent to Salisbury, began in 1896 when the Southern Railway moved its repair facility there from Company Shops, later named Burlington. The Spencer Shops, named for the line's president, operated until 1960 when a modern yard at Linwood replaced it. In 1983 the facility reopened as the North Carolina Transportation Museum (April–Oct., Tu.–Sat., 9–5; Sun., 1–5; Nov.–March, Tu.–Sat., 10–4; Sun., 1–4, free), featuring rides on old trains, the huge machine shop with cranes capable of lifting 150-ton locomotives, a thirty-seven stall roundhouse and displays of historic transportation equipment. Spencer's forty-block National Register-listed Historic District includes a group of century-old churches and other buildings.

Farther south toward Charlotte, Oak Ridge Farm (704-663-7085) at Mooresville offers bed and breakfast in an oak-shaded 1871 house; while at Lake Norman, owned by Duke Power Company, which operates there three power plants, the company's Energy Explorium (M.–Sat., 9–5; Sun., June–Aug., 12–6; Sept.–May, 12–5, free) contains energy-related exhibits. Nearby Davidson, founded in 1836 along with the town's Davidson College, Secretary of State Dean Rusk's alma mater, remains little changed from a century or so ago. In this lovely village survive such relics as the house once occupied by the college president, the town's oldest dwelling (1836); the c. 1851 Copeland House, now an art gallery; the c. 1848 Carolina Inn, once a hotel and now a college building; and the National Register-listed 1840s Eumenean and "Phi" (Philanthropic) Halls, built with funds the students raised to house rival literary societies. At Huntersville Register-listed Latta Place, a restored early nineteenth-century plantation, includes the Federal-style main house and outbuildings. Over at Kannapolis, home of Cannon Mills, the world's largest household textile company (for factory tours: 704-938-3200), you'll find bed and

breakfast at Plantation House (704-932-0812), and at nearby
Concord, site of one of the nation's earliest reform schools
(1910), you can tour the half-mile long, quarter-mile wide
Philip Morris cigarette factory (M.–F., 9–3, free), decorated
with the world's largest hanging quilt, paintings and a collection of postcards picturing North Carolina scenes. (The
firm's factories in Richmond, Virginia, and Louisville, Kentucky, also take visitors.) At Harrisburg the Memory Lane
Museum (daily, adm.), next to the Charlotte Motor Speedway, an upscale stock car stadium, houses a collection of
classic cars, and to the east lies the Reed Gold Mine (April–
Oct., M.–Sat., 9–5; Sun., 1–5; Nov.–March, Tu.–Sat., 10–4;
Sun., 1–4, free), site of the nation's first recorded gold find,
which led to the country's first gold rush, a claim also made
by Dahlonega, Georgia. In 1799 John Reed's son came across
a seventeen-pound rock which the family used as a doorstop
until 1802 when a Fayetteville jeweler recognized it as gold.
Reed proceeded to develop the gold deposits, by 1824 un-
earthing some $100,000 worth of the metal. Outsiders soon
flocked to the area, mined until 1912, an era recalled by
exhibits, trails through the property and a nineteenth-
century ore crushing machine.

At the Cotton Patch Gold Mine (March–Oct., 9–6, adm.)
in New London to the northeast you can pan for gold using
prospecting equipment available at the general store there.
Union County to the south, North Carolina's leading poultry producing area, took its name as a compromise between
political partisans unable to decide between Clay or Jackson
as the area's designation. Although nearby South Carolina
also claims the honor, Andrew Jackson was born in the area,
perhaps in North Carolina, in 1767. But there's no dispute
over his North Carolina career in law, which he studied in
Salisbury and practiced in Greensboro. Jackson's life in "the
Old North State," as residents fondly call their corner of

the country, and other regional history come alive at the outdoor amphitheater in Waxhaw, also known for its antique shops, with the performance of the drama *Listen and Remember* (June weekends, 8:30 p.m.). At Pineville, just south of Charlotte, log buildings recall the birthplace of another American president, James K. Polk, born on a farm there in 1795. Although Polk, the nation's first "dark horse" candidate, lived in Tennessee from age eleven, he returned to his home state to attend the University of North Carolina, where he ranked first in his class. Also south of Charlotte is Carowinds, the nation's only theme park located in two states—both Carolinas.

Charlotte, the largest city in the Carolinas with nearly three hundred and fifty thousand inhabitants, seemed to British General Charles Cornwallis a "damned hornet's nest," a complaint, or honor, recalled by the hornet depicted on the city's seal. A hotbed of Patriot sentiment, Charlotte passed the Mecklenburg Declaration, calling for independence from Great Britain, on May 20, 1775, a date which appears on the state flag. Now less a hornet's nest than a beehive of activity, Charlotte boasts two of the South's biggest banks, the Hornets basketball team and a humming economy. The Mint Museum (Tu., 10–10; W.–Sat., 10–5; Sun., 1–6, adm.), opened in 1936 as North Carolina's first art museum, recalls earlier economic activity when in 1837 the U.S. established in the city the first branch mint, which functioned until 1913, an operation that literally coined money, processing gold produced by the area's mines. For more current currency, you can tour the Federal Reserve Bank (704-336-7206), while other museums in the town include Discovery Place (June–Aug., M.–F., 9–6; Sept.–May, 9–5; year round, Sat. 9–6; Sun., 1–6, adm.), the state's largest science and technology museum; the 1774 National Register-listed Hezekiah Alexander Home (June–Aug., Tu.–F., 10–5; Sept.–May, Tu.–F., 1–5; year round, Sat. and Sun., 2–5, adm.); History Museum (Tu.–F., 10–5; Sat. and Sun., 2–5); and the Afro-American Cultural Center (Tu.–Sat., 10–6; Sun., 1–5, free). For flower and feathered-friend lovers, Wing Haven (Tu., W., Sun., 3–5, free) offers a bird sanctuary—one of the few where wild birds accept hand-feeding—and gardens started in 1927 almost single-handedly by the late Elizabeth Clarkson. In the center of town the Fourth Ward area, a restored Victorian-era neighborhood, lies near City-fair, a lively new (1988) marketplace, and Spirit Square, an art area with music and theater performances, workshops and galleries (M.–Sat., 9 a.m.–11 p.m., free). Bed and breakfast choices in Charlotte include Homeplace (704-365-1936), Morehead Inn (704-376-3357) in the Dilworth historic district, the Library Suite (704-334-8477) in the National Register-listed Overcarsh House, Fourth Ward (704-334-1485) and, at Mathews to the south, the Inn on Providence (704-366-6700).

Western North Carolina

South: Gastonia, Flat Rock, Hendersonville, Brevard—Central: Hickory, Valdese, Little Switzerland, Black Mountain—North: Jefferson, Boone, Linville, Asheville— West: Waynesville, Cherokee, Highlands, Franklin

In North Carolina, as with Virginia, Tennessee and Arkansas, the western section of the state differs in tone and heritage from the east. "From the very beginning there were fundamental differences between these two regions in physiography, national stocks, religion, social life, and economy," noted Hugh T. Lefler and William S. Powell in *Colonial North Carolina: A History.* "The east, which was settled largely by Englishmen and Highland Scots established an economy that was based on the plantation system with its unfree labor and aristocratic ideas. The west, on the other hand, was settled largely by Scotch-Irish and Germans, with an economic order of small farmers, free labor, and democratic ideals." From the central region it's convenient to head west either along the Interstate 40 corridor across the middle of the state, through the north on or near the Blue Ridge Parkway—these two itineraries are described later—or along the southern edge of the state.

On the southern route, after you cross the Catawba River just west of Charlotte you'll come to McAdenville, home of Aviary Gardens (Sun., 2–5), populated by lemurs, yellow baboons and other exotic animals. At Christmastime a million and a half people visit the town to see the holiday lighting displays. The 1894 Benedictine Monastery at Belmont, home of Sacred Heart College and the North Carolina Vocational Textile School, includes a church that served as the nation's only abbey cathedral from 1910 to 1977. Belmont is a rare surviving example of a company town. R. L. Stowe Mills, a textile firm there, is currently renovating 350 company-owned frame houses, built about 1920, which the corporation rents to its workers. The Schiele Museum of Natural History at Gastonia (Tu.–F., 9–5; Sat. and Sun., 2–5, free) offers not only exhibits but also a nature trail, planetarium and pioneer log structures. Another museum in Gaston County—where you'll find the unusual fish camp restaurants, some twenty eateries, many in the Belmont and the Dallas areas, at fishing resorts along the Catawba and South Fork Rivers—is the attractive County Museum of Art and History (Tu.–F., 10–5; Sat., 1–5; Sun., 2–5, free) at Dallas, installed in the 1852 Hoffman Hotel, featuring a collection of horse-drawn vehicles and textile history. Gaston claims to be where the American textile industry originated back in the mid-nineteenth century when mills along area waterways began to process raw materials from local farms. Around courthouse square in Dallas cluster century-old stores, antique houses and other relics of yesteryear. At Sherryville to the north the Carolina Freight Company operates the C. Grier Beam Truck Museum (F., 10–4; Sat., 10–5; Sun., 1–5, free), with a delightful display of old trucks dating from 1927.

A more antiquated form of transport survives at Polkville, west of Cherryville, where Patterson's Carriage Shop sells horse-drawn vehicles, harnesses and other such equine accessories and also offers bed and breakfast (704-538-3929) in a century-old farmhouse. Shelby County was the early home of W. J. Cash, author of the famous study *The Mind of the South,* and also of lawyer-preacher-actor-author Tom Dixon, Jr., whose 1905 novel *The Clansman* served as the basis for the famous movie *Birth of a Nation.* In mid-June Mooresboro, west of Shelby, hosts the annual Snuffy Jenkins Old Time and Bluegrass Music Festival. In the center of nearby Forest City stands a chimney-like rock construction that recalls the settlement's origins in 1855 as the village of Burnt Chimney, established near two chimneys that survived a fire which burned down a pioneer's house. Thinking the name undignified, the residents changed it in the 1880s to Forest City. In the pleasant little town of Rutherfordton, the county seat, stands the house of German settler Christopher Bechtler, who operated there a gold mine and who also ran a private mint between 1831 and 1857 that fabricated coins. Over the ages the Rocky Broad River carved through granite deposits the scenic Hickory Nut Gorge, a fourteen-mile long canyon where one-time stagecoach stops still offer hospitality to travelers. At Bat Cave, an antique center, you'll find the Stonehearth Inn (704-625–4027) and the Old Mill (704-625-4256), a chalet with a waterwheel and a grist stone forming part of its beamed premises. Between Lake Lure— setting for the 1987 movie *Dirty Dancing* and where the Lodge (704-625-2789) provides a pleasant place to stay—and Bat Cave lies Chimney Rock (8:30–4:30, Memorial Day–

Labor Day to 5:30, adm.), named for a three hundred and fifteen-foot monolith reached by an elevator built into the formation. From the Rock a two-hour trail leads past Exclamation Point to four hundred and four-foot Hickory Nut Falls, the highest in the East. Lodging choices at Chimney Rock include Dogwood Inn (704-625-4403), Gingerbread Inn (704-625-4038) and the historic 1917 Esmeralda Inn (704-625-9105), its lobby built of trees, where such stars as Mary Pickford, Gloria Swanson, Douglas Fairbanks, Clark Gable and other luminaries stayed, while in room nine of the Esmeralda Lew Wallace finished a play based on his famous novel *Ben Hur.*

Down by the South Carolina border lies Tryon, a popular retirement community, with a private library named after Georgia poet and former local resident Sidney Lanier. Brevard, which also serves as a hunting and horse center, as symbolized by the whimsical horse figure in town, offers for accommodations National Register-listed Pine Crest Inn (704-859-9135), with cottages, cabins and a dining room (reservations required for dinner, served 6:30–8:30); Stone Hedge Inn (704-859-9114); Melrose Inn (704-859-9419); Mill Farm Inn (704-859-6992); and L'Auberge (also 704-859-6992). The curiously named Isothermal Community College recalls Tryon's location within an isothermal belt, an area where prevailing winds and mountain contours combine to maintain winter temperatures warmer than at lower elevations. Near Saluda, which in early July celebrates Coon Dog Day, the rustic Bear Creek Lodge (704-749-2272) and Orchard Inn (704-749-5471), built in the early 1900s by the Southern Railway as an employee vacation resort, offer pleasant places to stay. There is also Woodfield Inn (800-247-2203 from 9 a.m. to 5 p.m. or 704-693-6016), listed on the National Register, in nearby Flat Rock, one of the state's most delightful and historic hostelries, originally a stagecoach stop opened in 1852 by Henry Tudor Farmer, who concocted the Lemon

Julep and invented the non-creak, non-creep Flat Rock
Rocker. Near the inn stand the c. 1845 Old Post Office,
now a secondhand bookshop, which served the mails until
the 1960s, and the Flat Rock Playhouse (performances late
June–early Sept., 704-693-0731), the State Theater of North
Carolina, installed in a red barn-like building.

Of special interest is historic St. John, built in the 1830s
as a private chapel by Charles Baring of the famous British
banking family and later deeded to the Episcopal diocese,
a sanctuary that served socialites who summered in the area,
some of whom remain there buried in the lovely graveyard
by the church. Among those interred is C. C. Memminger,
Charleston, South Carolina, banker and first Secretary of
the Treasury for the Confederacy, whose c. 1838 summer
house, Connemara, author Carl Sandburg later occupied for
twenty-two years, starting in 1945. A National Historic Site
(9–5, grounds, free; house, adm.), the white wooden house
crowns the crest of a hill that dominates the bucolic property.
The aroma of cedar trees perfumes the steep wooded trail
that climbs from the lake and stream below up to the dwelling, crammed with Sandburg memorabilia. Barns, animal
sheds and other outbuildings dot the farm, criss-crossed by
trails around the property. Connemara, which Sandburg described as "two hundred and forty acres of land and a million
acres of sky," is one of the choice sights in the South, and
not to be missed if you're anywhere near Flat Rock.

At nearby Hendersonville, seat of Henderson County, garnished with an estimated million apple trees that produce
two-thirds of North Carolina's crop of that fruit, the curiously configured Main Street curves gracefully back and
forth to create parking alcoves on alternate sides of the road.
For ten days before and during Labor Day Hendersonville,
whose lively Curb Market by regulation sells only home-
grown produce and handmade crafts, celebrates the North
Carolina Apple Festival. The core of the county's apple coun-

try lies near Edneyville, where fruit and cider stands line U.S. highway 64. Another rustic road is state highway 191 through the Mills River Valley. At Oakdale Cemetery in Hendersonville perches the doleful-looking angel carved by Asheville monument maker W. O. Wolfe, whose son Thomas immortalized the figure in the title of his novel *Look Homeward, Angel*. Accommodations in town include Waverly Inn (800-537-8195 and 704-693-9193), Claddagh Inn (704-697-7778) and the hilltop Echo Mountain Inn (704-693-9626), while nearby Mountain Home offers the festively named Forever Christmas Inn (704-692-1133) and the Mountain Home Inn (704-697-9090).

Off to the west the Cradle of Forestry in America (May–Oct., 10–6, adm.), a National Historic Site, traces the birth and growth of American forest management. In the late nineteenth century George Vanderbilt, who built Biltmore, the famous estate near Asheville, hired forester Gifford Pinchot to manage the financier's lands in the area. At Vanderbilt's Pisgah Forest, which became the nation's first large tract of managed woodland, the country's first forest school functioned between 1898 and 1909, an innovation recalled by exhibits, trails, Black Forest-type forest ranger lodges, an antique log loader and sawmill and other such remnants of the early days of forestry. In 1914 Vanderbilt's widow, Edith, gave the government eight thousand acres of woodlands, nucleus of the half-million-acre Pisgah National Forest, one of the nation's largest such preserves. Near the Cradle museum in the forest tumbles scenic Looking Glass Falls, while two miles away Sliding Rock, a sixty-foot water-slickened rock face, has for generations attracted mountain youngsters who flock there to slide down into an old-fashioned swimming hole. From late June to mid-August the nearby Brevard Music Center, established more than a half-century ago, presents classical and light music performances (704-884-2091).

Near Brevard the Ecusta Corporation, established in 1939,

manufactures from flax most of the nation's cigarette paper. Bed and breakfast choices in Brevard include Womble Inn (704-884-4770), the National Register-listed Inn at Brevard (704-884-2105), Pines Country Inn (704-877-3131), the Red House (704-884-9349) and, at Rosman, Red Lion Inn (704-884-6868), while the Sherwood Forest development (704-885-2091), a planned community for bird lovers, caters to Audubon Society members. More up-scale is the Greystone Inn (800-824-5766, in-state 704-966-4700), installed in a mansion on Lake Toxaway, the state's largest privately owned lake, where the Rockefellers, Fords, Firestones, Morgans, Vanderbilts and their peers summered in the early part of the century. A daily sunset cruise on the lake and other amenities help the resort retain its classy cachet. Near Toxaway rises the French Broad River, so named because this was the first major waterway encountered by the early settlers that flowed away from the British colonies and headed westward toward the French-controlled territory in the continent's interior. Near Knoxville, Tennessee, some hundred and sixty-five miles downstream, the French Broad merges with the Holston to form the Tennessee River which eventually drains into the Mississippi. Here, then, it can perhaps be said, is where the East first begins to come in touch with the West.

Returning now to the east, the itinerary across the state's center section to Asheville in the west begins at Hickory, where the former Claremont Central High School now serves as the Arts Center of Catawba Valley, featuring not only an art museum but also a science center (Tu.–F., 10–5; Sat., 10–4; Sun., 1–4, free), while Hickory Bed and Breakfast (703-324-0548) takes overnight guests. Nearby Valdese recalls the Waldensians, a persecuted Protestant sect founded in the Italian Alps in the twelfth century whose members moved to North Carolina to establish a communal settlement. Although the project failed, many Waldensians remained in the area and their descendants now dramatize the episode in *From This Day Forward,* presented from early July to mid-August in an outdoor theater (Th.–Sun., 8:15 p.m., 704-874-0176). The Waldensian Museum (5–8 performance evenings; Sun., 3–5, free) contains exhibits on the sect's history in North Carolina, while the 1899 Romanesque-style church, an outdoor museum at the amphitheater and tours of the Waldensian Bakery (F., free) offer further insights into the group. At Morganton, hometown of Watergate Senator Sam Ervin, the backyard of the house at 310 Shore Drive contains a totem pole in memory of another well-known personality, humorist H. Allen Smith. Morganton's Freedom High School, a large curved building, presents an unusual appearance, while in the Brown Mountain area on highway 181 north of town glimmer the mysterious "Brown Mountain Lights," curious multicolored glows that occasionally appear in the hill country.

At Pleasant Garden farther west two-century-old Carson House, listed on the National Register, a one-time stagecoach inn, now houses a pioneer history museum; while Little Switzerland to the north, one of the few towns directly on the Blue Ridge Parkway, is a mountain resort with vistas over the valleys below. Alpine Inn (704-765-5380), Switzerland Inn (800-654-4026) and the Big Lynn Lodge (704-765-4257), named for what was supposedly the world's largest and oldest (six hundred years) linden tree, offer accommodations in the town. Nearby Emerald Village (May–Oct., 9–5, to 6, June–Aug., adm.) is a gem-prospecting property located at the old McKinney mine that operated in the 1920s. At Old Fort, privately owned Grant's Museum (Tu.–Sat., 9–5; Sun., 1–5, adm.), with more than 150,000 Indian artifacts, and the Mountain Gateway Museum (M.–Sat., 9–5; Sun., 2–5, free) recall the area's early history when white settlers pushed into the region, then Cherokee territory, in the mid-1770s. Early in the Revolution the Ameri-

cans built a fort to secure the western frontier and to protect
settlers against the Cherokee, whose land the newcomers
acquired in the 1777 Treaty of Long Island, located at the
Holston River in Tennessee. The Inn at Old Fort (704-
668-9382) offers bed and breakfast, as do the Old House
(704-669-5196) at Ridgecrest and, at Black Mountain, Over
Yonder (704-669-6762), Blackberry Inn (704-669-8303),
Black Forest Lodge (June–Sept., 704-669-7124) and Red
Rocker Inn (April 15–Oct. 31, 704-669-5991), featuring huge
home-cooked dinners. At Black Mountain such establishments as Song of the Wood, a dulcimer and music shop,
preserve hill country crafts and ways. In mid-May and mid-
October Grey Eagle, a nonprofit organization, presents
music festivals (704-669-4546 from 2–6 p.m.). At the village
the famous avant-garde Black Mountain College functioned
until 1957, established in 1933 by a group of teachers who
left Rollins College in Winter Park, Florida. Faculty members
at the arts-oriented school included painters Josef Albers,
Ben Shahn and Robert Motherwell, dancer Merce Cunningham and musician John Cage. In 1987 a laid-back
latter-day version of the college, an informal non-accredited
school, started up at the old campus on the shore of Lake
Eden, but that operation has since closed. At nearby
Montreat, home of evangelist Billy Graham and the Conference Center of the Presbyterian Church, which houses the
group's archives, Glen Rock Inn (704-669-7511) provides
pleasant rooms. East of Asheville, just north of U.S. 70 the
Folk Art Center of the Southern Highland Handicraft Guild
(9–5, free) presents craft demonstrations, workshops and a
tasteful selection of handmade items for sale.

The itinerary from middle North Carolina toward Asheville through the north takes you west from Winston-Salem
into the Blue Ridge Mountains. In late May tiny Union
Grove hosts the Old Time Fiddler's and Bluegrass Festival
at Fiddler's Grove Campground, with music, dancing and

storytelling, while at equally small Elkin to the north Country Lane (919-366-2915) offers bed and breakfast. At Wilkesboro, west of Elkin, National Register-listed buildings recall the town as it developed a century and more ago: the 1860 jail, old houses and commercial structures, 1849 St. Paul's, the 1891 Smithey Hotel, and the imposing white 1902 Wilkes County Courthouse, as well as "Tory Oak" where English sympathizers were hung during the Revolution. On the seventy-five-acre Wilkes Community College campus bloom extensive gardens, with such special sections as eight hundred rosebushes and the Idea Gardens, which present tips for visitors with green thumbs. Alexander County to the south offers equally earthy attractions, with rock digging and sluicing at Emerald Hollow in Hiddenite, where the Hiddenite Center (M.–F., 9–4:30; Sat. and Sun., 2–5, adm.) houses folk and cultural displays and locally mined emeralds, while to the north, near the Virginia line, there's bed and breakfast at Turby-villa (919-372-8490) in Sparta, metropolis of the agricultural area with Allegheny County's only stoplight.

Between Sparta and Jefferson on U.S. 221 at New River, believed to be the oldest waterway in America and the world's second oldest, is an old-fashioned general store and outfitter where you can arrange trips on the ancient stream, twenty-six miles of it designated a National Scenic River. Shatley Springs Inn (919-982-2236) at Crumpler offers rustic cottages and country food, while at Laurel Springs Brugiss Farm (919-359-2995) takes bed and breakfast guests. In a warehouse just north of Laurel Springs, where you'll find another old-time general store, the New River Mountain Music Jamboree presents country and bluegrass music every Saturday evening at 8 (for information: 919-982-9414). At Glendale Springs beyond Index—so called when a local who consulted a book for a suggested name randomly looked first at the volume's index—the Glendale Springs Inn and

Restaurant (919-982-2102), listed on the National Register, occupies a century-old house used as WPA headquarters during construction of the nearby Blue Ridge Parkway. Religious frescoes by local painter Ben Long decorate area churches, including Holy Trinity in Glendale Springs and St. Mary's Episcopal at West Jefferson, where the Ashe County Cheese Company churns out cheddar and other varieties. Until 1975 Kraft Foods owned the firm (M.–Sat., 8–5, free), founded in 1930 and the Carolinas' only cheesemaker. Todd, to the south, boasts another venerable general store (1914) and the Elkland Shoppes, in an old schoolhouse, where you'll find antiques and other collectibles as well as bike rentals.

Continuing southwest, you'll come to Boone, well-supplied with Daniel Boone memories at the Boone Native Gardens, the outdoor *Horn in the West* drama (mid-June–late Aug., Tu.–Sun.), and the annual Wagon Train ceremony during the Frontier Days celebration. Between Boone and the nearby town of Blowing Rock a theme park (Memorial Day weekend–Sept., 9–6, shorter hours in Oct., adm.) called Tweetsie Railroad features a three-mile-long excursion on the old steam train. The Blowing Rock is an overhang three thousand feet above Johns River Gorge where air currents flowing upward return light objects cast over the edge, making this "the only place in the world where snow falls upside down," as Ripley noted in *Believe It or Not*. Nearby stands the National Register-listed 1882 Green Park Inn (704-295-3141) whose Divide Lounge takes its name from the eastern Continental Divide along the ridge there, while in the town of Blowing Rock a popular Arts in the Park show takes place once a month from May to October. Mystery Hill (June–Aug., 8–8; Sept.–May, 9–5, adm.), a commercial operation, features an antique collection, a "lifestyle" museum and "mystery" areas with various trick phenomena. At Goodwin Weavers in Blowing Rock craftsmen fabricate

cloth items on pre-Civil War looms, while High Mountain
Expeditions (704-295-4200) runs rafting, hiking, fishing and
coon hunting trips to the back country. Bed and breakfast
choices in Blowing Rock include Ragged Gardens Inn and
Restaurant (April–Jan., 704-295-9703), the Farm House
(June–Aug., 704-295-7361), Garden Ridge Inn (704-295-
3644), Maple Lodge (April–Feb., 704-295-3331) and Sunshine Inn (May–Nov., 704-295-3487). At nearby Cone Park
the Southern Highland Handicraft Guild shop occupies
the Moses Cone manor house.

Back to the west, Chapel Brook (704-297-4304) at
Vilas offers bed and breakfast, as do Bluestone Lodge
(704-963-5177), Mountainview Chateau (704-963-6593),
Taylor House (704-963-4271)—built by Foxes, Byrds and
Crows, names of the carpenters and plumbers—and Mast
Farm Inn (closed April and Dec., 704-963-5857) at Valle Crucis. Both the 1885 Mast Farm Inn and the nearby 1883 Mast
General Store (M.–Sat., 6:30–6:30; Sun., 1–6, free) complete
with potbelly stove, old post office, original fixtures and
other antique touches, are listed on the National Register.
The Valle Crucis Mission School Conference Center de-
scends from the Episcopal mission and monastery established
there in the mid-nineteenth century. Noah Llama Treks
(704-297-2171) in Valle Crucis runs two- to six-day treks
with llamas carrying your gear and provisions for the out-
ings. If you ever dreamed of walking wooded trails with
a llama lugging your pack, Valle Crucis is the place for you!
Beech Mountain, at 5,505 feet the highest town in eastern
America, serves in the winter as one of the area's ten ski
resorts, with others located at such places as Blowing Rock
(two) and nearby Banner Elk (four), where Archers Inn
(704-898-9004) offers pleasant rooms and where the Blue
Ridge Hearthside Craft Shop (summer, 9–6; winter, 10–5)
houses works by some three hundred artisans.

Through this area winds part of the North Carolina section of the Blue Ridge Parkway, a four hundred and seventy-mile long scenic road that extends at an average elevation of three thousand feet from near Front Royal, Virginia, to western North Carolina. Started in 1935 as a public works project, the Parkway was completed only in 1987 with the last seven and a half-mile link, which included an S-shaped free-standing stretch called the Linn Cove Viaduct—one of the nation's most complicated road construction jobs, a project based on techniques used in the Swiss Alps—that snakes around the granite face of Grandfather Mountain near Linville. Nearly 6,000-foot high Grandfather (April–Nov. 15, 8–dusk; winter, 9–4, adm.), perhaps the nation's only major privately owned mountain, includes a swinging bridge for pedestrians, hang gliding flights, wildlife and scenic trails. Also in the area are Linville Caverns (June–Labor Day, 9–6; April–May and Sept.–Oct., 9–5; March and Nov., 9–4:30; Dec.–Feb., weekends only, adm.), North Carolina's only commercial caves, as well as the Linville Gorge Wilderness and Linville Falls, a double cascade of waters that plunge into the gorge, one of the deepest canyons (2,000 feet) in the East. The 1821 Old Hampton Store and Grist Mill in Linville retains an old-fashioned atmosphere, while Eseeola Lodge (704-733-4311) offers rustic accommodations in a wood-shingled building. The fourth Sunday of June Linville hosts the annual Singing on the Mountain, a gospel songfest held since the mid-1920s, and in early July the annual Highland Games and gathering of Scottish clans enlivens the area. Bed and breakfast places abound in Spruce Pine, with Still Hollow (704-765-9380) and inns such as Fairway (704-765-4917), Pinebridge (704-765-5543) and Richmond (704-765-6993). The first week of August Spruce Pine hosts the North Carolina Mineral and Gem Festival, while the nearby Museum of North Carolina Minerals (mid-May–early Oct., 9–5, free) traces the history of mining in the area, rich with gemstones, kaolin, mica and feldspar.

The craft school at nearby Penland, one of the nation's largest and oldest (1929) such institutions, has attracted to the area a number of craftspeople. Bakersville Inn (704-688-3451) provides bed and breakfast at Bakersville, gateway to Roan Mountain on the Tennessee border where extensive rhododendron fields burst into color every June. Near Bakersville survives an old grist mill, no longer functioning, nestled in a rustic corner of the landscape. To the south, beyond Burnsville, where Hamrick Inn (704-675-5251) and Nu-Wray Inn (May–Dec., 704-682-2329) furnish bed and breakfast, rises 6,684-foot Mt. Mitchell, highest peak in the eastern U.S. You'll find more bed and breakfast places along the way: at Mars Hill, the Baird House (704-689-5722); at Marshall, Marshall House (704-649-9205); at Leicester, Greenfield (April–Oct., 704-683-2128); and the Dry Ridge Inn (704-658-3899), an 1849 former parsonage, at Weaverville. East of here lies the Zebulon B. Vance Birthplace (April–Oct., M.–Sat., 9–5; Sun., 1–5; Nov.–March, Tu.–Sat., 10–4; Sun., 1–4, free), which commemorates the four-time U.S. Senator and North Carolina's conciliatory, forward-looking Civil War chief executive, the state's "most beloved governor," adjudges Beth G. Crabtree in *North Carolina Governors.*

Asheville, western North Carolina's largest urban area, named its Houston Astros baseball farm team the Tourists, perhaps in tribute to the thousands of visitors that frequent the attractive town. Its location in the scenic wooded rolling hills, along with the city's open, spacious feeling, lend it a delightful ambiance long appreciated by tourists, natives and retirees from elsewhere. A rich variety of architectural styles, some rather eccentric—the tall tier-topped Buncombe County Courthouse, stone and brick Hogan's Watch Repair, the oddly angled S & W Cafeteria, Italianate St. Lawrence Church and many others—make the downtown area delightfully irregular. The Thomas Wolfe Memorial (April–Oct.,

M.–Sat., 9–5; Sun., 1–5; Nov.–March, Tu.–Sat., 10–4; Sun.,
10–4, adm.) preserves the dwelling, a boardinghouse run
by the author's mother, where Wolfe grew up. At Riverside
Cemetery on the north side of town repose not only Wolfe,
on whose marker appear his words, "The last voyage, the
longest, the best," but also William Sydney Porter, better
known as O. Henry. Other Asheville sights include the c.
1840 Smith-McDowell House (May–Oct., Tu.–Sat., 10–4;
Sun., 1–4; Nov.–April, Tu.–F., 10–2, adm.), the city's oldest
brick structure; the Colburn Mineral Museum (Tu.–F., 10–5;
Sat. and Sun., 1–5, adm.); the 1891 T. J. Morrison emporium, Asheville's oldest store; Green River Dulcimer, with
nicely crafted musical instruments; and the renowned two
hundred and fifty-room 1895 Biltmore Estate (9–5, grounds
to 8, adm.), the nation's largest private house, with gardens,
a winery, a restaurant and gift shops. On the opposite side
of town, to the north, lies the Grove Park Inn (800-438-5800,
in-state 800-222-9793), a magnificent hotel, dating from
1913, frequented by Franklin Roosevelt, Thomas Edison,
Henry Ford and any number of other notables, including
F. Scott Fitzgerald, who stayed there in 1936 to be close
to his wife, Zelda, confined to Asheville's Highland Hospital, where she died in a fire in 1948. The North Carolina
Homespun Museum (April–Oct., 9–4, adm.), with antique
cars as well as handcrafted furniture and other examples of
Appalachian folk art, occupies an old gatehouse next to the
Grove Park Inn, whose south fireplace mantel bears the inscription: "Take from this hearth its warmth, Take from
this room its charm, Take from this Inn its amity, Return
them not, but return."

For an unusual view of Asheville and the surrounding
countryside Land O' Sky Aeronautics at Skyland to the south
runs daily hot-air balloon excursions (704-684-2092). The
Farmer's Market brims with produce, crafts and other wares,
while summer Saturday nights the Shindig-on-the-Green

music jamboree enlivens downtown Asheville, seat of Buncombe County, a name that engendered the expression "bunk," inspired by local Congressman Felix Walker when he noted during a House debate that he needed to add his comments "for Buncombe." Asheville's dozen or so bed and breakfast establishments include Cornerstone Inn (704-253-5644), Flint Street Inns (704-253-6723), the Ray House (704-252-0106), Heritage Hill (704-254-9336), and three places listed on the National Register: Cedar Crest (704-252-1389), the Lion and the Rose (704-255-ROSE) and Albemarle Inn (704-255-0027), where Hungarian composer Bela Bartok lived when he composed his *Third Concerto for Piano.*

West of Asheville, North Carolina begins to taper into a tongue of territory facing away from the distant Atlantic coast and its early history and pointing toward the West and the new way of life the early pioneers found there. South of Candler you'll find cozy stream-side houses at Mountain Springs Cottages (704-665-1004), while at Canton the old Pressley Sapphire Mine (April–Oct., 8–6, adm.) invites you to prospect for gems. At Lake Junaluska lodges and an inn open from late spring to fall provide resort accommodations, and at Waynesville—home of the Museum of North Carolina Handicrafts (May 15–Nov. 15, W.–Sat, 10–5; Sun., 2–5, adm.), listed on the National Register—you'll also find rustic inns, including Hallcrest (704-456-6457), Swag (704-926-0430) and Forsyth (704-456-3537), as well as such bed and breakfast places as Haywood Street House (704-456-9831) and Palmer House (704-456-7521). At Maggie Valley— a ski resort in the winter, and in October site of the Clogging Hall of Fame competition, featuring foot-stomping dancers—the Old West supplies the motif for the Ghost Town theme park (May–Oct., adm.). If you fancy overnighting in a converted train depot the Balsam Lodge (704-456-6528), a bed and breakfast place in Balsam, is where

to go, and you'll also find bed and breakfast accommodations at Squire Watkins (704-586-5244), Dillsboro Inn
(704-586-3898) and century-old Jarrett House (704-586-9964)
in Dillsboro, where the Great Smoky Mountains Railway
operates train excursions (weekends in April, daily 9 and
2, May 15–Oct., 704-586-8811). Bradley's General Store in
Dillsboro retains its old-fashioned soda fountain, while
Enloe Market Place occupies land owned by the grandson
of Abraham Enloe, believed locally to be the real father of
Abraham Lincoln as Nancy Hanks supposedly became preg-
nant while working in the Enloe house before moving west
with Thomas Lincoln.

At nearby Sylva the handsome Jackson County Courthouse perches atop a rise. In this area where the Blue Ridge
Parkway ends, or begins, its long itinerary across North Car-
olina and Virginia, the road reaches its highest point, 6,053
feet at the Richland Balsam overlook. Nearby spreads the
Cherokee Indian Qually Boundary, nestled among the
Smoky Mountains. A re-created two-century-old Cherokee
village, an arts and crafts cooperative, the tribe's folk drama
Unto These Hills (mid-June–late Aug., M.–Sat., 8:45 p.m.;
8:30 in Aug., 704-497-2111), the Museum of the Cherokee
Indian (mid-June–Aug., M.–Sat., 9–8; Sun., 9–5; Sept.–mid-
June, 9–5, adm.), and other attractions recall the history of
the Cherokee, uprooted from their homeland in 1835 and
forced to move to Oklahoma. Thanks to the efforts of Tsali,
one of their leaders, a remnant of the Cherokee nation, about
a thousand people, remained in North Carolina and their
descendants now occupy the reservation, in some ways a
foreign country as treaties between the U.S. and the Tribal
Council govern the community's status. Adjacent Swan
County forms a curious enclave of the state, with more than
40 percent of the Great Smoky Mountains National Park
within its borders and 86 percent of its total area owned
by the U.S. Near the mountains rush the waters of the

Nantahala River, which you can float with such outfitters as the Nantahala Outdoor Center (704-488-6900), Great Smokies Rafting Company (704-488-6302) or Wildwater, Ltd. (800-451-9972), all near Bryson City, where National Register-listed 1895 Randolph House (704-488-3472) offers attractive accommodations.

To the south, toward South Carolina, lies Cashiers, where the High Hampton Inn resort (704-743-2411) occupies the property once owned by Wade Hampton, South Carolina governor and U.S. senator as well as Confederate general. Past the 3500-foot high town runs the Eastern Continental Divide, from which waters flow either toward the Atlantic or the Mississippi. Down by the South Carolina border plunge the 441-foot Whitewater Falls, the highest in the eastern part of the country. For years Highlands, just to the west, remained a quiet, exclusive resort where such long-time residents as Coca-Cola chairman Robert Woodruff occupied summer houses. More recently an influx of outsiders, many from Atlanta and southern Florida, has turned Highlands into somewhat of a boom town, with Main Street property selling for $350,000 an acre. Unchanged by all the activity, the 1880 Highlands Inn (704-526-9380) still presides over Main Street as the old dowager the place remains, its long front porch a perfect perch to watch the world amble by. The Playhouse Theater, arts and crafts fairs in July, August and October, and the unusual Scottish Tartans Museum, branch of the main collection in Comrie, Scotland, with more than two hundred plaids on display, provide diversions in Highlands, where the Old Edwards Inn (704-526-5036) also offers pleasant accommodations. The Gem and Mineral Museum (May–Oct., M.–Sat., 10–4; Sun., 1–4, free) reflects one facet of the area—the dozen mines where you can rummage for various precious stones. Many of the mining properties lie in the Cowee Valley north of Franklin, where Buttonwood Inn (704-369-8985) offers pleasant rooms. The third weekend in June the town hosts Festival of Festivals, featuring a sampling of twenty western North Carolina celebrations. At West Mill, north of the mine area, the mill no longer survives but the old Rickman Store remains as a relic of yesteryear.

Just west of Franklin passes a stretch of the 2,000-mile long Appalachian Trail, here nearing its end, or beginning, at Springer Mountain, Georgia. And here North Carolina begins to end. At Andrews the Walker Inn (704-321-5019) takes bed and breakfast guests, and farther north Fontana Village Resort overlooks Fontana Dam, highest in the TVA system. At Brasstown you'll find the John C. Campbell Folk School, the nation's only such institution, which teaches crafts, music, dances, homesteading and other traditional endeavors. And at Murphy ends our long tour of North Carolina. Hill Top House (704-837-8661) and Huntington Hall (704-837-9567) offer bed and breakfast there. The names of Tennessee and Peachtree streets point to the adjoining states. But before moving on from remote Murphy, at the far western edge of North Carolina, it's pleasant to linger a time, listening to the carillon bells that ring out twice a day from the Methodist church in town. Off to the west lie the territories settled by the pioneers who moved on from the coastal states, while back to the east stretches North Carolina and the haunts where its long past unfolded—land of Blackbeard and bluebloods, the fight for rights and the Wrights' flights, the uncivil Civil War, tobacco and textiles, frontiersmen, forests and furniture, all forming the fabric and history of "the Old North State."

North Carolina Practical Information

The North Carolina Division of Travel is at 430 North Salisbury Street, Raleigh, NC 27611; 800-VISITING or 919-733-4171. Both the North Carolina Hotel and Motel

Association and the Travel Council of North Carolina, which promotes tourism in the state, are at 1100 Raleigh Building, Raleigh, NC 27602, 919-821-1435.

Other state agencies include the Historic Sites Section, 310 North Blount Street, Raleigh, NC 27611, 919-733-7862, and the Division of Parks and Recreation, 512 North Salisbury, Raleigh, NC 27611, 919-733-4181. For information on federally operated areas: Blue Ridge Parkway, 700 Northwestern Bank Building, Asheville, NC 28801, 704-259-0779; Great Smoky Mountains National Park, Gatlinburg, TN 37738, 615-436-5615; National Forests, Box 2750, Asheville, NC 28802, 704-253-2352; Cape Hatteras National Seashores, Route 1, Box 675, Manteo, NC 27954, 919-473-2113.

North Carolina operates eight information centers on interstate highways: in the southwest on I-40 near Waynesville and I-26 near Tryon; in the south on I-85 near Kings Mountain, I-77 at Charlotte and I-95 near Rowland; in the north on I-77 near Dobson, on I-95 near Roanoke Rapids, and on I-85 near Norlina.

For information on popular tourist areas: in the east, Wilmington and Cape Fear region: 800-222-4757; New Bern, 919-637-3111; the Outer Banks, 919-637-9400; Fayetteville, 919-438-5311; in the Piedmont, Goldsboro, 919-734-2241; Chapel Hill, 919-967-7075; Charlotte, 800-231-4636, in-state 800-782-5544; Durham, 919-682-2133; Greensboro, 919-274-2282; Raleigh, 919-834-5900; Winston-Salem, 919-725-2361; in the west, Asheville, 800-548-1300; Hendersonville, 704-692-1413.

Bed and breakfast booking agencies include Bed and Biscuits, Box 19664, Raleigh, NC 27619, 919-787-2109 and Bed and Breakfasts in the Albemarle, Box 248, Everetts, NC 27825, 919-792-4584, while the North Carolina Bed and Breakfast Association is at Box 11215, Raleigh, NC 27604, 919-477-8430.

3. South Carolina

After the Spanish and the French tried unsuccessfully to settle along the Carolina coast, the English landed in the area in March 1670. Indians greeted the new arrivals by shouting "Hiddy doddy comorado Angles"—"English very good friends": an auspicious beginning for the promising new venture. The English had high hopes for the area. In 1699 Edward Randolph, collector of customs for the American colonies, commented in his report on Carolina: "If this place were duly encouraged it would be the most useful to the Crown of all the plantations upon the continent of America."

In the early days the colony made its way by trading in deerskins, buying the material from Indians in exchange for "English cottons, broadcloth of several colors, duffels, red and blue beads" and other such wares and trinkets, so a 1708 report noted. By that year Charleston, Carolina's only town until 1730, had developed sufficiently for John Oldmixon to note in his *British Empire in America* that the settlement was "so pleasantly green that . . . no prince in Europe, by all of his art, can make so pleasant a sight." Soon settlers started to grow cotton and tobacco, but the leading crop in the early days was rice, which enriched the owners of the low-country plantations along the Carolina coast. South Carolina's agricultural growth made the area the mainland's largest importer of slave labor, and by 1724 blacks in the low-country outnumbered the white population by three to one. In 1739 the first major slave insurrection occurred, with thirty-three whites killed, an insubordination a contemporary report blamed on the Spanish at St. Augus-

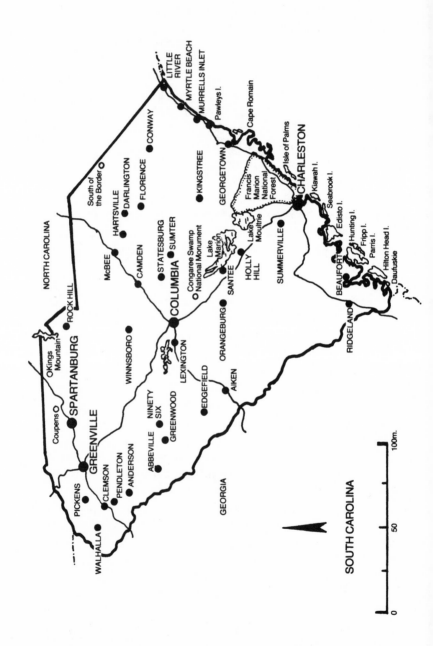

tine, "That den of thieves and ruffians! Receptacle of debtors, servants and slaves! Bane of industry and society!"

In 1719 the colony broke free from the Lords Proprietors, Charles II's eight cronies who for half a century had administered the land the king had given them, and Carolina became a royal domain run by crown-appointed governors. During the mid-eighteenth century the Carolina colony expanded as the governors promoted settlement of the up-country. In 1730 the British concluded a treaty with the Cherokee, that tribe conveniently serving as a buffer between Carolina and French Louisiana, and soon outlying settlements sprang up around the inland part of the territory, an area that—in contrast to civilized Charleston on the coast—remained so unruly the pioneers established vigilante groups called "Regulators" to bring a modicum of law and order into the back country. Between 1743 and 1756 James Glen, considered one of the best of the colonial administrators, ran the colony. Glen became known as the "energetic governor" for his efforts to deal with the Indians, to promote agriculture and to encourage trade.

The Revolution came early to South Carolina—earlier than anywhere else. The conflict in effect began on July 12, 1775, at Fort Charlotte in western South Carolina when Yankees for the first time ever forcibly seized British property in North America. In June 1776 South Carolinians sheltered in a palmetto log fort on Sullivan's Island near Charleston repulsed the British, an encounter memorialized in the state seal and flag, which bear representations of the palmetto tree, and in South Carolina's nickname, "the Palmetto State."

After the Revolution ended the rise of cotton as South Carolina's dominant crop began, a commodity so profitable other crops or industrial endeavors failed to tempt people. In his 1850s *Autobiography* William John Grayson observed that "The cultivation of a great staple like cotton . . . starves everything else. The farmer curtails and neglects all other crops." The cotton industry extended the plantation system to the up-country, thus increasing the demand for slaves, a development which eventually made South Carolina the leading advocate of slavery and states' rights. As early as 1832 the Nullification controversy—pitting the states' rights faction against the Unionists—foreshadowed the heated controversies that led to the Civil War. The federal government defused the explosive tensions by reducing tariffs, legislation which South Carolina had tried to "nullify," but this only temporarily eased sectional frictions, and on March 4, 1850, less than a month before his death, John C. Calhoun in his last speech pleaded with the North to accept the South the way it was.

Calhoun's plea failed to move the North and on December 20, 1860, South Carolina became the first state to secede. Although the state remained relatively free of military action the first three years of the war, nearly a fifth of South Carolina's white males died in the conflict and toward the end the Yankees targeted the South's most radically anti-Union area, with General William Tecumseh Sherman writing that "the whole army is burning with an insatiable desire to wreak vengeance in South Carolina. I almost tremble at her fate, but feel that she deserves all that seems to be in store for her." In February 1865 Grant burned Columbia, the state capital, and then inflicted on the state other damage. The Confederates fought back as best they could, in one skirmish routing out of bed Union Brigadier General Judson Kilpatrick, forced to flee without his trousers in what came to be called (at least by the Southerners) the Battle of Kilpatrick's Pants. In spite of General Sherman's vindictive comments much of South Carolina—including such treasures as Charleston and Beaufort—escaped unscathed, leaving the area with a rich heritage of antebellum ambiance and relics.

Although Louis B. Wright in *South Carolina: A Bicentennial*

History remarked on "the magnolia-and-moonlight syndrome, the tendency to interpret our past in overripe terms of romanticism," it is precisely that sort of carry-over from yesteryear that visitors to the state find so alluring—a kind of archaic, or perhaps even decadent, way of life from another era which survives in the sleepy up-country towns and at the stately plantation homes that seem to have strayed by mistake from the past into the twentieth century. As you tour the state you'll encounter a varied array of history, culture and natural features, from the architecturally rich old towns, some dating back two and a half centuries, to the verdant forests and large lakes that checker the landscape, to the hilly up-country terrain and low-country settlements and islands where past and present meet to form a pleasant mix that invites visitors to linger and to savor the delights of old South Carolina.

Carolina's Coast

Myrtle Beach—Conway—Pawleys Island—Georgetown—Around Charleston—Edisto—Beaufort—St. Helena—Hilton Head

Along South Carolina's two hundred-mile long coastline lie resorts, historic towns, wildlife preserves, sixteen major barrier islands and fully 20 percent, 420,000 acres, of the east coast's salt marshes. As James Henry Rice, Jr., describes this stretch of sea-side Carolina in *Glories of the Carolina Coast:* "In variety lies the charm of the coast. No description of one part can apply to another. . . . There is a change for each mile, often many changes to the mile." From the North Carolina state line south through Horry and most of Georgetown counties run the fifty-five miles of beaches known as the Grand Strand, a resort region that attracts more than half of South Carolina's out-of-state visitors. Tobacco and agricultural products once dominated the economy of Horry (pronounced "O'Ree" by the locals) County, now a tourist area with Myrtle Beach as its center.

As you cross the state line heading south from North Carolina you'll pass near a granite monument marking the site of Boundary House, a popular dueling spot as the line dividing North and South Carolina ran through the building. One famous encounter occurred in 1804 when General Benjamin Smith, later governor of North Carolina, received a chest wound in a pistol duel with his cousin, Captain Maurice Moore. Earlier, on May 9, 1775, Isaac Marion, brother of famous Revolutionary War General Frances "the Swamp Fox" Marion, received at the House news of the outbreak of war at the Battle of Lexington in Massachusetts.

Two miles south of the border lies Little River, a fishing village once called "Yankeetown" for its many settlers from the north—namely, North Carolina. As late as the first quarter of the eighteenth century pirates cruised in and out of the protected inlets of the Little River, one of the home ports and weigh stations for the Arthur Smith King Mackerel Tournament, said to be the world's largest fishing competition. Near the old Methodist church, which now shelters a restaurant, stands an antique and gift shop installed in a venerable one-time general store building furnished with long counters and an antique cash register. Stella's Guest House (803-249-1871) in Little River offers bed and breakfast. Inland, the town of Loris hosts the Bog-off, a chicken cooking contest, in mid-October; while Conway to the south, a pleasant town founded in 1734 under instructions from the British crown and embellished with a scattering of old houses, serves as seat of Horry County, the state's largest. The Horry County Museum (M.–Sat., 10–5, free) contains exhibits on the area's history, while the tiny Travelers' Chapel offers a mini-sanctuary for a few souls at a time.

A tobacco market operates at Conway between late July and mid-October (for information: 803-248-2273).

On the campus of Horry-Georgetown Tech on U.S. highway 501 near Conway you'll find the official Grand Strand Welcome Center, South Carolina's only community-sponsored such facility (803-626-6619), with information on the resort region's accommodations and attractions. The former far outnumber the latter, for the Myrtle Beach area offers more than 50,000 rooms at dozens of hotels, condos, cottages, at least one bed and breakfast establishment—the Spanish mission-style Serendipity Inn (803-449-5268)—and at some seven thousand campsites, enough for the region to call itself the "Camping Capital of the World." Myrtle Beach's population of 28,000 increases more than ten times in the summer when some 350,000 tourists invade the Grand Strand resort area, located halfway between New York City and Miami. The area offers wide beaches, watersports, golf courses galore (more than fifty of them), restaurants, nightspots and such come-ons or turn-offs as a wax museum (Feb.–Oct., 9–11, adm.); the Pavilion amusement park area (May–Sept., 1–12 midnight) with a sixty-foot Ferris wheel and an antique pipe organ and merry-go-round; a Ripley's Believe It or Not Museum (March 1–Nov. 28, 9–10, adm.); and the Waccamaw Pottery outlet, where before your very eyes workers craft various items. Embedded in concrete in front of the Myrtle Beach Convention Center are the footprints impressed on the moon's surface in 1972 by Charles M. Duke, honored at the state's Hall of Fame (M.–F., 9–5, free) inside the Center. Other honorees include musician "Dizzy" Gillespie, politician and Secretary of State James F. Byrnes, and other illustrious native sons and daughters.

Ocean Boulevard, Myrtle Beach's main tourist thoroughfare, runs along for miles, a relentlessly commercial strip lined with hotels, shops and other business establishments

frequented by crowds of pleasure seekers in various stages
of undress and sunburn. So congested, tacky and on-the-
beaten track is the Boulevard that, in a perverse way, it repays
a visit, if for no other reason than to see a section of South
Carolina that is the antithesis of the state's delightful back
roads and byways. You'll find some respite from the unre-
lieved commercialism at Myrtle Beach State Park (6–10,
adm.), which encompasses one of the last undeveloped natural areas along the state's northern coast. Old Civilian Conservation Corps-built structures in the park take you back
to the 1930s.

To the south, beyond the seafood restaurant enclave of
Murrells Inlet, lies another unspoiled state park, Huntington
Beach (6–10, adm.), with a boardwalk extending out into
the coastal salt marsh, in and near which bird life abounds.
In the park stands Atalaya, an unusual Moorish-Spanish-
style structure built in the early 1930s by New Yorkers
Archer Huntington and his wife, Anna, who created sculpture works in her studio there. Ramps rather than stairs lead
up to each entry door from the open courtyard, garnished
by the Sabal, or cabbage, palmetto, South Carolina's state
tree. Across from Huntington Beach Park is the entrance
to Brookgreen Gardens (9:30–4:45, adm.), founded by the
Huntingtons and marked with a lively-looking statue by the
sculptress showing two muscular fighting stallions. The Gardens, begun in 1931 on the grounds of a two-century-old
plantation, include more than four hundred and fifty works
of sculpture, with pieces by Saint-Gaudens, Daniel Chester
French, Gutzon Borglum, Carl Milles and Frederic Reming-
ton, as well as an arboretum, the moss-draped trees of Live
Oak Allée and more than two thousand types of plants.
In the area repose Governor Joseph Alston and Aaron Burr
Alston, husband and son of Theodosia Burr Alston, daughter of Aaron Burr, who disappeared off the North Carolina
coast when a storm sunk the "Patriot," the schooner she'd

taken from nearby Georgetown in 1812 to meet her famous father, but instead she met her Maker.

Not far south of Brookgreen Gardens lies Pawleys Island, a designation which refers both to the four-mile long, quarter of a mile wide sliver of land offshore, and to the mainland town on U.S. highway 17. Weathered beachhouses of no pretension line the shore on the island, traditionally known as an "arrogantly shabby" resort spot. Typifying that rather haughty modesty is the boast of Sea View Inn (803-237-4253), one of Pawleys' simple yet comfortable boardinghouses: "Here's what we don't have: TV, phones in the room, a swimming pool, air conditioners throughout." Another pleasant local hostelry is Tip Top Inn (803-237-2325), with a rocking chair-furnished long front porch. Since the late 1700s Pawleys Island has served as a summer resort, one of the oldest such retreats on the Atlantic coast. Back in those early days wealthy rice planters from the nearby Waccamaw Neck area sought sanctuary on the island to escape the threat of "summer fever," as they called yellow fever. Until the Siau Bridge opened in 1938 to replace the ferry, Pawleys remained isolated and virtually unfrequented by casual tourists. If you decide to visit Pawleys' haunts, keep your eye peeled for the "Gray Man," a ghost which, locals say, first spooked the island at the time of the devastating 1822 hurricane. Residents sighted the spirit again before the 1893 storm and also before Hurricane Hazel hit in 1954, giving rise to the legend that the Gray Man serves as a warning of stormy weather.

Out on the mainland along highway 17 nestles a pleasant tree-filled enclave called The Hammock Shops, one of the nation's most attractive shopping centers, a collection of more than twenty stores installed in old-time buildings that stand among moss-draped oaks and manicured gardens. At one establishment you'll find on sale the famous Pawleys Island rope hammock, invented in 1880 by Captain Joshua

John Ward, a riverboat pilot who carried rice and supplies between Georgetown and area plantations. Ward found the knot-filled hammocks then common aboard ships uncomfortable, so he designed a knotless open-weave version well ventilated for use during the low-country's humid summer nights. A. H. Lachicotte, Captain Josh's brother-in-law, began making the rope hammocks for friends, and in 1937 he started selling the popular product commercially in his general store at Pawleys Island. At a tin-roofed building next door to the hammock shop weavers braid the webby mats on wooden frames affixed to the wall. In the shopping compound stand the town's original post office (c. 1800) as well as an 1850 schoolhouse relocated there from a nearby rice plantation. Waverly, the plantation acquired by the Lachicotte family in 1871, survived as one of the last low-country rice-growing properties, the final harvest being gathered in 1911.

Rice was South Carolina's earliest money crop. The first fields began to yield the grain about 1685. Before then the state's main export was deerskins, bought from Indians who slaughtered the animals in great numbers, a massacre recalling the nineteenth-century decimation of buffalo on the great plains. When the rice plantations began to develop this both changed South Carolina's economy and established the low-country's social structure. The rice industry took root after Captain John Thurber, whose ship called in at Charleston harbor for repairs in 1685, gave less than a bushel of seed from Madagascar to Dr. Henry Woodward, thus introducing into the area "Carolina gold," a rice-type so called for its husk color. To impound fresh water for irrigation, planters built canals and dams, and in the following century and a half the rice industry thrived until competition from Texas and Louisiana eventually eliminated South Carolina's trade in the crop, and these days the state produces not a single grain of rice for commercial sale. Some one hundred and fifty rice plantations once filled the landscape along the Waccamaw River and across Waccamaw Neck, a strip of land between the ocean and the river. At one property, Brookgreen, proprietor Joshua John Ward owned eleven hundred slaves, at one time supposedly the nation's largest such holding. In mid-April every year visitors can tour some of the privately owned plantations in the region (for information: 803-546-5438). One latter-day spread in the area was Hobcaw Barony, the plantation of Bernard Baruch where the financier entertained such friends as Winston Churchill, Franklin Roosevelt, Omar Bradley, Mark Clark and other notables. The Belle W. Baruch Foundation, established to manage Hobcaw Barony, operates Bellefield Nature Center (M.–F., 10–5; Sat., 1–5, free), a small display facility at the estate's front gate, with exhibits on coastal ecology and wildlife. Tours of Hobcaw Barony, a wildlife refuge, are available only by appointment (803-546-4623).

Georgetown, the state's third-oldest town, is a history-filled settlement that dates from the early eighteenth century. But even before Elisha Screven laid out the town in 1729 the area attracted outsiders, for a Spanish expedition under Lucas Vasquez de Allyon founded a colony on Waccamaw Neck in 1526, the earliest European settlement in North America. The colony failed to take hold and later the English moved into the area. Soon after the English established Georgetown indigo replaced the Indian-supplied deerskin trade as Carolina's main product, while after the Revolution rice became the staple crop, with the region producing nearly half the nation's rice by 1840. Georgetown's Rice Museum (M.–F., 9:30–4:30; Sun., 2–4:30; Sat., April–Sept., 10–4:30. and Oct.–March, 10–1, adm.)—installed in the National Register-listed 1842 Old Market Building, whose clock tower (1845) serves as the town's landmark—traces the history of the rice industry and of the now-vanished plantation way of life, while the Winyah Indigo Society Hall (c. 1857), a club formed in 1740 "to talk over the latest news from London," recalls the indigo trade. Dues paid to the Society in indigo subsidized the only free school established (1757) between Charleston and North Carolina for a century. In the eighteenth century indigo blue dye colored British uniforms and the dress coats favored by gentlemen of the era. When wars in Europe depressed the rice price planters sought an alternate crop. Seventeen-year-old Eliza Lucas, daughter of an area rice grower, experimented a few years with indigo, finally in the early 1740s bringing in a crop that produced dyestuff satisfactory to London merchants. In her *Journal* the young Eliza expressed her hopes of "supplying our mother country with a manufacture for which she has so great a demand, and which she is now supplied with from the French colonies, and many thousand pounds per annum thereby lost to the nation." At the 1793 funeral of Eliza Lucas Pinckney, whose sons Thomas and Charles served as leading Revolutionary era figures, George Washington participated as a pallbearer.

Through the years the Georgetown area saw much history and many history makers. George Washington visited Clifton Plantation and addressed the townspeople in 1791; in 1821 the owners of Prospect Hill (now Arcadia) on the Waccamaw entertained President James Monroe, rolling out to the river for the occasion a real red carpet; President Martin van Buren visited the appropriately named White House Plantation on the Black River; and in 1894 President Grover Cleveland hunted ducks as a guest of the Annandale Gun Club. In Georgetown's Historic District, listed on the National Register, remain such mementos of yesteryear as 1750 Prince George Episcopal Church, listed on the National Register, whose chipped and pitted brick floors evidence use of the sanctuary as a stable by British Revolutionary War troops; Duncan Memorial Church, home of South Carolina's oldest Methodist congregation, established in 1785; the Rainey-Camlin House (c. 1760) where Joseph H. Rainey, the first black elected to the U.S. House of Representatives, lived. Also, such graveyards as the Screven Burial Ground where William Screven, father of the town's founder, reposes; the Baptist Cemetery, whose oldest grave dates from 1801; and the Hebrew Cemetery, one of the nation's oldest Jewish burial areas, some of its graves pre-dating the Revolution. Two show houses are open to the public—Man-Doyle House, c. 1775 (April–Oct., Tu.–F., tours on the hour, 10–3 except 1, adm.) and the 1760 antique-filled Kaminski House (M.–F., 10–5, adm.); while the Redstore-Tarbox Warehouse stands at the site where Theodosia Burr Alston, Aaron Burr's daughter, departed to her death in 1812 on the ill-fated "Patriot."

Two unusual ways to visit the area's attractions are the walking tour through the Historic District operated by Miss Nell Tours (Tu.–Th., 10:30 and 2:30. Sat. and Sun., 2:30 and 4:30 or by appointment, 803-546-3975, adm.) and an excursion on "The Island Queen" (May 1–Sept. 15, 10, 1, 4, evening; Sept. 16–Dec. 15 and March 1–April 30, 11, 2 and evening, adm.) which travels along rivers bordered by old plantations and ruins of the former rice-growing areas. Bed and breakfast places in Georgetown include the Shaw House (803-546-9663), 1790 House (803-546-4821), listed on the National Register, and Walton House (803-527-4330). On Wednesday evenings from June to August the old Strand Theater in town presents on stage *Ghosts of the Coast,* a spirited performance that recalls Georgetown's claim to be "the most haunted place in the South."

Sprawled across North, South and most of Cat Islands on the coast just southeast of Georgetown is the Tom Yawkey Wildlife Center, an unspoiled natural enclave with limited public use, access being available by boat only for weekly

guided field trips by prior arrangement (803-546-6814).
South of Georgetown survive two old rice plantations open
to the public. At 1740 Hopsewee Plantation overlooking the
Santee River (March–Oct., Tu.–F., 10–5, adm.) Thomas
Lynch, Jr., grew up, a signer of the Declaration of Independence and along with his father a member of the Continental
Congress. Hampton Plantation State Park (M.–Th., 9–6;
Sat., 10–3; Sun., 12–3, adm.) includes the 1730s restored
mansion that once served as centerpiece of the coastal rice
plantation that surrounded the house. Cutaway sections re-
veal the materials and construction techniques used to build
the showplace where George Washington spent the night
during his 1791 presidential tour of the South. In front of
the house stands a massive live oak named for Washington,
who supposedly persuaded the owners not to cut down the
tree, while in a nearby pine grove nestles the nearly three-
century-old St. James Church. In *Home by the River,*
Archibald Rutledge, South Carolina poet laureate who in
the 1930s retired to Hampton, his ancestral home, tells of
finding between the walls of the house a secret compartment
with a container holding a sketch that indicated the location
of a box hidden away on the grounds. As visions of a buried
treasure flitted through his head, Rutledge grabbed a shovel
and carefully paced off the steps just as the document directed, only to find at the spot indicated a huge, immovable
oak tree.

Hampton Plantation lies at the northern edge of Francis
Marion National Forest, which spreads for miles across much
of Georgetown County. In the Forest area to the south lies
the little town of McClellanville, which fairly oozes with
mossy Deep South charm. Two miles west of highway 17
near McClellanville stands 1768 St. James Santee Church,
a rather austere-looking brick and pine sanctuary. Three
miles off the coast stretches the nearly twenty-five-mile long
Cape Romain National Wildlife Refuge that occupies three

large barrier islands and a scattering of smaller ones. Although all the islands are open to the public for day use, only five thousand-acre Bulls can be reached by regular ferry (March–Dec., F., Sat. and Sun., Jan. and Feb., Sat. departure from Moores Landing at 8:30, return from Bulls at 4:30; for reservations: 803-884-0448). Eight ponds, the barrier beach and a maritime forest on Bulls contain a rich mix of wildlife, plants and natural features, some conveniently seen on a two-mile long interpretive trail. Along Boneyard Beach lie the twisty-limbed skeletons of dead oaks and cedars, while on the island's northeast side crumble the remains of an old fort that marks the spot where the first permanent European settlers stopped off on their way to Charleston in 1670. Rice plantations once operated on Bulls, named after Captain Bull who was aboard the 1670 ship. Over the years various families owned the island, which in 1930 the federal government acquired to add to the Romain Refuge, established in 1932.

Charleston is covered separately in the next section, but on the way into and out of the famous show city you may want to stop off at a few attractions near the town where South Carolina began. At Mt. Pleasant, between the Marion National Forest and Charleston, artisans weave sweetgrass baskets sold in the area, a three-century-old tradition that originated when rice plantation slaves adopted techniques they brought from West Africa to fabricate workbaskets. The craft waned after rice cultivation ended early in this century, but the technique survived in Mt. Pleasant, where an estimated one hundred weavers continue the tradition, confecting out of sweetgrass, palm-leaf strips and pine needles baskets, trays and other such items sold in Charleston and at the nearby sixty or so basket stands that line highway 17 near Mt. Pleasant. At Mt. Pleasant you'll also find a Confederate cemetery, an 1847 Presbyterian church, the house built (c. 1775) by colony treasurer Jacob Motte, and wide streets lined with moss-draped oaks. From the short remaining portion of the old Pitt Street Bridge, a span torn down in 1944 that once carried trolley cars between Mt. Pleasant and nearby Sullivan's Island, you can enjoy a scenic view of the Charleston skyline, ship traffic and Mt. Pleasant's Old Village waterfront homes. The restored 1888 Guilds Inn (803-881-0510) at Mt. Pleasant offers bed and breakfast, as does The Palmettos (803-883-3389), a late nineteenth-century house at Sullivan's Island, a historic stretch of land once dominated by Fort Moultrie, a federal outpost from Revolutionary times up to 1947.

On June 28, 1776 outmanned and outgunned colonists sheltered in a palmetto log fort withstood a British assault to win what some say was America's first decisive Revolutionary War victory. In a July 1 post-battle report to George Washington, General Charles Lee wrote: "I do assure you, my dear General, I never experienced a hotter fire—twelve full hours of it was continued without intermission." General William Tecumseh Sherman once served as commanding officer at Fort Moultrie, as did George Marshall, later General of the Army and Secretary of State, and at the base was stationed in the late 1820s (under the name E. A. Perry) Edgar Allen Poe, who described the area in his short story *The Gold Bug,* set on Sullivan's Island: "This island is a very singular one. It consists of little else than the sea sand, and is about three miles long. Its breadth at no point exceeds a quarter of a mile. It is separated from the mainland by a scarcely perceptible creek, oozing its way through a wilderness of reeds and slime. . . . Near the western extremity, where Fort Moultrie stands, and where are some miserable frame buildings, tenanted, during the summer, by the fugitives from Charleston dust and fever, may be found, indeed, the bristly palmetto." These days the buildings are more pleasant, with many of the Fort's former officers' quarters providing comfortable houses. In front of Fort Moultrie,

the third fort built on the site (1809) and now a museum
operated by the National Park Service (summer, 9–6; winter, 9–5, free), lies the grave of Seminole chief Osceola,
captured—in spite of his truce flag—during the Seminole
War of 1835 in Florida and imprisoned in a dungeon at the
fort where he died in 1838. On the adjacent Isle of Palms,
Major General Charles Cornwallis established a headquarters
in June 1776 as a staging point for the attack on Sullivan's
Island. After failing in the assault the British sailed for New
York and then in 1780 Cornwallis returned as second in command of the army that captured Charles Town. A year later,
in October 1781, he surrendered at Yorktown and the Revolutionary War was over.

Back a bit to the north you'll find tucked away near the
eastern branch of the Cooper River in the Francis Marion
National Forest some off-the-beaten-track sights that recall
the region's history. On state road 98 just north of Cainhoy
is the delightful little 1819 St. Thomas Church, embellished
with a delicate fan window over the entrance, while farther
up the road the Amoco Chemical Company office includes
in its lobby a display of area artifacts, such as age-old fossils
and mastodon remains, along with nineteenth-century rice
plantation objects. On the northeast side of French Quarter
Creek by the Cooper River rises a granite cross commemorating the Huguenots, French Protestants who settled along
the creek and elsewhere in the low-country in and near
Charleston. Rather puritanical and severe in their doctrines,
the Huguenots—who believed in education, thrift, hard
work and culture—in time became so successful there arose
in Carolina the common expression "rich as a Huguenot."
Farther north toward Huger stands the 1699 Middleburg
Plantation, South Carolina's oldest surviving wooden dwelling and a prototype of the low-country "single house." Remains of the original rice mill survive, as do a carriage house
and a commissary. The nearby 1763 Pompion (pronounced

"pumpkin") Hill, just by the Cooper River, is a simple but
elegant structure listed on the National Register, the state's
first Church of England edifice outside of Charleston, while
just west of Huger lies the site of the July 17, 1781, Revolutionary War Battle of Quinby Bridge in which Francis Marion participated.

The twenty-mile Swamp Fox Trail through the National
Forest commemorates Marion, known as the "Swamp Fox"
for his tactic of hiding his troops in Carolina's back country,
from which he'd sally forth to attack the British. Off to
the west at Moncks Corner near Lake Moultrie lies the new
Old Santee Canal State Park, which opened in the summer
of 1989. The park contains the southern end of the twenty-
two-mile long Santee Canal, completed in 1800—the nation's
first dug-channel canal—to connect the Santee River with
the Cooper in order to shorten the water route from up-
country cotton plantations to Charleston. Although the canal
operated until 1855, long before then railroads had diverted
traffic away from the waterway. Trails and boardwalks at
the park take you through the Biggin Creek basin, teeming
with low-country plant and animal life, and you can also
rent a canoe to float down the historic canal. You'll find
bed and breakfast at Moncks Corner at the Rice Hope
Plantation (803-761-4832) set on twelve acres of garden-
embellished grounds just by the Cooper River, and also in
the area are the old Strawberry Chapel and Mepkin Abbey,
a tranquil Trappist monastery with a garden and chapel
(9–4:30, free).

Continuing on to the South Carolina coast south of
Charleston, you'll first come to Folly Beach, where George
Gershwin and DuBose Heyward lived in the summer of
1934 as they worked on transforming the latter's novel *Porgy*
into the folk opera *Porgy and Bess*. In 1862 the Confederate
army decided to move its arms depot from the area, so slaves

loaded the weapons onto the steamer "Planter" for shipment to another fort. During the night Robert Smalls, one of the slave crew, navigated the ship into the hands of Federal forces. Smalls eventually became a general and then a U.S. congressman, and in 1863 he purchased the Beaufort (farther south on the coast) house, behind which he'd been born, previously owned by his master. On nearby Wadmalaw Island you'll find the nation's only tea plantation (tours, May–Oct., Tu. and Th., 11, by reservation only: 803-559-0383, free).

Kiawah Island now comprises one of those upscale resort and retirement communities common along the South Carolina coast. A so called "safari by jeep" (803-768-1111) on Kiawah will take you to alligator ponds, the antebellum Vanderhorst mansion and bird areas. As the birds fly, Edisto Island to the southwest lies rather near Kiawah, but to get there you have to return across the marshland to highway 17 to the north then head south to the coast again. A scattering of antebellum houses and old churches on Edisto recall the days when plantations that grew the coveted sea island cotton thrived in the area, first settled around 1690. The island's Presbyterian Church, listed on the National Register, houses the state's oldest congregation of that denomination (1696), while such mansions as Old House (c. 1750) and Seaside (c. 1802) recall the early plantation days. The Old Post Office restaurant, housed in a clapboard building that once served as the island's postal facility, specializes in grits as a main dinner course (Tu.–Sat., 6 p.m.–10 p.m.; closed Jan.) Edisto Beach State Park boasts a mile and a half long stretch of shell-littered sand, a thick forest of live oaks, an expanse of open salt marsh and a stand of some of the state's tallest palmetto trees. At the end of the four-mile long Indian Mound Trail stands a rise formed by seashells left by ancient Indians who inhabited the site, while an indentation northeast of the low hill is supposedly the remains of a rum runner's cave where ships from the Caribbean stored their bootleg liquor during Prohibition.

To proceed to the Beaufort area to the south you'll again have to return to highway 17, a roundabout route that will take you to Gardens Corner, just west of which—a half mile north of U.S. 17 on state road 721, delightfully canopied by branches of live oaks—nestle the lovely ruins of Prince William's Parish Church, originally constructed in 1745–55, burned by the British in 1779, rebuilt in 1826, and burned by Federal troops in 1865. This is one of South Carolina's most beguiling spots. Over the now roofless sanctuary, which hosts an outdoor service the second Sunday after Easter, stretch tree limbs, while the stark walls and a quartet of bare brick columns in front of the church seem forlorn remnants of the distant past. Before the altar lies the grave of William Bull (died 1755), who helped lay out the settlement at Savannah, Georgia, founded in 1733, and who served as lieutenant governor of South Carolina from 1737 to 1744. A few eighteenth-century graves lie in the small cemetery around the church, a functioning water pump by picnic tables lends a rustic touch and through the air sound the chirps and calls of birds that flit among the trees. All these elements and others combine to lend the secluded area a pleasantly melancholy atmosphere.

On the way south to Beaufort (pronounced "Bew-furt" in these parts) you'll pass the Marine Corps Air Station, in front of which stand three display planes and a sign proclaiming "The 'noise' you hear is the sound of freedom." Although Beaufort's outlying areas haven't escaped development—along the approach road stands a proliferation of unsightly fast food eateries, chain motels, franchised retail establishments and tacky shops—the old part of town down by the water remains one of the state's most alluring and unspoiled settlements. Like Natchez, Mississippi, or

Charleston, seventy miles northeast, or Savannah, forty-five miles to the southwest, Beaufort presents an architectural whole, an integrated appearance not unlike the pleasing visual harmony found in many European cities. Beaufort, South Carolina's second-oldest city, began in 1711 as a malaria-free summer resort for back-country plantation owners who over the years prospered from rice, then indigo and finally sea island cotton, a silky long staple fiber that brought great wealth to the town in the first half of the nineteenth century. The city owes its present state of preservation to its early surrender in the Civil War, a decision that saved the settlement from destruction. After the war cotton production, no longer economically viable without slave labor, declined and the arrival of the boll weevil in 1919 finally put an end to the crop. The town dozed away the years until the 1960s when a group of citizens formed the Historic Beaufort Foundation to restore the city's faded glories. Today Beaufort remains a splendid relic, a smaller and more intimate version of Charleston where the atmosphere of yesteryear lingers with an almost tangible presence.

Around Beaufort stand dozens of history-haunted houses, churches and other carryovers from the eighteenth and nineteenth centuries. As Beaufort native Pat Conroy noted in his novel *The Great Santini*, filmed at the beautifully proportioned Tidalholm in town as was *The Big Chill*, "Each house was a massive tribute to days long past." Two museum mansions open to the public recall those long-gone days: the 1840s Elliot House (M.–F., 11–3, adm.), a typical local residence in that it stands on a raised foundation and faces south toward the river to catch the vagrant breezes; and the 1790s John Mark Verdier House (Tu.–Sat., 11–4, adm.) where in 1825 the Marquis de Lafayette addressed the townspeople from the front porch and which Union forces used as their headquarters. A stroll around the old part of town will take you to such other historic structures as the Hepworth House, 214 New Street, believed to be Beaufort's oldest residence (c. 1717), which sports gun ports in its tabby walls; the spooky-looking Johnson House, 411 Craven, embellished with octagonal columns; the James Verdier House, 501 Pinckney, where the *Sea Island Lady,* as Francis Griswold called her in his novel of that name, lived; the Berners House, 201 Laurens, built in 1852 at the peak of the cotton prosperity, one of the few residences with still intact outbuildings; the striking St. Helena Episcopal Church, 501 Church, one of the nation's oldest churches (1724), used during the Civil War as a hospital, with tombstones serving as operating tables; the 1844 Greek Revival-style Baptist Church, 600 Charles Street; the Old Arsenal, a 1795 Gothic-style structure now housing the Beaufort Museum (M.–F., 10–12, 2–5; Sat., 10–12); and the National Cemetery (8–5, free), established in 1862, where 12,000 Union soldiers repose. Architectural and even whimsical details abound around town: at the Robert Small House, 511 Prince, listed on the National Register, appears a plaintive notice: "For dog's sake close the gate." At 800 Carteret stands the 1852 building that housed Beaufort College, a boys' school, its books taken by the Yankees after they captured Beaufort in 1861 and shipped off to New York for auction until Treasury Secretary S. P. Chase stopped the sales, proclaiming, "We do not war on libraries." An 1868 fire at the Smithsonian Institution in Washington destroyed most of the books, but the episode resurfaced as recently as 1940 when Congress authorized a $10,000 payment to compensate Beaufort for the plundered volumes.

Other Civil War memories remain in Beaufort at the Maxcy, or Secession, House at the corner of Craven and Church, an 1813 residence, built on the tabby foundations of a 1743 structure, where the first draft of South Carolina's Secession Ordinance was written. One of the leaders of the Secession movement—South Carolina became the first state to secede from the Union, on December 20, 1860—was the radical Confederate leader Robert Barnwell Rhett (born Smith), known as "the father of Secession," a Beaufort politician who in 1850 succeeded the renowned John C. Calhoun in the U.S. Senate. Disappointed at not being chosen president of the Confederate States of America, Rhett spent the Civil War sulking and criticizing Jefferson Davis. Bed and breakfast places in Beaufort include Old Point Inn (803-524-3177 or 525-6104); Trescott Inn (803-522-8552), a one-time plantation house bought after the Civil War by Congressman William Elliott and floated plank by plank to town on the Beaufort River; 1820 Rhett House Inn (803-524-9030); and 1852 Bay Street Inn (803-524-7720). The town's most elegant eating place is Anchorage House, a seafood and continental-style restaurant installed in a striking 1760-era mansion.

A few miles south of Beaufort lies the town of Port Royal, whose name recalls the early settlement French colonists led by Jean Ribaut tried to establish in the area. In the early 1560s French Huguenots landed in the St. Johns River area near St. Augustine, Florida. Fearing this area lay too close to Spanish territory to survive, the French sailed north and in 1562 landed at Santa Elena (St. Helen), an old Spanish harbor Ribaut renamed Port Royal. Ribaut, wrote his second-in-command, René Laudonnière, "found the place as pleasant as possible," with cedars "smelling so sweetly, that the very fragrant odor made the place seem exceedingly pleasant." But for the twenty-six men who volunteered to stay in the area, where they established a fort named Charlesfort after Charles IX of France, the outcome was hardly "exceedingly pleasant." When the fledgling colony's overbearing leader, Albert de la Pierra, punished one of the pioneers, a man named La Chère, by sending him to a barren island, the others rebelled, killed de la Pierra and rescued La Chère from almost certain death. Abandoning the settlement, the group soon departed for France on a makeshift ship. When the meager provisions ran out the men ate their leather shoes, and after exhausting that delicacy (no doubt the South's earliest example of "sole food"), the group drew lots to choose whom to sacrifice for nourishment. The recently reprieved La Chère's number came up, and his shipmates proceeded to dine on him.

On the grounds of the U.S. Marine Corps base at Parris Island, near Port Royal, stands a monument erected in 1926 by the Huguenot Society to Jean Ribaut and Charlesfort. Later excavations begun in 1979 determined that the site, near the eighth fairway of the base golf course, wasn't where the French established Charlesfort but, rather, the location of Fort San Marcos, a Spanish installation that guarded Santa Elena from 1566 to 1587. Since 1915 the Marines have trained recruits at Parris Island, there "separating the men from the boys" and, more recently, "the women from the girls," as some two thousand females a year graduate. A fifteen-mile loop driving tour takes you around the base to such sights as the Iwo Jima flag-raising monument and training areas such as an obstacle course, a bayonet course, a physical fitness course and a pugil stick (a pole with a boxing glove on each end) course. In the museum (M.–F., 7:30–4:30; Sat. and Sun., 9–4:30, free) a talking "D.I." (Drill Instructor) mannequin explains recruit training, while twice a week at the Grinder, the post's main parade ground, recruit graduation ceremonies take place, complete with the corps band, marching formations and the flags of all fifty states flying from poles over the reviewing stand.

Adjacent to Parris Island is St. Helena, a curious enclave, frozen in time, populated by Gullah-speaking descendants of slaves brought to the area to cultivate the rice plantations. In the eighteenth century the English settlers imported experienced West African rice workers, many from Sierra Leone. When landowners abandoned most of the rice plantations after the Civil War St. Helena remained cut off from the mainstream of American life and from the mainland, at least until the first bridge was completed in 1927. The local black culture thus survived virtually untouched by modern influences. In *Black Yeomanry,* T. J. Woofter, Jr., who studied the island in 1927, observed that the old days still lived at St. Helena, "in the songs and the dialect which fall so strangely on the ear, in the ox-drawn, two-wheeled carts which we so frequently pass, in the yeoman culture of small plots of land with its independent life not fashioned after a money economy. Long arms of the past reach down through tradition to shape the life of the people today." And even up to the present day a certain sense of self-contained isolation prevails on St. Helena. A more recent account in Patricia Jones-Jackson's 1987 *When Roots Die* notes: "Growing up as a black majority almost free from outside social influences . . . undoubtedly affected the attitudes and perceptions of the islanders, to the extent that few of them wish to leave the islands today."

Many old traditions survive on St. Helena, the most pronounced of which is the Gullah language, an English-based Creole enriched with many African words, a quarter of them from Sierra Leone's Krio. For years an internationally renowned witch doctor lived on St. Helena where he treated patients from near and far to de-hex them, a procedure still thought necessary as evidenced by the tufts of cotton stuck in screens and the light blue trim on windows and doors, both fiber and color meant to keep evil spirits away. An intricate network of consanguinity connects many of the island's sixty-two hundred residents, most of them descendants of slaves who, as freedmen after the Civil War, took over the terrain once owned by planters. On the forty-five square-mile island are no incorporated towns but only self-governing communities bound by family ties and church-centered activities.

In 1862 two women from Philadelphia established on St. Helena the South's first school for freed slaves—the Penn Normal, Industrial, and Agricultural School of Frogmore, installed in the St. Helena Baptist Church, which still stands. The Pennsylvanians later brought down from Philadelphia a prefabricated schoolhouse where for forty years they taught the locals. In recent years the institution, now called Penn Community Services, has functioned as a school, health clinic, farm bureau and agency for preserving the island's Gullah heritage. During the early 1960s Martin Luther King, Jr., and his associates met at Penn to plan the 1965 civil rights march from Selma to Montgomery, Alabama. Penn's York Bailey Museum contains a collection of farm tools, photos and clothes of the St. Helena culture. At 7 o'clock every other Sunday evening from September to May the institution hosts a program of spiritual singing. Near Penn, which lies beyond Frogmore, stands the 1855 Brick Church, where Miss Murray and Miss Towne, the school's founders, repose along with members of such early planter families as Fripp, Pritchard and McTureous. Not far from Penn stand, barely, the ruins of the 1740 Chapel of Ease, built for plantation owners who lived too far from the parish church of St. Helena in Beaufort. Along Lands End Road sometimes appears, so locals claim, a ghost called "The Light." You may not see "The Light" but along the way on Seaside Road you will pass many of the old plantation communities, such as Ann Fripp, Tombee, Dr. White and Big House. Life at Tombee—the island's oldest house, built in a T-shape so windows on three sides can brighten all the rooms—is recalled in the book *Tombee: Portrait of a Cotton Planter,* plantation owner Thomas B. Chaplin's journal of pre- and post-Civil War life on St. Helena. Around the island graze small horses, slightly larger than a Shetland pony, called the March Tackie, believed to be descendants of the steeds first brought to the area by the Spanish in the sixteenth century.

Two miles north of where Seaside Road crosses U.S. highway 21 lies Coffin Point Plantation, reached through a tunnel-like stretch formed by Spanish moss that drapes the live oaks that line the road. Built around 1800 by Ebenezer Coffin, the plantation was the largest and most prosperous on the island. In 1891 U.S. Senator James Cameron from Pennsylvania bought the property, which remained in the family until the 1950s, for use as a hunting lodge. His wife, Lizzie, was a friend of Henry Adams, who visited Coffin Point, painted watercolors of the place and mentions the house in *The Education of Henry Adams*. As you head back out to highway 21 you'll pass on the left after about half a mile the old slave cemetery, used these days by those early laborers' descendants who now comprise the Coffin Point community. A left turn on 21 will take you out to the Gay Fish Company docks, sheds and wharf, home port of a dozen or so shrimp boats. At the nearby Shrimp Shack, operated by members of the Gay family, you can get not only shrimp but also clams, shark steak and other seafood, served on a large screened porch overlooking the marsh and Harbor River, a tidal stream tinted at dusk by colorful sunsets.

St. Helena has so far escaped the development which has invaded such neighboring islands as Dataw to the north, a one-time indigo plantation and later a private hunting preserve where a subsidiary of Alcoa Aluminum Company is building a resort, and Fripp, a resort island with restricted access, named after Johannes Fripp, a sea captain given the property in appreciation for guarding the English-held coast against the Spanish. Off of Fripp and St. Helena islands lies Hunting Island State Park (6 until dark, parking fee), one-time haunt of Indians, pirates, antebellum gentlemen stalking deer and waterfowl, and affluent Northerners who used the three-by-one-mile territory as a private hunting area. Because of the island's strategic position near the shipping lane between Charleston and Savannah, a lighthouse was constructed there in 1859. After erosion wore away the base of the building, it fell into disuse, but in 1875 rose a new lighthouse, this time a quarter of a mile inland, away from the shifting sands and pieced together with easily dismantled cast-iron plates, a feature utilized in 1889 when the ocean again ate away the shore line. Moved away from the sea, the present structure functioned until 1933 and now serves as a local landmark whose one hundred and eighty-one steps lead to the top, from which the light once sent its beam eighteen miles out into the coastal waters. By the lighthouse stand the keeper's cottage, the oil house and several other buildings moved from the earlier site, now well offshore. On the sea side of Hunting stretches a long strip of white sand beach, while the inland side fronts on a marsh you can visit on a boardwalk that extends out into the wetland, and between the ocean and marsh lies a maritime forest thick with slash pine and palmetto trees.

To the south of the Beaufort-St. Helena area, beyond Port Royal Sound, lies Hilton Head, the largest of South Carolina's barrier islands—and, for that matter, second only to Long Island in size among the Atlantic coast barrier islands—and the first to be systematically developed as a resort. On the way there you'll pass through Bluffton, an attractive village perched high on a bluff of the May River estuary. In 1825 rice and cotton plantation owners established the town as a summer resort, which in the 1840s became known as the center of the Bluffton Movement, a protest campaign against the U.S. tariff bill of 1842. In 1844 the movement's leader, Congressman Robert Barnwell Rhett, addressed a gathering beneath the boughs of Secession Oak, as the tree came to be known, calling for South Carolina to nullify the bill or to secede. Fifteen years later many of the arguments Rhett mustered reappeared in the pre-Civil War debate over secession. Although many buildings vanished in the war, some antebellum structures survive at Bluffton, among them the Gothic-style 1854 Church of the Cross, an attractive sanctuary with vertical cypress siding and fan-light arches, and 1835 Fripp House Inn (803-757-2139), which offers bed and breakfast.

As for Hilton Head, these days it's a well developed, if not overdeveloped, resort island filled with fancy condos, recreational facilities and "sunbirds" from the North who perch in the area. Hilton Head took its name from Captain William Hilton who in 1663 sighted the island's northeast headland as he sailed into Port Royal Sound on an exploratory trip commissioned by planters on the Caribbean island of Barbados. Earlier that year the Lords Proprietors of Carolina had addressed to the "Gentlemen of Barbados" a proposal to settle in the colony, a place "where the air is, so we are informed, wonderous healthy and temperate, the land proper to bear such commodities . . . as wine, oil, currants, raisins, silks, & c." In his account of the voyage, Captain Hilton confirmed that "The air is clear and sweet, the country very pleasant and delightful; and we could wish that all they that want a happy settlement, of our English nation, were well transported thither." This positive report, published in London in 1664, did much to encourage the first English settlers to found a colony in Carolina in 1670.

Evidences of Hilton Head's early history have been somewhat overwhelmed by modern-day development, starting in 1954 when Sea Pines Plantation, the island's first planned community, was carved from five thousand acres of forest, marsh and beach. In the early days indigo and sea island cotton plantations operated, and during the Civil War Hilton Head was the scene of the nation's largest pre-World War II naval invasion when eighteen Union warships, supported by some fifty-five smaller craft, attacked Fort Walker on November 7, 1861 prior to the landing of some thirteen thousand Federal troops, who established the North's main Atlantic south coast blockade base. One surviving Hilton Head haunt of yesteryear is the Baynard family mausoleum, the island's largest antebellum structure, in the Zion Chapel of Ease cemetery where on moonless nights, so locals claim, a spectral funeral coach can sometimes be seen arriving from the old Baynard ruins at Sea Pines Plantation. You'll find bed and breakfast rooms on Hilton Head at By the Sea (803-671-2851), Halcyon (803-785-7912), Home Away (803-671-5578) and Marshwinds (803-671-9188).

Just south of Hilton Head lies Daufuskie Island, inhabited mainly by descendants of former slaves and reachable only by boat from Hilton Head. Parts of the car-free island, which South Carolina native Pat Conroy wrote about in his novel *The Water Is Wide,* is under resort development by the International Paper Company. Near the intersection of U.S. highway 278 and state road 46 a few miles west of Hilton Head is the Waddell Mariculture Research and Development Center, which researches the commercial cultivation of marine life (tours weekdays by appointment only: 803-757-3795), while the Savannah National Wildlife Refuge by the Georgia border includes a nature drive that winds along the dikes of several old rice plantations, affording a view of wildlife and waterfowl. Offshore, a few miles out to sea from Hilton Head, St. Helena and the other coastal islands in the area, hide South Carolina's least accessible sights—nine artificial fishing reefs and fish-rich shipwrecks. These reefs are created by a manmade material used to substitute for the rock formation that serves as the foundation of a natural reef. Barnacles encrusted on the reef material, rock or an artificial substance, attract feeding fish. The first known use of artificial reefs in the U.S. occurred in South Carolina in the late 1830s, and now the state boasts more than twenty such offshore installations, among them the newest, constructed in June

1984 out of concrete culvert pipe two and a half miles east of Hilton Head; the "Betsy Ross," a World War II ship sunk eighteen miles off Hilton Head; the sunken remains of the "General Gordon"; and a load of steel railroad tracks believed lost from a barge some years ago. Beyond these submerged reefs, coastal Carolina's last human evidences, stretch the long, lonely waters of the Atlantic.

Charleston

Ever since Charleston began in 1670 as South Carolina's first permanent settlement it's been the state's leading city. In the 1760s Alexander Hewat asserted in his book *The Rise and Progress of the Colonies of South Carolina and Georgia:* "With respect to the towns in Carolina, none of them, excepting Charleston, merit the smallest notice. Beaufort, Purysburgh, Jacksonburgh, Dorchester, Camden and Georgetown, are all inconsiderable villages, having in each no more than twenty, thirty, or at most forty dwelling houses. But Charleston, the capital of the Province, may be ranked with the first cities of British America, and yearly advances in size, riches and population." The city began when some one hundred and fifty English colonists settled at a site on the Ashley River near Town Creek where they founded Charles Town. An early report, September 9, 1670, to the Lords Proprietors noted that the settlers were short of clothing and that the supply of "powder was all damnified" when their ship had been damaged, and the colonists also called for a minister "by whose means corrupted youth might be very much reclaimed." Because they found the area near Town Creek unhealthy and difficult to defend against Indians, the settlers moved in 1680 to Oyster Point, the terrain between the Ashley and Cooper Rivers, and within two years a contem-

porary observer described the new town, the beginnings of
present-day Charleston, as "regularly laid out into large and
capacious streets, which to buildings is a great ornament
and beauty."

In the early eighteenth century problems with pirates and
Indians, as well as conflicts between the colonists and the
Lords Proprietors, hastened the end of the Proprietorship,
and in 1717 the people of Charles Town petitioned George
I "that this once flourishing Province may be added to those
under your happy protection," a request the king soon
granted. In the next few years plantation owners from the
countryside built versions of the "single house," those classic
Charleston residences featuring a width of one room, an
alignment perpendicular to the street and two or three tiers
of porches or "piazzas" as the Charlestonians call the breeze-
catching verandas. In the mid-eighteenth century Charleston
flourished, with a proliferation of buildings that still embellish the city. The era saw the opening of the English colonies'
first theater building (1736), start-up of the country's first
fire insurance company (1736), the founding of the nation's
first museum (1773), and the establishment of the St. Cecilia
Society, still the town's most exclusive organization, which
sponsors the St. Cecilia Ball, an event frequented by
Charleston's old-line families. The British, after their defeat
at nearby Fort Moultrie, returned to capture Charleston in
May 1780, and when the Revolution finally ended Charles
Town changed its name to Charleston, an Americanization
signaling a break with the English past.

In 1785 the state capital moved to Columbia from Charleston, which lost its importance in government but not its
dominating political, commercial and cultural position. For
a time the up-country regions remained rather raw and un-
civilized, not unlike how Charles Woodmason, an itinerant
Anglican minister, found that area in the late 1760s and early
1770s: "Thus You have the Travels of a Minister in the Wild

1. White Point Gardens – The Battery
2. Calhoun Mansion
3. Edmonston – Alston House
4. First Baptist Church
5. St. Michael's Church/Cabbage
    Roe Haywood – Washington
    House
6. Washington Square/City Hall
    Nathanial Russell House
8. Old Exchange Building
9. Rainbow Row
10. Hunley Museum
11. Huguenot Church/Dock Street
    Theatre/Old Slave Mart Museum
12. St. Philip's/Thomas Elfe Work-
    shop/Old Powder Magazine/
    Circular Congregational Church
13. City Market
14. Beth Elohim Synagogue
15. Marion Square/Old Citadel
16. US Customs Building
17. Colonial Lake
18. Manigault Mansion
19. Charleston Museum
20. Visitor's Information Center
21. WCSC Broadcasting Museum
22. The Citadel
23. Gibbes Memorial Art Building
24. Unitarian Church
25. Charleston marina (boats to Fort
    Sumter)

CHARLESTON

0   ¼   ½

Woods of America—Destitute often of the very Necessaries of Life—Sometimes starved—Often famished—Exposed to the burning Sun and the scorching Sands—Obliged to fight his Way thro' Banditti, profligates, Reprobates, and the lowest vilest Scum of Mankind." Charleston, meanwhile, became ever more refined, although the 1822 attempted slave insurrection led by Denmark Vesey, who'd bought his freedom for $600 in 1800 from the proceeds of a lottery he'd won, cast ominous shadows over the city's debonair but doomed way of life. When the shelling of Fort Sumter in Charleston harbor exploded on April 12, 1861, the town's aristocrats gathered at the Battery in a festive mood to watch the fireworks.

The opening salvos of the Civil War marked the beginning of the end of an era, and when David MacCrae, a British traveler, visited Charleston in 1868 he "found the old aristocracy still in the dust," with many of the once-genteel gentry "going about with ruin written on their faces." Fires and an 1886 earthquake damaged parts of the city, but many venerable treasures survived, such that Charleston now boasts more than seventy pre-Revolutionary War structures, one hundred and thirty-six late eighteenth-century buildings, and more than six hundred pre-1840 places. In the early part of this century these relics fell into a certain disrepair, but restoration began with the founding in 1920 of the Preservation Society of Charleston, a group that promoted passage in 1931 of the city's zoning ordinance, the nation's first legislation to protect an "old and historic" area, and in 1947 the Historic Charleston Foundation, established to preserve the city's architectural heritage, came into existence. By 1977 the historic city had become such a showplace that Gian Carlo Menotti chose Charleston as the site of the American Spoleto festival (803-722-2764), held for about two and a half weeks from late May to early June. These days the town survives as the best preserved, most authentic and perhaps most delightful major urban remnant of yesteryear in the United States. Although the lashing gales of Hurricane Hugo on September 21, 1989 damaged some of the city's houses, gardens and trees, Charleston's charm remains intact.

The best way to see old Charleston is on foot. The main part of the densely packed peninsula occupies only about one square mile, with two thousand houses, many of historic or cultural interest, crowding the area south of Broad Street, a corner of town known as "S.O.B." Six house museums open to the public give visitors an idea how wealthy planters and merchants lived in the old days: the 1828 Edmondston-Alston House (M.–Sat., 10–5; Sun., 2–5, adm.), which commands a splendid view of the harbor, contains a collection of original family paintings and antiques; the 1770 Heyward-Washington House (M.–Sat., 10–5; Sun., 1–5, adm.), residence of a signer of the Declaration of Independence, served as George Washington's abode ("The lodgings provided for me in this place were very good," the president noted in his diary) when the chief executive made his tour of South Carolina in 1791; the 1803 Joseph Manigault House (M.–Sat., 10–5; Sun., 1–5, adm.), with a long "piazza" (veranda) on the south side; the 1808 Nathaniel Russell House (M.–Sat., 10–5; Sun., 2–5, adm.), a neo-classical gem with a renowned free-standing circular staircase and a spacious garden; the c. 1876 Calhoun Mansion (10–4, adm.), the city's most ornate post-Civil War residence; and the 1817 Aiken-Rhett House (Tu.–Sat., 10–5; Sun., 1–5, adm.), occupied by Governor William Aiken from 1833 to 1887 and headquarters of Confederate General P. G. T. Beauregard during part of the Civil War.

Another old restored house (c. 1760) is the Thomas Elfe Workshop (M.–F., 10–5; Sat., 10–1, adm.), a small version of the Charleston "single house," where the city's most famous cabinetmaker lived and worked, creating his serenely classical showpieces, copies of which Historic Charleston Reproductions (M.–Sat., 10–5) offers for sale. The establishment also sells china with old Charleston patterns and Charleston-inspired fabrics, wallpapers and accessories. Another unusual old residence is the Pink House (M.–Sat., 10–5, free), an early eighteenth-century structure built of coral stone from the West Indies as a sailors' tavern and now an artist's studio and gallery.

Piety permeates Charleston, whose one hundred and eighty churches give the town the name "the Holy City." Noteworthy sanctuaries include the 1891 Circular Congregational (M.–F., 9–1, free), the fourth successor to the original 1806 church; the 1840 Congregation Beth Elohim (sanctuary M.–F., 10–12; museum, M.–F., 9:30–3, free), the nation's second-oldest synagogue and the oldest in continuous use; Emanuel African Methodist, successor to the 1791 "Free African Society" and the site of one-time slave Denmark Vesey's planning for the insurrection he hoped to lead; First Baptist (M.–F., 1–2, free), an 1821 church built to house a congregation established in 1682 founded by Maine Baptists who fled persecution by Puritans; the 1814 First Scots Presbyterian (M.–F., 8:30–5, free), sporting the Church of Scotland seal in the window over the main entrance but lacking bells, never replaced after the congregation voted to give them to the Confederacy in 1863; the 1845 French Huguenot Church (Feb.–May and Oct.–Nov., M.–Sat., 10–12, 2–4, free), the nation's last remaining such sanctuary, which during the 1800s held services coordinated with the tides so that Huguenots from river plantations could arrive on the ebb-tide and return on the flood; the Old Bethel Methodist Church (M.–F., 9–1, free); the 1706 Old St. Andrew's Episcopal (M.–F., 9–3, free), on Ashley River Road ten miles west of town, closed for more than half a century and reopened in 1948 as the oldest still operating house of worship in the Carolinas; the 1817 St. John's Lutheran (M.–F., 8:30–4:30, free), successor to a congregation established in 1742 by Henry Melchior Muhlenburg, "the father of Lutheranism in America"; the 1839 St. Mary's (M.–F., 8:30–4:30, free), the state's oldest Catholic church, whose graveyard contains the remains of local notables; St. Philip's Episcopal, which gave its bells—replaced only in 1976—to make cannons during the Civil War, and where Southern politician John C. Calhoun, Declaration of Independence signer Edward Rutledge, Constitution signer Charles Pinckney and DuBose Heyward, author of *Porgy,* repose; the 1811 Second Presbyterian, whose original sanctuary was so vast preachers had to shout to be heard; the 1787 Unitarian Church (open by appointment: 803-723-4617, free), with an elaborate fantracery ceiling, the city's second-oldest church building; and 1761 St. Michael's Episcopal (M.–Sat., 9–4:30, free), the city's oldest church edifice, George Washington's place of worship during his 1791 visit, whose eight well-traveled bells—they've crossed the ocean five times: imported from England in 1764, repatriated by the British in 1781, ransomed back, and sent to England for recasting after the Civil War and then returned—have for more than two centuries marked the hours for Charlestonians.

St. Michael's stands at Meeting and Broad, called the Four Corners of Law for God's, the city's, the state's and the federal government's, as symbolized by the church, City Hall and the county and federal courthouses. The City Hall council chamber (M.–F., 9–5, free) contains portraits of many prominent citizens, including a John Trumbull likeness of George Washington. Other artworks hang at Elizabeth O'Neill Verner's studio museum, with pastels and etchings by the Charleston native, and at the Gibbes Gallery (Tu.–Sat., 10–5; Sun. and M., 1–5, adm.), whose collection boasts more than three hundred miniature portraits, many of South Carolinians, while other local collections include the

Charleston Museum (9–5, adm.), the nation's oldest (1773), with displays relating to natural history and the history of the city and state; the Confederate Museum (Tu., Th., Sat., 12–3, summer, 11–4, adm.), housed in the 1841 Market Hall, operated since 1898 by the Daughters of the Confederacy; the Old Exchange and Provost Dungeon (M.–Sat., 9–4:30; Sun., 12–4:30, adm.), with wax figures that recall the Revolutionary War-era British prison; Patriot's Point Naval and Maritime Museum (summer, 9–6; winter, 9–5, adm.), with tours of the "U.S.S. Yorktown" aircraft carrier and other craft, such as a nuclear-powered merchant ship and a submarine; and—if ships are your cup of tea—the Charleston Naval Base (Sat.–Sun., 1–4, free), the Navy's third-largest home port and biggest submarine installation, with more than seventy-five craft based there.

Other martial attractions include the American Military Museum (M.–Sat., 10–6; Sun., 1–6, adm.), with a huge collection of uniforms and artifacts from all the services, and The Citadel (8–6, free), established in 1842 and one of the nation's two remaining state military colleges (the other is Virginia Military Institute), with a museum (Sun.–F., 2–5; Sat., 9–5, free) containing exhibits on the school and its graduates, including Generals Mark Clark and William Westmoreland, and presenting on Fridays at 3:45 during the school year a full-dress parade. Another local educational institution is the College of Charleston, founded in 1758 and, when the city began financing it in 1839, the nation's first municipal college.

Other relics of the early days include the 1713 Powder Magazine (M.–F., 9:30–4, adm.), now headquarters of the South Carolina Society of Colonial Dames of America; the 1804 Market (9:30–5, free), filled with cafes and specialty shops; and the Dock Street Theatre (M.–F., 10–5, adm.), opened in 1736 as the nation's first building designed solely for theatrical purposes. Stage plays still take place there,

while two film presentations which will serve to introduce
you to the city are the movie *Dear Charleston* (on the hour
10–4, except 1, adm.) and the multimedia *Charleston Adventure* (9–5, adm.). Other ways to get to know the city include
tours by bicycle or pedal-driven carriages, buses, trolley-like
buses, carriages, ships, and on foot with cassettes, with a
group or with a private guide. For information on firms
offering these various tours you can contact the Charleston Convention and Visitors Bureau, 85 Calhoun Street,
803-723-7641; open 8:30–5:30, from November through February, 8:30–5.

One of the delights of visiting Charleston is to amble
on your own through the old area south of Broad between
"where the Ashley and the Cooper rivers come together to
form the Atlantic Ocean," as the locals like to claim. As
you wander through the old section you'll discover for yourself any number of hidden corners, architectural details and
beguiling vistas and perspectives. Decorated fireplugs in the
area resemble midget sentries, and twisty, pinched ways like
Zig-Zag Alley invite exploration. Old-time lantern-like
lights stand on the streets, many paved with flint nodules
or cobblestones brought from England as ballast on sailing
ships. Along Tradd stands one of the city's densest concen-
trations of early eighteenth-century houses; on East Bay
stretches "Rainbow Row," pastel-hued homes whose inhabitants in the old days would issue party invitations on sta-
tionary matching the house's color so recipients would
immediately know the party's venue; Legare (pronounced
"luh-gree") Street, between numbers 8 and 32, offers picturesque scenes; the "single houses"—the width of a single
room—at 90, 92 and 94 Church Street exhibit "three variations on a theme," as a Charleston historian once observed;
the building at 89-91 Church was Cabbage Row, inspiration
for the Catfish Row of *Porgy and Bess,* and at 76 Church
a plaque marks the spot where DuBose Heyward lived while

he wrote *Porgy,* the novel that inspired Gershwin's 1935 folk opera. The character of Porgy was based on Samuel Smalls, known as Goat Sammy, a beggar who worked the business section of town in a wheeled soapbox drawn by a malodorous goat. When you cross Water Street, Church curves to form a small plaza canopied by the limbs of an old oak, near which stands the 1743 George Eveleigh house, one of the area's rare residences facing the street. Most homes align their sides to the street, with a long piazza on the south side, an arrangement which gave rise to Charleston's "north side manners." This convention makes it impolite to peer from one's north windows and intrude on the privacy of your neighbor's piazza and garden, two of Charleston's most distinctive features which inspired William Dean Howells to note in 1915: "The galleries give the city its peculiar grace, and the gardens its noble extent." The many gardens that embellish the city's residential areas perhaps stem in part from the early planters who settled there. Alice R. Huger Smith observes in her 1917 book *Dwelling Houses of Charleston:* "There was a constant interchange between town and country, and Charleston's social organization never became in those [early] years purely urban, nor did the life of the countryside become purely rural. Architecturally, this continuity is especially noticable."

North of the "S.O.B." quarter lie such other neighborhoods as Ansonborough, a section where the Historic Charleston Foundation carried out its first major restoration project; and the East Side, an architecturally rich but dilapidated four by eight-block area where, after the Civil War, more than three thousand freed black carpenters, ironsmiths, tailors and other craftsmen lived. The city's newest area, which opened in the spring of 1990, is Waterfront Park on the Cooper River at the foot of the Vendue Range quarter in the old historic district. In March and April more than eighty private homes and other sites are open to the public (for information: 803-723-1623), while in September and October candlelight walking tours visit some of the show-places (803-723-5879).

Beyond Charleston's core attractions lie other sights worth seeing. Out in the harbor, perched on a small manmade island, stands Fort Sumter (8:30–7, adm.), a National Monument, where the Civil War began on April 12, 1861, with a Confederate artillery and mortar barrage that led President Lincoln to declare that "the last ray of hope for preserving the Union peaceably expired at the assault on Fort Sumter," while Southern President Jefferson Davis hailed the outpost as the place "where was first given to the breeze the flag of the Confederacy." Of the Confederate shelling and cannon balls Abner Doubleday, later famous for another kind of ball game (baseball), wrote that the scene "was really terrific. The roaring and crackling of the flames, the dense masses of whirling smoke, the bursting of the enemy's shells, and our own, and the sound of masonry falling in every direction, made the fort a pandemonium." Armaments, ruins, the restored forty-foot walls built with seven million bricks and other remnants of the era recall the siege.

Charles Town Landing 1670 (9–5, summer to 6, adm.), on the Ashley River north of town, harkens back to an earlier era in the city's history—the time more than three centuries ago when colonists established South Carolina's first permanent English settlement. Exhibits, a replica of a seventeenth-century trading ship, copies of colonial-era buildings and other displays give the flavor of the colony's formative days. Out on John's Island off highway 700 grows the fourteen-hundred-year-old Angel Oak, a splendid specimen whose twisty, gnarled branches spread one hundred and fifty feet. A trio of show gardens garnish the landscape north of Charleston. Magnolia Plantation (8–dusk, adm.), occupied over the years by eight generations of Draytons, blooms with one of the nation's largest collections of azaleas and camellias. Nearby Middleton Place (9–5, adm.), a magnificent property, features the nation's oldest landscaped garden, the restored antique-crammed main house (c. 1755) and exquisite grounds. Cypress Gardens (9–5, adm.) includes a flower-filled cypress swamp where Francis "the Swamp Fox" Marion used to hide during the Revolutionary War. Near Magnolia Plantation stands 1742 Drayton Hall (tours on the hour 10 to 3, March–Oct., 10–5, adm.), a handsome Georgian-style mansion with splendid architectural details and the only Ashley River plantation house to survive the Civil War intact, supposedly because a quick-witted Confederate officer defended the property by bringing there smallpox-infected slaves. Another showplace, Boone Hall Plantation (April 1–Labor Day, M.–Sat., 8:30–6:30; Sun., 1–5; rest of year, M.–Sat., 9–5; Sun, 1–4, adm.)—off highway 17 six miles northeast of Charleston—was rebuilt in 1935 as a copy of the original mid-eighteenth-century mansion and stands at the end of a three-quarter-mile long alley of oak trees, first planted in 1743. To the northwest of Charleston lies Old Dorchester State Park, where a few remains still evidence what was pre-Revolutionary War South Carolina's third largest town (after Charles Town and Beaufort), founded by Congregational church members from Dorchester, Massachusetts. Nearby Summerville, a one-time health resort, includes lush gardens, flower-filled parks and old houses in a National Register-listed historic district.

The Charleston area boasts nearly one hundred bed and breakfast establishments and one Bed No Breakfast (803-723-4450). Many of the places are represented by Historic Charleston Bed and Breakfast (803-722-6606), Charleston East Bed and Breakfast (803-884-8208) and Charleston Society Bed and Breakfast (803-723-4948). Less expensive places include: Ann Harper's (803-723-3947), Bailey House (803-723-6807), Cannonboro Inn (803-723-8572), and Rutledge Museum Inn and Guest House (803-722-7551).

Up-Country

Columbia—Columbia to the East:
Camden—Sumter—Hartsville—Cheraw—Florence—Columbia
to the South:
Orangeburg—Santee—Aiken—Edgefield—McCormick—Columbia
to the North: Winnsboro—Lancaster—Rock
Hill—York—Kings Mountain—Cowpens—Cherokee
Foothills Scenic Highway—Spartanburg—
Greenville—Pendleton—Clemson—Greenwood

From the time South Carolina began, with the founding of Charleston in 1670, the state has been divided into two regions—"Low-Country and Up-Country, terms that have a special meaning in South Carolina," observed Louis B. Wright in *South Carolina: A Bicentennial History.* "Low-Country and Up-Country in South Carolina had distinct and separate cultures, the result of topography and of the types of people who settled the different regions." For many years the up-country area remained rough-hewn and raw in contrast with the genteel plantation-dominated way of life along the coast and at Charleston. South Carolinian J. Gordon Coogler's famous couplet might well describe the rather uncouth up-country of the early days: "Alas! for the South, her books have grown fewer— / She never was much given to literature." (This verse rhymes in Deep Southern.) After its founding in the center of the state in 1786 as one of the nation's first planned communities, Columbia became the new state capital, a development that somewhat civilized at least part of the up-country, such that by 1848 Alexander McKay, a British traveler, noted of the seat of government: "Columbia is, on the whole, rather an interesting little town. There is about it an air of neatness and elegance, which betokens it to be the residence of a superior class of people."

Still today Columbia remains a pleasant place with an ambiance of understated well-being. Like Austin, Texas; Madison, Wisconsin; and, in the South, Baton Rouge, Louisiana, Columbia is one of the nation's few cities to boast both the state capital and the state university, enhancements that have furnished the town with a number of attractions. Government buildings include the c. 1855 State House (tours on the half hour, M.–F., 9–4, free), set in a well-statued parklike enclave and with a veritable museum of paintings, plaques and historical markers inside; the lovely Governor's Green, which encompasses gardens, the ironwork-bedecked Lace House and the Governor's Mansion (Tu.–Th., 9:30–11:30, 2:45, free, by appointment only: 803-737-1710), formerly part of a military school that burned in 1865; the Department of Archives and History (M.–F., 9–2:30, free), with historical documents and displays; and the South Carolina Criminal Justice Hall of Fame (M.–F., 8:30–5, free), a museum featuring exhibits on the history and present-day activities of the state's law enforcement procedures. Other collections in town include the Museum of Art and Gibbes Planetarium (Tu.–F., 10–5; Sat. and Sun., 1–5, adm.); the Confederate Relic Room and Museum (M.–F., 9–5, free); the Fort Jackson Museum (Tu.–Sun., 1–4, free), with displays on recruit training and on the history of the military base, where the practice of wearing special unit patches originated; Mann-Simons Cottage (Tu.–F., 10–4; Sat., 11–2, by appointment only: 803-252-1450, adm.), housing a museum of African-American culture; Riverbanks Zoo (9–4, to 6 summer weekends, adm.), specializing in endangered species; the new (1988) South Carolina State Museum (M.–Sat., 10–5; Sun., 1–5, adm.), featuring four floors of exhibits on science, history, art and natural history installed in the cavernous 1894 building that housed Columbia Mills, the world's first totally electric textile mill; and the University's McKissick Museum (M.–F., 9–4; Sat., 10–5; Sun., 1–5, closed weekends in summer, free), with an eclectic range of items, including the Movietonews Exhibit, based on the famous Movie Tone newsreels. Also on campus, which boasts the 1840 South Caroliniana Library, the nation's first separate college library building, curves the central "Horseshoe," the original university area (1805–50), lined with National Register-listed nineteenth-century Georgian-style structures.

Other venerable Columbia buildings include Chestnut Cottage, home of Mary Boykin Chesnut who wrote *Mary Chesnut's Civil War,* a well-known account of the South during the war years; the Palmetto Building downtown, its facade embellished with terra cotta designs and palmetto tree motifs; the Town Theatre, which houses the nation's first community troupe (1924); and The Big Apple, a former black nightspot housed in a one-time synagogue built in 1910. Columbia churches include the 1859 First Baptist, site of the First Secession Convention, held in December 1860, a session removed to Charleston because of a smallpox scare in the capital; 1846 Trinity Cathedral, modeled after York Minster in England, whose graveyard contains the tombs of six former governors and Secretary of State James F. Byrnes; and 1853 First Presbyterian, where Anne Pamela Cunningham, who in 1853 spearheaded the drive to save George Washington's Mount Vernon, and the parents of Woodrow Wilson repose. The Wilson Boyhood Home (Tu.–Sat., 10–4; Sun., 2–5, adm.), listed on the National Register, contains memorabilia of the U.S. President, who lived there in the 1870s. Other museum houses in town include the 1818 Hampton-Preston Mansion (Tu.–Sat., 10–4; Sun., 2–5, adm.), also Register-listed, with elaborate family furnishings, and, just across the street, the Robert Mills House (Tu.–Sat., 10–4; Sun., 2–5, adm.), designed by Mills, protege of Thomas Jefferson and architect of the Washington Monument.

The Riverfront Park and Historic Columbia Canal offers a glimpse of a turn-of-the-century waterworks and a waterway built more than one hundred and fifty years ago. Town founder Thomas Taylor and family members repose in the Taylor Burial Ground, while other early Columbia citizens, including two mayors, lie in the cemetery of the Hebrew Benevolent Society, organized in 1822, a still-functioning charitable organization. On the Federal Land Bank Building at Taylor and Marion Streets, artist Blue Sky painted a mural of a highway advancing through a tunnel so realistic that visitors, it's said, occasionally consider entering it—a hard way to leave town. You'll find bed and breakfast in Columbia at Claussen's Inn at Five Points (803-765-0440).

Around Columbia lie a few nearby attractions, such as Lake Murray, site of what was upon its completion in 1930 the world's largest earthen dam, where Dreher Island State Park offers recreational facilities. By the lake at Irmo—named in 1890 from the last names of two railroad officials, Irdell and Mosley—the Cat's Tale (803-732-1959) offers bed and breakfast; while up at Little Mountain to the north—beyond White Rock, so named as Indians supposedly gathered there flint rock to make arrowheads—the annual Reunion, South Carolina's oldest folk festival, takes place in early August (for information: 308-345-3902). You'll also find bed and breakfast at the Pompey Town Inn (803-359-9100) in Lexington, to the west of Columbia, an attractive little town, originally called Saxe Gotha by the German settlers, whose County Museum (Tu.–Sat., 10–4; Sun., 1–4, adm.) includes a group of old regional houses, among them the 1772 Conley Log Cabin; the 1774 Senn House; the Hazelins House, once a Lutheran seminary where in 1891 an evangelist named Charlie Tillman wrote the spiritual "Give Me That Old Time Religion"; and the Oak Grove Schoolhouse (c. 1820), where students occasionally locked out the teacher, who retaliated by putting a board atop the chimney to smoke the pranksters into the open. The town's century-old cotton mill, which manufactured a heavy red material used for prison uniforms in California, has been restored as a shopping area.

As you head east out of Columbia you'll pass Sesquicentennial State Park, known by the less syllabic designation "Sesqui," which occupies land purchased with proceeds of souvenir half-dollars minted and sold in 1937 to commemorate the state's one hundred and fiftieth anniversary. On the park grounds stands a 1756 log cabin built in a style favored by pioneers from Germany. Camden, established in 1732, holds the distinction for being South Carolina's oldest inland city. Historic Camden (June 1–Aug. 31, Tu.–F., 10–5; Sat., 10–5; Sun., 1–5; Sept. 1–May 31, Tu.–F., 10–4; Sat., 10–5; Sun., 1–5, adm.) comprises old dwellings—including Kershaw House, where English General Cornwallis headquartered—dioramas and displays which recall the area's Revolutionary War era, when the British twice defeated the Americans in major local encounters. In 1825 the Marquis de Lafayette visited Camden to dedicate a monument to Baron De Kalb, the German who commanded the American army in the South, mortally wounded in the August 16, 1780, Battle of Camden, an encounter watched by thirteen-year-old Andrew Jackson from the stockade where the British had impounded him. At Ivy Lodge (c. 1780), 1205 Broad, once lived Dr. Simon Baruch, who performed the first known successful operation to remove a perforated appendix, but he's perhaps better known as the father of financier Bernard M. Baruch. More than sixty attractive old homes grace the Historic District in Camden, where the Archives (M.–F., 8–12, 1–5, free) include old documents as well as artifacts from the town's past. Camden's 1759 Quaker Cemetery contains as markers nothing but simple arched brick monuments as the Quakers considered more elaborate memorials too ostentatious.

North of Camden, once a dueling center, lies Springdale

Race Course, home of the Colonial Cup Steeplechase and the Carolina Cup, at whose training center you can watch the horses go through their paces (from 7:30 to 9:30 in the morning). Bed and breakfast in Camden is available at Greenleaf Inn (803-425-1806), once the home of Lincoln's brother-in-law, and at Aberdeen (803-432-9861 weekdays, 803-432-2524 evenings and weekends), while four miles east of town HoField Garden (M.–F., 8–7; Sat., 8–2) offers summer visitors "pick-'em-yourself" fruits and vegetables.

Down at Sumter you'll find Swan Lake Iris Gardens (8–dark, free) which, true to its name, displays irises and swans; the Williams-Brice Museum and Archives (museum, Tu.–Sat., 10–5; Sun., 2–5; archives, W.–Sat., 2–5, free) with period furniture and genealogical records; the Sumter Gallery of Art (M.–F., 11–5; Sat. and Sun. Sept.–May, 2–5, free); and the National Register-listed 1840 house of artist Elizabeth White. At Sumter lives—or did as late as 1989, when she was ninety-seven—Daisy Cave, the last surviving widow of a Confederate veteran, Henry Cave, age seventy-five when she married him in the 1920s. North of U.S. highway 378, on state road 261 near Stateburg, stands the 1850 Church of the Holy Cross, a Gothic Revival-style sanctuary in a peaceful rustic setting. There repose Revolutionary War hero Thomas Sumter, after whom Fort Sumter at Charleston is named, and American diplomat Joel Poinsett, whose name survives in "poinsettia," a flower he discovered in Mexico, and whom Poinsett State Park to the south commemorates. At the village of Mayesville, east of Sumter, Windsong Bed and Breakfast (803-453-5004) offers accommodations.

Woods Bay State Park, farther east, includes a fifteen hundred-acre egg-shaped swamp sunk into a depression, typical of other elliptical sinkholes in the region, formed as meteorite scars, some scientists say, or an area where springs once agitated the terrain. In late July every year Lake City to the east celebrates the Tobacco Festival, with displays of the leaf and an auctioneer contest. Nearby Truluck Vineyards (Tu.–Sat., 10:30–5:30, free), nestled among the tobacco fields, offers tours and tastings, and the Brownton Museum (F. and Sat., 9:30–4:30; Sun., 2–4:30, adm.), farther east on highway 341, contains a collection of mid-nineteenth-century farm buildings. North of Woods Bay lies Lee State Park, with a scenic roadway past natural areas, an old sawmill and the pasture that watered drought-stricken cattle brought by train from the parched Western states during the Dust Bowl era. Bethune, to the northwest, hosts every April a Chicken Strut in commemoration of the town's distinction as the nation's largest egg producer. If you ever dreamed of seeing a Chicken Strut festival April in Bethune—not April in Paris—is the place to be. Nearby Hartsville offers Kalmia Gardens Arboretum (8–5, free), a small museum (M.–F., 10–5; Sun., 3–5, free) housed in the 1908 train depot—the caboose parked there contains railroad arti-facts—and the H. B. Robinson Information Center (M.–F., 8:30–4:30, free) at the state's first commercial nuclear gene-rating facility, with displays on atomic power.

West of town stands the Jacob Kelley House (c. 1820) where Sherman headquartered for two days in 1865 (Feb.–Nov., first Sunday of the month, 3–5, free). In mid-April Darlington, whose museum (M.–F., free) occupies the for-mer county jail, celebrates a Renaissance Faire, with a madri-gal banquet and other entertainments (for information: 803-395-2310). In 1866 freedmen, former slaves, established the St. James Church on Pease Street which, according to tradition, Federal occupation troops supplied with a bell they'd lifted from nearby St. John's Academy, located in the town's historic district. The NMPA Stock Car Hall of Fame/Joe Weatherly Museum (9–5, adm.) claims the world's

largest collection of race cars. On North Main a mural by
Blue Sky depicts Darlington, a center for late-summer tobacco auctions of a century ago.

As you head north to what's known as the Old Cheraws
corner of Carolina you'll pass through Society Hill, a hamlet
(population: nine hundred) settled by Welsh Baptists in 1736,
where in 1777 the St. David's Society established one of
the nation's first free public schools, an institution that
turned the town into an intellectual center. Early houses and
such buildings as Trinity Church (c. 1834), the Old Library
(c. 1822), the Coker-Rogers (c. 1860) and the Sompayrae
Stores (c. 1813) survive to recall Society Hill's one-time cultural importance. Off to the west stretches the Sandhills National Wildlife Refuge and the Sandhills State Forest, named
for the strip of sandy terrain that cuts across part of South
Carolina, dunes formed when the ocean reached the area.
The refuge and forest preserve part of the million-year-old
sand hills, many elsewhere damaged by latter-day plantings
of pine and scrub oak. Just north of Cheraw State Park,
South Carolina's oldest such facility (1934), lies Cheraw,
which immodestly calls itself "the prettiest town in Dixie."
Established around 1740 as a trading post on the Great Pee
Dee River, the longest stream that flows into the North Atlantic, photogenic Cheraw boasts a rich collection of antique
buildings, among them tiered-steeple St. David's Episcopal
(1768), the last church built in South Carolina under authority of King George, whose cemetery contains what's supposedly the nation's oldest monument to Confederate dead; the
Merchant's Bank (1835), the last to honor Confederate currency, still a bank (First Citizens) but no longer accepting
Dixie money; and the early nineteenth-century structures
around the Town Green, including the Town Hall, Market
Hall, the Inglis-McIver Law Office and the Lyceum Museum
(M.–F., 8–5, free), with history displays. Antique-filled
Spears Bed and Breakfast in Cheraw offers accommodations

(803-537-7733). Chesterfield, northwest of Cheraw, an attractive town with turn-of-the-century structures, serves as seat of Chesterfield County, the first to call for secession from the Union.

East of Cheraw lies Bennettsville, where the Marlboro County Historical Museum (M.–F., 10–1; Tu.–Th., 2–5, free) houses a medical museum and other artifacts from the past, also recalled by the 1827 Jennings-Brown House and the 1833 Female Academy. Marlboro County—where, locals claim, the rich farmland once sold not by the acre but by the pound—took its name from England's Duke of Marlborough, whose Blenheim Palace estate (where Winston Churchill was born) near Oxford gave its title to the town of Blenheim, perched by mineral springs whose waters the Blenheim Ginger Ale Company (tours available) uses to manufacture a spicy beverage. In tiny Clio, east of Bennettsville, you'll find mansions built when cotton brought great prosperity to the area. Around Clio, which supposedly had more millionaires per capita than any place in the nation, cotton still grows, and in the fall you can see in the area the ginning operation. Also surviving from the old days is Calhoun's store, built in 1905 and frozen in its appearance as of 1925 when a depression brought the region to a standstill.

Just by the North Carolina line lies South of the Border, a rather garish tourist stop, or perhaps trap, with a Mexican motif, a theme symbolized by the neon-encrusted sombrero-topped figure and by Pedro's, the name used to designate the village-like compound of six eateries, twelve gift shops, a huge (three hundred rooms) motel and other facilities. At nearby Dillon stands the National Register-listed Dillon House (open by appointment: 803-774-9051, free), a museum that recalls town founder James W. Dillon, and near town rises the Dillon Marriage Chapel (M.–F., after 5, for emergency use on weekends: 803-774-2671) where more than seven thousand knots are tied annually. To the south lies Little Pee Dee State Park, which occupies part of an area once called "The Devil's Woodyard." The two Pee Dee Rivers and the Pee Dee region, which take their name from the Pedee Indians, might have been immortalized in Stephen Foster's famous song "Old Folks at Home," but second thoughts induced the composer to revise the lyrics, which originally read, "Way down upon the Pee Dee River." During the tobacco season in August and September auctions take place (visitors welcome) at the huge warehouse at Dillon and at Mullins, where you'll find bed and breakfast at Webster Manor (803-464-9632). Tobacco warehouses that hold auctions also operate in the region at such towns as Lake City, Timmonsville, Lamar, Hemingway and Pamplico.

At Marion survive a scattering of turn-of-the-century relics, among them the Old Town Hall and the Opera House (M.–F., 9–4, free) and the Marion Museum (M., W., Th., F., 9–12, 1–5, free), installed in an old schoolhouse. Although restored in 1970, the 1853 Marion County Courthouse retains an antiquated touch of individualism, with each iron step proudly bearing the metal worker's name, "Hayward Bartlett, Baltimore." Near the bridge over the Great Pee Dee River beyond Pee Dee, west of Marion, once operated a Confederate navy yard, where the wooden gunboat "C.S.S. Pee Dee" was launched in November 1864, only to be burned the following March to prevent its capture by Federal forces.

On the way to Florence you'll pass Mars Bluff, where the Wilmington and Manchester Railroad wanted to establish a depot in the 1850s. Colonel Eli Gregg, owner of the settlement's largest store, refused the request so the line founded Florence, named for the baby daughter of the rail company's president. Located halfway between New York and Miami, Florence became a major railroad center, site of one of the three re-icing plants once used on the Florida–New York run to refrigerate perishable produce. The Florence Museum (Tu.–Sat., 10–5; Sun., 2–5, free) contains displays on history, art and science; the Air and Missile Museum (9–5, adm.) offers planes, weapons and astronaut Alan Shepherd's space suit; and in Timrod Park stands a memorial to Henry Timrod, so-called Confederate poet laureate, who in 1859 taught in the one-room schoolhouse there.

Returning now to Columbia, here's the itinerary from the state capital to the south. To the southwest lie the little towns of Pelion, which in early August hosts the annual Peanut Party (for information: 803-894-3535), and Salley, where in late November the Chitlin' Strut (803-258-3331) enlivens things, while nearby Springfield hosts a Frog Jump and Egg Strike, a messy testing of shell strength. To the southeast of Columbia stretches Congaree Swamp National Monument (8:30–5), remnant of the great chain of swamps that once checkered the landscape from the Chesapeake Bay to east Texas. The area includes some ninety species of trees, fully half of Europe's total number of types. Trails take you through thick forests, their towering trees nourished by fertile soils deposited when the ten or so annual floods wash nutrient-rich dirt into the area. Animals survive the floods by retreating to high points; a park ranger once saw a trio of pigs perched atop a floating log to ride out the surging waters. At nearby St. Matthews—which in late April celebrates the annual Purple Martin Festival (803-874-3791) to mark the bird's return to the area—you'll find the Calhoun County Museum (M.–F., 9–4, free), with history exhibits that recall the era when the surrounding region included some of the state's first inland plantations.

Off to the east lies the Santee Cooper country where Lakes Marion and Moultrie, connected by a six and a half-mile long channel, brim with fleshy fish that challenge anglers. The waters there yielded the world's record channel catfish, a fifty-eight-pound specimen. Santee State Park offers accommodations in unusual "rondette" cabins (803-854-2408), some perched on piers that extend into the lake. A trail and visitor center at the Santee National Wildlife Refuge (M.–F., 8–4:30, free) offers an introduction to the migratory birds that frequent the enclave, located along the Atlantic Flyway. The town of Eutawville stands at the site where the Battle of Eutaw Springs took place on September 8, 1781—only six weeks before Cornwallis's surrender at Yorktown—as the last major Revolutionary War engagement in South Carolina, which suffered from more Yankee-British encounters during the conflict, a hundred and thirty-seven, than any other state.

To the south lies Francis Beidler Forest (Tu.–Sun., 9–5, adm.), which encompasses the Four Hole Swamp and the world's largest stand of bald cypress and tupelo gum trees, while back to the northwest is Orangeburg, named for the Prince of Orange, son-in-law of England's King George II, where you'll find the Edisto Memorial Gardens (8–dusk, free), a National Fish Hatchery (M.–F., 8–4, free), and the Stanback Museum and Planetarium (Sept.–May, 9–4:30, adm.). Residents of the town of North near Orangeburg, which in early January hosts the annual Grand American Coon Hunt, sometimes confuse outsiders by stating they are from North, South Carolina.

Other attractions around Orangeburg County include the Farm Museum (open by appointment: 803-247-5143 or 247-2952, free) at Neeses, which boasts the state's first (1981) and only mushroom farm; an old train depot at Cope, center of one of the nation's first Rural Free Delivery (R.F.D.) mail routes; and Branchville, established in 1734, site of what was supposedly the world's first railroad junction, where the tracks of the line from Charleston branched off to Hamburg and to Columbia. On the line began the nation's first scheduled steam railway service on December 25, 1830, and by 1833 the one hundred and thirty-six-mile route between

Charleston and Hamburg had become the world's longest railway. Branchville's 1877 depot, listed on the National Register, houses a museum filled with train memorabilia. At nearby Rowesville is Cattle Creek Campground, an old-fashioned meeting area established by Methodists in 1786. The encampment—the present buildings date from 1899—thrived under Bishop Francis Asbury, an early religious leader, who vividly recorded in his *Journal* impressions of a trip he made in 1786 through South Carolina. At one point he complained about the "wickedness, mills and stills: a prophet of strong drink would be acceptable to many of these people." Another entry noted: "I could not but admire the curiosity of the people—my wig was as great a subject of speculation as some wonderful animal from Africa or India would have been."

In the little town of Smoaks, south of Branchville, stands Trinity Methodist Church, a lovely white wood American Gothic structure, and farther south lies Walterboro, with an attractive group of homes and churches in the Historic District, the 1820 Little Library, and the 1822 Colleton County Courthouse, its brick stuccoed to resemble stone. County residents consume more rice per capita than anywhere else in the U.S., a taste celebrated at Walterboro's annual Rice Festival, held in late April. Early nineteenth-century homes stand along U.S. highway 17-A near Hendersonville, and at Jacksonboro, once called Pon Pon, sat the first South Carolina legislature when the city served as provisional state capital in 1782 while Charleston was under siege. Along the county's northeastern border snakes the Edisto, the world's longest free-flowing black-water stream, the "black" referring both to the color of the tannin-rich spring water and to the absence of white-water riffles and other disturbances. For information on kayak or canoe rentals for trips on the fifty-six-mile water trail: 803-549-9595. At Ridgeland off to the southwest the Pratt Memorial Library (M.–F., 11–6, free) houses a large collection of rare books, Civil War relics, old maps and prints, and Indian artifacts. The hamlet of Switzerland recalls Jean Pierre Purry of Neufchatel, Switzerland, who in 1731 founded the nearby settlement of Purrysburg on land given him by the king of England. At Estill, back to the north, the John Lawton House (803-625-3240) offers bed and breakfast. Near the courthouse at Hampton, the county seat, stands the 1878 Jail which houses a history museum upstairs (Tu. and Th., 4–6, free), while up at Brunson the 1906 Town Hall once stood on stilts to cover the town's artesian well.

North of Allendale, seat of South Carolina's newest county (1919), lies Barnwell, with the 1831 St. Andrew's Church, the 1857 Gothic-style Church of the Holy Apostles, used as a stable by General Sherman's forces, the County Museum (W., Th., Sun., 2:30–5:30; F., 10–1, free) and, in courthouse square, a century-and-a-half-old vertical sundial, said to be the nation's only surviving such relic. North of town bubble Healing Springs, source of medicinal mineral water, and nearby is the 1850 Baptist church which once baptized members in the springs. East of Barnwell lies Bamberg, with a historic district embellished with antebellum houses. Near town is the reconstructed Woodlands Plantation (open by appointment: 803-245-4427, free), home of author William Gilmore Simms. Off to the west lurks the Savannah River Plant, which produces tritium, a gas used to enhance the power of nuclear warheads. When the federal government acquired some 250,000 acres for the plant, operated for years by the du Pont Company, many landowners moved their houses, with at least one entire settlement, Ellenton, being transported north where it rematerialized under the name New Ellenton.

Aiken is a horsy, fancy sort of city where in the late nineteenth-century wealthy Yankees wintered and where, these days, some of the nation's fastest steeds get their training. The town's Whitney Field, opened in 1882, is the nation's oldest polo grounds. The Thoroughbred Hall of Fame (Oct.–June, Tu.–Sun., 2–5, free) houses racing exhibits, while the Aiken County Historical Museum (M., W., F., 10–4, free) includes an 1808 log house, a restored one-room schoolhouse and a replica of "The Best Friend," the nation's first passenger steam engine, which blew up within a year of starting service in the winter of 1830 when a disgruntled fireman sat on the safety valve lever until the engine exploded, the fireman going up with it. Attracted by Aiken's fair weather, in December 1882 German astronomers set up their instruments to observe the transit of Venus between the sun and the earth, an event commemorated by a marker in the gardens of the Henderson home, Laurens Street and Edgefield Avenue.

At Graniteville, near Aiken, began the South's first cotton mill (1847), the beginnings of the region's extensive textile industry. Old mill houses that line the canal along Blue Row recall the era, while to the south Redcliff Plantation State Park includes the 1850s mansion of Governor James Henry Hammon (Sat., 10–3; Sun., 12–3, adm.). Various towns scattered around the area offer bed and breakfast rooms: in Aiken, the Briar Patch (803-649-2010), the Brodie Residence (803-648-1455), the Chancellor Carroll House (803-649-5396), Holley Inn (803-648-4265), Pine Knoll Inn (803-649-5939) and National Register-listed Willcox Inn (803-649-1377), which hosted the Astors, the Vanderbilts, Winston Churchill and other celebrities; at Montmorenci, Annie's Inn (803-649-6836); at Beach Island, the Cedars (803-827-0248); at North Augusta, Bloom Hill (803-593-2573). Bed and breakfast accommodations are also available at Edgefield—home of long-time U.S. Senator Strom Thurmond and where exhibits at the Pottersville Museum (F.–M., W., 9–6, free) recall the area's nineteenth-century pottery trade—at the Inn On Main (803-637-3364) and the Plantation House (803-637-3789) in the National Register-listed Historic District; in Johnston, "Peach Capital of the World," at Cox House Inn (803-275-3346); and in Leesville, at Able House Inn (803-532-2763). In and around McCormick, which sits atop some five miles of gold-mine tunnels and which was named for reaper inventor Cyrus H. McCormick, who donated some of the land the town occupies, are such antiquated grist grinders as Price's, Calhoun and Dorn's Mills, all listed on the National Register; the Guillebeau House (c. 1770), last surviving structure of the French Huguenots who settled in the area in 1764; and the 1747 John de la Howe School, one of the nation's first privately funded child-care institutions. Hickory Knob State Park, tucked into the woods by Clarks Hill Lake, is a country-club-like resort area with rustic cabins (for reservations: 803-443-2151), a golf course and a wide range of recreational facilities.

Returning once again to Columbia, the itinerary north from the state capital takes you first up to Winnsboro, self-described as "the Charleston of the up-country." In the town's central section, which forms a National Register Historic District, you'll find the Fairfield County Museum (M., W., F., 10:30–12:30, 1:30–4:30, second and fourth Sunday of the month, 2–4, free), housed in a Federal-style building (c. 1830); the 1833 boxy brick building that sports what's supposedly the nation's longest continuously running town clock; and the 1823 courthouse. Over at Ridgeway to the east are the 1853 Century House, Confederate General Beauregard's headquarters; the Old Ruff Store (1847)—across from which stands what is claimed to be the world's smallest police station, a claim also asserted by Carrabelle in northern Florida—and out on highway 34 just east of town is a recently revived gold mine. North of Ridgeway lies the picturesque hamlet of White Oak, listed on the National Register in 1985, while to the northeast—beyond Great Falls, known locally as Flopeye, so called for an early droopy-lidded general store owner named Andy Morrison—is Lancaster, where much history lingers. At the County Courthouse (c. 1825), designed by Charleston's Robert Mills, one of America's first professional architects, occurred what was supposedly the nation's last witchcraft trial (1813). Murals of local residents decorate some of the town's buildings, while nearby Springs Industries claims to be the South's largest textile mill under one roof. About a mile and a half north of the courthouse stood Barr's Tavern where George Washington breakfasted on May 27, 1791, paying by giving the proprietor's young daughter half a Spanish dollar the president cut with his sword. The Wade-Beckham House (803-285-1105) near Lancaster offers bed and breakfast in a restored 1830 farmhouse.

About three miles west of highway 21 is Waxhaw Presbyterian, up-state Carolina's first church, established in 1755, where Andrew Jackson was baptized and where his father reposes. Although North Carolina claims otherwise, Andrew Jackson was apparently born (1767) in the area now occupied by Andrew Jackson State Park, where a museum contains displays recalling the back country during the pioneer era when the future president grew up in the area. The National Register-listed Historic District at Chester to the west includes Aaron Burr Rock, which the former vice-president mounted in 1807 to plead for rescue from his guards, taking him to Richmond, Virginia, to be tried for treason.

Farther north—beyond Historic Brattonsville (March–Oct., Tu. and Th., 10–4; Sun., 2–5, adm.), a restored settlement which shows the evolution of the Bratton family and a social system from bygone times—lies Rock Hill, with flower-filled Glencairn Gardens (open during daylight hours, free); Winthrop College, its campus a National Historic District; and the Museum of York County (Tu.–Sat., 10–5; Sun.,

1–5, adm.), which features animal exhibits. Near the Gardens is Oakland Inn (803-329-8147), which offers bed and breakfast. At Fort Mill just to the north is the Heritage USA theme park, once controlled by televangelist Jim Bakker whom the federal government accused of defrauding his followers by selling lifetime lodging rights at the facility. Nearby York, where the National Register-listed Brandon House (803-684-2353) furnishes bed and breakfast, boasts one of the nation's largest Register-listed Historic Districts, an enclave with more than one hundred and eighty landmarks. In York County lies South Carolina's only Indian community, inhabited by Catawba who, in a Federal District Court suit, claim title to more than 144,000 acres in the county. Exhibits and a battlefield trail at Kings Mountain National Military Park up near the North Carolina border recall the famous 1780 victory by the "over-mountain" men who marched to the area from the Watauga River in Tennessee. The rag-tag band of volunteers defeated the British in one of the Revolutionary War's most pivotal encounters. British commander Patrick Ferguson, who maneuvered his men by blowing signals on a large silver whistle, had taunted the makeshift American force as "back water men . . . a set of mongrels," but the "over-mountain" men gained their revenge by killing the cocky major.

At nearby Kings Mountain State Park a dozen or so old buildings in the History Farm recreate a mid-nineteenth-century up-country farmstead. Cowpens National Battlefield (9–5, free) to the west—beyond Gaffney, over which towers a million-gallon peach-shaped water tank—recalls another crucial American Revolutionary War victory when Colonel William Washington, a distant cousin of George, led a cavalry charge on January 17, 1781, which broke the power of the British forces. Off to the west of Cowpens—whose name recalls the cattle herds that once grazed there, tended by America's first cowboys—stretches Cherokee

Foothills Scenic Highway, a hundred and thirty-mile long road that takes you through the northern South Carolina hill country to or near such sights as 1909 Campbell Bridge, the state's only surviving covered bridge; 1820 Poinsett Bridge, a rough stone Gothic arch, the state's oldest span; thirty-five hundred and forty-eight-foot Sassafras Mountain, South Carolina's highest point; an abandoned 1850s railway tunnel on a line intended to link Charleston and the Middle West; and waterfalls, scenic outlooks and a series of state parks, among them Caesars Head, with a splendid view of the Blue Ridge Mountains, Table Rock, Keowee Toxaway, with Cherokee artifacts on display; and the nearby Duke Power Company World of Energy facility that traces the history of electricity; and Oconee, near which survives Oconee Station, the up-country's oldest building, a former trading post.

South of Cowpens lies Spartanburg, named for the so-called "Spartan Rifles" regiment that in 1781 helped rout the British at Cowpens. At Walnut Grove Plantation (April–Oct., Tu.–Sat., 11–5; Sun., 2–5, adm.) lived Kate Moore Barry, a Yankee scout during the battle of Cowpens. Another antique local residence is the Price House (c. 1795), a rather severe-looking Dutch-style brick box (Tu.–Sat., 11–5; Sun., 2–5, adm.) where Thomas Price operated a "house of entertainment"—an establishment to bed and board stagecoach travelers. The County Regional Museum (mid-Sept.–May, Tu.–Sat., 10–12, 3–5; Sun., 3–5, June–mid-Sept., closed Sun., free) offers scale models of Walnut Grove and the Price House, as well as exhibits on the area's history. Nearby Croft State Park occupies a World War II infantry training center, an installation where former Secretary of State Henry Kissinger obtained his U.S. citizenship papers. National Register-listed Nicholls-Crook Plantation (803-583-7337) in Spartanburg offers bed and breakfast.

Some distance south of Spartanburg lie Laurens—where

Andrew Johnson, Lincoln's successor, operated a tailor shop, and where the unusual 1859 Octagonal House stands—and Rose Hill State Park with the restored 1832 plantation mansion (Sat. and Sun., 1–4, adm.) of William Henry Gist, "the Secession Governor." An ardent secessionist, Gist lost his son and his cousin, graphically named States Rights Gist, in the war he helped bring about. Tiny Prosperity to the south in Newberry County—supposedly so called as the pioneers found the land so fruitful it was "as pretty as a new berry"—changed its name from Frog Level to a more enticing designation.

Greenville, back to the north, offers some unusually good museums, among them the County Art Museum, (Tu.–Sat., 10–5; Sun., 1–5, free), with a collection of works by Andrew Wyeth; the Art Gallery (Tu.–Sun., 2–5, free), featuring works with a religious theme by such artists as Rembrandt, Rubens, Titian and Van Dyke, on the campus of Bob Jones University, the world's largest nondenominational Christian liberal arts institution, with fifty-five hundred students; the relatively new (1987) Cultural Exchange Center (Th., 2–6; F., 7–9; Sat., 10–4; Sun., 3–5. free), dedicated to black history and culture; and the more than three hundred textiles from around the world on display at Liberty Life Corporation (M.–F., 9:30–5, by appointment only: 803-268-8111, free). Out on the northern edge of town nestles Furman University, occupying a dreamy parklike enclave filled with trees, flowers and other garnishments. Nearby lies Paris Mountain State Park, named for Richard Pearis, the area's first white settler, an Indian trader who married a squaw, and whose property the state confiscated when he sided with the British during the Revolutionary War. True to its name, Pumpkintown to the north hosts a Pumpkin Festival in mid-October (803-878-9937), while at Pickens off to the west even law-abiders go to jail—a Gothic-like crenellated building—there to visit the Pickens County Museum which contains both history (M. and F., 2–5; W., 9–12; Th., 9–12, 1–4, free) and art (Tu., 1–5; W.–F., 9–12 and 1–5; Sun., 3–5, free) sections. The 1825 Hagood Mill, a weathered wood installation by a rocky stream, still goes about its daily grind. Around the county you'll find such towns as Nine Times and Six Mile, thought to have been named by early-day soldiers or trappers to describe each settlement's location.

South of Pickens, beyond Central—named for its position as midpoint of the old Atlanta and Charlotte Airline Railroad—lies Pendleton, center of the so called Pendleton District comprised of Anderson, Oconee and Pickens counties, an area delineated in 1789 out of lands ceded by the Cherokee. The District's visitor center occupies the c. 1850 Hunter's Store, which contains displays, crafts and information on one of the country's largest historic districts. In the middle of the picturesque village green stands Farmers Society Hall, started in 1826 as a courthouse but completed as a meeting place, the nation's oldest such assembly building in continuous use. The Agricultural Museum (open by appointment: 803-646-3782, free) west of town contains antique items, including an early cotton gin pre-dating Eli Whitney's 1793 version, that recall the early days of farming in the Pendleton District. Liberty Hall Inn (803-646-7500) offers bed and breakfast accommodations in Pendleton, as does the Chisman House (803-639-2939) in nearby Clemson, home of Clemson University, which occupies land given a century ago by Thomas G. Clemson, son-in-law of U.S. Senator and Southern leader John C. Calhoun, whose mansion (Tu.–Sat., 10–12, 1–5:30; Sun., 2–6, free) stands on the campus. One of the delights of visiting the university is to sample the delicious ice cream concocted at the dairy school's Newman Hall. Nearby Seneca took its name from the Iroquois, who settled in the area after previous tribes of Cherokee and Creek arrived there. It's believed that the nation's first tomatoes were cultivated around Seneca from seeds brought there by the Creek. Chauga River House (803-647-9587) at Long Creek, in Sumter National Forest to the west, provides bed and breakfast. Wildwater, Ltd. (803-647-9587) and Southeastern Expeditions (803-647-9083) at Long Creek outfit rafting trips on the Chattooga River, where scenes from the movie *Deliverance* were filmed.

North of Anderson, where you'll find a National Register-listed historic district—the Evergreen Inn there (803-225-1109) furnishes bed and breakfast—is the Jockey Lot and Farmer's Market, a huge emporium offering produce, antiques and flea market items. Route 81 out of Anderson is the Savannah River Scenic Highway, which to the south takes you to Calhoun Falls, named for the family of John C. Calhoun, born at Calhoun Mill not far from the village of Mt. Carmel. Abbeville calls itself "the Birthplace of the Confederacy," the original secession document having originated there. Ironically, the town also witnessed the death of the Confederacy when the South's War Council, Jefferson Davis presiding, decided on May 2, 1865, to disband the Confederate army during a meeting held at the Burt-Stark House (Sat., 1-5 and by appointment: 803-459-2475, adm.). The Abbeville Historic District includes the 1908 Opera House (M.–Fr., 9–5, free), other old buildings and two bed and breakfast establishments, Painted Lady (803-459-8171) and the restored 1903 Belmont Inn (803-459-9625).

Greenwood to the east, well-garnished with flowers at the Park Seed Company's greenhouses and experimental gardens (M.–F., 8–4:30, free), hosts every year in late July the Festival of Flowers. Near Greenwood, which claims the world's widest Main Street, at three hundred and sixteen feet, is the Ninety Six National Historic Site (9–5, free) where the South's first Revolutionary War land battle took place in November 1775, while in the Cedar Springs District near Bradley lies a two-century-old cemetery where ancestors of publisher William Randolph Hearst repose. The city and county took its name from the log house an early settler dubbed Green Wood, a name which well describes the verdant forested area typical of South Carolina's up-country. Here we can end our tour of the state, in a corner of Carolina so fondly recalled by Greenwood native Louis B. Wright, who in *South Carolina: A Bicentennial History* remembered his home county as "a region of red hills and piney woods; of springtime with green fields, snowy dogwoods, and the soft red of woodbine; of autumn days when damp hickory leaves, kicked up as we hunted for scaly-bark and pig-nuts, gave off a fragrance like spice; of wild grapevines laden with purple muscadines, sweet, juicy, and pungent."

South Carolina Practical Information

The South Carolina Division of Tourism: P.O. Box 71, Columbia, SC 29202; 803-734-0235. Other government agencies include: Division of State Parks, 803-734-0156; Department of Archives and History, 803-734-8577; Arts Commission, 803-734-8696; Museum Commission, 803-737-4921.

South Carolina operates ten highway travel information centers. To the north near the North Carolina state line: U.S. 17 near Little River, I-95 near Dillon, I-77 near Fort Mill, I-85 near Blacksburg, and I-26 near Landrum; to the west near the Georgia line: I-85 near Fair Play, I-20 at North Augusta, I-95 near Hardeville, and on U.S. 301 near Allendale; and on I-95 near Santee and Lake Marion.

Tourist offices in areas popular with visitors include: Myrtle Beach, 803-448-1629; Charleston, 800-845-7108; Columbia, 803-254-0479; Hilton Head, 803-785-3673; York County, 803-329-5200; Beaufort, 803-524-3163; the horse country around Aiken, 803-649-7981; the up-country area,

803-233-2690; the Old Ninety Six area, 803-223-1559; the low-country and resort islands area, 803-726-5536; the Georgetown area, 803-546-8436.

Bed and breakfast agencies in the Charleston area are: Historic Charleston Bed and Breakfast, 43 Legare Street, Charleston, SC 29401, 803-722-6606; Charleston Society Bed and Breakfast, 84 Murray Boulevard, Charleston, SC 29401, 803-723-4948; and Charleston East Bed and Breakfast League, 1031 Tall Pine Road, Mt. Pleasant, SC 29464, 803-884-8208.

II

The Deep South

4. Georgia

The exploration and settlement of all new lands is fraught with danger and difficulty. When German settlers known as the Salzburgers reached the Savannah area soon after the city's founding in 1733, they recalled the old-country proverb about emigration to undeveloped regions: "Dem Ersten, Tod; dem Zweiten, Not; dem Dritten, Brot"—first comes death, then hardship, finally bread. Although in 1717 Sir Robert Montgomery—who offered a penny an acre to the Lords Proprietors of Carolina for a large wedge of Georgia—described the area as "the most delightful Country of the Universe," a century later Captain Basil Hall, who trekked from Savannah across Georgia in 1828, noted in *Travels in North America* that "the maps of these regions were not yet dotted with cities and villages, nor webbed over with lines of roads and canals. Whether the time will ever come when these things shall appear is doubtful; for every step of this first day's journey was through swamps, where millions of fevers and agues seemed to be waiting to devour any one who should come near."

Perhaps Hall's departure from Savannah's civilized precincts into the rough back country distressed him. By then Savannah had become the genteel and picturesque place it remains today. In her *Southern Tour,* published in 1831, Anne Royall averred that "Savannah is the first city of the South, by a long way." James Oglethorpe, an Oxford graduate who had fought the Turks and at age twenty-six was elected to Parliament, founded Savannah, and Georgia, as a place where disadvantaged Englishmen could get a new start in life. Two centuries before, Spanish explorer Hernando de Soto, during

GEORGIA

0   50   100m.

his passage across Georgia, had been "much given to the sport of killing Indians," as the Hidalgo of Elvas's contemporary account put it. But the English parlayed with the redskins, and Oglethorpe concluded a treaty with them enabling the Europeans to occupy the Savannah area "for as long as the sun shines or the water runs." A year later, in 1734, Oglethorpe took the obliging chief and five braves to London where, decorated in war paint, they met George II, after whom the new colony was named. In 1752 the trustees, who had organized the Georgia colonization project in return for a twenty-year concession, returned the area to the king, whose third governor, James Wright, ruled the region for twenty-two years, during which time he coped with the Stamp Act of 1765, a much-hated law that created fierce opposition to the crown and marked the beginnings of the breach between the colonists and the king, a conflict culminating in the events of 1776. After the March 1776 Battle of the Rice Boats, when the British blocked eleven rice-laden Yankee ships trying to sail out of the Savannah River, the Georgia Congress fled to Augusta where they prepared the first written document creating a government for the territory. But Georgia was a strongly loyalist state, thanks to Governor Wright's popularity and to the colony's many English-born residents. Kenneth Coleman, in *The American Revolution in Georgia,* maintains that if "left to themselves" Georgians wouldn't have joined the Revolution.

After the war the state suffered from the Yazoo Fraud, the greatest land speculation in the nation's history, a promotion organized in 1795 by bribing Georgia legislators to approve the sale of some fifty million acres at about a cent and a half an acre. The following year the assembly rescinded the Yazoo Act, with the bill and related papers being burned on February 15, 1796, by the sun's rays focused through a magnifying glass as if the judgment of heaven was being brought to bear on the underhanded legislation. Litigation over land titles was finally settled only in 1810 when the U.S. Supreme Court, in the first case declaring a state statute unconstitutional, ruled in *Fletcher* v. *Peck* that purchases of land under the 1795 act remained valid as they "were not stained by that guilt which infected the original transaction."

Once the land problem was resolved, Georgia began to develop. In 1819 the Savannah Steam Ship Company sent to Liverpool the "Savannah," the first steam-assisted ship to cross the Atlantic, and in 1833 the legislature chartered the Georgia Railroad to run from Athens to Augusta, a line that gradually grew until it finally reached a village on the Chattahoochee River named White Hall (later called Terminus, Marthasville and, these days, known as Atlanta). Meanwhile, around the Dahlonega area in the north Georgia hills, one of the nation's first gold rushes brought further prosperity to the state.

As the century moved on, the cotton economy in Georgia rapidly developed, thanks in part to the cotton gin New Englander Eli Whitney invented in 1793 on a plantation near Savannah. In 1826 Georgia's 150,000-bale crop made the state the world's leading cotton producer, and by the eve of the Civil War more than one-third of the 118,000 families in Georgia owned a total of nearly 500,000 slaves, with each able-bodied man worth eighteen hundred dollars. Unlike its loyalist attitude during the Revolution and unlike some other Southern states, secession in Georgia was a popular move, with only a few Northern sympathizers, like Judge Garnett Andrews, voicing such warnings as, "Poor fools! They may ring bells now, but they will wring their hands—yes, and their hearts, too—before they are done with it." But the main sentiment was epitomized in the April 15, 1861, *Macon Telegraph* headline, which screamed, "War! War!! War!!! 75,000 Barbarians Coming Down on the South." Perhaps this language wasn't completely exaggerated, for General Sherman's barbaric "March to the Sea" left more than 25,000 Southerners dead in the hundred or so miles between Chattanooga and Atlanta, which he burned to the ground before proceeding on to Savannah. On the way there Sherman's men tore up two hundred miles of track, heating the rails on bonfires of cross-ties and twisting the metal around telegraph poles to make what the troops dubbed "Sherman's neckties."

Although Atlanta quickly recovered, thanks in part to Northern opportunists who flocked to the area, the war so retarded the region that President Franklin Roosevelt, who frequented Warm Springs to bathe in the mineral waters to help his polio, called Georgia an unfinished state as it seemed not to have recovered from the conflict. But this failure to finish itself has left Georgia with a rich residue of antebellum Old South ambiance and sights. Any number of towns scattered around the state, the largest east of the Mississippi, boast delightful old houses along tree-filled streets and a pleasantly laid-back atmosphere, as well as a surprisingly rich collection of historical attractions. The inscription on the statue at Capitol Square in Atlanta of Eugene Talmadge, who brought his cow to graze on the lawn of the governor's mansion when he served as chief executive, reads: "I may surprise you, but I will never deceive you." For Georgia's many varied travel attractions, this could perhaps be rephrased: "I may surprise you, but I will never disappoint you."

Atlanta

The great metropolis that is today Atlanta once bore the rather end-game name of Terminal, so called as the settlement began in 1837 as the southern terminus of the Western and Atlantic Railroad, the nation's first state-owned line. Local tradition says that the line's chief engineer, J. Edgar

Thomson, coined the word "Atlanta" in 1845 to evoke the town's rail link to the sea. Within twenty years Atlanta, the hub of four railroads, served as the South's transportation nexus, a fateful accomplishment as the city's importance led to its destruction by General William Tecumseh Sherman. Asked after the Civil War why he annihilated the city, Sherman raised his thin, bony hand, fingers outstretched, and explained, "Atlanta was like my hand. The palm was the city or hub. The fingers were its spokes—in this case the railroads. I knew that if I could destroy those railroads, the last link of the Confederacy would be broken."

After the Yankees burned the city, destroying two-thirds of its houses and all of its businesses—Atlanta quickly bounced back and in 1868 became the state capital. In the early part of the twentieth century a land boom exploded in Atlanta, led by such colorful characters as Jack Smith, whose favorite beverage was "cow and corn," a mixture of corn whisky and milk, who constructed a building called The House That Jack Built. Later, in the 1920s, the Chamber of Commerce's "Forward Atlanta" program became the country's first national campaign to market a city. When Alderman William B. Hartsfield convinced federal officials back then to make Atlanta a stop on the new New York to Miami mail route the city purchased a landing field that evolved into Hartsfield International, which by some measures is the world's busiest airport today, boarding a daily average of some 70,000 passengers. All of the helter-skelter growth enjoyed by Atlanta in recent years has made the city a rather hyperactive and congested place, with sky-scraper-lined and car-clogged Peachtree Street downtown— one of the city's thirty or so arteries bearing the name "Peachtree"—symbolizing the pell-mell expansion experienced by the metropolis. As a result, traces of the Old South have become scarce in Atlanta. Medora Field Perkerson wrote in *White Columns in Georgia* that "it is Gone with the Wind country that the majority of Atlanta's first-time visitors wish to see—a land of legend, of cotton and camellias, mint juleps and magnolias and all the rest of it." Although that Atlanta is for the most part "gone with the wind," you'll find in the metropolis a number of attractions of historic or cultural interest.

For a faint breath of past "winds," the Atlanta Fulton County Library downtown contains a display of Margaret Mitchell's personal items, including the typewriter she used to create *Gone with the Wind,* much of which she drafted at the Crescent Apartments, Tenth Street and Crescent Avenue, where the author, who dubbed the place "The Dump," lived from 1925 to 1932. Residences of other famous Atlantans include the delightful Wren's Nest (Tu.–Sat., 10–5; Sun., 2–5, adm.), listed on the National Register, where Joel Chandler Harris, author of the *Uncle Remus Tales,* lived; the house (10–4:30, to 3:30 Labor Day through May, free) where Martin Luther King, Jr., was born, located in the King National Historic Site in the "Sweet Auburn" neighborhood, so named by the grandfather of Maynard Jackson, Atlanta's first black mayor, an area crammed with historic buildings of the black community, including headquarters of the Atlanta Life Insurance Company, the nation's largest black-owned such firm, whose founder, one-time slave Alonzo Franklin Herndon, lived in a 1910 National Register-listed mansion (Tu.–Sat., 10–4, free) which houses antiques, art and family archives. Hammonds House (Tu.–F., 10–6; Sat. and Sun., 1–5, free) contains exhibits of black art, while other showhouses include Rhodes Memorial Hall (M.–F., 11–4, adm.), listed on the National Register, a Rhine River-type castle, now headquarters for the Georgia Trust for Historic Preservation; the Governor's Mansion (Tu.–Th., 10–11:30, free), a 1968 Greek Revival-style dwelling garnished with three hundred rose bushes on eighteen acres of grounds; and Callanwolde Fine Arts Center (M.–Sat., 10–5, adm.), a 1920

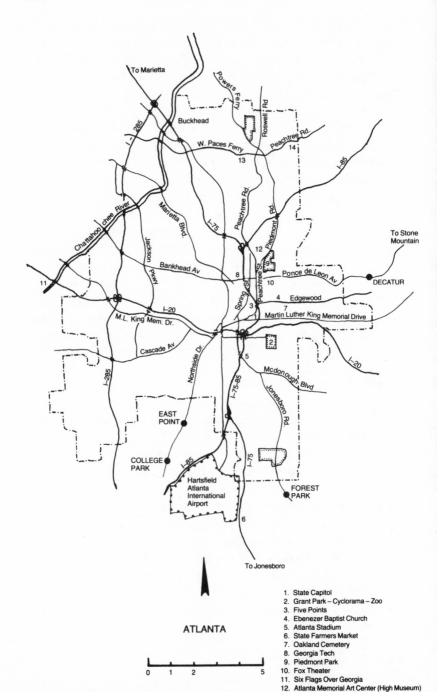

ATLANTA

0   1   2   5

1. State Capitol
2. Grant Park – Cyclorama – Zoo
3. Five Points
4. Ebenezer Baptist Church
5. Atlanta Stadium
6. State Farmers Market
7. Oakland Cemetery
8. Georgia Tech
9. Piedmont Park
10. Fox Theater
11. Six Flags Over Georgia
12. Atlanta Memorial Art Center (High Museum)
13. Atlanta Historical Society
14. Toy Museum of Atlanta

Tudor-style mansion built for a son of Asa G. Candler, founder of Coca-Cola Company. For the Candlers, things went better with Coke. "The Candlers were our royal family," wrote Thomas Stokes in his 1940 *Chips Off My Shoulder.* "Atlanta was the Candlers and Coca-Cola, and the Candlers and Coca-Cola were Atlanta." In 1888 Asa Candler, an Atlanta pharmaceutical company owner, acquired a controlling interest in the new beverage firm from Dr. John Styth Pemberton, who two years before had produced the first Coke syrup, supposedly in a three-legged brass pot in his backyard, after which the drink went on sale, as a "brain tonic," at Jacobs' Pharmacy for five cents a glass. During the first year sales averaged nine drinks a day, but after Candler acquired sole ownership in 1891 for a total cost of $2,300, sales began to take off, and by 1894 the first syrup manufacturing plant outside Atlanta started up in Dallas. That year Joseph A. Biedenharn of Vicksburg, Mississippi, installed bottling machinery in the rear of his drugstore, thus becoming the first person to put Coca-Cola in bottles. With that innovation began the franchising system that led to the large-scale bottling of the beverage, now sold in more than one hundred and fifty-five countries.

Another century-old industry is commemorated in the Telephone Museum (M.–F., 11–1), which contains a collection of antique phones and displays on the history of telecommunications. Atlanta boasts the world's largest toll-free dialing zone, with more than one million phones in the thirty-three hundred square-mile metropolitan area. Other Atlanta museums include the High Museum of Art (Tu.–Sat., 10–5; W. to 9; Sun., 12–5, adm.) and its annex at the Georgia-Pacific Center downtown (M.–F., 11–5, free); a museum in the Federal Reserve Bank (M.–F., 9–4, free) that traces the evolution of currency, the history of money and the development of a private banking system; the Atlanta Historical Society out in Buckhead (M.–Sat., 9–5:30; Sun.,

12–5, adm.) and the downtown branch (M.–Sat., 10–6, free) in the 1911 Hillyer Trust Building; the African American Panoramic Experience (Tu.–F., 10–5; W. to 6; Sat., 10–4, adm.), featuring African wood sculpture; the new (1988) Sci-Trek Science and Technology Museum; the Emory University Museum of Art and Archeology (Tu.–Sat., 11–4:30, free); the Jimmy Carter Library and Museum (M.–Sat., 9–4:45; Sun., 12–4:45, adm.); and the unique Center for Puppetry Arts (M.–F., 9–12; Sat., 10–3:30, adm.), with more than two hundred puppets from around the world as well as puppet shows.

History lingers in Atlanta at the old Fox Theatre (tours, April–Oct., M. and Th., 10; Sat., 10 and 11:30, adm.), a National Register-listed 1929 Moorish-Egyptian Art Deco curiosity; the 1889 wooden Inman Park barn-like Trolley Barn, one of the city's oldest buildings; the Georgia Department of Archives and History (M.–F., 8–4:30; Sat., 9:30–3:15, free), installed in a striking seventeen-story windowless marble box-like structure; the 1889 State Capitol, whose dome glistens with gold from Dahlonega in northern Georgia, site of the nation's first gold rush; and the Cyclorama (May–Sept., 9:30–5:30; Oct.–April, 9:30–4:30, adm.), featuring a multimedia show based on an immense 1885 cylindrical canvas depicting the 1864 Battle of Atlanta. At the 1850 Oakland Cemetery (sunrise to sunset, free) repose many of Atlanta's extinguished leading lights, including golfer Bobby Jones and now gone-with-the-wind author Margaret Mitchell, while more lively attractions include the Zoo (M.–F., 10–5; Sat. and Sun., 10–6, adm.) where gorillas and orangutangs run wild in their special habitat areas, and the Botanical Garden (Tu.–Sat., 9–6; Sun., 12–6, adm.). The CNN Center offers tours (on the hour, M.–F., 10–5; Sat. and Sun., 10–4, adm.) of the Cable News Network headquarters, while other company tours include the *Atlanta Journal Constitution* (404-526-5691); Delta Air Lines

(404-765-2554), the state's largest single employer; and WSB Radio and TV (404-897-7369), the South's first radio station, established in 1922 by the *Journal,* and the nation's first to use musical notes for its call letters.

The New Georgia Railroad will take you on an eighteen-mile circuit of Atlanta on an old-time steam train (404-656-0768) that leaves from the 1869 Freight Depot, downtown's oldest building, near Underground Atlanta, a complex of shops and restaurants that reopened in June 1989 after nearly a decade of expansion and renovation. For horse-drawn carriage rides around Atlanta you can call Pegasus, 404-681-2740; while for young people's itineraries contact ABC Children's Tours, 404-451-2884; and for guided walking tours through historic areas of town, held April through October, call the Atlanta Preservation Center, 404-522-4345. On your own you might want to drive through some of the magnificent residential areas around Atlanta, the nation's most densely wooded metropolitan area. The show areas impressed even irascible H. L. Mencken, who adjudged, after touring such areas as Druid Hills and Habersham Road, that Atlanta was the nation's loveliest city.

With some 50,000 hotel rooms, including the 1,684 at the Marriott, the South's biggest hotel, Atlanta doesn't lack for places to stay. If you fancy bed and breakfast accommodations you can book them through Atlanta Hospitality (404-493-1930) and Bed and Breakfast in Atlanta (404-875-0525, M.-F. 9–12, 2–5), or contact such establishments as Marlow House, in Marietta (404-426-1881); Beverly Hills Inn, in Buckhead (404-233-8520); D. P. Cook House, near McDonough Square (404-957-7562); RMF, in the Candler Park area (404-525-5712); and Shellmont, in midtown (404-872-9290). For meals, locals frequent such places as Paschal's, a coffee shop and restaurant, haunt of black politicians, specializing in fried chicken; Mary Mac's, Thelma's Kitchen, Aleck's Barbeque Heaven, Auburn Ave-

nue Rib Shack and Harold's Barbeque, all simple and, in
some cases, seedy local joints; Manuel's Tavern, a favorite
of politicians and journalists, with plenty of cold beer and
hot chili; the legendary Varsity, across from Georgia Tech,
the world's largest drive-in, specializing in hot dogs; Patrick's, in the Little Five Points area, a vaguely bohemian
corner of town; Murphy's, Capo's or Indigo's in the pleasantly lively Virginia Highland neighborhood; and, for food
at rock bottom prices, courtesy of the state's taxpayers, the
cafeteria at 2 Martin Luther King, Jr. Drive, S.W., just across
the street from the Capitol, where a traditional Southern
meal will cost a few dollars.

From Atlanta to the East

Stone Mountain—Monroe—Athens—Madison—
Milledgeville—Washington—Thomson—Augusta

The interstates and the other main highways that vein the
Georgia map all lead to, or from, Atlanta whose Hartsfield
International Airport, the world's busiest, serves some fifty
million passengers annually, handles 800,000 landings and
take-offs every year and offers more scheduled flights than
any other airport on earth. All roads, most flights and many
itineraries lead to Atlanta, the state capital and population
center whose more than two million residents give it nearly
40 percent of Georgia's inhabitants. From Atlanta fan out
roads in all directions, each offering sights of historic, scenic
or cultural interest. With Atlanta as the starting point you
can head east through antebellum towns to Augusta (this
section), north to the hill country (the next section) and
south (the third section) to below the Fall Line, a series of
low rises—once the shore of a prehistoric ocean—that cuts

across the state from Columbus via Macon and Milledgeville to Augusta, dividing the Piedmont Plateau from the Coastal Plain.

As you leave Atlanta to the east you'll pass through Decatur, with a scattering of antique buildings, including the old courthouse, Agnes Scott College, the 1891 depot and a historic cemetery, last resting place of Rebecca Latimer Felton, first female U.S. Senator, and of Charles Murphey, delegate to the Secession Convention, who avowed he hoped he'd never live to see Georgia leave the Union—a wish granted to him. To the north, at Chamblee, more than thirty antique stores occupy nineteenth-century structures, and to the east you'll reach Stone Mountain, one of Georgia's most famous tourist attractions, centerpiece of an enclave filled with sights that seem to encapsulate many of the state's themes. Around the huge granite formation—embellished with the world's largest high-relief sculpture, carvings of Confederate heroes Jefferson Davis, Robert E. Lee and "Stonewall" Jackson, here literally a stone wall—cluster an old-fashioned scenic railroad line, an antique auto and music museum featuring more than forty old cars and period music machines, an antebellum plantation with nineteen restored nineteenth-century buildings moved to the site, a paddlewheel riverboat offering excursions on the lake, a beach, boating and fishing facilities, an ice skating rink, twenty-seven holes of golf, hiking and biking trails and other amenities, amusements and distractions.

Back in 1916 the family that owned the mountain deeded the dome's face to the Confederate Monumental Association, giving the organization twelve years to complete a memorial on the granite rock. After sculptor Gutzon Borglum finished Robert E. Lee's head in 1924 twenty local celebrities dined, perched on the huge figure's shoulder. Borglum later abandoned the project and moved west to carve the presidential figures on Mount Rushmore in South Dakota. Only in 1970

was the carving, thirty-six stories high and the length of
a football field, finally finished. During the summer a laser
show (every night from May through Labor Day, weekends
through Oct), featuring beams that project colorful designs
onto the mountainside, brightens the grey granite, while
throughout the year Stone Mountain hosts such celebrations
as Kite Day, a March event in which contestants try to keep
their kites aloft long enough to beat the current record of
twenty-five hours; the mid-September Yellow Daisy Festival,
with one of the South's largest arts and crafts shows and
other events marking the flower's annual blooming; and the
late October Scottish Festival and Highland Games with bagpipes, kilted clans and pageantry. (For information on the
special events: 404-498-5633.) If you want to stay at Stone
Mountain, the enclave offers more than four hundred campsites (for reservations: 404-498-5710), the Inn (404-469-3311)
and the new Evergreen Resort (404-879-9900 or 800-722-
1000), opened in 1989.

To the northeast of Stone Mountain lies Gwinnett County,
once a sleepy rural area but in the mid-1980s the nation's
fastest-growing county. Named for Button Gwinnett, a
signer of the Declaration of Independence and an author of
the Georgia Constitution killed in a duel with a political
rival who called him a scoundrel, the county grew from
fewer than twenty thousand people after the war to more
than three hundred thousand now. But a scattering of old-
time corners remain, among them the rather church-like
courthouse in Lawrenceville, where you'll also find the Georgia Historical Aviation Museum; the attractive hamlet of
Grayson (population: five hundred and sixty); and Lilburn,
where a group of old buildings now filled with antique and
craft shops (M.–Sat., 9–5) survive. On Yellow River near
Lilburn stretches the Wildlife Game Ranch (June–Aug.,
9:30–9; Sept.–May, 9:30–6, adm.), a twenty-four-acre preserve with buffalo, mountain lions, deer and other wildlife.

Winder, farther east, is the hometown of Richard B. Russell, the nation's youngest U.S. Senator (thirty-three) when elected to the first of his seven terms. Every year in June more than a hundred members of the Russell clan gather for a family reunion at the old homestead in Winder.

To the north near Hoschton, where Hill House offers bed and breakfast (404-654-3425), lies Chateau Elan (M.–Sat., 10–4; to 6 May through Sept., free), a relatively new Irish-owned winery that produces some forty thousand cases a year. The visitor center, which resembles a French Renaissance-era country house, contains a bistro, boutique and history of wine exhibits. The Chateau Elan property, still being developed, will eventually include an inn, conference center and other enhancements. The nearby town of Braselton is a curiosity, as the settlement has for years been privately owned, most recently by actress Kim Basinger who in 1989 bought the community from descendants of William Harrison Braselton, founder of the settlement in 1876. Twenty-four family members owned shares in the town of five hundred residents when Basinger acquired it. South of Winder the streets of Bethlehem bear Christmas-related names, while south of the village the 1874 Kilgore Mill covered bridge spans the Appalachee River between Barrow and Walton counties.

Nearby Fort Yargo State Park (7–10, free) includes a 1793 fort or blockhouse built of hand-hewn pine logs that bear bullet-hole marks. At Jefferson, seat of adjacent Jackson County—named for James Jackson, who refused to serve when elected governor in 1788 on the ground he was too young (thirty) to hold such an office, and who once uttered the heartfelt sentiment, "If you cut my heart open, you will find 'Georgia' engraved on it"—is the Crawford W. Long Museum (Tu.–Sat., 10–12, 1–5; Sun., 2–5, free), a memorial to the physician who pioneered the use of ether as an anesthetic. Displays installed in the office where Dr. Long performed the first operation with ether include his personal memorabilia, photos and the story of the development of anesthesia. Long, whose roommate at the University of Georgia at nearby Athens was Alexander H. Stephens, Vice-president of the Confederacy, attended the University of Pennsylvania medical school and began pacticing at Jefferson, where in the early 1840s he discovered that party guests who inhaled ether for a "high" didn't feel pain. In 1842 Long used the substance when he operated on a patient to remove two neck tumors, and so originated ether as an anesthetic.

Athens is an attractive, hilly city dominated by the huge University of Georgia (for tours: 404-542-3354), which sprawls across the town down into a hollow and back up again. In 1785 Georgia chartered the school, the nation's first state university, which started in 1801 as Franklin College, perched on a small plateau above the Oconee River. (The University of North Carolina, chartered four years after the Georgia institution, began operations in 1795.) Bemused and curious Indians peeked from behind bushes at the school's first classes, held outdoors beneath trees. Back in 1853 student regulations prohibited on campus such threats to decorum as duels, dogs, defacing, dramas, liquor and women, as well as "hallooing, loud talking, jumping, dancing, or any other boisterous noise." Such rules are no longer in effect. The university's original quadrangle borders the downtown area, part of which is a National Historic District with such structures as the Church-Waddel-Brumby House, the city's oldest residence (c. 1820); the Tinsley-Stern House (c. 1830); the Art Deco-style Georgia Theatre; the Morton Theatre, built by Monroe "Pink" Morton, a black business-man and politician, one of the nation's four still-existing black vaudeville stages; and the 1904 City Hall, perched on Athens's highest point, with the unique double-barreled cannon built in 1863 to fire two balls connected by a chain aimed to sweep across the battlefield. The concept misfired and the weapon is now a showpiece on the City Hall lawn pointed north—just in case. Other handsome houses line Milledge and Prince Avenues, while around the 1858 university president's home, acquired by the school in 1949, stand stately tall columns. A similarly column-embellished dwelling is the 1840 Taylor-Grady House (M.-F., 10-3, adm.) where Henry Grady, later editor of the *Atlanta Constitution,* lived with his family while attending the university. Grady, who died in 1889 at age thirty-eight of pneumonia contracted on a trip to Boston, became famous for his moderate, modernistic ideas, holding that "the New South should wear the halo and absorb the romance of the olden times, but it should get away from the retarding philosophy of the Old South." At a program in New York City in December 1886 Grady followed to the podium General William Tecumseh Sherman, the warrior who'd set Atlanta aflame. During his remarks Sherman had apologized for the "incidents of war," as the Union leader described the burning and destruction he caused, to which Grady responded that "some people think that he is kind of a careless man about fire."

Museums in Athens include the Georgia Museum of Art (M.-Sat., 9-5; Sun., 1-5, closed in Aug.); the U.S. Navy Supply Corps Museum, with displays on the service's uniforms, Revolutionary War artifacts, ship models and other nautical exhibits; Butts-Mehre Heritage Hall (M.-F., 8-5, free), featuring a collection of university sports memorabilia; the State Botanical Garden of Georgia (May–Sept., 8-8; Oct.–April, 8-5, free), with the glossy and glassy new visitor center and conservatory complex; and Founders Memorial Garden and Museum House (M.-F., 9-12, 1-4, adm.), established to commemorate the world's first garden club, founded in Athens in 1891. Above cobbled Finley Street at Dearing stands another specimen of Athens plant life—the curious "tree that owns itself." It seems that in 1875 Colonel W. H. Jackson deeded the tree to itself, the document of conveyance relating that "for and in consideration of the great affection which he bears said tree, and his great desire to see it protected [grantor] has conveyed, and by these presents do convey unto the said oak tree entire possession of itself and of all land within eight feet of it on all sides." The present tree, successor to the original, thus occupies an oak-owned no-man's-land. You'll find bed and breakfast accommodations in Athens at the Serpentine (404-354-1177) near the university campus, as well as at a country home outside town (404-546-9740).

Near Athens—hometown of National Football League star quarterback Fran Tarkenton and seat of Clarke County, smallest of the state's hundred and fifty-nine counties but eleventh-largest in population—once operated Smithsonia, an extensive convict-lease farm owned by James M. Smith. Under the lease system, a kind of peonage that survived in Georgia until 1908, landowners would pay the state as little as fifty dollars a year for prisoners. In some cases the convicts would be subleased at a markup or used as collateral to secure bank loans. When Smith died in 1915 he left an estate estimated at five million dollars, with some of the assets in bonds so old they crumbled away when removed from the vault. The plantation eventually fell into decay and its railroad was sold as scrap metal.

Before heading east toward the South Carolina border you may want to drop down to Watkinsville, about twelve miles south of Athens, to see the Historic District there which includes nearly forty old structures along Main Street. At Eagle Tavern (M.–F., 9–5, free), originally built as a fort to protect settlers against Indians and in 1801 remodeled into an inn, supposedly met the committee that decided where to locate the University of Georgia, the group agreeing that Watkinsville was too raucous a place for such a serious enterprise. Off highway 15 four and a half miles south of Watkinsville stands Elder Mill Covered Bridge, a short boxy span that crosses Rose Creek. East of Athens lies Elbert County, where William W. Bibb, both territorial and state governor of Alabama and a U.S. senator from Georgia, practiced medicine in the early nineteenth century. Bibb resigned from the Senate in 1816 as a matter of conscience after the legislators awarded themselves a fixed salary—the munificent sum of $1,800 a year—to replace a lesser per diem stipend. Pocking the terrain around Elberton are thirty-seven granite quarries from which workers extract the blue-grey stone. The Granite Museum and Exhibit (2–5, free) at Elberton, which supposedly produces more granite monuments than any other city in the world, contains displays on the industry. In the center of town rises the rather attractive courthouse, with a pleasing combination of arches and angles, while other local buildings of interest include the 1858 Christmas Tree House, Historical Society Headquarters, where German immigrant George Loehr set up Georgia's first Christmas tree, and the Nancy Hart Log Cabin, off highway 17 south of town, where Hart, doctor, markswoman and Colonial spy, lived during the Revolutionary War era. On highway 72 southeast of Elberton are Wahachee Creek Farms, one of the nation's leading Polled Hereford breeders (visitors welcome), and the grave of the Reverend Daniel Tucker (died 1818), whose name survives in the famous "Old Dan Tucker" folk song, while seven miles north of town stands the Stonehenge-like inscribed granite slabs, the so-called Georgia Guidestones, bearing in various languages admonitions and philosophical ruminations.

Farther north out of Elberton you'll reach Royston, a rather drab place whose one claim to fame is that baseball superstar Ty Cobb grew up there. On the main roads into Royston stand billboards picturing the famous "Georgia Peach" clad in his old-fashioned Detroit Tigers uniform. Cobb lived in a house that stood where the Pruitte Funeral Home, just behind Cunningham's furniture store ("since

1905") now rises. A small plaque to the star, whose lifetime batting average was .367, stands in the outdoor courtyard of City Hall, and the "Peach" reposes in a cemetery just south of town, the large boxy mausoleum bearing over its door the name "Cobb," while in the middle of the left wall inside an inscription reads "Tyrus Raymond Cobb, December 18, 1886, January 17, 1961." If you linger in Cobb country until dusk the Hartwell Inn (404-376-3967) at Hartwell near Royston offers bed and breakfast.

Returning now to Stone Mountain, where this itinerary began, the road east toward Augusta takes you to a series of delightful antebellum towns filled with history. At Conyers is the Old Jail Museum and the Monastery of the Holy Ghost (7–6:15, free), established in 1944 by a group of monks who live a self-sufficient life at the lovely enclave, where plantings, a lake, a greenhouse (Th.–Sat., 10–12, 2:30–4:30) and other serenities afford a contemplative atmosphere. A shop at the monastery offers homemade breads baked by the monks. At Oxford, a few miles east, antebellum homes comprise the National Register-listed Historic District, while a Confederate cemetery, the recently restored Methodist church (c. 1841) and Oxford College, a branch of Atlanta's Emory University, also invite you to linger. North and south of Interstate 20—off which, on highway 11 south, the Fox Vineyards offers tours and tastings (404-787-5402)—lie two towns with curious names: Newborn, so called as the residents wanted their town "born anew" after hearing sermons from evangelist Sam P. Jones, and Social Circle where a plaque in regard to the unusual name stands against a gazebo-like construction in the middle of the main street to explain that locals invited a stranger to join a party as the gathering was a "social circle" where outsiders were welcome. At Rutledge, just to the east, Jones Cottage (404-557-2516), next to Hard Labor Creek State Park—so named for a stream there Indians found difficult to ford or, some say, by over-

worked slaves in the area—offers bed and breakfast accommodations. You'll also find bed and breakfast at the Brady
Inn (404-342-4400) and the Three Chimneys (404-342-4802),
both near the main square in Madison, a delightful old town
which is one of Georgia's most attractive settlements.

Known as "the town Sherman refused to burn" on his
devastating March to the Sea, tree-filled Madison, which
in 1864 *Harper's Weekly* called Georgia's "most picturesque
town," boasts thirty-five structures listed on the National
Register. One curiosity is that in the middle of town stands
not the courthouse, usually a county seat's centerpiece, but
the post office. The Morgan County government building
lies nearby with its facade angled to face the corner, an unusual and vaguely disconcerting alignment also seen in the
Hunter House (c. 1883), Hunter Street and South Main,
where the sides angle away from the central section. Around
the square stand old buildings with antique facades housing
commercial establishments, such as the *Madisonian* newspaper and Baldwin's Drug Store, brightened by an old-time
shiny red Coca-Cola sign out front. The Madison-Morgan
Cultural Center (M.–F., 10–4:30; Sat. and Sun., 2–5, adm.)
offers history displays and art exhibits, while in mid-May
and the first weekend in December visitors can tour some
of the old homes in town (for information: 404-342-4454).
The Presbyterian church (c. 1842), on Johnson just off South
Main, is an especially delightful little structure, with its windows edged with lintels and neatly angled roof lines, while
the low, angular Hardee's a few blocks east of the square,
built to conform with Madison's Historic District zoning
ordinance, may be the nation's most attractive fast-food
chain outlet. Local lore in Madison has it that the loss by
a card sharp—or perhaps better called dull—of his wife's
house in a poker game led to passage by the state legislature
of the Married Woman's Property Act, which gave a wife
the right to own property in her own name.

Nearby Greensboro, like Madison, boasts a Historic District with antebellum and Victorian-era homes and churches, among which are the 1850 Greek Revival-style courthouse, listed on the National Register; the turn-of-the-century Mill Village structures; and the early nineteenth-century "Gaol" used until 1895 to house prisoners in dungeons modeled after the medieval "bastille," with unlit and unventilated cells. More on the bright side, pleasantly named Happy Times (404-453-7433) offers bed and breakfast in Greensboro, which in April 1989 hosted the first annual Masters of Croquet tournament, with fifty-seven wielders of the mallet competing at the Port Armor Country Club. West of town snakes the upper portion of Lake Oconee, Georgia's second-largest lake, formed in 1979 when Georgia Power Company completed Wallace Dam downstream. Around the lake you'll find fishing, swimming and other recreational facilities as well as campsites at Lawrence Shoals (404-485-5494), Old Salem (404-467-2850) and Parks Ferry (404-453-4308). In Greene County, north of Greensboro, remain relics of the area's early days: at Penfield 1833 Old Mercer University, listed on the National Register, and the pre-Revolutionary War Shiloh Cemetery; at Union Point century-old Chipman-Union hosiery mill, also Register-listed and open for tours (404-486-2112); and at Scull Shoals, a village founded in 1784, the site of Georgia's first paper mill.

Before continuing east to visit the sights between Greensboro and Augusta it's worth heading south to see a scattering of attractions below Interstate 20. The little town of Monticello on the edge of Oconee National Forest boasts an old-time square with turn-of-the-century buildings. Eatonton to the east preserves memories of native son Joel Chandler Harris and his Uncle Remus tales. Born impoverished in Putnam County in 1848, Harris applied at age thirteen for a job as printer's devil for *The Countryman,* a weekly published at Turnwold, a plantation in the area. The magazine's owner, planter and lawyer Joseph Addison Turner, guided Harris in the boy's early writings, published in *The Countryman.* Harris later worked for *The Atlanta Constitution,* which began printing the soon-famous stories featuring Uncle Remus, Br'er Rabbit, Br'er Fox and other such characters. On the courthouse lawn in Eatonton—also hometown of author Alice Walker, whose novel *The Color Purple* won the Pulitzer Prize—stands a rather grotesque statue of Br'er Rabbit, a lumpy looking hare with blue legs and wearing a bright red coat. The Uncle Remus Museum (M.–Sat., 10–12, 1–5; Sun., 2–5, closed Tu., Sept.–May., adm.), installed in an old slave cabin, houses exhibits relating to the stories and Harris memorabilia. Around town stand such other venerable structures as the 1817 Bledsoe-Green House and Museum (M.–F., 8:30–4:30), the 1811 Thompkins Inn and the 1816 Bronson House (Tu.–Sun., 1–5, free), headquarters of the local Historical Society. Near Eatonton lies the Rock Eagle Effigy, a huge Indian-built eagle-shaped quartz rock design, believed to be more than five thousand years old. East of Eatonton lies the village of Sparta, embellished with a number of nineteenth-century houses, an attractive courthouse square and the old Hotel Lafayette (open by appointment: 404-444-5550, free), where Civil War refugees once found shelter.

Milledgeville, to the south, is one of Georgia's most historic and interesting towns. The city, which served as Georgia's capital from 1803 to 1868, retains its original grid of wide, tree-lined streets filled with venerable Federal-style structures. Among the showplaces are the Old Governor's Mansion (Tu.–Sat., 9–5; Sun., 1–5, adm.), where ten Georgia chief executives resided; the 1812 Stetson-Sanford House (by appointment only: 912-452-4687, adm.), widely praised for its design and workmanship; St. Stephens Church, used by Union troops as a stable; and the nearby Old State Capitol

(1807), now the administration building for Georgia Military College, whose campus contains the Museum and Archives of Georgia Education (M.–F., 12–5; Sat., 10–12:30; Sun., 4–5:30) and, in the Bussel Library, the Flannery O'Connor Room (M.–F., 9–5, free). Born in Savannah in 1925, young Flannery was taken to Milledgeville, her mother's hometown, in the mid-1930s when the child's father contracted lupus, a degenerative disease which in 1964 also took the famous author's life. The family lived in a spacious 1820 white frame house on Green Street where Flannery's mother had grown up with fifteen brothers and sisters. Young Flannery began to write when she attended Peabody High School, and she continued her literary efforts at Georgia State College for Women, a few blocks from home. Later she and her mother moved to Andalusia Farm, a family property five miles north of town, and there O'Connor created the short stories that made her famous, rather grotesque tales shadowed with dark images, such as this passage from *Everything That Rises Must Converge*: "The sky was a dying violet and the houses stood out darkly against it, bulbous liver-colored monstrosities of a uniform ugliness." Teachers occasionally brought schoolchildren to the dairy farm where O'Connor lived. "They see the ponies and the peacocks and the swan and the geese and the ducks," O'Connor related, "and then they come by my window and I stick my head out and the teacher says, 'And this is Miss Flannery. Flannery is an author.' So they go home having seen a peacock and a donkey and a duck and a goose and an author." Before leaving Milledgeville you might want to visit the Hard Twist Ranch, home of Sara Finney, an artist known for her carved fruits and vegetables, and if you're in the area the fourth weekend of April or the third weekend of October the Brown's Crossing Craftsmen Fair, held at a nineteenth-century cotton ginning site nine miles west of town, attracts nearly two hundred artisans from around the nation. For meals, Willis House in Milledgeville is a popular local restaurant. Milledgeville's mental hospital boasts what's supposedly the world's largest kitchen, capable of preparing thirty thousand meals a day.

At Toomsboro, south of Milledgeville, is the Swampland Opera House, with country, gospel and bluegrass music every Saturday, while back to the north lies Hamburg State Park, featuring a photogenic still-functioning 1850 water-powered grist mill with a country store and a museum displaying old-time agricultural tools. Little Louisville, to the southeast, served as Georgia's capital from 1796 to 1805, but the town never developed in the same way its Kentucky namesake did. The village, which on July 24, 1952 suffered from the state's highest recorded temperature, 112°, boasts a 1758 market and a pre-Revolutionary cemetery with thirty graves.

Up toward Washington lies the A. H. Stephens State Historic Park, with 1875 Liberty Hall, the politician's residence, and the adjacent Confederate Museum (Tu.–Sat., 9–5; Sun., 2–5:30, adm.), which contains one of the state's best collections of Civil War memorabilia. Stephens served as a U.S. congressman both before and after the War, as Vice-president of the Confederacy during the conflict, and briefly as governor of Georgia until he died in 1882 four months after his inauguration. Stephens, a moderate who opposed secession, once delivered an oration which no less a public speaker than Abe Lincoln adjudged "the very best speech of an hour's length I have ever heard. My old, withered dry eyes are full of tears yet." Stephens lost his liberty at Liberty Hall when Federal troops arrested him there on May 11, 1865, but in October of that year the Northerners released him from prison and Stephens returned to his property, where he now reposes beneath a monument that bears the words: "I am afraid of nothing on the earth, above the earth, or below the earth, except to do wrong."

To the northeast of the Stephens Memorial lies Washington, another of those mid-Georgia antebellum towns filled with stately old homes, one once occupied by the fiery Confederate partisian Robert Toombs, a planter and lawyer. Toombs, a radical Southern fanatic known as the "Unreconstructed Rebel," was the opposite of the moderate and reasonable Alex Stephens. Toombs, a U.S. Senator and Confederate Secretary of State, once threatened, "I will drink every drop of blood the Yankees shed." Most Georgians prefer Coca-Cola. During the Civil War he resigned from the Confederate cabinet and returned to his Washington house (Tu.–Sat., 9–5; Sun., 2–5:30, adm.), there to brood and to criticize the South's conduct of the war. After the conflict ended Toombs fled abroad, then later returned home, boasting, "I am not loyal to the existing government of the United States and do not wish to be suspected of loyalty." Washington, incorporated on January 23, 1780—it claims it was the nation's first town to be named for the President, but Washington, Virginia, took its designation in 1775—boasts four National Register districts and fully fourteen individual properties listed on the Register, among them the Toombs House and the Washington-Wilkes Historical Museum (Tu.–Sat., 10–5; Sun., 2–5, adm.) with Old South, Confederate and Indian items installed in an 1830 dwelling. More history resides in the Mary Willis Library, one of the state's oldest privately owned libraries (1888), with a collection of antiques as well as books. In the Washington region are two Register-listed attractions: Callaway Plantation (April 15–Oct. 15, M.–Sat., 10–5; Sun., 2–5, adm.), a working plantation five miles west on highway 78, featuring a group of old buildings and the adjacent 1800 house (relocated there) where Georgia governor George R. Gilmer lived, and the Kettle Creek Battlefield, off highway 44 eight miles southwest of town, where the Revolutionaries broke the hold of British forces on Georgia and so saved the state from surrender. Bed and breakfast establishments in Washington include Water Oak Cottage (404-678-3548), Anderson's Guest Cottage (404-678-7538), Liberty Street (404-678-3107) and the Olmsteads (404-678-1050).

Campgrounds, recreation areas, marinas and parks border the waters of Clarks Hill Lake (for information: 404-722-3770) to the east, the largest U.S. Army Corps of Engineers project east of the Mississippi, while to the south toward Augusta lies Thomson, known as the Camellia City. In front of the restored old train depot stands a woman's statue honoring females of the South who supported the Confederate cause. Historic residences include the Rock House (c. 1785), Georgia's oldest documented dwelling (open by appointment: 404-595-5584) and Hickory Hill, a lovely white-columned mansion (privately owned) where U.S. Senator Tom Watson, a populist politician who sponsored legislation establishing the Rural Free Delivery mail service, resided. Through McDuffie County runs the Bartram Trail (for information: 404-595-5584), named for noted naturalist William Bartram who visited the area in 1773 and 1774. On his trek the scientist passed through Wrightsborough, seven miles west of Thomson, where Quakers established a village in 1768. An 1810 church and an old cemetery recall the Quakers' early presence there. At Appling, northeast of Thomson, stands the 1771 Olakiokee Church, Georgia's oldest Baptist sanctuary. One way to see the area is with the Upcountry Plantation Tour (for information: 404-595-5584; minimum of ten persons), so named as the excursion travels in an area near the Fall Line, a geographic region above Augusta known in Colonial times as "up-country." Another way to glimpse the countryside is by riding to hounds: from November through March the Belle Meade Hunt chases foxes on Wednesdays and Sundays (visitors welcome: 404-595-4830).

To complete your tour of the central section of Georgia

east of Atlanta continue on to Augusta, the state's second-oldest city, after Savannah. Much history lingers in old Augusta, one of those tree-filled, slow-paced, house-beautiful cities that typify the antebellum South. Even the masthead of the *Augusta Chronicle* recalls yesteryear: "The South's Oldest Newspaper—Established 1785." After James Oglethorpe, the Englishman who established the colony of Georgia, founded Augusta as a military outpost in 1736 he reported back to London: "The settlement of Augusta is of great Service, it being . . . the Key of all the Indian Country." War-whooping Cherokee threatened the village during the French and Indian War, and during the Revolution Light Horse Harry Lee captured the town from the British. After the Revolution Augusta served as state capital for ten years. In 1791 President Washington visited the city, where in 1802 Parson Weems first published his famous fictitious tale recounting Washington's refusal to lie about cutting down the cherry tree. In the early nineteenth century the world's longest railroad connected Charleston, South Carolina, a hundred and forty miles east, with Hamburg, just across the river. Because of the area's rail transportation and the river, which furnished water power for factories, Augusta became the site of the 1862 Confederate Powderworks, supposedly the world's largest munitions plant, whose obelisque-like chimney survives as the nation's only remaining Confederate-commissioned construction.

In more recent times Augusta has hosted the Masters Golf Tournament, first held in 1934 on a course built where a well-known nursery previously operated. Around town remain many remnants of Augusta's early days. Along the Augusta Canal—started in 1844 and enlarged between 1872 and 1875 by Chinese laborers whose descendants form one of the nation's oldest Chinese communities—stand Sibley, King and Enterprise Mills, all listed on the National Register. The Cotton Exchange near Riverwalk, a pleasant promenade

along the Savannah River, recalls the days a century and
more ago when Augusta functioned as the world's second-
largest (after Memphis) inland cotton market. So many bales
of cotton filled the town's sidewalks back then that local
children, so the story goes, could frolic along the bales for
a mile without ever returning to earth. Sacred Heart, a brick-
embellished church deconsecrated in the early 1970s, now
serves as a cultural center (M., Tu., W., F., 8:30–5; Sun.,
1–4, adm.); St. Paul's (M.–F., 9–5; summer to 4, free), which
occupies the site where Augusta's original fort stood, shelters
the tomb of Leonidas K. Polk, known as "the fighting bishop
of the Confederacy"; and at the First Presbyterian Church
(M.–F., 9–4:30, free), designed by the architect who created
the Washington Monument, the Reverend Joseph R. Wilson,
father of Woodrow Wilson, served from 1858 to 1870. Woodrow Wilson grew up in a house two blocks down Telfair
Street.

Other historic houses in Augusta include Ware's Folly
(Tu.–F., 10–5; Sun., 1–4, adm.), a lovely mansion, now the
Herbert Institute of Art, which Nicholas Ware, later mayor
and U.S. Senator, spent the exorbitant sum of forty thousand
dollars to build in 1818; Meadow Garden (Tu.–Sat., 10–4;
Sun., 1–5, adm.), the townhouse of Declaration of Independence signer George Walton, which is Augusta's oldest residence (c. 1794) and the first structure in Georgia to undergo
historic preservation; and the Ezekiel Harris Home (M.–F.,
9–4; Sat., 10–4; Sun., 1–4, adm.), the city's second-oldest
dwelling (1797), a New England-type place perched on a
hill overlooking Augusta. The Augusta-Richmond County
Museum (Tu.–Sat., 10–5; Sun., 2–5, adm.) fills the 1802
building erected for the Academy, one of the nation's first
high schools for boys, while the Augusta Council of Garden
Clubs (M.–F., 9–1; Sat., 9–12) occupies the 1835 Old Medical
College, one of the country's first medical schools. In the
Broad Street district, listed on the National Register, rise

both the Old Market Column—sole remnant of a supposedly preacher-damned building destroyed by an 1878 cyclone—and a seventy-two-foot high Confederate Monument bearing four life-size statues of Southern generals and topped by Berry Benson, a lowly—but here high-placed—private.

Dozens of additional historic structures fill such districts as Harrisburg, Telfair, Greene Street, Summerville and Olde Town, known locally as Pinch Gut for the tight waistline styles neighborhood ladies wore in Victorian times. Augusta College occupies buildings constructed between 1827 and 1829 as part of the U.S. Arsenal. The College president resides in the National Register-listed house where poet and novelist Stephen Vincent Benét, whose father served as arsenal commandant, grew up, while in the Laney Walker neighborhood, at 1112 Eighth Street, stands the dwelling where novelist Frank Yerby, author of *The Foxes of Harrow, The Vixens* and other books, lived. Perrin Guest House Inn (404-736-3737) and Telfair Inn (404-724-3315) offer bed and breakfast accommodations in Augusta, whose azalea-scented ambiance, Old South atmosphere and many historical corners provide a good summary of antebellum Georgia.

From Atlanta to the North

Northwest:
Marietta—Cartersville—Rome—Dalton—Northeast: Lake Lanier—Gainesville—Dahlonega—Helen—Dillard

In the northern part of Georgia rises the state's hill country, with winding roads that climb and dip their way through the mountains. Here the people and the attractions differ from the Old South plantations and antebellum houses scattered around the central and southern sections of the state.

Back in the 1840s Emily Burke, who came from New Hampshire to teach in Savannah, claimed that "Those who . . . live in the northern part of the state . . . differ much in their manners and customs from the people in the low country. They have no idea of style and refinement in living." Such was one observer's opinion, a century and a half ago. The routes out of Atlanta to the northwest, the north and the northeast will take you to Indian country, old mining towns and Alpine-like villages high in the hills. Northwest of Atlanta, beyond Smyrna, called the Jonquil City, lies Marietta, where Civil War memories abound. Marietta, hometown of World War II General Lucius D. Clay, is one of only two U.S. cities with cemeteries for both Union and Confederate dead, many killed in an encounter recalled at the nearby Kennesaw Mountain National Battlefield Park (8:30–6, free), where cannons and earthworks remain to evoke the attempt to stop General Sherman's march to Atlanta in June 1864. Nearby rises the one-time cotton gin that now serves as the Big Shanty Museum (9:30–5:30, Dec.–Feb., Sun., 12–5:30, adm.) housing "The General," the old steam engine, sporting a bulbous black smoke stack and a pointy red cowcatcher, that Northerners stole in 1862, a feat for which they won the first Medals of Honor ever awarded. Martial matters survive at Kennesaw these days, for in 1982 the city council enacted an ordinance requiring every household to retain a gun on the premises. At Marietta—which offers bed and breakfast accommodations at The Blue and Gray (404-425-0392) and at the Marlow and the Stanley Houses (404-426-1887)—you'll also find the Historic Brumby Rocker Shop and Museum (M.–F., 10–12, adm.), featuring antiques, old catalogs and secrets of making a Brumby Rocker, perhaps Georgia's oldest product (1875) still in production. Marietta is the site of the famous 1915 lynching of Leo Frank, a Jewish pencil company manager convicted of murdering Mary Phagan, an employee of the

factory. A band of men—accompanied by a legal advisor
and by auto mechanics to repair breakdowns—drove over
to the state prison at Milledgeville to the east, abducted Frank
and brought him back to Marietta where they hung the victim from a tree limb.

East of Marietta lies Roswell, a century-and-a-half-old
community filled with historic buildings. When Sherman's
forces swept through the state in 1864 they left Roswell virtually untouched, destroying only the town's mills. Left
standing was a treasure trove of old structures, among them
Allenbrook (c. 1845), now the visitor center (M.–F., 10–4),
where the Ivy Woolen Mill manager once lived; Mimosa
(c. 1842), dubbed Phoenix Hall as, like the mythical bird,
it rose out of its own ashes when rebuilt just after it burned
during an overheated housewarming; and National Register-
listed Bulloch Hall (c. 1840), now a cultural center (open
by appointment: 404-992-1731), childhood home of Mittie
Bulloch, mother of Theodore Roosevelt, who in 1905 spoke
from the bandstand in the 1840s-vintage town square, the
center of Roswell's National Historic District. Another well-
known Washington figure, Dean Rusk, Secretary of State
from 1961 to 1969, was born in Cherokee County to the
north.

Just outside Cartersville, to the northwest of Marietta,
rise the Etowah Indian Mounds (Tu.–Sat., 9–5; Sun., 2–5:30,
adm.), millenium-old flat-topped earthen knolls which
served as ceremonial sites. A museum contains artifacts and
displays relating to the ancient Indians who lived in the area.
Four more museums enrich the small town of Cartersville:
Etowah Historical Museum houses artifacts from yesteryear;
the Etowah Arts Gallery (Tu., 7–9 p.m.; Th. and F., 10–3;
Sat., 12–4), installed in an old commercial building with
lyre motifs on the facade, offers crafts and fine arts; the
Roselawn Museum (M.–F., 9–5, adm.), in a late nineteenth-
century house owned by evangelist Samuel Porter Jones,

contains ironwork, stained glass and Civil War memorabilia; and the Weinman Mineral Center (Tu.–Sat., 10–5; Sun., 2–5), which occupies a rather forbidding cube-like white brick building, exhibits Georgia rocks and minerals and has a simulated limestone cave, complete with waterfall. The brick wall on the side of Young Brothers Pharmacy bears the newly restored (1989) "Drink Coca-Cola" sign, painted in 1894 as the beverage's first such advertising site in the U.S. On the banks of the Etowah River near Allatoona Lake, which begins only three miles from downtown, stands the 1850s Cooper's Iron Works furnace, remnant of a factory that manufactured ammunition during the Civil War. Mark Anthony Cooper, who established the operation, erected at a site not far from the nearby Allatoona Dam an unusual friendship monument to honor the thirty-eight acquaintances who helped him during a financial crisis. Just outside Cartersville stand the 1886 Euharlee Covered Bridge and the 1859 Stilesboro Academy, used during the Civil War as a sewing center for items worn by Confederate soldiers.

Off to the far west at Cave Spring lies another old schoolbuilding, the Hearn Dormitory Inn (open by appointment: 404-777-3382), an 1830s dorm built for the Hearn Manual Labor School. The Inn is one of the various attractions in Rolater Park, listed on the National Register, where you'll also find the cave and mineral spring that give Cave Spring its name; an 1851 Baptist church, with a balcony where slaves worshiped; and an acre and a half swimming pool, the state's second largest, shaped like Georgia. Not to be upstaged, Cedartown, south of Cave Spring, also boasts a rustic water source, Big Spring, as well as the 1848 Old Mill, renovated and opened as a restaurant in 1960 (Tu.–Sat., evenings).

In Georgia all roads don't lead to Rome but three rivers do. The Etowah and the Oostanaula meet in the northwestern Georgia town to form the Coosa. Seven hills rise in Rome, just as at the town's Italian namesake, and at the entrance to City Hall stands a replica of the famous Romulus and Remus statue on the Capitoline in Europe's Rome with an inscription (in Latin) that reads: "This statue of the Capitoline Wolf, as a forecast of prosperity and glory, has been sent from Ancient Rome to New Rome during the consulship of Benito Mussolini, in the year 1929." Thus does a memento of Italy's Il Duce decorate a corner of Georgia, U.S.A. The city received its name when the five founders, unable to agree on what to call the place, put slips of paper in a beaver hat with each entry bearing the suggestions— Hillsboro, Hamburg, Warsaw, Pittsburg and Rome, the last being drawn by chance. The town's most famous landmark, the 1871 City Clock Tower, listed on the National Register, in fact serves as a water tower. Perched on one of Rome's rises is National Register-listed Myrtle Hill Cemetery, with the graves of the first Mrs. Woodrow Wilson and the World War I "Known Soldier" and scenic views onto downtown, an area called "Between the Rivers," through which runs well-named Broad Street, the state's second-widest artery. Next to the restored 1901 train depot, now the visitor center, stands the massive 1847 Noble Machine Shop Lathe, which survived the November 1864 destruction of the Noble Iron Works by Federal troops but which still bears scars inflicted by sledge hammers the Northerners used to smash the machine.

With Floyd Junior College, Baptist-related Shorter College, Darlington prep school and Berry College, Rome is an education center. Berry, whose twenty-eight thousand-acre campus—with one hundred separate buildings—is the world's largest, began a century ago when founder Martha Berry established a school to educate children of the hill folk. Mrs. Berry persuaded Andrew Carnegie to give $50,000 and Henry Ford and other tycoons also made substantial contributions. On the campus, open to visitors, spins a huge (forty-two foot) waterwheel, delicately perched on a stone pillar, while opposite the College stands the Martha Berry Museum and Art Gallery (Tu.–Sat., 10–5; Sun., 1–5, adm.) and 1847 Oak Hill (Tu.–Sat., 10–5; Sun., 1–5, adm.), the family home. For tours of the college's animal feeding center, equestrian facility or dairy barns, call 404-236-2223. Not far from the campus is the Chieftains Museum (Tu.–F., 11–3; Sun., 2–5, free), home of Cherokee leader Ca-nung-de-cla-geh, better known as Major Ridge, major being the rank he earned while helping Andrew Jackson fight the Creek. The museum recalls the history of the Cherokee leader, who in the 1830s signed the fateful Treaty of New Echota, which led to the Trail of Tears emigration to Oklahoma, a forced march resulting in the murder of Major Ridge by resentful tribesmen. Near Calhoun, northeast of Rome, lies the New Echota State Historic Site (Tu.–Sat., 9–5; Sun., 2–5:30, adm.), location of the Cherokee national capital, established in 1825. Period buildings and displays, including a sheet of the *Phoenix,* the first Indian newspaper, published in 1828, trace the history of the tribe, whose headquarters remained at the site until 1838 when the Trail of Tears trek westward began. Another relic of yesteryear at Calhoun is the Confederate Cemetery where some four hundred soldiers who fell in the May 1864 Battle of Resaca repose, while at the Mercer Air Museum stands an outdoor collection of seventeen aircraft dating back to 1944. From May to October Calhoun hosts a popular country music show (7:30 and 10 p.m., 404-629-0226).

Dalton, to the north, calls itself "the carpet capital of the world," no exaggeration as an estimated 60 percent of the earth's carpeting originates here, manufactured in more than two hundred plants employing some 28,000 workers. The industry began in the early part of the century when Catherine Evans Whitener, a farm girl, fashioned a tufted bedspread she sold for $2.50. Soon other local women started to fabricate tufted items and eventually local factories began turning out tufted carpets. Georgia's main industry is textiles, with Dalton, which boasts more than two hundred carpet mill outlets, the leading textile center. The West Point-Pepperell factory, employing fifteen hundred workers, offers tours of the rug operation (404-278-1100). Amy's Place (404-226-2481) provides bed and breakfast in Dalton, which every August holds the Old Time Fiddlin' Convention. On highway 2, ten miles northeast of Dalton, stands the 1859 Prater Mill (Sat. and Sun., 10–6, adm.), listed on the National Register, a hand-hewn pine timber structure in the Appalachian foothills. Across the road from the rustic mill— setting for a crafts fair held on Mother's Day weekend in May and Columbus Day weekend in October—stands an old-fashioned country store. Up in the far northwestern corner of Georgia in Walker County, once so isolated that until 1942 it could be entered only by way of Alabama or Tennessee, is the Chickamauga portion of the Chickamauga and Chattanooga National Military Park (the Chattanooga section is described in the Tennessee chapter), the nation's first and largest such facility, dedicated in 1895, which commemorates the bloodiest battle in U.S. history, with 34,000 Union and Confederate soldiers killed. The visitor center (8–4:45, to 5:45 in summer, free) houses three hundred and fifty-five weapons, one of the world's best collections of American arms, while a seven-mile driving tour takes you through the battlefield to such places as the terrain where the Confederates breached the Federal line, the point where Union troops rallied to defend against the Rebels and other strategic sites. The village of Chickamauga contains a group of frontier era and Victorian buildings, many nominated for listing on the National Register, while in the town of Rossville on the Georgia-Tennessee line is the 1797 Ross House (spring and fall, Sat. and Sun., 2–6; summer, daily 2–6), a two-story log cabin where Cherokee Indian chief John Ross lived.

Back toward the center of the state, east of Dalton, lies

Chatsworth, a village nestled at the base of Fort Mountain, so named for the ruins of an ancient stone fortification. Atop Fort Mountain, considered the terminus of the Blue Ridge Mountain chain, is a cluster of craft shops. Nine miles southeast of town Carters Dam, the highest earth-filled dam east of the Mississippi, retains behind it Georgia's deepest lake (four hundred feet when full); while three miles west of Chatsworth stands the Chief Vann House (Tu.–Sat., 9–5; Sun., 2–5, adm.), built in 1804 by a Cherokee leader and sporting Indian carvings, period furnishings and a cantilevered stairway. To the north near the Tennessee line stretches the Cohutta Wilderness area of the Chattahoochee National Forest. Through the area, which includes the southern end of the Appalachian Mountain chain, run the Conasauga and the Jacks rivers, two of Georgia's best wild trout streams. The village of Blue Ridge, an attractive mountain settlement, boasts the Chattahoochee National Fish Hatchery (M.–F., 7:30–4; Sat. and Sun., 8–3:30, free) and Lake Blue Ridge, formed in 1930 by what was then the longest earthen dam (a hundred feet) in the eastern U.S. Fannin County is one of the nation's few areas with deposits of staurolite, a mineral commonly known as "Fairy Crosses," popular with collectors. Creekside Farms (404-632-3851) near Blue Ridge offers bed and breakfast in a farmhouse by a trout stream, while the Bed and Breakfast Hideaway Homes service (404-632-2411) represents north Georgia mountain area residences that take bed and breakfast guests.

To the south lies Ellijay, known as Georgia's apple capital. The second weekend in October the area celebrates the annual Apple Festival. Here the turn-of-the-century Hyatt Hotel building now serves as the courthouse for Gilmer County, which also boasts a covered bridge with open sides. To the east of Ellijay begins (or ends) the famous Appalachian Trail, seventy-eight miles of which pass through Georgia. To the south is Jasper, center of the Georgia marble industry, which every October hosts a Marble Festival (for information and for tours of a quarry during the Festival: 404-692-5600). Chunks of Georgia, second nationally in marble production, traveled north to serve the government in Washington, D.C., for the state's marble comprises the Lincoln Memorial. John's Mill, west of Jasper, is a rustic corner of Pickens County, while south of town lies Tate House, a pink marble mansion built in 1926 by Georgia Marble Company president Sam Tate as his residence and as a showcase for the stone mined from his quarries. Dining, lodging and guided tours at the beautifully restored house, listed on the National Register, are available by reservation (404-342-7515).

The hill people of the Piedmont in this part of Georgia differ from the so-called "Crackers" who dwell in the pine-covered flatland of the Coastal Plain south of the Fall Line. According to Floyd C. and Charles Hubert Watkins in their reminiscence *Yesterday in the Hills* about the folks in and around Ball Ground just south of Tate, "One of the greatest pleasures of the hill people was talk." A certain "Freeman Weaver enjoyed talking more than anybody. . . . He knew everything about every person [in the area]. . . . When Freeman drove through the [region] and saw a neighbor plowing, he stopped, hitched his horse to a tree, walked across the plowed field, stopped his friend, and began to talk. Sometimes he hindered the neighbor's work from the middle of the afternoon until dark. No one knew how to stop his talking." Who knows?—as you wind your way through the hilly back roads of the Piedmont, perhaps you'll come across Freeman jawing away. Don't stop.

Some miles off to the east stretches Lake Sidney Lanier, known as "the Houseboat Capital of the World." At least one firm, Three Buoys, offers houseboats for rent (800-262-3454). Lake Lanier Islands, at the lake's south edge, comprises a twelve hundred-acre family resort filled with recreational facilities. Near the resort the Chattahoochee River, celebrated in Georgia poet Sidney Lanier's "Song of the Chattahoochee," begins its flow to Atlanta and then on to form the western border of the state. The Chattahoochee River National Recreation Area includes a forty-eight-mile stretch of the stream popular for float trips, which you can start at the put-in points of Johnson Ferry and Powers Island (for information: 404-955-6931). Paces Mill, the last takeout point, lies at the very edge of Atlanta, whose western boundary the Chattahoochee in part forms. Gainesville, near the northern edge of Lake Sidney Lanier, contains the Georgia Mountains Museum (M.–Sat., 10–4; Sun., 2–5), with exhibits on the area's history, crafts on display and on sale, and an exhibit on the Mark Trail comic strip. The Railroad Museum, housed in a renovated baggage car, includes displays on Gainesville's rail history, while broad, tree-lined Green Street encompasses a Historic District with a relatively unspoiled group of neo-classical-style buildings. Poultry Park, with its gardens and statuary, recalls Gainesville's claim as "the Broiler Capital of the World," as does the town's whimsical ordinance that makes it illegal to eat fried chicken with a fork. Dunlap House (404-536-0200) in Gainesville offers bed and breakfast accommodations.

Northwest of the city lies the interesting old mining town of Dahlonega, site of the nation's first major gold rush (1828)—an honor also claimed by North Carolina—recalled in the Gold Museum (Tu.–Sat., 9–5; Sun., 2–5:30, adm.), installed in the handsome 1836 brick courthouse, whose square is listed on the National Register. Southern politico John C. Calhoun supposedly extracted $800,000 worth of gold from his mine, while defeated presidential candidate Samuel J. Tilden also prospered from a mine in the area, which attracted roughnecks, smoothies and prospectors. According to local lore, at the nearby settlement of Auraria, also called Knucklesville, now a ghost town, every stone had at one time or another struck someone's skull. In 1838 the federal government established a branch mint at Dahlonega which functioned until 1861, later serving as a building for North Georgia College. In 1849 mint manager Matthew F. Stephenson stood on the courthouse steps imploring miners not to depart for greener—or yellower— pastures out at the California gold fields. Stephenson's claim that gold still remained in the Dahlonega area became famous as the saying, "There's gold in them thar hills." Latter-day prospectors might want to try their hand at panning for gold out at Crisson's Gold Mine (April–Nov., 10–6, adm.). Two unusual bed and breakfast places at Dahlonega are the Worley Homestead (404-864-7002), an 1840s residence owned by an early owner's great-granddaughter, and the Smith House (404-864-3566), an inn best known for its huge family-style meals (closed M.), devoured on a summer Sunday by as many as 3,000 people. The Mountain Top Lodge (404-864-5257), a secluded inn nestled in a wooded hilly area, also offers bed and breakfast rooms, as do Dogwood Haven (404-754-4256) and Stonehenge (404-745-4675) at Blairsville to the north, and the Victorian Inn (404-745-4786), adjacent to Brasstown Bald, at 4,784 feet Georgia's highest mountain, where a visitor center houses exhibits on the area and an observation tower affords views out to four states. At Blairsville stands the 1898 red brick former Union County Courthouse, now (in part) a historical museum, and south of town is the Georgia Mountain Experiment Station (M.–F., 8–5) where the state university carries out agricultural research programs. At Hiawassee, north of Brasstown Bald, the Georgia Mountain Fair (404-896-4191) presents spring and fall festivals featuring country and gospel music, with craft shows, a pioneer village and other musical performances and events throughout the summer.

Between Neels Gap and the town of Helen runs the fourteen-mile long Richard B. Russell Scenic Highway

(Georgia highway 348), which climbs and dips its way through the Chattahoochee National Forest, across the Appalachian Trail and past splendid mountain vistas. A one-time lumber mill town rebuilt as a Bavarian Alpine village, Helen hosts throughout the year a steady series of celebrations, such as the January Fasching Karnival, a Mayfest, a Balloon Festival in June, and an Oktoberfest (for dates and information: 404-878-2181). Bed and breakfast places in Helen include the Glen-Kenimer-Tucker House (404-878-2364), the Hilltop Haus (404-878-2519 or 878-2388) and Stovall Haus (404-878-3355). The National Register-listed Old Sautee Store (M.–Sat., 9:30–5:30; Sun., 1–6, free) east of Helen contains a large collection of antique store memorabilia and a gift shop featuring Scandinavian items, while north of Helen in the Chattahoochee National Forest nestles the Anna Ruby Falls Scenic Area (7–10, adm.), an unusual twin waterfall near Unicoi State Park where you'll find in the main lodge a well-stocked craft shop (9–5) with a wide variety of Appalachian handicrafts.

South of Helen on the way to Cleveland you'll pass the 1876 Nora Mill Granary and Store, while in Cleveland the Babyland General Hospital (M.–Sat., 9–5; Sun., 1–5, free), a one-time clinic, now houses the maternity ward where the Cabbage Patch Kids dolls are "born." This is one of those rather eccentric but endearing corners of Americana one finds on the back roads and byways of the U.S.A. Over the speaker rings out the announcement, "There's a cabbage in labor. All staff to the delivery room, STAT," and in the maternity area the bald-headed babies nestle in the leafy cabbage plants awaiting adoption. Those who opt to adopt must vow "with all your heart to be the best parent in the world." Up the way, via Tearbritches Trail, lies the Moody Hollow General Store where the Furskin Bears, also available for acquisition, tend the old-time emporium. A particularly attractive shop in Cleveland is Rosehips, which specializes in

Appalachian crafts, some made on the spot by resident weavers, potters, quilters and other artisans. For bed and breakfast in the Cleveland area, contact McCollum Home (404-865-2666), RuSharon (404-865-5738) and Towering Oaks (404-865-6760). Bed and breakfast is also available in Clarkesville off to the east at Burns-Sutton House (404-754-5565) and at the evocatively named Charm House (404-754-9347). Two attractive area inns are Laprade's (404-947-3312), which occupies facilities originally built in 1916 to house and feed engineers and workers building Lake Burton for the Georgia Power Company, and Glen-Ella Springs (404-754-7295), on Bear Gap Road by Panther Creek, a rustic century-old hostelry and restaurant.

At Cornelia, south of Clarkesville, a huge red-hued apple monument, complete with a stem bearing three leaves, perches atop a white base, and nearby the decade-old Habersham Winery (M.–Sat., 10–5; Sun., 1–6, free) offers tours and tastings. On highway 197 ten miles north of Clarkesville the Mark of the Potter (10–6, free), located in the converted 1930 Grandpa Watts' Grist Mill on the Soque River, offers an attractive selection of stoneware and other craft items. At Toccoa, east of Clarkesville, plunge the one hundred and eighty-six-foot Toccoa Falls (8–7, adm.) on the campus of the local college, while a restored hydroelectric plant serves to recall the early days of water-generated power. Six miles east of Toccoa, where you'll find bed and breakfast at Habersham Manor House (404-886-6496), lies Travelers Rest (Tu.–Sat., 9–5; Sun., 2–5:30), a National Historic Landmark, built as a stagecoach inn and plantation house in 1775. At Tallulah Falls, to the northeast of Clarkesville, you'll find the Old Time General Store, housed in a turn-of-the-century building with original furnishings, and Tallulah Gorge, believed to be North America's oldest such natural feature. Anatano Farm at tiny Lakemont offers bed and breakfast rooms (404-786-6442).

Halfway between Tallulah Falls and Clayton to the north you'll pass the Lofty Branch Craftsman's Marketplace, a complex of workshops, artists' studios and a retail store featuring attractive handicrafts and hosting spring (late May) and fall (mid-October) festivals (for information: 404-782-5246). East of Clayton, forming Georgia's border with South Carolina, flows the Chattooga, selected as one of the nation's top ten white-water rivers. For rafting, canoeing or kayaking through the six-mile rapids and whirlpool-filled stretch of the Chattooga, where scenes from the movie *Deliverance* were filmed, contact Southeastern Expeditions (404-329-0433) or Wildwater, Ltd. (800-451-9972). To the northeast of Clayton—where you'll find bed and breakfast rooms at the English Inn (404-782-4411) and the Kennett Home (404-782-3186)—lies Sky Valley, which boasts Georgia's only ski resort, the nation's southernmost such area, while near Mountain City north of Clayton 1896 York House (404-746-2068), listed on the National Register, offers bed along with breakfast in bed served on a silver tray.

At the northern edge of Raburn County—more than half occupied by a National Forest and home of the high school teacher Eliot Wigginton, who created the famous *Foxfire* series of books on mountain country customs and crafts—lies the metropolis of Dillard (population: two hundred). The Copecrest Resort (404-746-2134) five miles west of the hamlet caters to square-dance groups, while at the Raburn Gap Elementary School the Top of Georgia Jamboree presents country music and dancing (June–Aug., 8 p.m.). For more than two centuries the Dillard family has lived in this far northeastern corner of Georgia, for years operating there Dillard House Inn (800-541-0671), an attractive resort in a valley surrounded by the Blue Ridge Mountains. Here at this rustic retreat would be a pleasant place to linger and to finish your tour of north Georgia's hill country.

From Atlanta to the South

Southeast: Macon—Perry—Valdosta—Thomasville
Southwest: Newnan—Warm Springs—
Columbus—Andersonville—Plains—Americus—Albany

South of Atlanta lie the Georgia haunts of Presidents Franklin Roosevelt and Jimmy Carter, Civil War sites and the plantation country. The route to the southwestern part of the state is covered below. On the way out of Atlanta toward Macon to the southeast you'll pass Forest Park, home of what is supposedly the world's largest Farmer's Market, and the nation's largest privately owned food emporium, a twenty-four-hour-a-day wholesale and retail operation filled with both everyday and exotic wares, the latter offered by Pakistanis, Indians, Thais, Laotians, Ecuadorians, Ethiopians and other ethnic groups. The Jonesboro Historic District includes twenty-two old places, among them the 1898 courthouse where Margaret Mitchell researched *Gone with the Wind*. The author summered on her grandmother's Jonesboro-area plantation, there absorbing the antebellum atmosphere that inspired the famous novel. On the Flint River stands Ashley Oaks, a handsome two-story dwelling constructed of bricks handmade by slaves. Treetops (404-471-9733) at Jonesboro offers bed and breakfast rooms. The nearby town of Fayetteville fairly reeks of a pre-Civil War atmosphere. Fife House (M.–Sat., 9–4, free), believed to be the nation's only unaltered antebellum residence, from 1855 to 1857 housed faculty and students of the Fayetteville Academy, whose most famous coed was *Gone with the Wind's* Scarlett O'Hara. Margaret Mitchell Library (M.–F., 1–6; Sat., 10–2), established by the famous novel's author, contains one of the South's most complete Civil War reference collections, as well as *Gone with the Wind* memorabilia. The 1825 Fayette County Courthouse (M., Tu., Thu., F., 8–4:30; W., Sat., 8–12) is Georgia's oldest continuously used such facility.

Tiny Senoia off to the west offers two bed and breakfast places: Culpepper House (404-599-8182) and the Veranda (404-599-3905). The turn-of-the-century Coca-Cola bottling and Baggarly Buggy building houses a collection of horse and buggy days equipment and artifacts (open by appointment: 404-599-6624). McDonough, to the east of Fayetteville, boasts an attractive town square, its turn-of-the-century courthouse and old jail listed on the National Register, while the Shingle Roof Campground is Georgia's oldest such Methodist meeting place in continuous use. In Jackson to the south rises the venerable (1823) Indian Spring Hotel, built by Creek Indian Chief William McIntosh. Griffen, back to the west, contains such historic structures as the Bailey-Tebault House, a handsome Greek Revival-style dwelling listed on the National Register; the mid-nineteenth-century Lewis-Mills House, also an attractive Register-listed Greek Revival-style residence; and the Dovetown Hosiery Mill, built about 1921 as Georgia's first silk hosiery manufacturer and now J. Henry's restaurant and retail shops. The village of Experiment just north of Griffen recalls the five-mile stretch of road constructed near there in 1919 as the state's first experimental concrete highway. At Barnesville, down the road to the south, there's a Downtown Historic District with an 1870s-era hardware store, one of the state's oldest, stocked with hundreds of vintage items. The shop once served as showroom for the Smith Buggy Company, one of the four local such manufacturers that made Barnesville "the Buggy Capital of the World."

To the southwest at Thomaston the Guest House (404-647-1203) offers bed and breakfast rooms and just to the east of Barnesville lies Forsyth, whose courthouse square and surrounding eight blocks boast forty mid-nineteenth-century structures listed on the National Register. The Whistle Stop Museum, housed in an 1899 train depot, contains Creek Indian artifacts and the 1880s-vintage typesetters desk used by Uncle Remus author Joel Chandler Harris when he apprenticed at the *Monroe Advertiser*. A Country Place (912-994-2705) near Forsyth provides bed and breakfast accommodations, while twelve miles south of town on highway 83 hides the little-known hamlet of Culloden, a pre-Civil War settlement with an 1802 Methodist church. Off to the east of Forsyth lie Percale, established in 1966 and named for the cotton fabric, and Juliette, where the 1927 grist mill was once the world's largest waterpowered such installation. Nearby Jarrell Plantation (Tu.–Sat., 9–5, Sun., 2–5:30, adm.) is a seven and a half-acre working farm with equipment and installations spanning the years from the 1840s to the 1940s. You'll find another relic from yesteryear at nearby Clinton, a hamlet of three hundred people where a dozen or so early nineteenth-century structures present a picture of how a typical Georgia frontier era county seat looked. Of Georgia's early county seats only Clinton, a New England-type settlement, once the state's fourth-largest town, has survived virtually untouched by time. The Clinton Female Seminary was supposedly the forerunner of the world's first institution chartered to grant degrees to women. A roadside park at Clinton contains huge granite outcroppings which mark a bit of the Fall Line, the geologic formation separating Piedmont from the Low Country.

Just south of Clinton lies Macon, Georgia's third-largest city, laid out in 1823 on a plan that followed the design of the ancient Gardens of Babylon, providing for large park-filled blocks and wide streets. Located on the Fall Line, Macon nestles in a green valley where the Piedmont Plateau slopes north to the mountains and the Coastal Plain stretches nearly two hundred miles south to the sea. Around Macon stand dozens of lovely old buildings, more than fifty of them listed on the National Register and most furnished not only with antiques but also with memories of yesteryear. Among the show places, all Register-listed, are the mid-nineteenth-century Hay House (Tu.–Sat., 10:30–4:30, Sun., 2–4, adm.), an Italian Renaissance Revival-style pile surrounded by balconies and topped by a kind of cupola; the Old Cannonball House (Tu.–F., 10:30–1; 2:30–5; Sat. and Sun., 1:30–4, adm.), struck in 1864 by a projectile that bounced off a column, smashed through a window and landed in the main hallway; the 1906 restored Grand Opera House (tours, M.–F. at 10, 12, 2, adm.), believed the South's largest stage; the 1889 Old Macon Library, with an attractive high-vaulted second-floor reading room; the 1840 Holt-Peeler-Snow House, birthplace of Nanaline Holt, mother of billionairess Doris Duke; the Woodruff House, dating from the 1830s, scene of a ball held for Winnie Davis, Jefferson Davis's daughter, and once owned by Colonel Joseph Bond, who in 1857 sold 2,200 bales of cotton for $100,000, the era's largest such transaction; the Lanier Cottage (M.–F., 9–1, 2–4; Sat., 9:30–12:30, adm.), where poet Sidney Lanier was born in 1842; and First Presbyterian Church, which Lanier attended, and Christ Episcopal, where he married. In the Municipal Auditorium, topped by the world's largest copper-covered dome, murals depict the area's history from Spanish explorer Hernando de Soto's 1540 visit to World War I, while murals in the New Federal Building also picture the town's past.

Museums in Macon include Ocmulgee National Monument (9–5, adm.), part of the largest archeological development east of the Mississippi, with artifacts from six distinct Indian cultures which occupied the site; the Museum of Arts and Science and Mark Smith Planetarium (M.–Th. and Sat., 9–5; F., 9–9; Sun., 1–5, adm.); and the Harriet Tubman Historical and Cultural Museum (M.–F., 10–5; Sat. and Sun., 2–5, free), with art exhibits and displays relating to black culture. The fourth week in March Macon mounts an elaborate Cherry Blossom Festival, featuring the city's 115,000 Yoshino cherry trees, then in full bloom, and dozens of exhibits, music performances, dances, balls and other festive events (for information: 912-744-7429). Macon's bed and breakfast places include Carriage Stop Inn (912-743-9740), 1842 Inn (912-741-1842), Victorian Village (912-743-3333) and La Petite Maison (912-742-4674). The Brown and Williamson Tobacco Company factory in Macon offers plant tours (M.–F., 8:30–4, by reservation: 912-743-0561), while at tiny Lizella west of Macon you'll find another factory, Middle Georgia, which retains much of the original nineteenth-century machinery and equipment used to make whiskey jugs back in the old days. On the courthouse lawn at nearby Knoxville stands a statue of Joanna Troutman, who in 1835 designed the Texas Lone Star flag that Georgia volunteers carried in the Texan struggle for independence from Mexico. At Roberta, just to the west, lies Troutman's pre-1835 home as well as a downtown Historic District with an old jail and vintage general store.

South of Macon lies Peach County, created on July 18, 1924 as the newest of Georgia's one hundred and fifty-nine such units—more than any other state except Texas—which are subdivided into political sections with the curious and antiquated designation "militia districts." In Peach County, one of Georgia's main peach-producing areas, the blossoms peak in mid-March and the fruit is available from June to August. You'll find the best views of the trees along U.S. highway 341. Other plantings embellish the Fort Valley area, home of the American Camellia Society, where those flowers bloom from November to March. A gallery (M.–F., 8:30–12, 1–4, free) at the Society's gardens houses a collection of Boehm porcelain. Fort Valley—so named when the 1825 post office application in the name of Fox Valley was misread in Washington—also boasts the Blue Bird Body Company, the world's largest school bus manufacturer (tours available: 912-825-2021). At Marshallville, three miles south of the Camellia Society headquarters, Suite Revenge (912-967-2252) offers bed and breakfast. Stately old houses in Marshallville recall the early days of the town's prosperity, nurtured by the Elberta peach, developed in the 1870s by Samuel Henry Rumph, who also invented the refrigerated boxcar to transport the fruit to northern markets. A few miles south of town Georgia's only remaining ferry, a fifty-foot cable-drawn steel barge, operates across the Flint River (honk for service during daylight hours).

Thanks to the highway network that intersects at Perry, the town is called "The Crossroads of Georgia" and its more than one thousand hotel and motel rooms give it the additional designation of "The Motel City." This two-slogans-for-one town makes up in a small way for the fact that the legislature has never officially adopted a slogan for the State of Georgia. Perry boasts the nation's only golf ball mold manufacturer, and another industrial facility, the Heileman brewery, offers tours (M.–F., 9–4; for reservations: 912-987-3639). The recently opened Georgia Agricenter at Perry held its first fair in October 1989. Back to the north a few miles at Robins Air Force Base, which offers tours by prior arrangement (912-926-2137), you'll find the Museum of Aviation (Tu.–Sun., 10–5, free). The fast-expanding museum, which has steadily added exhibit and hangar space, boasts more than fifty historic aircraft as well as displays of aviation memorabilia dating back to World War I, including the General Robert L. Scott—"God Is My Co-pilot"—collection. If you're heading toward Savannah, Dublin, off to the east beyond Allentown—whose unusual location puts it at the junction of fully four counties: Bleckley, Laurens, Twiggs and Wilkinson—offers a small history museum (Tu., Th.,

Sat., 1–5) installed in the former Carnegie Library; the 1811 Chappell Mill, still in operation; and Fish Trap Cut, ancient Indian-built mounds and a canal by the Oconee River believed to have served as a fish trap. True to its name, Dublin mounts a St. Patricks Festival for two weeks in early March. At a track on highway 129 in Hawkinsville, southwest of Dublin, harness-race horses train from November until early March before heading north for the racing season. Known as "the City of Thirteen Highways" for the many routes that intersect there, Hawkinsville boasts a National Register-listed 1883 steam-powered fire-fighting pumper, displayed on the lawn of the 1907 Opera House.

Down at Eastman, off to the southwest, the Dodge Hill Inn (912-374-2644) offers bed and breakfast rooms, and a mile south of nearby Chauncey lies the oddly named village of Suomi, the Finnish word for Finland, but no fen-land or swamp soaks the area, the designation having originated, so it's believed, from Finnish loggers brought to the area to cut timber and work in the sawmills there. The logging industry is recalled at the town of Lumber City on the Ocmulgee River to the southeast, location in the mid-nineteenth century of the South's largest sawmill. Due south of Eastman lies Fitzgerald, whose Blue and Gray Museum (April–Sept., M.–F., 2–5, off season by appointment: 912-423-5375, adm.) contains a rare and perhaps unique combination of both Union and Confederate Civil War relics, a mix due to the fact that Union veterans founded the town in 1865. It was in this area, not far from Irwinville, where Confederate President Jefferson Davis was captured on May 16, 1865.

Although Cordele, back to the northwest, claims to be "The Watermelon Capital of the World," it's a peanut industry operation that offers tours there—the Paul Hattaway firm, which manufacturers peanut-shelling equipment (half-hour tours, M.–F.). Ashburn to the south boasts the world's largest peanut monument as well as the world's biggest shelling plant (open for tours: 912-567-3311). At Tifton, to the south on Interstate 75, the Agrirama (June through Labor Day, 9–6; Labor Day to May 31, M.–Sat., 9–5; Sun., 12:30–5, adm.) encompasses antique buildings, a country store, old-fashioned craft demonstrations, a sawmill, a cotton gin, and other relics of yesteryear which combine to form a living history museum operated by the state of Georgia. From July through September the Wiregrass Opry performs on Saturday nights. Myron Bed and Breakfast (912-382-0959) offers accommodations in the turn-of-the-century Grand Hotel downtown. A village to the east of Tifton presents a true Enigma—the town's name.

Continuing south toward Florida you'll reach Moultrie, seat of Colquitt County, a rich agricultural area which is one of Georgia's leading producers of tobacco, peanuts, corn and cotton. In the center of town stands the White House-like courthouse, while in the County Library (M.–Sat., 8:30–5:30; Tu., to 8) you'll find a large collection of genealogical material on the entire eastern U.S. and on migration patterns to the West. In mid-October the huge Sunbelt Agricultural Exposition takes place at Moultrie, which calls itself "the Quail Capital of the World," quail hunting being offered at such places as Ashburn Hill Plantation (912-985-5069), Boggy Pond (912-985-8585), Pinefields Plantation (912-985-2086) and Quail Ridge (912-769-3201). Back toward the interstate lies the town of Berlin, which during World War I changed its name to Lens; while nearby Adel, originally called Puddleville, took its new name (in 1889) by selecting out the four middle letters of Philadelphia. At Valdosta, called "the Azalea City" and once the nation's smallest town with a streetcar system, you'll find three National Register Historic Districts and such showplaces as 1889 Crescent House (F., 2–5), so called for the columned, gracefully curved front porch; and Barber House (M.–F., 9–5), built in 1915 for E. R. Barber, the world's second bottler of Coca-

Cola. Tiny Needmore, off to the east of Valdosta, received its name when customers of a general store there complained about needing more merchandise.

Thomasville off to the west is a photogenic town with a gracious atmosphere. In the late nineteenth century wealthy Northerners began to winter in Thomasville, some staying in one of the six resort hotels there, others occupying such "cottages" as the sixteen-room 1884 Lapham-Patterson House (Tu.–Sat., 9–5; Sun., 2–5:30, adm.), listed on the National Register, and still others staying at their own plantation, such as Pebble Hill (Tu.–Sat., 10–5; Sun., 1–5, adm.), a magnificent property owned by the Hanna family of Cleveland and rebuilt after a 1930s fire under the direction of Abram Garfield, son of U.S. President James A. Garfield. The famous Cleveland family recalls Ogden Nash's verse, in the introduction to the *Savannah Cookbook,* about the well-known "remark made by the late Mark Hanna:/'I care not who makes our Presidents as long as/I can eat in Savannah.'" At well-garnished Thomasville you'll find the Rose Test Gardens (mid-April to mid-Nov. during daylight hours, free) where some two thousand rose plants grow; Big Oak, believed to be Georgia's largest live oak; and Paradise Park, a twenty-six-acre forest in the middle of town. Additional historical areas in Thomasville include Confederate Prison, a park where a few ditches that formed part of the jail remain, and the Old Cemetery where native son Henry Ossian Flipper, West Point's first black graduate (1877), reposes. One Thomasville native daughter who became known is actress Joanne Woodward. For accommodations in the area Quail Country Bed and Breakfast (912-226-7218 or 226-6882) can make reservations for you, while Magnolia Inn (912-228-4876 or 228-7915), Neel House (912-228-6000) and Susina Plantation Inn (912-377-9644) offer bed and breakfast rooms. To the west of Thomasville lies Cairo, Georgia's cane grinding and syrup center as well

as "the Okra Capital of the World" and the town where
baseball star Jackie Robinson was born. Cairo's Roddenberry
Memorial Library (M.–W. and F., 9–6; Th., 9–8; Sat., 9–12,
free) contains history, wildlife and art exhibits. Every November the hamlet of Cavalry to the south holds a Mule
Day celebration.

Returning now to Atlanta, if you're headed southwest out
of the metropolis the itinerary will first take you to Lithia
Springs off to the west, site of one of the world's three
mineral springs with lithium in the water, of the Family
Doctor Museum (M.–F., 9–5; Sat., 10–12, free), and of the
Lithia Springs Water and Bottling Company. Nearby Doug-
lasville occupies a site once known as Skint Chestnut, so
called for the bark-skinned tree there Indians used as a landmark. At Carrollton off to the west is the Southwire Company, the world's largest privately owned rod and cable
manufacturing company (for tours: 404-832-4242, ext. 4572),
and the world's largest record manufacturing plant, operated
by CBS. Fairburn, back to the east, an attractive and peaceful
town with the historic old Campbell County Courthouse,
presents every year on six weekends in late April, May and
June the Georgia Renaissance Festival (for information: 404-
964-8575) featuring costumed merrymakers, jugglers, fire
eaters, jousting, archery, artisans and other past-time pas-
times.

To the southwest lies Newnan, a medical center during
the Civil War where seven hospitals treated wounded of both
sides. Because of the town's hospital status General Sherman
spared Newnan, many of whose antebellum homes survive
in their original state. The Male Academy Museum (Tu.–
Thu., 10–12, 1–3; Sat. and Sun., 2–5, adm.), installed in
the town's 1883 boys' school building, contains Civil War
artifacts and a large collection of period clothing. Newnan's
Parrot Camp Soucy House (404-253-4846) offers bed and
breakfast. At the village of Sharpsburg in Coweta County

antique and craft shops occupy the restored old mercantile buildings. Grand Ole Opry star Minnie Pearl was once a drama coach at Dunaway Gardens in the northern part of the county, while at White Oak in the south was born novelist Erskine Caldwell, whose father served as pastor at the Presbyterian church there. The contents of Caldwell's most famous book, *Tobacco Road*, may be fiction but not the title, for a Tobacco Road does exist in Georgia, a route extending from Wilkes County to one-time tobacco market Augusta over which mules and oxen drew carts carrying hogsheads packed with tobacco. The road south takes you down to LaGrange, perched next to West Point Lake, which snakes across the state line into Alabama. Around the lake cluster any number of recreational facilities (for information: 404-645-2937).

LaGrange College, established in 1831, is Georgia's oldest independent non-tax-supported institution of higher education, while other historic corners of town include National Register-listed Bellevue (Tu.–Sat., 10–12, 2–6; Sun., 2–5, adm.), the 1859 home of U.S. Senator Benjamin Hill, and the 1892 Troup County Jail which these days houses an art gallery (Tu.–F., 9–5; Sat., 9–4; Sun., 1–5, free). On the college campus is the Lamar Dodd Art Center (M.–F., free), named for the man many consider to be Georgia's greatest living artist. The 1929 Callaway Memorial Tower echoes the design of the famous Campanile in Venice's St. Mark's Square, while the statue of Marquis de Lafayette, for whose estate in France LaGrange was named, duplicates the statue of the famous Frenchman that stands in LePuy, France. At Greenville to the east the 1832 Samples Plantation Inn (404-672-4765) offers bed and breakfast in a lovely neoclassical-style house. Tiny Woodbury, off to the east, once claimed to be the "Pimento Capital of the World," but somehow the village has renounced the title. Perhaps the pimento powers that be moved the capital elsewhere.

Warm Springs, home of Franklin Roosevelt's Little White House, nestles in the hills to the south. Eight years after Roosevelt first visited Warm Springs in 1924 to try the waters for his polio he moved into his own home there. The simple yet comfortable three-bedroom residence, which soon became known the world over as "the Little White House" (9–5, June–Aug., weekends to 6, adm.), perches on the edge of a forested hill that falls off sharply beneath a terrace just beyond the house. Visitors enter through the kitchen, where a hand-scrawled note written by the cook reads: "Daisy Bonner cook the 1st meal and the last one in this cottage for the President Roosevelt." On an easel in the living-dining room rests the famous portrait of the president left unfinished after he died in the house on April 12, 1945. At the nearby museum exhibits trace FDR's political career and his frequent visits to Warm Springs. One rare scene in a twelve-minute movie on Roosevelt's visits to the area shows the President with his leg braces visible over his trousers, an image never revealed to the public during FDR's lifetime. To get an idea of the treatments Roosevelt found so beneficial for his polio it's worth visiting the warm springs area, about two miles from the Little White House. In Georgia Hall at the March of Dimes-funded institution for polio sufferers FDR would traditionally attend Thanksgiving dinner with his fellow victims of the disease.

A rather delightful group of nineteenth-century buildings embellishes the center of Warm Springs, near which, by the Southern Railroad tracks, stands a plaque marking the site of the old depot where Roosevelt arrived and departed between 1924 and 1945. In April 1939 his parting comment there was, "I'll see you in the fall if we don't have war." In April, six years later, Roosevelt was dead, and from this spot on April 13, 1945, the body of the thirty-second president was transported to its final resting place at Hyde Park, New York—the last journey from Warm Springs and the end of an era. Around rustic Meriwether County, where covered bridges stand at Red Oak and at White Oak Creeks, live the sort of down-home folks who, FDR once observed, gave him "a better perspective of life, or a better sense of proportion about all sorts of things, from peanuts to politics."

Over at Pine Mountain to the west lies Callaway Gardens, an unusually attractive resort (800-282-8181 or 404-663-2281) criss-crossed with trails and with such delightful enclaves as Mr. Cason's Vegetable Garden, with more than four hundred varieties of fruits, vegetables and herbs, a pioneer log cabin, and an octagonal glass-enclosed conservatory that houses a thousand butterflies. The nearby village of Pine Mountain includes a group of old-time shops, among them Kimbrough Brothers General Store, in continuous operation since 1892. At Hamilton, six miles south of Callaway Gardens, Wedgwood Bed and Breakfast (404-628-5659) offers accommodations.

Columbus, the region's leading city, was established in 1828 on the banks of the Chattahoochee River at the foot of a series of falls that provided waterpower for industry and made the settlement the northernmost navigable port on Georgia's longest river. Columbus boasts such National Register-listed sights as the Rankin House, embellished with wrought-iron trim; the 1828 Walker-Peters-Langdon House, the city's oldest dwelling, now headquarters for the Historic Columbus Foundation, which operates the Heritage Tour to many of the city's old houses (404-322-0756); the restored 1871 Springer Opera House, with three tiers of boxes and gold tulip-shaped lights; and the cottage (moved from the countryside) occupied from 1855 to 1860 by Dr. John Styth Pemberton, who originated the formula for Coca-Cola. The Chattahoochee Promenade links such local attractions as the Columbus Naval Museum (Tu.–Sat., 10–5; Sun., 2–5, free), which houses hulls of Civil War gunboats raised from the bottom of the Chattahoochee a century after they were sunk by Confederates to prevent capture by Yankee forces, and the Columbus Ironworks, a large factory along the river once used to manufacture cannons for the South and now attractively restored as the city's Convention and Trade Center. The Columbus Museum (M.–F., 10–5; Sat., 2–5, free), featuring fine arts and historical displays, opened its new building in April 1989.

At nearby Fort Benning, named for local-boy-made-good Confederate General Henry L. Benning, the world's largest infantry camp at two hundred and eighty-four square miles, you'll find the National Infantry Museum (Tu.–F., 10–4:30; Sat. and Sun., 12:30–4:30, free), with an extensive collection of small arms, while on the base rises stately Riverside, the commanding general's residence. Company tours in Columbus include snack packager Tom's Foods (Sept.–May, Tu., and Wed., 9:30, 10:30 and 1, by appointment: 404-323-2721, ext. 131); Sunshine Biscuits (Tu.–F., 9 and 1, by appointment: 404-689-0150) and the *Columbus Ledger-Enquirer* (by appointment: 404-324-5526), successor to the paper founded in 1828 by Mirabeau Buonaparte Lamar, later President of the Republic of Texas. Julian La Rose Harris, son of Joel Chandler Harris, edited the paper in 1926 when the daily, then called the *Enquirer-Sun,* won a Pulitzer Prize. Columbus's most famous writer was Carson McCullers, like her sister Georgia author Flannery O'Conner, from Milledgeville, a sickly type and one who favored what might be called the Southern Grotesque style of writing, typified by such works as *The Ballad of the Sad Café* which depicts love, lovelessness and loneliness in a "dreary" Georgia town, "empty, white with dust," with "peach trees [that] seem to grow more crooked every summer." Bed and breakfast in Columbus is available at the 1863 DeLoffre House (404-324-1144).

Heading south from Columbus you'll come to Lumpkin, home of Westville (M.–F., 10–5; Sun., 1–5, adm.), a recreation of the 1850s way of life before the Industrial Revolution with old buildings relocated there from the countryside and with craft demonstrations. The Bedingfield Inn (Tu.–Sun., 1–5, adm.) is a restored 1836 stagecoach hostelry, while the Hatchett Drug Store (Tu.–Sun., 1–5, adm.), with a collection of antique items, served as town apothecary from 1875 to 1950. Off to the east lies Preston, near which was born Walter F. George, who served thirty-four years in the U.S. Senate, never losing an election. In 1922 George delayed taking his seat so Rebecca Latimer Felton, the nation's first female Senator, appointed by Georgia's governor, could serve for two days. A feminist, temperance fighter, newspaper columnist, Felton died in 1930 at age ninety-five and reposes in Decatur, near Atlanta.

The hometown of Georgia's most famous politician, Jimmy Carter, is at Plains, just to the southeast of Preston. The seemingly plain name of Plains doesn't originate from the area's geographical features but from an older crossroads about a mile north of town called the Plains of Dura, a designation for the area near Babylon where Nebuchadnezzar erected a colossal golden image he ordered his subjects to worship. A visit to Plains, a town of some seven hundred people, gives you an idea of the deep roots Jimmy Carter, whose ancestors arrived in the area in the eighteenth century, has there. There is something heartwarming and basic and, yes, plain about Plains, far from the greater world beyond— the world of power politics and international vexations—to which the town's native son ventured forth, later returning to his roots. The Carter National Historic Site includes the President's boyhood home, his current residence, Plains High School and the train depot, now a museum, that served as campaign headquarters for the 1976 election. Plains Bed and Breakfast (912-824-7252) and Plains Country Inn (912-824-4410) offer rooms.

Nearby Americus, the county seat, takes its name from

explorer Americus Vespucius or, some say, from the "merry cusses," as the happy-go-lucky early settlers called themselves. Downtown's centerpiece, the 1892 Windsor Hotel, a red brick pile listed on the National Register, has recently undergone restoration. A marker at Souther Field, north of town, recalls Charles A. Lindbergh's first solo flight, which took place there. Merriwood Country Inn near Americus offers bed and breakfast (912-924-4992).

Ten miles northeast of Plains lies Andersonville, or Camp Sumter as it was officially known, the largest of the Confederate Civil War military prisons. Established in 1864, Andersonville held more than 55,000 Union soldiers during the camp's fourteen months of existence, and at the prison nearly 13,000 of the inmates died. The Andersonville National Historic Site includes a visitor center with historical exhibits, the prison site and a national cemetery, the nation's only place with a memorial to all American prisoners of war, a bronze statue portraying three enfeebled men. In May 1989 survivors of the infamous Stalag 17 Nazi prisoner-of-war camp gathered at Andersonville to dedicate a granite memorial to American POWs imprisoned in Europe. The hamlet of Andersonville (population: three hundred), which served as the Southwestern Railroad terminal where 45,000 Federal prisoners of war arrived in 1864 and early 1865, is a picture out of the past, with a museum housed in a nineteenth-century depot, the Pennington St. James log church, designed by the same architect who planned St. John the Divine in New York City, and other relics of the old days.

Continuing to the south, Dawson claims to be the world's largest Spanish-peanut market—perhaps Spain boasts a town that's the largest Georgia-peanut market—while Cuthbert to the west is an attractive town with thirty mid-nineteenth-century houses listed on the National Register, including the 1856 King-Stapelton House and the 1888 residence where jazz musician Fletcher Henderson was born. Andrew College, chartered in 1854, holds the distinction of being the nation's second-oldest college authorized to grant degrees to women, while the Shellman Historic District includes the Scottish American Heritage Center. More Georgia-born musicians originated at Albany to the south, hometown of trumpeter Harry James and of composer and pianist Ray Charles. Known as "the Pecan Capital of the World," Albany raises, in addition to nuts, animals at the Chehaw Wild Animal Park (9–5, adm.), a wildlife preserve where elephants, giraffes, lions, bears and other such beasts roam. The Thronateeska Heritage Foundation (Tu.–Sun., 2–5, free) contains local history and natural science exhibits, while old buildings include 1860 Smith House, the town's first brick dwelling, and 1859 St. Teresa's Church, the state's oldest Catholic sanctuary in continuous use, both listed on the National Register. The Marine Corps Logistics Base at Albany controls supplies for the entire corps. Outside town along the Flint River begins a thirty-mile stretch of sand dunes, believed by some geologists to have once been the Gulf of Mexico shore.

To complete your tour of Georgia south of Atlanta, you'll find over at Blakely, southwest of Albany, the Kolomoki Indian mounds (Tu.–Sat., 9–5; Sun., 2–5), a National Historic Landmark, and on courthouse square a peanut monument and the last remaining Confederate flagpole (1861). Nine miles west off highway 62 stretches the nearly hundred-foot long late nineteenth-century Coheelee Creek Covered Bridge. At Colquitt, to the southeast, is a twenty-three-foot Indian head carved from a red oak tree by Hungarian sculptor Peter Toth, who spent his career creating Indian memorials in different states. In the far southwestern corner of the state lies Lake Seminole—source of Florida's Apalachicola River—formed by the 1957 Jim Woodruff Dam that impounds the Chattahoochee and Flint Rivers, now three times as deep as their three-foot depth before the dam. Seminole County

borders two states, Alabama and Florida, so Georgia here
has run out of space.

Savannah, the Coast and the Southeast

Savannah is one of those rare places where the town itself,
rather than any particular landmark or any single museum
or individual sight, is the main attraction. The city began
in 1733 when James Oglethorpe led the first settlers from
England to a bluff at the mouth of the Savannah River. The
purpose of the new colony was to give an opportunity to
the disadvantaged of London, "gentlemen of decayed circumstances" as Oglethorpe described them. Benjamin Mar-
tyn, Secretary for the Trustees who ran the trust that held
rights to the new colony, explained in 1733 that "as every
wise government, like the Bees, should not suffer any
Drones in the State, these poor should be situated in such
Places, where they might be easy themselves, and useful to
the Commonwealth." Although the first group included a
few "Grumbletonians," as Thomas Causton, the colony's
storekeeper and bailiff wrote to his wife, the new venture
survived and soon attracted more settlers, among them
Scots, Italians, Germans, Greeks and Irish. A century after
Savannah's founding Anne Royall—disproving the complaint
of Georgia pioneer Mary Boykin Chesnut, who grouched
in her *Diary from Dixie* that English travelers came "with
three P's, Pen, Paper, Prejudices"—noted in her 1831 account
of a tour through the South that "Savannah is the first city
of the south, by a long way. The citizens are wealthy, sober,
intelligent, hospitable, industrious, and high-minded, to a
degree which few towns in the United States can reach."
Such a treasure did Savannah become that when William
Tecumseh Sherman took the city after his famous "March

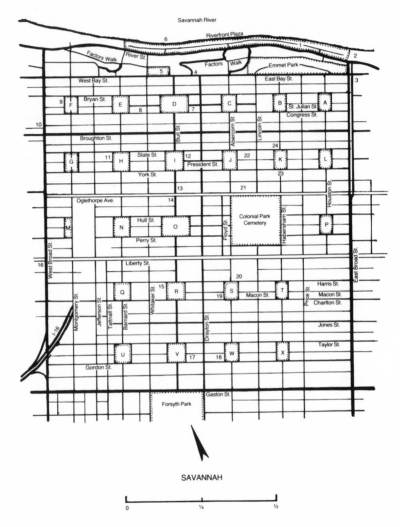

SAVANNAH

0　　　　　　¼　　　　　　½

A.	Washington Square	1.	Ships of the Sea Museum
B.	Warren Square.	2.	The Waving Girl
C.	Reynolds Square	3.	Pirates' House/Trustees' Garden
D.	Johnson Square	4.	Cotton Exchange
E.	Ellis Square	5.	City Hall
F.	Franklin Square	6.	Savannah River Cruises
G.	Liberty Square	7.	Christ Church
H.	Wright Square	8.	Tic Toc Museum
I.	Telfair Square	9.	First African Baptist Church
J.	Oglethorpe Square	10.	Scarborough House
K.	Columbia Square	11.	Telfair Mansion (Art Museum)
L.	Greene Square	12.	Lutheran Church of the Ascension
M.	Elbert Square	13.	Juliette Gordon Low Girl Scout Center
N.	Orleans Square	14.	Independent Presbyterian Church
O.	Chippewa Square	15.	Green-Meldrim Home
P.	Crawford Square	16.	Savannah Visitors' Center
Q.	Pulaski Square	17.	Temple Mikve Israel
R.	Madison Square	18.	Wesley Monumental Church
S.	Lafayette Square	19.	Andrew Low House
T.	Troup Square	20.	Cathedral of St. John the Baptist
U.	Chatham Square	21.	Marshall Row
V.	Monterrey Square	22.	Owens-Thomas House
W.	Calhoun Square	23.	Bethesda Gate

to the Sea," the Union general informed President Lincoln
on December 22, 1864: "I beg to present you as a Christmas
Gift the City of Savannah." Others, however, thought less
of the town: John M. Harney, who in 1820 abandoned the
city after failing to establish there the *Georgian* newspaper,
bid an ascerbic "Farewell to Savannah" in a poem that began,
"Farewell, oh, Savannah, forever farewell,/Thou hot bed of
rogues, that threshold of hell," a place "Where man is worth
nothing, except in one sense,/Which they always compute
in pounds, shillings and pence." He ends: "I leave you,
Savannah—a curse that is far/The worst of all curses—to
remain as you are!"

Harney's curse became a blessing for today's visitors to
the city, for Savannah has indeed remained much as it was
in the old days, a town of spacious squares and gracious
houses, trees and statues and a rather laid-back pace uncom-
mon on the eve of the twenty-first century. Savannah may
even be mislaid-back, rather too backward-looking: Betsy
Fancher in *Savannah: A Renaissance of the Heart* suggests that
"Ancestor worship is Savannah's besetting sin." A good
place to introduce yourself to the city's delights is at the
visitor center (M.–F., 8:30–5; Sat. and Sun., 9–5), installed
in the restored Civil War-era Central of Georgia depot,
where you'll also find the Great Savannah Exposition (9–5,
adm.), a multimedia presentation and collection of historic
artifacts that recall the city's two-and-a-half-century past.
To visit Savannah, which boasts the nation's largest National
Historic Landmark District, takes a few days; to see
Savannah—all the hidden corners, architectural details, and,
in at least one case, ghost-haunted (the dwelling at 506 East
Julian Street) houses—would take months. Among the
showplaces are the 1848 house of Andrew Low (M.–Sat.,
10:30–4, adm.), whose son married Juliette Gordon, founder
of the Girl Scouts, at the residence in 1912, and the Low
Girl Scout National Center (M., Tu., Th.–Sat., 10–4; Sun.,

12:30–4:30 except Dec. and Jan., adm.), birth house of Juliette Gordon; the 1852 Green Meldrim House (Tu., Th.–Sat., 10–4, adm.), known for its stained glass windows, where General Sherman headquartered at the end of his "March to the Sea."

Savannah museums include the Telfair Academy of Arts and Sciences (Tu.–Sat., 10–5; Sun., 2–5, adm.), the Savannah Science Museum (Tu.–Sat., 10–5; Sun., 2–5, adm.), and such ocean-oriented institutions as the Skidaway Marine Science Complex (M.–F., 9–4; Sat. and Sun., 12–5, free), with exhibits on the flora and fauna of the Continental Shelf, the Ships of the Sea Museum (10–5, adm.), and Tybee Lighthouse and Museum (summer, 10–6; winter, 1–5, adm.) at Tybee Island, location of Fort Screven, one of Savannah's historic military installations, which also include Fort Jackson (March–Dec., Tu.–Sat., 9–5, adm.), the Civil War Fort McAllister (Tu.–Sat., 9–5; Sun., 2–5:30, adm.), and Fort Pulaski National Monument (summer, 8:30–6:45, winter, 8:30–5:15, adm.). At Colonial Park Cemetery repose many early settlers, including Button Gwinnett, signer of the Declaration of Independence and not much else—collectors find his signature exceedingly rare—while at tree- and flower-filled Bonaventure Cemetery poet Conrad Aiken and composer Johnny Mercer perhaps combine their words and music through eternity. Factor's Walk, a cobblestone way near the river lined with nineteenth-century cotton buildings, and the 1852 U.S. Customs House recall Savannah's early commercial enterprises. Where the Customs House now stands lived James Oglethorpe, and at this site founder of Methodism John Wesley preached his first Savannah sermon.

Soon after Wesley arrived in Savannah in the spring of 1735 he met Miss Sophia Hopkey, who received from the thirty-three-year-old bachelor at least spiritual, if not carnal, attentions. When Wesley turned from matters of eternity to more temporal subjects and proposed marriage, Sophia rebuffed him, in March 1737 marrying William Williamson, who became so enraged when Wesley refused to give his wife Communion he sued the preacher for £1,000. The case caused a furor and everyone in the colony took sides. Wesley demanded an immediate trial but when the proceedings were delayed he snuck away under cover of night to Charleston, South Carolina, from where he returned to London. In Reynolds Square stands a statue of Wesley, while at Christ Episcopal, the colony's first church, he preached and established what's believed to be the world's first Sunday school (1736). Other historic religious buildings include Wesley Monumental Methodist, where the Massie School survives as the only remaining original building of Georgia's oldest chartered school system; Independent Presbyterian, where in 1885 Woodrow Wilson married Ellen Axson, the pastor's granddaughter; First African Baptist, the nation's first black congregation, established in 1788 (the present structure dates from 1859); and Temple Mickve Israel, the nation's third-oldest synagogue (1733) and the oldest Reform congregation.

For meals in Savannah Mrs. Wilkes' Dining Room, 107 West Jones, is a legendary local eatery, with family style all-you-can-eat home cooking (11:30–3). For bed and breakfast Savannah Historic Inns and Guest Houses (800-262-4667 from 1–5 p.m.) can book at area establishments, among which are Barrister House (912-234-0621), Charlton Court (912-236-2895), Comer House (912-234-2923), Harris House (912-236-8828) and Timmons House (912-233-4456). Also, such inns as Liberty (912-233-1007), Magnolia Place (912-236-7674), Old Harbour (912-234-4100), Planters (912-232-5678), Pulaski Square (912-232-8055) and 17Hundred90 Inn (912-236-7122).

Before heading away from the ocean to the attractions in the hinterland west of Savannah, the island-clotted coastal area south of the city is worth exploring. Any number of wildlife refuges and wilderness areas nestle along the coast, rife with rivers, inlets, marshes and other watery indentations. As you head south out of Savannah you'll pass near Midway, where in 1752 there settled a group of New England Puritans who for several generations had lived in South Carolina. The 1792 church they built, the fourth on the site, survives beneath an ancient oak as a lovely rememberance of Georgia's early days. At Hinesville off to the west is a Military Museum (M.–F., 1–5; Sat. and Sun., 2–6) and the old Liberty County Jail, where the Arts Council Director now serves time, while at Sunbury to the east, Georgia's second-largest seaport in colonial times, a visitor center recalls the area's history.

Farther south lies Blackbeard Island, the site where pirate Edward Teach, better and more graphically known as Blackbeard, established his headquarters in 1716; while the adjacent Sapelo Island National Estuarine Sanctuary, once the home of tobacco magnate R. J. Reynolds, offers tours of the remote preserve (Sept.–May, W. and Sat., June–Aug., W., F. and Sat., March–Oct., all-day tours last W. of month; for information and reservations: 912-437-4192). At the gateway to the sanctuary, Darien, settled in 1735 by Scottish Highlanders who brought to the New World the game of golf, stands Christ Chapel, called "the littlest church in the United States"—ten by fifteen feet, with seats for twelve—and the reconstructed Fort King George (Tu.–Sat., 9–5; Sun., 2–5:30, free), the first English presence in Georgia (1721). Open Gates (912-437-6985) in Darien offers bed and breakfast. On the way down to Brunswick, route to the so called "Golden Isles," you'll pass the Hofwyl (rhymes with "waffle")-Broadfield Plantation (Tu.–Sat., 9–5; Sun., 2–5, adm.), a splendid surviving example of the many coastal rice farms that once operated in the area, few of which managed to survive the Civil War. At the property, where rice was cultivated until 1915, remain the old dikes, outbuildings and a typical "low-country" plantation house quite unlike classic antebellum cotton plantation mansions.

Brunswick, like Savannah, was laid out (in 1771) on a grid pattern. The town remained one of the few in America not to change the English names of its streets during the Revolution. The 1907 Glynn County Courthouse, one of the South's most imposing such structures, stands in a four-acre park garnished with moss-hung oaks. Brunswick boasts a couple of especially storied such trees, including Lover's Oak, under which an Indian met his maiden, and Lanier Oak, where in the 1870s Sidney Lanier wrote his poem "Marshes of Glynn" which, from a nearby park, "Stretch leisurely off, in a pleasant plain,/To the terminal blue of the main," as Lanier described the swampy area. The Mary Miller Doll Museum (M.–Sat., 11–5; Sun., 2–5, adm.) includes more than 3,000 dolls from three centuries ago to the present, while at the Shrimp Docks in Brunswick, called "the Shrimp Capital of the World," you can see shrimpers unloading their catch most weekdays in late afternoon. For a good introduction to the coast's ecological, biological and natural features, it's worth visiting the Coastal Marine Exhibit (M.–F., 8–5), a State of Georgia facility.

The road from Brunswick takes you out to Saint Simons, one of the "Golden Isles," so called by the Spaniards in the sixteenth century, not for gold—they found none there—but for the islands' lustrous beaches and radiant natural beauty. On the way you'll pass Bloody Marsh, site of the 1742 battle in which Oglethorpe's small band of hardys defeated the more numerous Spanish in a surprise attack, a crucial victory that led to Spain's withdrawal from the area and to the definitive establishment of England's culture and language in the region. Had Oglethorpe not triumphed, this sentence, and all the others in the book, might well have been written in la idioma español y no en inglés. As you reach St. Simons, to your left lies Epworth by the Sea which occupies the former Hamilton Plantation site where slave cabins and a museum recall antebellum days. Bordering the property to the south is Gascoigne Bluff, whose oak trees supplied timber used to build the Brooklyn Bridge and U.S. Navy ships, including "Old Ironsides," better described as "Old Oaksides." On the southern edge of the island rises the 1872 St. Simons Lighthouse and the adjacent Museum of Coastal History (summer, M.–Sat., 10–5; Sun., 1:30–4; winter, Tu.–Sat., 1–4; Sun., 1:30–4, adm.), both listed on the National Register, with history displays, antiques and early tools and agricultural artifacts. To the north lies Christ Church (summer, 2–5; winter, 1–4), rebuilt in 1884 by Reverend Anson Phelps Dodge whose life inspired local writer Eugenia Price's novel *Beloved Invader*. Nearby is Fort Frederica, built by Oglethorpe in 1736 to defend against the Spanish, where the installation's foundations (summer, 8–5:45; winter, 8–5) and historical displays at the visitor center (summer, 9–5:45; winter, 9–5) recall the colonial period. Country Hearth Inn (912-638-7805) on St. Simons offers bed and breakfast rooms.

Off St. Simons lie two delightful island enclaves. To the north stretches Little St. Simons, a completely unspoiled 10,000-acre privately owned property, reached only by boat, which in recent years has opened guest accommodations to outsiders (912-638-7472); while to the east perches Sea Island, home of the impeccably kept resort called The Cloister (800-SEA-ISLAND or 912-638-3611), built in the 1920s by Hudson Motor Car founder Howard E. Coffin. Sea Island gave its name to the famous long staple cotton grown on area plantations such as Hampton, where in 1804 Aaron Burr, then Vice-president, spent a month after the duel in which he killed Alexander Hamilton, and where English actress Fanny Kemble, married to Major Pierce Butler of Philadelphia, lived in 1838–39, an experience that inspired her famous *Journal of a Residence on a Georgian Plantation,* whose strong antislavery tone helped convince England not to support the Confederate cause.

Farther down the coast you'll find two other islands. Jekyll was developed in the late nineteenth century as a millionaires' retreat, while Cumberland remained an undeveloped wilderness area. Named for an English nobleman who helped promote Oglethorpe's colonization of Georgia, Jekyll was purchased in 1886 for $125,000 by a group of financiers who established there the ultra-exclusive Jekyll Island Club, which by the turn of the century boasted a membership that supposedly represented an estimated one-sixth of the world's wealth. Five years after the club finally closed its doors in 1942 the state of Georgia bought the grounds and buildings for $675,000, the modern-day equivalent of the purchase of Manhattan Island. Thirty-two of the original structures still stand, among them the clubhouse and the "cottages" Morgans, Rockefellers, Goulds and others called home in the winter. Predating the influx of big bucks is Horton House, a two-story ruin dating from 1742 and one of the state's oldest structures built of tabby, an oyster shell-based material. Nearby lies the cemetery of the du Bignon family, who owned the island and grew Sea Island cotton there prior to the millionaires, and the tabby ruins of Georgia's first brewery, which supplied ale to troops and settlers at Fort Frederica on St. Simons Island.

Cumberland, the southernmost barrier island along the Georgia shore, was once a plantation area cultivated by the English colonists. In 1881 Thomas Carnegie, brother of financier Andrew Carnegie, bought an estate on the south end of the island but, unlike Jekyll, no colony developed in the area, which remains virtually untouched by the hand or wallet of man, a pristine state assured for posterity when much of the terrain became the Cumberland Island National Seashore in 1972. Bird and animal life, fifty-foot high dunes, twisty-limbed live oaks, sparkling white sand beaches and other gifts of nature abound on the island, reached only by ferry from St. Mary's (daily in summer, daily ex. Tu. and W. in winter, 9 and 11:45; for reservations: 912-882-4335). St. Mary's is believed to be the nation's second-oldest city, where much history reposes in Oak Grove Cemetery (c. 1780), whose inscriptions in French recall Acadians driven by the English out of Nova Scotia in 1755. The McIntosh sugar mill tabby ruins in St. Mary's are among the oldest industrial remnants in Georgia (c. 1825), while the town's Toonerville Trolley (also claimed by Louisville, Kentucky) became nationally known when cartoonist Roy Crane featured it in his strip "Wash Tubbs and Easy" in the 1930s.

Inland, off to the west beyond Kingsland—whose every street once bore the name of a member of the family of William H. King, once southeast Georgia's largest landowner—stretches, or sinks, the nearly seven hundred square-mile Okefenokee ("land of the trembling earth") Swamp, whose most famous denizens were the characters in Walt Kelly's "Pogo" comic strip. In 1889 the state sold the swamp for 12½ cents an acre to a company that planned to drain the area and turn the terrain into farmland. When this proved impossible, the Hebard Lumber Company bought the swamp and cut its virgin pine and cypress for timber, an activity that destroyed the habitats of much of the area's wildlife. In 1935 the company sold about half of the swamp to the state, which transferred the property to the federal government. You can enter the National Wildlife Refuge south of Folkston via a spur road that leads to the Suwannee Canal Recreation Area; from Edith, to the west, into Stephen C. Foster State Park; and from Okefenokee, to the north, an approach that takes you to the Okefenokee Swamp Park (spring and summer, 9–6:30; fall and winter, 9–5:30, adm.), a privately run nonprofit operation with various display areas, shows, boat tours and other attractions and activities.

At Waycross, north of the swamp, you'll find two museums, the Okefenokee Heritage Center (Tu.–Sat., 10–5; Sun., 2–4, adm.), with a rather mixed group of displays on history, science and art, and the Southern Forest World (Tu.–Sat., 10–5; Sun., 2–4, free), featuring forestry exhibits on the lumber industry's development in Georgia, 70 percent covered by forests, and in the South, with a thirty-eight-foot tall model of a loblolly pine in which you climb to exhibits upstairs. Waycross also boasts the J. H. Swisher & Sons factory which makes the famous King Edward cigars (tours by reservation: 912-283-3601), as well as the huge Seaboard Coastline Railroad repair facility and also North America's largest computer-controlled rail classification yard. To the north lies Baxley, one of the nation's first small municipalities to construct a waterworks system, home of Caroline Pafford Miller, who in 1933 won a Pulitzer Prize for *Lamb in His Bosom*. Baxley serves as seat of sparsely populated Appling County where Georgia's first commercially produced turpentine was processed in 1858 at Tar Landing on the Altamaha River, by which Georgia Power's Edwin I. Hatch nuclear power plant stands (visitor center open M.–F., 9–5; Sun., 1–5, free).

Jesup, to the east, boasts what is supposedly the world's largest pulp-producing mill, operated by ITT Rayonier, and the National Register-listed 1903 boxy brick courthouse topped by a tower with outsized clock faces. From Jesup the road north takes you to Claxton, home of the well-known Claxton Fruit Cake and site of the annual Rattlesnake Roundup the second weekend in March, held since 1968 when an Evans County boy was fanged by a rattler, and off to the west lies Lyons, with the Robert Toombs Inn (912-526-4489), offering bed and breakfast; the hamlet of Santa Claus (population: two hundred seventy-five), which promotes the holiday spirit by having no police department or traffic lights and with its streets named Candy Cane Lane, December Drive, Rudolph Way and Sleigh, Dancer, Prancer, Reindeer and Noel; and Vidalia, home of nationally known Vidalia sweet onions.

To the north of Vidalia is Swainsboro, where you'll find bed and breakfast rooms at Edenfield House Inn (912-237-3007) and to the northeast lies Metter, with a restored 1930 lumber mill. Five miles east on highway 46 stands the 1839 Old Lake Church, among the oldest Baptist sanctuaries in continuous existence—the predecessor church dated from 1823—across from which stretches one of Georgia's largest country cemeteries. At nearby Statesboro—whose Trellis Garden Inn (912-489-8781) and Statesboro Inn (912-489-8628) offer bed and breakfast—lived blues singer Willie Mc-Tell, who performed around town in the 1940s at tobacco warehouses and on the steps of the Jaeckel Hotel and whose song "Statesboro Blues" became well known in the 1960s when played by the Allman Brothers Band. A few miles to the northwest is the whimsically named community of Hopeulikit, while farther north lie Millen, with a National Fish Hatchery (M.–F., 9–4, free) and Sylvania, six miles north of which stands the 1815 Dell-Goodall House, no doubt Georgia's most durable residence, for all the neighboring dwellings disappeared in a fire and flood after Lorenzo Goodall, a travelling Methodist preacher, put a curse on the entire town except the one house that survived, a place that took him in after villagers stoned him. The blessed Dell-Goodall House is perhaps a propitious place to end a tour of the Georgia countryside and of Georgia.

Georgia Practical Information

For tourist information: The Georgia Department of Industry and Trade, P.O. Box 1776, Atlanta, GA. 30301; 404-656-3590. For state park and historic site information: 800-3GA-PARK, in-state; 800-5GA-PARK, outside Georgia. Georgia operates roadside visitor information centers in the north at Ringold and Lavonia; in the west at Tallapoosa, West Point, Columbus and Plains; in the south at Valdosta and Kingsland; in the east at Savannah, Sylvania and Augusta.

Phone numbers of some of the tourist offices in the most popular areas are: Athens, 404-549-6800; Atlanta, 404-521-6600; Augusta, 404-826-4722; Columbus, 404-322-1613; Jekyll Island, 912-635-3400; Macon, 912-743-3401; Milledgeville, 912-452-4687; Rome, 404-295-5576; Savannah, 912-944-0456.

Booking agencies for bed and breakfast accommodations in Atlanta are: Atlanta Hospitality, 404-493-1930, and Bed and Breakfast in Atlanta, 404-875-0525 (open M.–F. 9–12, 2–5); in the Thomasville area, Quail Country Bed and Breakfast, 912–226–7218 and 226–6882; in the hill country near Blue Ridge, in the north-central part of the state, Bed and Breakfast Hideaway Homes, 404-632-2411.

III

The Sun South

11. Florida

Florida seems less Southern than most of the states in this book. From the very early days the area was an appendage to the region and to the continent more than just geographically. Unlike states in the North, which took their names from Europe or derived them from Europeans—New York, New Hampshire, Pennsylvania, Delaware—or those in the South with Indian designations, such as Arkansas, Tennessee and Mississippi, the word denoting the peninsula came from the Spanish, "Florida"—as Ponce de Leon christened the area on April 2, 1513—being the first permanent name given by Europeans to a place on the North American continent.

The French, very briefly, and then the Spanish, the English and the Indians fought over Florida, with the Spaniards dominating the area for more than two centuries until the British traded Havana for the peninsula in 1763. Twenty years later the British returned Florida to Spain, following which numerous Spanish-American border disputes broke out, culminating in Andrew Jackson's capture of Pensacola in 1813. Then, in 1821 in that city, Jackson formally took possession of Florida from the Spanish. The United States found itself with a foreign country populated by Spanish and Indians, a land in which only little more than a half-century before had the English language been introduced when the British acquired the territory. The first Atlantic coast colony settled by Europeans thus became the last in that region to fall under American jurisdiction and influence.

Through the middle part of the nineteenth century, from 1818 to 1858, the Americans fought the Indians in a series of three Seminole wars. During this period Florida joined

the Union, in 1845, and began to develop. The first railroad
started at St. Joseph in the Panhandle in 1836, and in 1855
the legislature passed the first Internal Improvement Act,
which encouraged further rail development and a canal transportation system. But the Civil War brought these advances
to a halt: "In no phase of Florida's life does there appear
to have been any greater collapse and disorganization brought
by the Civil War than in its program of internal improve-
ments," maintains Kathryn Abbey Hanna in *Florida: Land
of Change*. As late as the 1880s Florida remained a frontier
territory, with no city larger than 10,000 inhabitants. Toward the end of the century two entrepreneurs began to
develop the state's railroad system, with Henry Plant's line
reaching Tampa on the west coast in 1884 and Henry Flagler's rails pushing down the east coast to St. Augustine a
few years later. These developments mark the very beginnings of Florida's economic growth and tourist trade, which
now attracts more than thirty million visitors a year, some
of whom return to retire there, giving the state the nation's
oldest population, with a median age of more than thirty-six.

Prior to that late nineteenth-century spurt of rails to
Tampa and St. Augustine, Florida's salubrious climate had
remained unexploited but not unnoticed. Speaking of St.
Augustine, naturalist Bernard Romans noted in his 1775 *A
Concise Natural History of East and West Florida* that "I do
not think, that on all the continent, there is a more healthy
spot; burials have been less frequent here than any where
else . . . the Spanish inhabitants live here to a great age."
In 1885 the American Medical Association endorsed Pinellas
Point, site of today's St. Petersburg, as the nation's healthiest
spot, while one of the earliest guides to the state, published
by the American News Company after the Civil War (that
archaic handbook includes none of Florida's west coast, covers the east coast only as far south as Sanford, north of
Orlando, and omits Miami on the map), presciently pre-

dicted: "The wonderful salubrity of the climate of Florida is its greatest attraction, and is destined to make it to America what the South of France and Italy are to Europe,—the refuge of those who seek to escape the rigor of a Northern winter." This, of course, came to pass and, as Kenneth L. Roberts noted in *Florida,* published in 1926: "Nothing in Florida starts a visitor's day quite so pleasantly as does an adverse weather report from the North." During the mid-'20s land speculation raged. So called "binder boys" would contract for property, getting binders on land they intended to sell before making even the first payment.

The resulting bust, land panic and Depression only delayed Florida's development, which took off after the war with space-age rockets at Cape Canaveral, Walt Disney World, the citrus industry's juicy profits and retirement communities. In 1949 the legislature enacted a citrus law to update the industry, and in 1950 Bumper 8, a German V-2 rocket carrying a WAC Corporal missile, became the first rocket launched from Cape Canaveral. In 1958 the National Aeronautics and Space Administration began operations at Canaveral, and in 1966 Disney announced plans for the theme park near Orlando. Walt Disney World started operations in 1971, and the company opened EPCOT in 1982. In 1960—pre-Disney and NASA—Florida ranked tenth in the nation with a population of nearly five million, while in the late '80s the state, with twelve and a half million people, had become the nation's fourth most populous, and by 2000 it is projected to be the third-largest in the Union. About nine hundred new residents move to Florida every day. Florida boasts eight of the nation's top ten fastest-growing areas of the 1980s, led by Naples whose population increased by more than 60 percent, while Ocala, Fort Pierce and Fort Myers–Cape Coral all grew by more than 50 percent during the decade.

Signs of this pell-mell growth appear everywhere, from the high-rise condos and apartments that line the coasts to

the proliferation of tourist attractions featuring menageries of monkeys, dolphins, parrots, acres of gardens and any number of "worlds"—theme parks that enable you to experience a touch of foreign lands and exotic adventures while still being able to drink water from the tap. Florida's first state flag bore the motto, "Let us alone." The present banner might well read: "Keep coming." But Florida is more than just the seaside resort areas, the tourist come-ons, the manufactured attractions catering to the huge flow of visitors that arrive in search of sun, amusement and pleasure. If you look hard enough, rummaging a bit in the back areas beyond the main roads, away from big cities and removed from beachfront conurbations, you'll find some attractive and pleasant places of historical and cultural interest, many described in the pages that follow. To know the real Florida, Gloria Jahoda wrote in *Florida: A Bicentennial History,* "you must know its seasons and its wild places, the white little town squares beyond the superhighways, the clear-windowed Baptist churches in the pinewoods and the bougainvilleas in Hobe Sound gardens and the palms in Jacksonville's Hemming Park, where the sparrows chatter at night." Such is the sort of Florida that awaits the off-the-beaten-track traveler to the state.

The Panhandle and Western Florida

Pensacola—Tallahassee—Gainesville—Cedar Key—Tampa—St. Petersburg—Sarasota— Fort Myers—Naples

Although St. Augustine, established on Florida's east coast in 1565, is considered the nation's oldest city, Pensacola, in the Panhandle to the west, occupies the site where the country's very first substantial colonization attempt took place. In 1559 Tristan de Luna y Arellano led a group of fifteen hundred settlers and soldiers to Pensacola Bay where a hurricane greeted them and destroyed most of their supplies. Harassed by hostile Indians, the settlement lasted for two years before disbanding. The following few years the French tried to establish a foothold along the east coast, finally in 1564 founding a fort that led to the beginnings of the competing Spanish colony of St. Augustine the following year. Thus did the Europeans finally take hold there in eastern Florida, but it was in the west, at Pensacola, where the very first colony in the United States once stood, and still today the city, with its old buildings and historic atmosphere, recalls early days in the Florida peninsula. The Spanish established the present city in 1752, a heritage that survives in such parts of town as Seville Square and nearby Zaragoza, Cervantes and Intendencia Streets.

In and around Seville Square stand historic houses and museums that give the flavor of old Pensacola. The Pensacola Historical Museum (M.–Sat., 9–4:30, free) occupies the 1832 Old Christ Church, listed on the National Register and Florida's oldest church; the Pensacola Museum of Art (Tu.–Sat., 10–5, free) inhabits the former city jail; and the Hispanic Building, once a warehouse, shelters the West Florida Museum of History (M.–Sat., 10–4:30, free). The nearby Piney Woods Sawmill recalls the days a century and more ago when the region experienced a lumber boom, echoes of which remain in the wooden buildings around picturesque Seville Square. Among them is the 1871 National Register-listed Dorr House, 311 South Adams, a classic revival-style wood structure owned by Eben Dorr, originally from Maine, who branded the hands of a man named Jonathan Walker for stealing slaves, an incident poet John Greenleaf Whittier recounted in his verse "The Branded Hand." Dorr (died 1846) reposes in St. Michael's Cemetery, a burial ground filled with ghosts of the past a few blocks north of Seville Square. Figures buried there include Don Francisco Moreno (died 1882), patriarch of twenty-seven children, seventy-five grandchildren and one hundred and twenty-seven great-grandchildren; Joseph Noriega (died 1827), the last "alcalde" (mayor) of Spanish Pensacola, who participated in the 1821 flag ceremony at which Andrew Jackson took possession of Florida for the United States; John Hunt (died 1851), whose tomb is a replica of Napoleon's; and Jose Roig, who occupies the cemetery's earliest known grave, 1812, although earlier burials took place at St. Michael's, established about 1791.

A few blocks west of the cemetery runs Palafox, Pensacola's main commercial street, named for the Spanish military commander who defended Zaragoza, Spain, against Napoleon's army. Wooden buildings once lined the street, but after an 1880 fire Pensacolians rebuilt the area with brick structures embellished by ornate New Orleans-style wrought-iron metal work. Palafox's ten-story American National Bank Building, listed on the National Register, was Florida's tallest structure when completed in 1909, and the street's Register-listed Saenger Theater, designed by New Orleans architect Emile Weil and inaugurated April 2, 1925, with the screening of Cecil B. DeMille's original *Ten Commandments,* recalls the golden era of movie palaces. Other venerable structures fill the sixty-block North Hill Preservation District, where one of the century-old residences houses the Hopkins Boarding House, 900 North Spring, a restaurant serving huge family-style meals with food so plentiful no "boarding house reach" is necessary. (Tu.–Sat., from 11 for lunch; dinner, 5:15–7). Back down in town you'll find the Seville Quarter dining and entertainment complex, featuring seven eateries and nightspots, among them Rosie O'Grady's well-named Good Time Emporium, decorated with old English and nautical fixtures. Perched on the edge of a huge bay just by the Gulf of Mexico, water-logged

Pensacola fairly swims in a nautical ambiance, one contributor to that atmosphere being the Naval Air Station, the city's biggest employer with 10,000 sailors and nearly as many civilian employees. At the base, the nation's first and the world's largest naval air facility, the Pensacola Naval Aviation Museum (9–5, free) houses an extensive collection of air-related displays and equipment, including the Skylab command module, fifty or so aircraft and the NC-4, the first plane to cross the Atlantic, a three-week flight in May 1919 from New York to Lisbon via Newfoundland and the Azores. Although Sherman Field at the Air Station isn't very heavenly, the Blue Angels, the famous precision flying team, are headquartered there, while just across from the Aviation Museum stands Fort San Carlos de Barrancas, a Spanish installation located about where Tristan de Luna established the first European settlement in the U.S. in 1559. (An earlier colony, founded in 1526 near Georgetown, South Carolina, failed to take hold.) The fort, open to visitors (9:30–5, free), forms part of the Gulf Islands National Seashore, a federal historic and nature preserve that stretches along the Florida and Mississippi coasts.

Other units in the Florida section of the National Seashore include the remains of 1834 Fort Pickens (9–5, free), a one-time Union redoubt where Apache chief Geronimo was imprisoned, reached via the Pensacola Bay Bridge, "the world's longest fishing pier"; the Naval Live Oaks groves, with trees once coveted for use in building ships; and the village of Gulf Breeze, whose zoo boasts Colossus, a friendly five-hundred-and-ten-pound gorilla, the largest in captivity, who for fifteen years grew up without ever seeing another gorilla. Even more water wets the Pensacola area in the Blackwater River State Park, with a hiking trail used by Indians and followed by Andrew Jackson when he traveled to Florida in 1818, and with the gentle river, a pleasant canoeing stream (outfitters in the town of Milton, once called Scratch Ankle for the area's many bothersome briars, rent boats) which winds its way beneath hangings of Spanish moss. Back in Pensacola you'll find bed and breakfast rooms at the Jablonski residence, 508 Decatur Avenue (904-455-6781).

Between Pensacola and Tallahassee, the state capital nearly two hundred miles east, lie some other Panhandle attractions. Inland, north of the Gulf, you'll find near Lakewood on the Alabama border Florida's highest point, Britton Hill, a three hundred and forty-five-foot peak topped by the remains of an old church. De Funiak Springs to the south boasts what is supposedly one of the world's few perfectly round lakes; a late nineteenth-century Chautauqua assembly building modeled after the famous New York concert and lecture facility; and the 1887 Walton-De Funiak Public Library, believed the state's oldest in its original quarters, which houses not only books but also a collection of European armor donated by Wallace Bruce, president of the Chautauqua winter program. Two towns farther east offer unusual celebrations: In early August Wausau hosts its annual Possum Festival, featuring possum meals and a parade (for information: 904-638-0250); while at Chipley the annual Panhandle Watermelon Festival takes place the last weekend of June. The Falling Waters State Recreation Area south of Chipley (8–sunset, free) claims Florida's only waterfall, a cascade that plunges into a one-hundred-foot sinkhole, while east of Chipley Florida Caverns State Park (8–sunset, free) encompasses a labyrinth of limestone caves. It was at Sylvania, his home near Marianna just to the south, where Florida's Civil War governor John Milton, a descendant of the famous English poet of that name, took his life on April Fools Day 1865 not long after declaring in his last message to the legislature that "death would be preferable to reunion."

To the north of Marianna lies the hamlet of Two Egg, supposedly named when an early-day customer asked for a couple of eggs at the country store there. Farther east, on highway 271, spreads Torreya State Park, with the 1849 Gregory mansion, a cotton planter's home, and the unique torreya tree, also known as gopher wood, which grows along the banks of the Apalachicola River in the immediate area. Local myth holds that the area served as Adam and Eve's home, the Apalachicola supposedly being the world's only river with "four heads"—as Genesis, Chapter 2, verse 10 describes the Garden of Eden's stream—formed by two rivers and two inlets to the north in Georgia.

Along the shore road between Pensacola and Tallahassee you'll come first to the huge Eglin Air Force Base, the world's largest such facility and, at more than seven hundred square miles, two-thirds the size of Rhode Island. On the base you'll find the Air Force Armament Museum, with missiles, bombs, jet fighters and other weapons on display, and the McKinley Climatic Laboratory, the world's largest environmental test chamber, which can simulate all sorts of weather, from tropical monsoons to jungle heat up to a hundred and sixty-five degrees and blizzards with as much as four feet of snow in twenty-four hours. Occasionally schoolchildren visit the lab to experience such un-Florida-like fun as throwing snowballs or sculpting snowmen. For information on the Eglin Air Base attractions and tour schedules: 904-244-8191 or 882-3933. In Valparaiso just by the base the Historical Society Museum (Tu.–Sat., 11–4, free) houses a collection of old documents and historical artifacts, and at Fort Walton Beach on the coast the Temple Mound Museum (Tu.–Sat., 11–4; Sun., 1–4, free) contains exhibits on the pre-Columbian societies that once inhabited the area. Fort Walton Beach also has the Camp Walton School House Museum (Tu. and Th., 9–4; W., 9–2, free), a bright white structure restored to its appearance a half-century and more ago. Destin, perched on a narrow strip of land between Choctawhatchee Bay and the Gulf of Mexico, was once a peaceful fishing village whose early days in the 1830s are recalled by displays at the Old Destin Post Office Museum (M. and W., 1:30–4:30, Sat., 9:30–12:30, free), while the oddly eclectic Museum of the Sea and Indian (March–Oct., 8–6; Nov.–Feb., 9–4, adm.) offers exhibits on the deep blue sea and on redskins. In 1933 a wooden bridge connected the "world's luckiest fishing village," as the town calls itself, to the mainland and over time and over the bridge the outside world gradually encroached on the one-time tranquil seaside area. By now all along the white sand shore stand high-rise condos and apartment buildings, not to mention shopping centers, restaurants and other commercial establishments.

For relief from this rather forbidding stretch you can visit an antebellum mansion on grounds well garnished by Spanish moss-draped old oaks at Eden State Gardens near Point Washington. A local lumber baron built the antique-furnished white-columned house (9–4, closed W. and Th., Sept. 16–April 30), once a social center for Panhandle society. On the coast to the south, just west of Seagrove Beach, perches the new town of Seaside, so new it doesn't yet appear on most maps. Pastel-colored frame houses and a human scale make Seaside one of Florida's most attractive developments. Farther north, between Freeport and Niceville, one of Florida's few wineries, Alaqua Vineyards, offers tours and tastings (Tu.–Sat., 1–5, free). Near Panama City is a third Panhandle coast military reservation, Tyndall Air Force Base, smaller than the Naval Air Station at Pensacola and the Eglin installation but perhaps more notable in that Tyndall, which opened the morning the U.S. entered World War II, counted among its first students Hollywood luminary Clark Gable, who studied gunnery there. At Panama City the Museum of Man in the Sea (9–5, adm.) houses oceanography and marine life exhibits, while the Institute of Diving at the adjacent town of Panama City Beach contains displays on underwater activities (9–5, adm.). Panama City was the locale where the famous 1963 U.S. Supreme Court Constitutional law decision of *Gideon* v. *Wainwright* began, for after Clarence Gideon was convicted there of burglary the high court held that the proceedings were defective as the defendant lacked legal counsel. On retrial, Gideon was acquitted. So many rural Georgians and Alabamians frequent the rather tacky resorts near Panama City—so called by its founder as the site lies on a direct line between Chicago and the Central American town of the same name—that the area has become known as the "Redneck Riviera."

Farther east the resort atmosphere gradually gives way to less commercial regions. Port St. Joe—a once wild and wooly (and cottony) cotton-shipping port which originally bore the more pious name Saint Joseph—boasts the state's first railroad, a mule-powered line that started on April 14, 1836, to link St. Joseph Bay with Lake Wimico, and also Florida's first Constitutional Convention, held 1838–9. Port St. Joe's Constitution Convention State Museum (M.–Sat., 9–5; Sun., 1–5, free)—with early Florida artifacts and antique train equipment—commemorates the city's two "firsts." Narrow St. Joseph Peninsula, dotted with towering dunes and with saltwater marshes that attract bird life, stretches along the coast like a pincer; while the nearby unspoiled St. Vincent National Wildlife Refuge (reached only by boat: 904-653-8808), a once privately owned thirteen-thousand-acre nature preserve, also shelters birds and animals. Apalach-icola, just to the east, serves as Florida's oyster center, providing 90 percent of the state's supply, cultivated in more than 10,000 acres of offshore beds harvested with tongs. Every year in early November the Florida Seafood Festival—one of the state's oldest (successor to a jamboree started in 1915) and best-known such events—celebrates the town's oyster farming and fishing industries.

In 1851 Dr. John Gorrie of Apalachicola patented a device for making ice, needed to cool feverish malaria patients. After failing to win acceptance for the invention, forerunner of modern-day refrigeration and air conditioning, Gorrie suffered a nervous breakdown and died in 1855 at age fifty-two, but his work is now honored at the John Gorrie Museum (Th.–M., 8–5, adm.), with a replica of his machine (the Smithsonian in Washington owns the original) and by his statue in the nation's capital, one of the two Floridians represented there. (The other Florida citizen so honored is General Edmund Kirby Smith, a St. Augustine native, who at Galveston, Texas, surrendered the last Confederate force to the Yankees on June 2, 1865. So independently did Smith run the Trans-Mississippi Department for the Confederates that the area came to be called "Kirby Smithdom." At the time the West Point graduate died in March 1893 he was the sole surviving Civil War full general of either side.)

Across from the Gorrie Museum in Apalachicola stands Trinity Church, one of the state's oldest sanctuaries (1830s) and said to be the nation's first prefabricated church, sections of which were cut in New York and sent by schooner to its present site. North of Apalachicola lies Fort Gadsden State Historic Site (8–sunset, free), with a small display of Indian relics and British arms recalling the outpost destroyed by Americans in 1816, rebuilt by order of Andrew Jackson in 1818 and since then crumbled away, as forlorn as the nearby cemetery where grave robbers who plundered the tombs left only slight indentations in the earth. To the north and east stretches Apalachicola National Forest, a huge preserve, with many recreational facilities, extending for more than a half-million acres across parts of four counties to the edge of Tallahassee. Back in Apalachicola, the Gorrie Bridge takes you ahead in time as well as place, as on it you cross from the Central to the Eastern time zone. At the end of the span a toll bridge takes you to St. George Island, an unspoiled state park with more than nine miles of dune-pocked undeveloped beaches, while from the nearby seaside town of Carrabelle—which boasts the world's smallest police station (a claim also asserted by Ridgeway in central South Carolina), installed in a telephone booth—you can take a ferry to Dog Island, another pristine beach area.

Farther east, on the coast, the St. Marks National Wildlife Refuge encompasses a nature preserve with trails, alligator-filled marshes and bird life, including Florida's only Canada Geese wintering area. A visitor center (M.–F., 8–4:30; Sat. and Sun., 1–5, free) houses displays and offers an observation deck over the marshland, while a scenic drive takes you to the 1831 St. Marks Lighthouse, one of the South's oldest, built with stones from Fort San Marcos de Apalache, a 1679 Spanish outpost a few miles north where a museum (9–5, free) traces the history of the fortress, also used by British, French and Confederate forces and in 1818 captured by Andrew Jackson. A path takes you through the area to Confederate earthworks, a powder magazine and past the walls along the Wakulla River and on to the site of the original Spanish enclave where the Wakulla and St. Marks rivers meet. Just around the corner from the museum stands Posey's, perhaps the best known of the many oyster bars along the coast. A sign on the facade of the establishment, open only from September to April, proclaims "Home of Topless Oysters."

To the north toward Tallahassee lies, or flows, Wakulla Springs (9:30–5:30, adm.), said to be the deepest in the world, a hundred and eighty-five feet. The primitive 4,000-acre wildlife and nature preserve there remains so primeval that *The Creature from the Black Lagoon* was filmed in the area in the 1950s. Glass-bottom boats and cruise craft take you through the unspoiled enclave where alligators lurk and twisted cypress trees grow. The park was donated to the state by financier Ed Ball, who in 1937 built the Wakulla Springs Lodge as a private retreat (for rooms: 904-640-7011 or 224-5950). The dining room of the Spanish-style inn, whose wood ceiling beams bear painted motifs depicting

Florida scenes and flowers, serves tasty Southern cooking, so you might want to eat at the lodge even if you don't stay there. Ball, who died in 1981 at age ninety-three, was one of Florida's great latter-day characters and the last of the old-time pre-boom businessmen. He married the sister of Alfred I. du Pont of the famous E. I. du Pont de Nemours chemical company family. After du Pont died in 1935 Ball took over his brother-in-law's estate and proceeded to build up St. Joe Paper, a Jacksonville-based holding company which owns, among other assets, the parent firm of Florida East Coast Railway, a line that runs the three hundred and fifty-one miles between Jacksonville and Miami, and a million acres of Florida land, mostly in timber, or about one thirty-seventh of the entire state. History buffs may want to stop off on the way to nearby Tallahassee to see Natural Bridge Battlefield State Historic Site (8–sunset, free), where Confederates carried out a surprise attack on March 6, 1865, and blocked Union troops from marching to Tallahassee, the only state capital east of the Mississippi the Yankees didn't capture.

Tallahassee was founded in 1823 at a point about halfway between St. Augustine and Pensacola, capitals of East and of West Florida, to serve as the new seat of government. With its moss-draped oak trees and antebellum mansions, Tallahassee still retains some of the flavor of the old days and the Old South. Paradoxically, northern Florida tends to resemble the South, while the southern part of the state, with its many retirees, seems in some ways like the North. An observation deck on the twenty-second floor atop the Capitol building affords an overview of the attractive, tree-filled city. The Capitol Gallery on that floor, as well as the Old Capitol Gallery in the restored former statehouse (1902), contain art exhibits featuring Florida artists (M.–F., 8–4:30; Sat. and Sun., 11–3 for the Capitol; 12–4 for the Old Capitol, free). More artwork embellishes LeMoyne Art Center and

Sculpture Garden (Tu.–Sat., 10–5; Sun., 2–5, free), while
the Museum of Florida History (M.–F., 9–4:30; Sat., 10–
4:30; Sun., 12–4:30, free) houses displays on the state ranging
from prehistoric times to the state's space and Disney era,
and the Junior Museum (Tu.–Sat., 9–5; Sun., 2–5, adm.),
out near the airport, occupies an 1880-vintage pioneer farm
with a grist mill, old schoolhouse and the restored home
of Prince Achille Murat, Napoleon's nephew, who met his
future wife, George Washington's grand-niece, in Tallahassee. Murat, whose various Florida plantation operations
eventually failed, liked to chew tobacco, a dirty habit his
wife, Catherine, coped with by giving him a St. Bernard
dog into whose fur the prince could spit so as not to soil
the floor. Another Frenchman, the famous Marquis de Lafayette, who had spent $200,000 of his own funds to support
the American Revolution, received from a grateful Congress
in 1824 a township of U.S. land located wherever he chose.
Because of the property boom then exciting Florida specula-
tors and the state's mild climate, the marquis selected terrain
in Tallahassee, the Lafayette Grant as the township is called,
now bounded by Meridian Road on the west, approximately
Gaines Street on the south, and extending six miles to the
east and the north. In 1831 Layfayette induced fifty or sixty
Norman peasants to settle on his land and cultivate vineyards, olive groves, mulberry trees and silkworms, but the
colony failed and the land was sold. The Lafayette Vineyards
and Winery (M.–Sat., 10–6; Sun., 12–6; Sept.–Feb. closed
M., free) echoes by its name the Frenchman's early holdings
in the area.

Memories of other local property owners survive at such
showplaces as Killearn, a 1920s mansion (9–5, adm.) north
of town set in a more than three-hundred-acre park filled
with camellias and azaleas, called the Maclay Ornamental
Gardens (8–sunset), and The Grove, an 1836 residence, built
by Richard Keith Call, twice territorial governor of Florida.

In January 1861 Northern sympathizer Call stood on the front steps of the house to answer taunts by Secessionists after Florida had left the Union by stating, "Well, gentlemen, all I wish to say to you is that you have just opened the gates of hell." In 1941 LeRoy Collins, governor from 1955–61, and his wife, Mary Call Darby, Call's great-granddaughter, bought The Grove and moved in to the old family homestead. Near The Grove on the grounds of the governor's mansion stands no grove but a single sample of the state tree, perhaps Florida's northernmost orange tree, for the famous citrus farms lie farther south. Not that Tallahassee's climate is severe: most of the time the weather's benign, but on February 13, 1899, the city suffered from the state's lowest recorded temperature, − 2° Fahrenheit. Other attractions at Tallahassee include Lake Jackson Mounds State Archeological Site north of town, with ancient Indian mounds, the Butler Mill Trail up to where an 1880s grist mill once stood, and the history-haunted lakeside place where in 1539 Spanish explorer Hernando de Soto is believed to have celebrated the first Christmas mass in the territory that became the United States; the mid-nineteenth-century Old Union Bank Building (Tu.–F., 10–1; Sat. and Sun., 1–4, free); the antebellum-era Calhoun Street Historical District; and two universities: Florida State (alumni include movie stars Burt Reynolds and Faye Dunaway), whose most elevated subject is the Flying High Circus, which presents a three-ring event every spring (for information: 904-644- 4874), and Florida Agricultural and Mechanical, with the Black Archives Research Center and Museum (M.–F., 9– 4, free).

Off to the east of Tallahassee you'll edge away from the Panhandle and proceed toward the main part of the peninsula. Although the state's lowest temperature was recorded in Tallahassee, nearby Monticello suffered from the highest in history, 109° on June 29, 1931. Monticello is an attractive town, crammed with more than a hundred historic structures, among them the 1890 Opera House, antebellum homes dating from the King Cotton days before a boll-weevil infestation dethroned the monarch of crops, and the silvery-domed courthouse supposedly modeled after Thomas Jefferson's Monticello in Virginia but resembling more a kind of mini-White House. Prince Achille Murat, whose Tallahassee house is mentioned above, also lived in the Monticello area, where the cooks on his cotton plantation served such treats as sheep ears, buzzard meat and alligator tail. To the east of Monticello lies Madison, embellished by the antebellum Wardlaw-Smith House, listed on the National Register, which occupies an entire block on the main street. The past lingers in Madison at the Confederate Memorial Park, located where a blockhouse once stood to help locals defend against Seminole Indian attacks, and in the boast that John Cabell Breckenridge, the Confederate War Secretary, spent a night in the town in 1865 as he fled from the country after General Robert E. Lee surrendered the South.

Farther to the east you'll find at Live Oak and at White Springs canoe outfitters for float trips on the renowned Suwannee River, whose praises are widely sung in Stephen Foster's song. The composer, who never laid eyes on the stream he immortalized, is commemorated at the Stephen Foster Folk Culture Center (9–5, adm.) at White Springs where the attractions include dioramas depicting the songwriter's compositions, among them Florida's state song, "Old Folks at Home"; the "Belle of the Suwannee" riverboat; a banjo-strumming black man; and a ninety-three-bell carillon that rings out Foster favorites. Every year around Memorial Day weekend the Florida Folk Festival—featuring music, crafts, baptisms in the river, storytellers, meals of black-eyed peas and collard greens—takes place at the Center (for information: 904-397-2192). Suwannee River State Park back to the west of White Springs offers water recreation, an overlook above the confluence of the Suwannee and the

Withlacoochee and remains of a Confederate defensive installation. East of White Springs you'll find the Osceola National Forest, which includes Olustee Battlefield State Historic Site, locale of the state's largest Civil War battle, an 1864 Confederate victory that blocked Federal troops from advancing into Florida, so preventing the Northerners from cutting off interior supply lines. In early 1990 at nearby Lake City the Florida Sports Hall of Fame, at the junction of I-75 and U.S. 90, opened.

Bradford County, to the south, takes its name from Captain Richard Bradford, the first Florida officer killed in the Civil War, October 1861, while Gainesville, farther south, took its name—but not without some controversy—from Indian fighter General Edmund Pendleton Gaines. In 1853, when Alachua County moved the county seat, a prominent citizen named William H. Lewis wanted the new settlement to be called Lewisville. At a barbecue dinner the locals agreed that if the town gained the courthouse it would be called Gainesville and if the town were to lose the honor Lewisville would designate the place. But either name beats Hog Town, as Gainesville was once called. On the University of Florida campus in Gainesville you'll find the Florida State Museum (M.–Sat., 9–5; Sun., 1–5, free), with archeological displays and replicas of a cave and of a Mayan palace, while near the museum at the Lake Alice Wildlife Preserve slither and doze king-size alligators. The university boasts the world's largest citrus research center, one of the nation's few hyperbaric chambers used for treating near-drowning victims, and what's said to be the country's largest academic program on a single campus, with more than one hundred undergraduate majors available.

The little town of Windsor, too small to appear on Florida's official highway map (the hamlet lies near Newmans Lake east of Gainesville) hosts every year in early May a Zucchini Festival (for information: 904-377-2346). Near

Gainesville are two natural areas, The Devil's Millhopper State Geological Site (8–sunset, free), a five-acre hundred-foot-deep sinkhole overgrown with subtropical rain forest vegetation, and Payne's Prairie State Preserve (8–sunset, free), a grassy swatch where Indians once lived and where buffalo now roam, with an overlook and a visitor center containing exhibits on the area's history. At nearby Cross Creek—not far from the attractive little town of Micanopy, filled with nineteenth-century architecture—stands the home of author Marjorie Kinnan Rawlings, who settled in the area in 1928. The Yearling Restaurant (Tu.–Sat., noon–10; Sun., 1–8:30) recalls Rawlings' Pulitzer Prize-winning novel of that name, while the eatery's exotic fare—fried alligator tail, cooter (soft-shelled turtle) and other such delicacies—recalls the unusual regional recipes collected in the author's *Cross Creek Cookery*. The writer's late nineteenth-century three-sectioned home (Th.–M., 10–11:30; 1–4:30, adm.)—comprised of porch and living room, bedrooms, and kitchen and dining room—remains little changed from the days she lived there. An outhouse indicates the primitive conditions Rawlings found when she bought the house, a wood-burning stove outfits the kitchen, a living room closet serves as a bar, and throughout the residence typewriters wait silently for inspired fingers. But gone is the renowned writer, buried at the nearby town of Island Grove, and now, as she once described the area, "Cross Creek belongs to the wind and the rain, to the sun and seasons, to the cosmic secrecy of seed, and above all, to time."

Returning to the Tallahassee area, another possible route that will take you south from the capital toward the center of the state passes through Perry, home of the Forest Capital State Museum (9–5), with forestry exhibits on turpentine production, pine tree propagation, Florida's more than three hundred species of trees, and also a century-old Cracker Homestead, that nickname for Floridians stemming from the cracking cattle-whips cowboys in the state used. From the main highway south extend side roads to isolated seaside towns in an area so primitive and wild it's come to be known as the Hidden Coast. This is Florida as it was before land booms, condos and tourist attractions and traps arrived in the state. These remote coastal communities bear such names as Spring Warrior Camp, Jug Island, Fish Creek and Steinhatchee. Unless you want to hazard the logging trails that link some of the hamlets, you have to return to U.S. highway 19 before heading out to the next shore village. If you have time for only one such town Steinhatchee is perhaps the best choice, for the settlement boasts such rather basic but colorful seafood places as Cooey's Restaurant, started in the 1930s and since expanded.

Farther south on the coast, beyond the Suwannee River, which flows into the Gulf of Mexico there, lies picturesque Cedar Key, another out-of-the-way unspoiled town with an ambiance out of the distant past. Still today Cedar Key remains like Key West no doubt was a half-century and more ago. Cedar Key might well be named "low key," so laid-back is the village of seven hundred persons perched on an isolated island three miles off the coast. No fast-food establishments quicken sleepy Cedar Key's slow pace; no bright brand name signs link the town with motel chains from the outside world; no glossy shopping centers crowd out the mix of down-home local stores. Somewhat seedy Cedar Key is an understated sort of place, an old-fashioned enclave unpossessed by the twentieth century. A good introduction to the town is the Island Hotel, installed in a nearly century-and-a-half-old galleried building made of "tabby," a mixture of crushed oyster shells, sand and lime. The Island, listed on the National Register, seems to epitomize Cedar Key's relaxed atmosphere. In the plant-filled lobby of the ten-room hotel (904-543-5111), which once served as a general store, a gun-runner's lair, and to house both Confederate and

Union troops during the Civil War, stands antique furniture, while the cedar-scented bar contains colorful murals painted in the 1940s by an artist who traded her work for a room at the Island. Once the state's largest city, Cedar Key is small enough to cover on foot. A short stroll along a causeway takes you out to the pier, where a cluster of restaurants serve seafood and offer views of the Gulf. Back in the center of town is the Cedar Key Historical Society Museum (M.–F., 10–5; Sun., 1–5, adm.), while a mile or so from the center stands the Cedar Key State Museum (9–5, adm.). Exhibits at these two museums trace the town's colorful past and its prosperity, which started with completion of the trans-Florida railroad from near Jacksonville on the east coast out to the key. A few years later Eberhard Faber established a mill to process grooved pencil slats from cedar wood, and by 1880 Cedar Key—with pencil companies, a thriving lumber industry, shipyards and freight traffic—had become a boom town where the elegant two-hundred-room Suwannee Hotel catered to fashionable travelers. In the late nineteenth century the supply of cedar and pine timber began to dwindle and the mills started to close. Then, in 1896, a tidal wave and a fire—supposedly started when the postmistress poured kerosene on hot coals while heating coffee for her husband—destroyed much of the village, which gradually settled into the sleepy but delightful fishing settlement it is today. In 1989 the state approved construction of a marina at the nearby privately owned undeveloped 160-acre island of Atsena Otie, uninhabited since the turn of the century, so the Cedar Key area may, alas, soon be updated.

Cedar Key lies in Levy County, named for David Levy Yulee, a member of the 1838 constitutional convention held at Port St. Joe and later Florida's first U.S. senator. Yulee's grandmother, daughter of an English physician, was captured by Barbary pirates as she sailed for the West Indies and the corsairs sold her at a slave market in Fez to Jacoub ben Youli, grand vizier to the Sultan of Morocco. During an uprising she smuggled her son Moses out to Gibraltar, escaping from the sultan's harem. Later Moses married and settled in Florida where his son, David, was born in 1811. David later married the daughter of a Kentucky governor and developed a five-thousand-acre sugar plantation in Homosassa, south of Cedar Key. On the way to the Yulee Sugar Mill State Historic Site there you'll pass the Cross Florida Barge Canal, just south of Inglis, an uncompleted project—intended to cut a channel for freight ships to enter north-central Florida—started and abandoned several times, most recently under pressure by ecologists, in 1971. Yankeetown, just west of Inglis, suffered from a twenty-four-hour rainfall of thirty-eight and seven-tenths inches, a national record, on September 5–6, 1950. Florida, for reasons unknown, is the thunderstorm center of the Northern Hemisphere, and in the entire world only the central part of South Africa experiences tempests more frequent than those over the Florida peninsula. As early as 1821 James Grant Forbes commented on the phenomenon in *Sketches, Historical and Topographical of the Floridas:* "Thunderstorms, accompanied by vivid lightning, which rise generally in the south and south west, are violent and transient." Forbes tells of one "Mr. Jesse Fish, Jun. who was found dead in the fields, with his horse, after a violent storm, which he had endeavoured to avert by an umbrella with brass mounting, which it is confidentally believed caused his death." Thus did a Fish die in the rain. The Yulee Mill Historic Site recalls the sugar plantation David Levy Yulee operated for thirteen years, beginning in 1851. A self-guided tour takes you through the partially restored facility, which supplied the Southern army with sugar products until the Yankees destroyed the property in 1864.

At Inverness, a bit inland, the Crown Hotel, 109 North Seminole Avenue (904-344-5555) offers bed and breakfast ac-

commodations, while farther north, near Ocala, lies Florida's thoroughbred country, with neatly kept horse farms,
many along U.S. highway 301, some of them open to visitors (for information: 904-629-8051). Just east of Ocala,
where the relatively new Appleton Museum houses a varied
collection of art and artifacts, stretches Ocala National Forest, the country's southernmost such enclave, with the
world's largest stand of sand pine and well-wetted by such
water sources as Alexander Springs, Juniper Springs, Salt
Springs and Silver Glen Springs. Silver Springs (9–5:30,
adm.) near Ocala, which emits about a half-billion gallons
of water a day, the nation's largest flow from a single source,
has been a tourist attraction for a century, with steamboats
carrying sightseers along the Oklawaha River from Palatka,
one hundred and thirty-six miles to the northeast. One early
visitor to the springs, author Harriet Beecher Stowe, opined
"there is nothing on earth comparable to it." Glass-bottom
boats—a craft invented at Silver Springs—take tourists
through the watery precincts, past jungle animals whose ancestors were brought there for use in the original Tarzan
movies filmed in the area.

Up at Anthony, just north of Ocala, is the Florida Heritage
Winery and Vineyards, offering free tours and tastings,
while back down on the coast, south of the Yulee Sugar
Mill, flows another tourist-oriented spring at Weeki Wachee
("winding waters"), populated by mermaids who perform
acrobatics, or aquabatics, as you watch through four-inch-
thick underwater windows. Just up the street looms a forty-
eight-foot tall concrete dinosaur that houses a local gas
station, the service bays installed in the beast's flank. Rather
less commercialized than Weeki Wachee Spring is the nearby
village of Masaryktown, settled by Czechs in 1925. After
failing in their attempt to grow oranges the Czechs switched
to chickens and to good effect, for eventually the town entered the *Guinness Book of World Records* as home of the fastest

chicken-pluckers on earth (nearby Spring Hill hosts the annual world's championship plucking contest). You'll see around Masaryktown an occasional "kroje"—a traditional costume—and strudel is featured on many dessert menus, while the Kavarcik Motel offers Old World hospitality.

The town of St. Leo, a few miles to the southeast, is a religious community with an other-world atmosphere far removed from Florida's usual ambiance. St. Leo Abbey and College comprise the village, a green and serene enclave that affords a pleasant retreat from the frequently over-built and over-touristed coastal areas. Benedictine monks from the Carolinas founded St. Leo in 1889, and in 1936 the brothers began work on the Abbey church, built of handmade bricks and red cedar from the surrounding grounds and completed in twelve years. The sanctuary is sometimes described as "the church built with orange juice," revenue from the Abbey's citrus groves having defrayed part of the construction costs. The church sports thirty-nine striking stained-glass windows, and behind the building perches a terrace where you can enjoy a view over peaceful Lake Jovita. At nearby Zephyrhills, home of an annual parachuting competition, two places offer bed and breakfast: Colonial Park Inn, highway 54 west (813-782-4505) and the Burr residence, 4431 North 23rd Street (813-788-4788).

Before heading over to the Tampa–St. Petersburg area you may want to visit a few more inland attractions. Plant City, south of Zephyrhills, retains an easygoing small-town flavor, the primary local flavor being strawberries, for the area produces one of the nation's largest crops of that fruit. Paying tribute to the product are the annual Florida Strawberry Festival in early March and a huge berry perched atop the town's water tower. A few buildings around Plant City sport murals of locals painted by resident John Briggs. Nearby Lakeland, with its ten large and other lesser lakes, is one of Florida's more attractive cities. Florida Southern College, which occu-

pies a parklike site, once an orange grove, overlooking sparkling Lake Hollingsworth, boasts the largest group of Frank
Lloyd Wright buildings in one place. Scattered about the
campus, listed on the National Register, are seven structures
designed by the renowned architect, among them the 1941
Annie Pfeiffer Chapel, Wright's first creation at the college,
and the Polk Science Building, the last, finished in 1958.
Rising above the Science Center's long, low lines—a characteristic Wright configuration—is the contrasting bulge of
a planetarium dome which, during the Christmas season,
bears a face and hat in its role as Florida's largest (and no
doubt only) snowman. Also on campus is a curious little
enclave called the Hindu Garden of Meditation, decorated
with cow and elephant statues and with a small red sandstone
temple that in a way resembles a Wright creation but which
was dismantled into two hundred and thirty-nine sections
in India and shipped to the college as a gift from a Methodist
missionary.

Lakeland also serves as home of the Florida Citrus Commission, the industry's supervisory organization. For a juicy
citrus tour the Minute Maid plant in Auburndale to the east
takes visitors in the spring and winter, and Winter Haven,
just to the south, mounts an eleven-day Florida Citrus Festival every year in mid-February. Just outside Winter Haven
lies Cypress Gardens (8–dusk, adm.), one of Florida's older
(1930s) and better-known tourist attractions, featuring water
ski performances, the state's only ice-skating shows, walking
paths, a small zoo and other such mild-mannered activities;
while at nearby Lake Wales nestles another botanical area,
the Bok Tower Gardens (8–5:30, adm.), listed on the National Register, where a fifty-three-bell carillon sounds forth
(brief selections every half hour, a concert at 3 daily) from
a "singing" tower given to the state in 1929 by *Ladies Home
Journal* editor Edward Bok, buried at the foot of the marble
and coquina structure. You'll also find at Lake Wales Spook

Hill, a road at Fifth and North Avenue where your car will seem to roll uphill, an optical illusion you can produce by shifting into neutral and pausing at the bottom of the steep drive. Late winter and spring in Lake Wales brings performances in an amphitheater of the Black Hills Passion Play (for schedules and reservations: 813-676-1492), while another local religious attraction is the three-hundred-thousand-piece mosaic of Leonardo da Vinci's painting "The Last Supper" at Masterpiece Gardens (9–5:30, adm.). For supper—hopefully not your last—or other meals and for rooms the Chalet Suzanne Country Inn and Restaurant (813-676-6011) is a well-known Lake Wales establishment, with an elegant dining area and rooms furnished in such exotic styles as Moroccan, Mexican, Italian and Indian. Florida produces 80 percent of the world's phosphate, used primarily in fertilizer. Lunar-like landscapes disfigure the area around Bartow, to the west of Lake Wales, a phosphate mining region known as Bone Valley, so called as the digging equipment occasionally dredges up prehistoric fossils, some of which are on display at the Bone Valley Phosphate Museum. Some miles south of Bartow lies Arcadia, site of weekly cattle auctions (for information: 813-494-4033) and of Oak Ridge Cemetery, last resting place of twenty-three Englishmen, Royal Air Force cadets who died during World War II while training in the area.

Back on the coast the region around and near Tampa Bay offers a varied group of attractions. If you've bypassed the inland area and continued down the coast road from points north you'll pass through New Port Richey, a congested and urbanized town with the one redeeming feature of hosting the world's largest barbecue, given by the local Sertoma Club at its annual Chasco Festival on the banks of the Pithlachascotee River. So if you ever hankered for a picnic on the Pithlachascotee, New Port Richey is definitely the place to go. Tarpon Springs, just to the south, retains the Greek ambiance first brought there around the turn of the century when divers from the old country arrived to harvest the rich sponge beds just off the coast. Along Dodecanese Boulevard stand the sponge docks, now used to berth fishing craft, as synthetic materials have for the most part replaced natural sponges. The Spongerama (10–6, free) contains exhibits on the early sponging days, while part of the 1907 Sponge Exchange, now occupied by shops, survives as a remnant of the industry's high tide. These days the town's main business, apart from tourism, is boat building, with shipyards such as Peer Lovfald turning out customized yachts for fancy sailors. Tarpon Springs began as a rather fancy place when Hamilton Disston of Philadelphia established the town as a resort for well-heeled Easterners after he acquired a bit of Florida land—four million acres at twenty-five cents an acre—in 1881. This so called "Disston Sale" enabled the state to repay bondholders, who otherwise might have foreclosed and forced the sale of public lands at even lower prices. Kathryn Abbey Hanna in *Florida: Land of Change* regards this transaction as a key event in the state's development, maintaining that "The significance of his [Disston's] influence cannot be overstated." Tarpon Springs also boasts two churches of note: the 1943 St. Nicholas Greek Orthodox Cathedral, a Byzantine-style structure crammed with icons, and the Universalist Church (Oct.–May, Tu.–Sun., 2–5, free), decorated with eleven paintings by George Inness, Jr., son of the more famous artist of the same name who owned a home in Tarpon Springs. The town has a bed and breakfast establishment—Spring Bayou Inn, 32 West Tarpon Avenue (813-938-9333)—as does Palm Harbor, just to the south: Florida Suncoast B and B, 119 Rosewood Drive (813-784-5118).

Tampa's beginnings date from 1824 when the American government built Fort Brooke, one of a series established to defend against the Seminole Indians, but the town's true

development began only sixty years later when railroad magnate Henry Plant extended his line to Tampa Bay, an area,
the entrepreneur observed, he then found "slumbering as
it had been for years." Needled by one-time partner and
later rival Henry Flagler, who developed railroads and hotel
properties on Florida's east coast, with the question "Where
is Tampa Bay?" Plant replied, "Just follow the crowd." In
1891 Plant built the minaret-topped Moorish-style Tampa
Bay Hotel, which now houses the University of Tampa and
a small museum (Tu.–Sat., 10–4, free) containing Plant's collection of furniture and art objects. Other local museums
and displays include one devoted to Science and Industry
(10–4:30, adm.), sporting a sign outside promising (or
threatening) "Hurricanes every hour!" and the Tampa Museum (Tu., Th., F., 10–6; W., 10–9; Sat., 9–5; Sun., 1–5,
free), an art gallery perched on the banks of the Hillsborough
River in downtown Tampa, now an area of glossy high-rises
housing banks, hotels and offices. Overshadowed by the skyscrapers, Franklin Street's 1930s Art Deco-style shops and
the 1926 Tampa Theater remain to recall the town's pre-
boom days, as does the nearby 1905 Sacred Heart Church,
adorned with a large rose window. Moored downtown, off
Bayshore Boulevard, whose six and a half-mile sidewalk is
supposedly the longest continuous such way in the world,
is the "Jose Gasparilla," a modern-day craft (1954), said to
be the world's only fully rigged pirate ship, which stars in
the raucous Mardi Gras-like Gasparilla Invasion held every
February, the same month Tampa, Florida's third-largest city
(after Jacksonville and Miami), hosts the State Fair.

As the nation's seventh-largest port, Tampa possesses a
waterfront that bustles with activity, so if you're a sea buff
you may enjoy watching banana boats unload at the Twiggs
Street docks or the shrimp boats, the state's largest fleet
devoted to those crustaceans, bringing their catch in at
Hooker's Point at the end of Bermuda Avenue. On the west

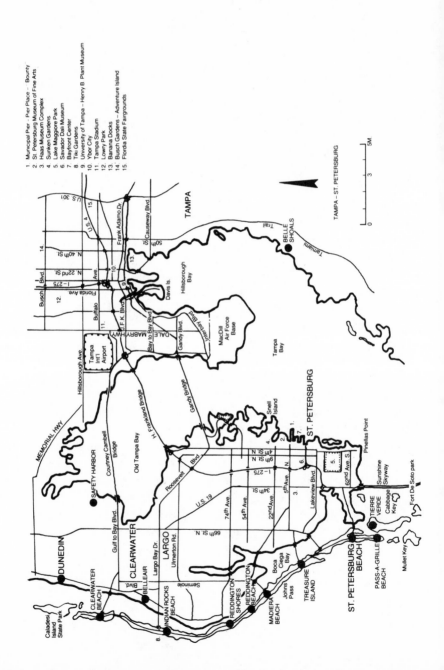

1   Municipal Pier – Pier Place – Bounty
2   St. Petersburg Museum of Fine Arts
3   Haas Museum Complex
4   Sunken Gardens
5   Lake Maggiore Park
6   Savador Dali Museum
7   Bayfront Center
8   Tiki Gardens
9   University of Tampa – Henry B. Plant Museum
10 Ybor City
11 Tampa Stadium
12 Lowry Park
13 Banana Docks
14 Busch Gardens – Adventure Island
15 Flordia State Fairgrounds

side of town lies Tampa International Airport, chosen by more than one authority as the best in the nation, and Tampa Stadium, near which Columbus Drive—called by locals "Boliche Boulevard," boliches being sausage-stuffed beef—is lined with Latin cafes, while to the north spreads Busch Gardens (9:30–6, longer in summer; for hours and information: 813-971-8282, adm.), Florida's second-most popular tourist attraction, after Disney World. The Busch facility is a simulated "Dark Continent" African theme park with animals, rides and tame versions of such exotic distant places as Timbuktu, Nairobi and the Congo, and if those foreign-like enclaves make you homesick you can always tour the less alien precincts of the Anheuser-Busch brewery on the property. In 1990 the park opened its newest theme area, the eighth, called The Crown Colony. At little Lutz, north of Tampa, is Lake Como, home of one of the nation's largest and oldest nudist colonies. Back in Tampa you'll find an unusual restaurant, Bern's Steak House, 1208 South Howard, with what's supposedly the world's largest wine cellar, a half-million bottles representing some seven thousand varieties. The establishment—which serves pampered steaks, caressed vegetables from its own organic farm, fresh caviar and other such delicacies—sells the wine list for more than what meals cost in most restaurants.

The most interesting and least modernized section of Tampa is Ybor City, a Cuban quarter established in 1886 when Vincente Martinez Ybor moved his cigar factory there from Key West. According to *The Immigrant World of Ybor City* by Gary R. Mormino and George E. Pozzetta, that first year workers produced a million cigars; in 1900 they turned out twenty million and in 1919 production peaked at more than four hundred million stogies fabricated by some twelve thousand workmen. Ybor Square, the tastefully restored original factory, now houses antiques, craft and collectibles shops and cafes as well as such other establishments

as the Tampa Rico Cigar Company where workers of Cuban
descent still hand-make cigars the old way using wooden
molds (M.–F., 10–4). Signs at the atmospheric and aromatic
shop proclaim, "Thank you for smoking." Turn-of-the-
century structures line the streets of Ybor City, a National
Historic District, with the excellent Ybor City State Museum (9–5, adm.) installed in one old building, the Ferlita
Bakery, which until 1973 produced Cuban-type bread, described by a sign in front of the former neighborhood shop:
"Tampa's Latin Loaf is like no other bread in the world.
It is leavened with emotion, flavored with tradition, and eaten
with a large helping of nostalgia." A reasonable facsimile
of this delicacy can be found at La Segunda Central Bakery
in Ybor City, 2515 15th Street, or in sandwich form at such
places as La Tropicana, 1822 East 7th Street, where a giant
loaf of Cuban bread decorates the premises. Ybor City's
most famous restaurant is the Columbia, an eleven-room,
sixteen-hundred-seat establishment built in 1905, featuring
Latin food and tile-embellished mock Spanish architecture.

Another unusual area eating place is the Italian baroque
garden spot in Clearwater, west of Tampa, called the Kapok
Tree Restaurant. Fountains, statuary, crystal chandeliers, columns and the site's sole surviving kapok tree, planted in
the 1870s from seeds brought to the area from the Far East,
embellish the establishment. Another Henry Plant hotel, the
1897 Belleview Biltmore, listed on the National Register,
still stands at Clearwater, as does the old Fort Harrison
Hotel, which now serves as area headquarters of the
California-based Church of Scientology. The Clearwater
premises of the *St. Petersburg Times* and *Evening Independent*
boasts rather futuristic touches with a windmill and solar
panel power sources, while the town's Peace Memorial
Church sports a striking pink hue as if mocking the skin
color of "sunbirds" from the North who remained too long
on the nearby beach. To the north of Clearwater lies

Dunedin, founded by settlers from Scotland, where a home-country shop, 1401 Main Street, offers a huge stock of tartan goods; while at Indian Shores, south of Clearwater, is the Suncoast Seabird Sanctuary (9–dusk, free), an infirmary for injured and sick wild birds which hosts more than five hundred feathered patients at any one time. Farther south, near the tip of Sand Key, stands the rather funky Don CeSar, a pink pile of a hotel, listed on the National Register, which opened in 1928. During the Depression the establishment hit hard times and eventually became an army hospital, the bistro serving as the morgue, but these days the Don CeSar is back in business as a hotel (813-360-1881, 800-247-9810). Fort De Soto Park, on the very south edge of the key, remains an unspoiled area with the ruins of a century-old fort and pristine beaches.

St. Petersburg, as with Tampa, began to develop after the railroad arrived, in this case the Orange Belt Line built in 1885 by Peter Demens, who named the town for his birthplace in Russia. St. Pete is a slow-paced sunny city—its seven hundred consecutive days of sunshine set a world's record—with a sort of seedy air about it, perhaps typified by the once elegant but now deteriorated 1925 Vinoy Park Hotel, north of which, on Shell Island, lies one of the town's more attractive residential districts. Elsewhere, at the splendid house at 510 Park Street, the last designed by famous Florida architect Addison Mizner, is a plaque that recalls the 1528 landing of Panfilo de Narvaez, whose expedition to conquer Florida ended in failure but inspired survivor Cabeza de Vaca's famous account of the New World, a narrative people refused to believe. In the 3500 block of Second Avenue South stand other historical homes that comprise an enclave including the Turner House, the Lowe House and the Haas Museum (Th.–Sun., 1–5; closed Sept., adm.), with an old dental office, barber shop, railroad station, antiques and other Florida relics. The Museum of Fine Arts (Tu.–Sat., 10–5; Sun.,

1–5, adm.) contains a mixed group of European, pre-Columbian and American works, while the nearby Salvador Dali Museum (Tu.–Sat., 10–5; Sun., 12–5, adm.) displays works only by the eccentric Spanish artist. Housed in a ten-thousand-square-foot gallery in a revamped former marine warehouse, the museum is said to be the world's largest devoted to only one person's art. Other St. Petersburg attractions include the touristy Sunken Gardens (9–sunset, adm.), an enclave of tropical plantings; Haslam's, Florida's largest used-book store, 2025 Central Avenue, with some 300,000 volumes; the Shuffleboard Hall of Fame, at the north edge of pensioner-popular Mirror Lake; the unusual 1916 open-air post office, at Central Avenue and Fourth Street North; and The Pier, renovated in 1988, which features an inverted bayside pyramid with shops selling imported wares and a restaurant. A more colorful place to eat is the Chattaway, 358 22nd Avenue South, best described as a fancy shack, with an old bathtub used as a planter, a miscellany of items decorating the walls, and respectable home cooking. The Albemarle Hotel, 145 Third Avenue Northeast (813-822-4097), offers bed and breakfast, while through B and B Suncoast Accommodations (813-360-1753) you can make reservations at other area bed and breakfast places.

Beyond the splendid Sunshine Skyway toll bridge that gracefully spans the edge of Tampa Bay you'll find the Gamble Plantation State Historic Site where an elegant, many-pillared (eighteen in all) mansion, the oldest home on Florida's west coast (mid-1840s), stands; the Madira Bickel Mound Historic Memorial, commemorating a two-millennium-old Indian settlement; and the ruins of "Braden Castle," built by sugar planter Joseph Braden, after whom nearby Bradenton is named. At the town of Ellenton you may see some of the distinctively dressed Mennonites who've settled there in recent years, while to the north the village of Ruskin, named after English intellectual and critic John

Ruskin, was founded to be a communal colony with a college modeled after Oxford, but these days the town functions in a more practical vein as one of the nation's leading tomato producers. Perched on the shore west of Bradenton is the De Soto National Memorial, a small enclave that commemorates the arrival there of Spanish explorer Hernando de Soto, who reached the New World in May 1539 to begin the first major exploration of the North American interior, a three-year trek which took his band of adventurers through areas now occupied by Southern states. A museum houses a model of the caravel de Soto's fleet used, armor and such old-time weapons as a crossbow, halberd (a kind of spear) and an arquebus (an oversized matchlock-operated gun). Also at the Memorial is a re-creation of Camp Ucita, de Soto's original encampment, where visitors can try on suits of armor, perhaps the only place in the nation that offers the chance to don such attire. Through Bradenton, where the world's highest percentage of mobile home residents live, or at least pause, runs a river called the Manatee, named for the once-thriving but now scarce sea cows that Columbus thought were mermaids when he espied them in 1492. At least twelve hundred manatees still survive, but boats and other hazards kill fifty or so a year, a loss difficult to replace as the females produce only one new calf every three years. A good place to get the flavor of Florida's citrus industry is at Mixon's Farm in Bradenton, a three hundred and fifty-acre grove with a packing house and a shop with free orange juice and mail order fruit selections for sale.

Sarasota to the south is one of the favorite perches of the so-called sunbirds, Northerners who flock to warm weather in the winter. In 1884 the Florida Mortgage & Investment Company, Ltd., owned by Scotsman John Gillespie, who two years later built in the area the nation's first golf course, started to develop the tiny community then called Sara Sota. Among the company's board members was

the Archbishop of Canterbury, so Sarasota certainly started
off with heavenly connections. In 1910 Mrs. Potter Palmer,
whose family gave its name to the Palmer House Hotel in
Chicago, arrived from that city and purchased land in
Sarasota—she later gave to Florida the Myakka River State
Park, a huge unspoiled wildlife refuge (8–sunset) east of the
city—and soon northern socialites started to winter in the
area. John and Mable Ringling, who first visited Sarasota
in 1911, decided to build there a thirty-room Venetian-style
mansion called Ca'd'Zan, completed in 1926, now the city's
leading tourist attraction (M.–F., 9–7; Sat., 9–5; Sun., 11–6,
adm.), with not only the residence but also the Ringling
Museum of Art, featuring a large collection of Rubens
works, a circus museum and the gem-like eighteenth-century
Asolo Theater imported from a castle in Italy. The first
weekend in March a Medieval Fair, with minstrels, jousting
matches, a human chess game and other such archaic activities, take place on the grounds of the Ringling Art Museum.
The New College campus of the University of South Florida,
north of the Ringling complex, includes several buildings
designed by the renowned architect I. M. Pei. An unusual,
if not unique, eating place in Sarasota is Fiddler's, tucked
away on a side street, at 6557 Gateway, operated entirely
by one person, a Yugoslavian woman named Carol Mount
(Tu.–Sat., 5–8). Beyond Lido Key and its fancy St. Armands
Circle shopping quarter stretches twelve-mile long Longboat
Key, lined with high-rise condos and apartments, while to
the south lies less developed Siesta Key, a one-time art colony
and commercial fishing area, now a maze of canal-side
houses, where authors Mackinlay Kantor and John D. Mac-
Donald once lived. Venice, to the south, originated as the
planned retirement community of the Brotherhood of Railroad Engineers, but now it's best known as winter home
of the Ringling Brothers Barnum and Bailey Circus and the
Ringling Clown College, established in 1967 to teach aspir-

ing jesters juggling, tumbling, unicycle riding and other such tricks. Less lighthearted are the exhibits—murder weapons, electric chairs and law enforcement items—at the Police Museum not far from Port Charlotte to the east of Venice. The nearby Warm Mineral Springs (9–5, adm.) is thought by some to be the Fountain of Youth sought by Ponce de Leon, commemorated at the Ponce de Leon Historical Park and Shrine at Punta Gorda, which marks the location of the first attempt, in 1521, to settle the present United States, an effort that ended after a poisoned Calusa Indian arrow took the explorer's life.

In the 1970s the Fort Myers-Cape Coral area was the nation's fastest-growing metropolitan region, the population nearly doubling in ten years. As usual, inventor Thomas Edison had the idea first, for he arrived in 1886 at age thirty-nine after doctors warned him to seek a better climate for his failing health. The house built—or, rather, assembled, as it was prefabricated—by Edison, who survived to age eighty-four, remains as a splendid monument to the great man and his inventive ways—he received more than a thousand patents. Edison constructed Florida's first modern-day swimming pool, reinforced with bamboo and still leakproof, and in the garden he planted royal palms, trees from South America and the Far East, including Florida's largest banyan, and a goldenrod he hoped to use in making synthetic rubber, a project supported by his Fort Myers neighbors Harvey Firestone and Henry Ford, whose six-room residence, called the Mangoes, opened as a museum in January 1990. A museum at the Edison Winter Home (9–4; Sun., 12:30–4, adm.) contains photos, personal items, light bulbs the inventor developed and a small tinfoil strip that plays "Mary Had a Little Lamb"—the world's first record. At the Shellpoint Village retirement community is a huge model train operation patterned after Florida's Gulf Coast Railroad sysem (M., W., F., 1–3, free), and the city's Historical Museum (Tu.–F.,

9–4:30; Sat. and Sun., 1–5) includes a scale model of turn-of-the-century Fort Myers, while south of the city lies the site of the southernmost Civil War battle, fought February 20, 1865. Also to the south is the Honey Bee Observatory (9:30–5, free), where you can observe the busy little bees in their hives and buy orange blossom honey. At Alva off to the east Eden Vineyards opened in December 1989, featuring a nature trail, tram ride through the vineyards and tastings in an old-style reception center modeled after a Florida farmhouse of the mid-1800s, while just north of town the Shell Factory (9–6, free) boasts what it claims is the world's largest selection of those gifts from the sea.

The 1933 old post office in downtown Fort Myers was built of coral and seashells collected on the nearby keys and islands, one of which, Sanibel, is held to be among the world's three best shelling areas, along with Jeffreys Bay in Africa and the Sulu Islands in the Philippines. For some years local residents fought construction of a causeway from the mainland to Sanibel and adjacent Captiva Island, a case that finally ended in the U.S. Supreme Court. The bridge builders won and in 1963 completed the span, but eleven years later Sanibel seceded from Lee County and established its own administration, which limited development on the island, now partly occupied by the J. N. "Ding" Darling National Wildlife Refuge, frequented by crimson-winged roseate spoonbills and other birds. The Sanibel-Captiva Conservation Foundation, installed in an attractive weathered wood structure, contains exhibits on these two fragile barrier islands, while at Sanibel's southern tip stands the century-old lighthouse, a local landmark since 1884. Other islands to the north fleck the coastal waters, among them two bits of land reachable only by water: Useppa, a one-time millionaires' retreat used to train Cubans for the Bay of Pigs invasion and now a private club, but open to the public, with the pleasantly old-fashioned Collier Inn, and Cabbage Key, whose Hide-Away Inn and Restaurant (813-283-2278) was converted into a hotel from the 1938 house of mystery novelist Mary Roberts Rinehart. Also relatively unspoiled are Pine Island, with the pleasant towns of Bokeelia and St. James City at the north and south ends, and Gasparilla, a quiet slow-paced place, reached by a privately owned causeway, with the comfortable but rather formal Gasparilla Inn (813-964-2201), bike paths, huge banyan trees and an atmosphere so laid-back three streets bear the names "Dam if I Know, "Dam if I Care" and "Dam if I Will."

To complete your tour of western Florida you can head south from Fort Myers to the Naples and Marco Island area, the west coast's most southern resorts. On the way you'll pass near Estero the curious Koreshan community, a State Historic Site (8–sunset, free), where in 1894 a visionary named Cyrus Reed Teed, who called himself "Koresh," brought his followers from Chicago to establish a communal religious settlement by the Estero River. Koresh convinced his followers he was immortal, so when the leader died in 1908 his disciples placed the body on a cypress plank to await his reincarnation. Teed remained moribund and in a few weeks his corpse was removed to a bathtub, soon thereafter swept away by a hurricane. Both tub and contents disappeared forever, but many of the buildings erected by the Koreshans still stand, the most complete survivor being Art Hall, a kind of meeting and lecture room with charts, a globe and measuring instruments the sect used to study its theory that the earth was a hollow sphere with the sun in the center and life on the inside. In October the abandoned settlement celebrates its Koreshan Unity Solar Festival (for information: 813-992-0311). Off to the east lies Corkscrew Swamp Sanctuary (9–5, free), a six-thousand-acre National Audubon Society preserve with the nation's largest stand of virgin bald cypress trees and a flock of rare wood storks which nest there from December through March. Corkscrew

Swamp lies, or sinks, at the northern edge of Big Cyprus National Preserve, a remote swamp through which runs a mostly unpaved country road, number 94, via Seminole Indian settlements, Sunniland and its eccentric little cafe, and Ochopee, which boasts what's said to be the nation's smallest post office and where the National Park Service operates a visitor center.

Naples on the coast, a town of about twenty thousand people, is an elegant and handsome place which supposedly has more millionares per capita than any other city in the country. During the 1980s Naples was the nation's fastest-growing metropolitan area. In town is the fourteen-acre Conservancy Nature Center (M.–Sat., 9–5; May–Oct., closed Sat., free) and the tastefully restored Old Marine Market, installed in an antique tin-roofed building, while along the north shore no fast-food, low-life or high-rise establishments mar the seven-mile long beach, from which extends into the Gulf a century-old thousand-foot long fishing pier that once boasted its own narrow gauge railway. South of Naples lies Marco Island, actually three islands, the middle one—bordered by beaches with talc-like sand—highly developed as a tourist area, while Old Marco, with its picturesque inn, and the quiet fishing village of Goodland remain less commercial. Local atmosphere and characters prevail at water-side Stan's Idle Hour Restaurant in Goodland, an unspoiled corner of Marco. Along the coast lie the Ten Thousand Islands, a labyrinth of mangrove swamps and islets you can explore on tours that leave from Everglades City, the western entrance to the Everglades National Park; for information: 305-247-6211. Here in this primitive area, near the tip of the peninsula on the verge of the primeval Everglades, you are removed from the tourist's version of Florida, which now seems an eternity and a world away.

Eastern Florida

Jacksonville—Saint Augustine—Cape Canaveral—Orlando and Disney World—Palm Beach—Miami—The Everglades—The Keys

Florida was first settled in the west, at Pensacola, when Spanish colonists established an outpost in the New World in 1559. This was also the very first settlement of any permanence in the area of the present United States. A year after the Spaniards abandoned the colony in 1561 a French expedition commanded by Huguenot navy officers reached Florida, discovering on May 1 a waterway they named the River of May, now known as the St. Johns. In 1564 one of the officers, René de Laudonnière, returned to establish La Caroline, a fort on the south bank of the St. Johns. These French incursions into the New World alarmed Spain's Philip II, who in 1564 organized an expedition which managed to capture Fort Caroline, after which the Spaniards set up a colony called Saint Augustine, by now the nation's oldest city. Reminders of much of this early history survive in the state's northeastern corner, where monuments, buildings and St. Augustine itself recall the time four centuries ago when both Florida and the United States had their origins.

Having been under eight flags, Amelia Island in the state's very northeastern corner is a kind of microcosm of Florida history. French, Spanish, British, American Patriots (1812), Green Cross of Florida (1817), Mexican, Confederate and U.S. banners flew over the area, a skein of occupiers remembered in the Isle of Eight Flags Shrimp Festival held the first weekend in May. At the very northern tip of the thirteen and a half mile-long island stands Fort Clinch, used during the Civil War and for training in the Spanish-American War. Built of European-style brick masonry unique in the U.S.,

the fort presents the first weekend of every month a costumed reenactment of the outpost's 1864 occupation. In the
town of Fernandina Beach thirty blocks comprise the Centre
Street historic district, listed on the National Register, with
pre-Civil War and Victorian-era houses, one of which, Bailey
House, 28 Seventh Street (904-261-5390), offers bed and
breakfast accommodations, as does the 1735 House, 584
South Fletcher (904-261-5878). Out at the beach two bedrooms wallpapered with nautical charts provide sleeping
quarters in a lighthouse (904-261-4148), whose every room
is guaranteed to offer an ocean view. More elegant, and definitely more spacious, accommodations can be found at
Amelia Island Plantation (800-874-6878, 800-342-6841 in-
state), which occupies nine hundred acres at the south end
of the island. The resort includes three golf courses, fishing
ponds reserved for children under twelve, trails and a nature
preserve. Although it's hard to imagine as you stroll along
balmy Amelia Island's beaches of talc-like white sand—
crushed quartz washed by erosion from the Appalachian
Mountains—Florida's heaviest recorded snowfall, five inches
in January 1800, took place not far away at Point Peter near
the mouth of St. Marys River. So in spite of poet Wallace
Stevens' observation that "There is no Spring in Florida,"
seasons do exist in the peninsula, for the northeastern part
of the state lies north of the somewhat seasonless tropical
zone.

Jacksonville, with over a half-million inhabitants, more
than Miami's three hundred and fifty thousand, is Florida's
largest city and the nation's largest by area, at eight hundred
and forty-one square miles. The state's very earliest history
is commemorated at Fort Caroline National Memorial (9–5,
free), a replica of the outpost established by the French Huguenots in 1564, and at Mayport, one of the nation's oldest
fishing communities, whose name recalls the River of May,

as the French dubbed the St. Johns, the nation's only major river that flows from south to north. The old St. Johns Lighthouse, listed on the National Register, stands on the grounds of the Naval Station, where you can tour aircraft carriers and other ships (Sat., 10–4:30; Sun., 1–4:30, free). From picturesque Mayport, also home to the Marine Science Education Center (M.–F., 9–4, free), a school with an ocean museum, departs the ferry to Fort George Island. There you'll find another carry-over from the old days, 1792 Kingsley Plantation (tours at 9:30, 11, 1:30, 3, adm.), the oldest such property in Florida, where Zephaniah Kingsley, a Scotsman—his niece became famous as Whistler's mother—imported to the estate thousands of slaves whom he trained and then resold at a handsome profit. It was promoter Henry M. Flagler's steel bridge across the St. Johns in 1890 that eliminated the need for a ferry and permitted the first through trains from New York to St. Augustine and points south along Florida's east coast, a development that led to the state's increasing popularity as a vacation and retirement spot.

Writing in 1886 under the evocative pen-name Sylvia Sunshine, Abbie M. Brooks asserted in the equally evocatively entitled *Petals Plucked from Sunny Climes* that Florida suited "those fretted by the rough edges of corroding care to retire and find a respite from their struggles." In her 1873 *Palmetto-Leaves* Harriet Beecher Stowe, better known as author of *Uncle Tom's Cabin,* told of Florida's many charms but cautioned Northerners not to expect greenery, for what "one never fails to miss and regret here, is the grass. The *nakedness* of the land is an expression that often comes over one." In 1867 Stowe moved to a riverside cottage at Mandarin, now in south Jacksonville, where she wrote and served as a tourist attraction, the St. Johns River steamboat companies paying the noted author to sit on her veranda when the ships

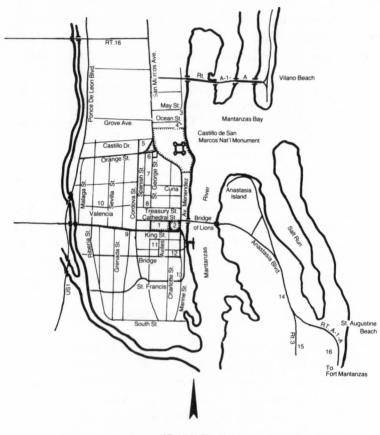

ST. AUGUSTINE

| 0 | ¼ | ½ |

1. Plaza de la Constitucion/
   Cathedral of St. Augustine
2. Market
3. Fountain of Youth
4. Mission of Nombrede Dios/Shrine
   of Our Lady de la Leche
5. City   Visitors   Information
   Center/Zero Milestone/Old Drug
   Store
6. City Gates/Oldest Wooden
   Schoolhouse
7. San Augustin Antiguo
8. Sanchez House/Dr. Peck House
9. Lightner Museum/Zorayda Castle/
   Flagler College
10. Flagler Memorial Church
11. Oldest Store Museum
12. Ximenez Fatio House
13. Oldest House
14. St. Augustine Alligator Farm
15. St. Augustine Amphitheatre
16. Coquina Quarries

passed by. The house isn't open to visitors but it's a pleasant drive south on highway 13 to reach the village of Mandarin and the historic home.

On the campus of Jacksonville University stands the restored cottage of another creative type, English composer Frederick Delius, whose two-year stay in Jacksonville in the mid-1880s inspired such compositions as his *Florida Suite*. Museums in Jacksonville include the Cummer Gallery of Art (Tu.–F., 10–4; Sat., 12–5, free), featuring a large collection of Meissen porcelain; the Museum of Arts and Sciences (Tu.–F., 9–5; Sat., 11–5; Sun., 1–5, adm.), with a planetarium and history and natural history exhibits; and the Jacksonville Art Museum (Tu.–F., 10–4; Th. to 10; Sat. and Sun., 1–5; closed Aug., free), with an extensive Oriental porcelain collection. Jacksonville's Friendship Fountain emits a jet that rises a hundred and twenty feet, nearly a quarter the height of the thirty-seven-story Independent Life Insurance Company headquarters, one of the state's tallest buildings, while in Jessie Ball du Pont State Park stands Treaty Oak, believed to be eight hundred years old, with a limb span wider than the Friendship Fountain's spray is high.

As you head south to St. Augustine you'll pass Ponte Vedra Beach, where four Germans on a sabotage mission landed the night of June 17, 1942. Authorities captured the intruders, who less than two months later died in the electric chair. St. Augustine, like almost every place based on a superlative—in this case "the nation's oldest city"—has become touristy. The four-hundred-year-old town boasts the Oldest House, an early eighteenth-century coquina (shell rock) wall and cedar beam residence (9–5:30, adm.), the Oldest Wooden Schoolhouse (9–5, adm.), the Old Spanish Cemetery, the Old Jail (M.–Sat., 8–6; Sun., 9–7, adm.), the San Agustin Antiguo restoration area (9–5, adm.) with reconstructed Spanish-colonial era houses, the Oldest Store (M.–

Sat., 9–5; Sun., 12–5, adm.), a turn-of-the-century emporium, and the 1893 Alligator Farm (June 1–Aug. 31, 9–6; Sept.–May, 9–5, adm.), "the world's original alligator attraction" and thus perhaps the oldest such facility.

A natural spring at the Fountain of Youth Park evokes the town's earliest history, when Ponce de Leon arrived in 1513 to claim the region for Spain and to search for an elixir that would keep him young, but the explorer found neither youth nor old age in the New World, for he died of a wound from an Indian arrow. De Leon left behind as the territory's designation "Florida," the first permanent name, predating even "America," given by Europeans on the North American continent. A two hundred and eight-foot stainless steel cross on the grounds of the original Nombre de Dios Mission (the present chapel dates from 1915), near the Fountain of Youth Park, marks the early Spanish presence, commemorating where St. Augustine founder Pedro Menendez de Aviles celebrated the continent's first mass. Spain's influence survives in the city's architecture and the street names, with the Lightner Museum (9–5, adm.) in the old Alcazar Hotel at Cordova and King, and Flagler College installed in the former Ponce de Leon Hotel at Sevilla and King, both occupying Hispanic-style structures; while the Zorayda Castle (9–5:30, adm.), originally a gambling casino, reproduces part of the Alhambra in Granada. The town's most imposing monument is the Castillo de San Marcos (end Oct.–end April, 8:30–5:15; rest of year, 9–5:45, free), besieged five times but never taken, a substantial pile with walls sixteen feet thick at the base and thirty feet high, which took a quarter of a century to build (1672–95). At St. Augustine you'll find a wide selection of bed and breakfast establishments, including the Victorian House, 11 Cadiz (904-824-5214), Wescott Guest House, 146 Avenida Menendez (904-824-4301), Casa de Solano, 21 Aviles (904-824-3555), Sailor's Rest, 298 St. George (904-824-3817), St. Francis Inn, 279

St. George (904-824-6068) and Kenwood Inn, 38 Marine (904-824-2116).

The coast road south out of St. Augustine takes you to 1742 Fort Matanzas (9–4:30, free), an outpost of Castillo de San Marcos, and then on to Marineland (8–5:30, adm.), one of those typical Florida theme parks, among the state's oldest (1938), featuring porpoise shows, aquatic displays and a perfectly shocking electric eel exhibit with a volt meter to register the charge emitted. Inland Palatka, on the St. Johns River, is a foliage and flower-filled town, some of the plants sprouting in Ravine State Gardens (8–sunset). To the south, near De Leon Springs, where Bed and Breakfast Register of Volusia County can book accommodations for you (904-985-5068 and 738-1515), lies Ponce de Leon Springs, thought by some to be the explorer's Fountain of Youth—a museum there houses Indian artifacts retrieved from the waters—and DeLand, named after a baking powder magnate, known for its century-old city-subsidized shade trees. Hat tycoon John B. Stetson gave DeLand a head start by funding Stetson University in 1886, and the same year there arrived in town China-born Lue Gim Gong, who in 1888 created a cold-resistant type of orange still an important product for the state's citrus industry. Near DeLand are two state parks, Blue Spring (8–sunset, free), with an 1872 restored country house (9–4) and with Florida's second-largest (by volume) spring, where manatees winter from September to March, and Hontoon Island (8–sunset, free) in the St. Johns River, accessible only by boat. The little town of Cassadaga is populated, or haunted, by spiritualists, while more mundane matters echo at De Bary to the south, the town having been founded by Baron Frederick DeBary, the American agent for Mumms champagne, who built there a Bavarian-style castle.

Back on the coast, near Flagler Beach south of Marineland, is the Bulow Plantation Ruins Historic Memorial, where remnants of Charles Bulow's early nineteenth-century sugar mill and mansion, destroyed during the Seminole Indian wars, survive. Ormond Beach, settled in 1873 when a Connecticut lock company established a health resort for its employees threatened with tuberculosis, developed into what came to be called the "millionaire's colony" after Henry Flagler extended his rail line south and acquired the Ormond Hotel, listed on the National Register, which once hosted the rich and now serves as a retirement home. One monied local resident of bygone times was John D. Rockefeller, Sr., who spent more than twenty winters in Ormond until he died in 1937 at age ninety-seven at his mansion, The Casements, also listed on the National Register, now a cultural center, as is the nearby Florida estate of artist Malcolm Frazier, whose house serves as the Ormond Beach Memorial Art Gallery and Gardens (12–5; closed W., free). Ormond Beach claims the title "birthplace of speed," as the wealthy sunbirds who wintered there, men with names such as Chevrolet, Olds, Ford, set up a racecourse on the hard-packed beach and began to compete in setting speed records, accelerating the pace from R. E. Olds' fifty-seven miles per hour in 1902 to Sir Malcolm Campbell's 1935 five miles a minute (two hundred seventy-seven miles per hour). Daytona Beach, with its International Speedway (tours 9–5, adm.), a two and a half-mile track opened in 1959, now claims to be the speedster's mecca, the famous Daytona 500 roaring into action every February. You can still drive on part of Daytona's beach, but you won't be setting any records as the speed limit is now ten miles per hour. Daytona's so-called three coasts—waterfront strips that border on the ocean and on both banks of the Halifax River—give the town an ample supply of liquid vistas, while liquid refreshments flow every spring break when thousands (more than 400,000) of college students crowd the resort town.

Perhaps some of the revelers find their way to the local

cultural and historic attractions, such as the Museum of Arts and Sciences (Tu.–Sun., 9–4, adm.), with a good collection of Cuban paintings, the 1887 Ponce de Leon Inlet Lighthouse with memorabilia of the landmark housed in the keeper's cottage (10–5; summer, 10–8, adm.) and, near New Smyrna Beach to the south, the New Smyrna Sugar Mill Historical Memorial which commemorates Florida's first commercial production of sugar and the colony founded in 1767 by Dr. Andrew Turnbull, who induced fifteen hundred Greeks, Italians and Minorcans to settle in the area. Turnbull named the colony, established on a land grant he'd received from the British government, for the Smyrna, Greece, birthplace of his wife, daughter of a Greek merchant. While traveling in the Byzantine-governed Levant, "I observed that the Christian Subjects in that Empire were in General disposed to [flee] from the calamities which they groaned under in that despotic Government," Turnbull noted in his *Narrative,* concluding that the inhabitants of the area would therefore "be a very proper people for Settling in his Majesty's Southern Provinces of North America." But the settlers at New Smyrna groaned under even more calamities in Florida and in 1777 the colony disbanded, leaving behind, however, a system of irrigation and drainage canals still used today, as well as now-ruined wells, houses and indigo vats, mute witnesses to the failed experiment.

A century later, in the 1860s, a native of Barbados named Douglas Dummett arrived in the area where he developed the now well-known Indian River citrus fruits, so called for the Indian River section of the Intracoastal Waterway. On an island in the middle of Canova Drive in New Smyrna lies the grave of Dummett's son, Charles, buried there in 1860 after the sixteen-year-old boy died in a hunting accident. Highway A1A to the south presents attractive vistas on the way to Turtle Mound State Archeological Site, a rise formed by six centuries of oyster shells discarded by ancient

Indians. As the highest point along the shore for miles the shell hill, reached by a boardwalk to the top, served as a landmark and appeared on maps as early as the sixteenth century. Beyond the Mound stretches Canaveral National Seashore, twenty-five miles of unmarred beach, one of the last undeveloped waterfront sections on Florida's east coast. Just to the south, next to the famous space center, nestles Merritt Island National Wildlife Refuge, where flocks of birds make their home. Birds have flocked to the area without fear, little disturbed by the takings-off and goings-on at the adjacent Space Center. When the original Long Range Proving Ground was being built in the early 1950s security officials noticed observers in the area peering through binoculars. The curious onlookers proved not to be cloak and dagger agents but beak and feather fanciers, members of the local Audubon Society checking on how the activity was affecting the birds. Back in the old days, before the space era and before World War II, the area, as Fred H. Langworthy notes in *Thunder at Cape Canaveral,* "was a drowsy world, a somnolent world of quiet sand dunes and whispering sea, of sunny days and starlit nights and lazy Sundays spent a-fishing under the warm Florida sun."

Canaveral—"canebreak"—was so named when the Spanish erected a fort there in 1565, but the U.S. Geographic Board took only three hours to change the four-hundred-year-old designation when President Lyndon Johnson decreed that the area should be called Cape Kennedy. Floridians refused to accept the change and in 1973 the original name was restored. Although a government facility, Cape Canaveral uses a private contractor to operate the Spaceport tours, which take you to the Space History Museum, rocket exhibits, the space shuttle launch site, a movie filmed from space shown on a five-and-a-half-story screen, the vast Vehicle Assembly Building—large enough to contain the entire volume of New York City's Empire State Building—the Astronaut

Training Building and other facilities at the Center, the last stop before the moon. In early 1990 the U.S. Astronaut Hall of Fame (9–6, adm.) opened at the U.S. Space Camp, which offers five day programs for fourth to seventh grade children (for information: 1-800-63-SPACE) at a facility a few miles west of the Spaceport.

On the way to Orlando and the Walt Disney World complex to the west you'll pass through the hamlet of Christmas. Christmas comes only once a year except at the village there in Orange County where you can find Christmas all year around, for an all-season symbol of the town's festive name stands on highway 50—a towering permanent Christmas tree festooned with colorful tinsel streamers and oversized ornaments. The tradition began in 1952 when local residents planted a red cedar as the permanent holiday tree. A sign by the present tree, successor to earlier ones, explains: "The permanent Christmas tree at Christmas, Florida, is the symbol of love and good will and the Christmas spirit every day in the year." Alongside the grove where the permanent Christmas tree rises runs Fort Christmas Road which takes you to a reproduction of a century-and-a-half-old fortress (Tu.–Sat., 10–5; Sun., 1–5, free), built at Christmastime 1837 as a supply depot for use during the Second Seminole War. The reconstructed fort contains displays that trace the history of the Indian wars in Florida. An echo of those wars sounds in the designation of the now nationally-known tourist city to the west named for Orlando Reeves, a soldier who died fighting the Seminole. Orlando, which is to tourism what Washington is to politics, boasts 64,000 hotel rooms, second only to New York City (about 100,000). It was a quarter of a century ago when real estate agents representing the Disney Company secretly bought twenty-eight thousand acres of land just south of town, the terrain now occupied by Walt Disney World. Before proceeding on to that world-renowned World it's worth stopping off to see a few sights in the Orlando area. At Maitland to the north you'll find the Maitland Art Center (Tu.–F., 10–4; Sat. and Sun., 1–4, free), installed in an Aztec-Mayan-motif decorated building embellished with an attractive garden and courtyard area, and the well-feathered Audubon House (M.–Sat., 10–4, free), an art gallery, gift shop, aviary (closed M.) and a nest full of bird-connected items. Julia Switlick in Maitland runs a bed and breakfast place at 504 Oak Lane (407-339-6473), while the pleasant nearby town of Winter Park offers bed and breakfast at Chelsea-on-the-Bank, 412 East Fairbanks (407-629-4189) and Park Plaza Gardens, 307 Park Avenue (407-647-1072), with reservations at other such establishments available through B and B of Florida, P.O. Box 1316, Winter Park, FL 32790 (407-628-3233), and at Bed & Breakfast of Orlando, 8205 Banyan Boulevard, Orlando, FL 32819 (407-870-8407).

Winter Park serves as a kind of cultural enclave for the area, with the Crealde School of Art (M.–F.), the Morse Gallery of Art (Tu.–Sat., 9:30–4; Sun., 1–4), featuring Tiffany glass, and two museums on the campus of Rollins College, the Cornell Fine Arts Center (Tu.–F., 10–5; Sat. and Sun., 1–5, free), with the world's largest watch-key collection, and the Beal Maltbie Shell Museum (M.–F., 10–12, 1–4, adm.), while the College's Walk of Fame includes eight hundred stones from places connected with famous people. Around Orlando you'll find near Longwood to the north Big Tree Park, which boasts "the Senator," one of the nation's largest and oldest (three thousand years) bald cypress trees; to the west at Winter Garden the Central Florida Railroad Museum (Sun., 2–5, free) and, near Claremont, two-hundred-foot-high Citrus Tower, from which you can see some seventeen million orange trees that comprise about a third of Florida's groves. In Orlando itself are the Leu Gardens (9–5, adm.) and House (Th.–Sat., 10–4; Sun., 1–4, adm.), with forty-seven acres of botanical displays and a turn-of-the-century residence; the Orange County Historical Museum (Tu.–F., 10–4; Sat. and Sun., 2–5, free), containing displays on the development of Mosquito County, as the area was called in the early days; the Orlando Science Center (M.–Th., 9–5; F., 9–9; Sat., 12–9; Sun., 12–5, adm.), featuring a reptile collection. Also there are the city's few surviving old buildings, some on Orange Avenue—the Belle Epoque-style Kress store, the Egyptian-style First National Bank, Art Deco McCroy's—and the Church Street stretch of turn-of-the-century structures, one housing the atmospheric Rosie O'Grady's Goodtime Emporium in the old Orlando Hotel near the station. One unusual attraction in Orlando is the ceremony—featuring a band, parade and pageantry—held every Friday morning at 9:45 to mark the graduation of six hundred or so navy boot camp recruits (for information: 407-644-1100), while an unusual museum (M.–F., 9–4, free) at Tupperware World Headquarters in Kissimmee to the southwest beyond Disney World contains a collection of historic food containers from Egyptian times to the present.

Kissimmee is cowboy country, a rather un-Florida-like area where you'll find cattle ranches, a weekly cattle auction held on Wednesdays (for information: 800-432-9199 in Florida, 800-327-9159 out-of-state), a twice-yearly professional rodeo called Silver Spurs, and headquarters of the Florida Cattlemen's Association, with beef lunches served in connection with the weekly auction. The pyramid-like Monument of States in Kissimmee includes stones from every state and twenty-one foreign countries, while the Medieval Times Dinner Tournament in town (407-396-1518, 800-432-0768 in Florida, 800-327-4024 out-of-state) lets you dine in millennium-old style with serving wenches, jousting knights and colorful pageantry out of the middle ages, all in contrast to futuristic Xanadu in Kissimmee, a computer-enhanced futuristic house (10–10, adm.) occupying ultra-modern white polyurethane quarters. Next to Medieval Times lies the new Medieval life area, a three-acre re-creation of an old time European hamlet, with artisans, birds of prey demonstrations and other Medieval-era entertainment. Two bed and breakfast places in Kissimmee are Beaumont House, 206 South Beaumont (407-846-7916) and Old Town Lodge and Guest Quarters, 8 South Orlando (407-847-7053).

In the Orlando orbit revolve a number of special worlds, among them Sea World, Alligator World, Circus World and—perhaps the world's most famous "World"—Walt Disney World, really more of a kingdom (non-magic) since Disney in effect exercises sovereignty over forty-two square miles, twice the area of Manhattan, bearing the rather mundane name Reedy Creek Improvement District. Disney World claims to be the top tourist attraction on earth, with a yearly attendance of twenty-five million visitors, or "guests," as the Disney organization calls paying customers. The modern-day theme park—a manufactured environment aimed to create an enclave different enough to be exciting yet not so unfamiliar as to be disquieting—is an American invention with antecedents such as Coney Island, world's fairs, and pleasure parks like Copenhagen's famous Tivoli, and Vauxhall Gardens, a seventeenth-century London attraction that featured musical performances, unusual architecture (or "parkitecture," as some call the modern version of the art), statuary and dioramas. Charles Dickens's description of those enchanting London Gardens in *Sketches by Boz* could well serve to describe the delight visitors find at the Magic Kingdom and Epcot ("Experimental Prototype Community of Tomorrow"), Disney World's two main units: "The temples and saloons and cosmoramas and fountains glittered before our eyes . . . a few hundred thousands of additional lamps dazzled our senses; and we were happy."

It takes a full four or five days to visit the Disney complex, but for those lacking that kind of time here are some practical pointers that may help expedite a visit: attendance is lowest

in May, September and January and, contrary to common
assumptions, not weekends but Monday through Wednesday
are the most crowded days, with Friday the least busy; to
avoid heavy arriving traffic it's best to travel on access roads
before 8 a.m.; once you enter the Magic Kingdom or Epcot
proceed immediately to the rear part of the park and begin
there, working your way back to the gate; skip the 3 p.m.
Mickey Mouse parade in the Magic Kingdom in order to
take advantage of reduced lines at many of the attractions;
eat at off-peak hours and visit during normal eating times;
to set priorities, ask fellow "guests" which attractions they
most and least enjoyed. Disney World is a world in motion,
with new features constantly being added. In 1989 the
Disney-M.G.M. Studios Theme Park opened, with actual
on-camera performing areas and glimpses of behind-the-
scenes movie and TV production facilities and techniques,
a new attraction perhaps instigated by the previously announced opening in 1990 of Universal Studios Florida, a
similar functioning sound stage and production complex in
Orlando, and perhaps also based on the observation of Mae
West (for whom Key West is not named) that "Too much
of a good thing is wonderful."

Leaving the fantasy environs of Fantasyland, movie studios, cartoon characters, enclaves of artificial foreign lands
and controlled experiences may cause reentry problems and
require some adjustment: after all, in the big wide world
beyond Disney World you're no longer a guest but, once
again, a tourist. To resume your tour of eastern Florida it's
well to return to the coast and continue south of Cape Canaveral, passing through Cocoa—picked from a box of Baker's
Cocoa when locals changed the name of the town from Indian River City—and the adjacent town of Rockledge, a
long-time winter resort filled with lovely old homes, and
then on to Melbourne, which offers the Brevard Art Center
and Museum, a botanical garden at the Florida Institute of

Technology, and a missile display at Patrick Air Force Base, as well as waves favored by surfers at Melbourne Beach, site of the annual professional surfing competition.

At Sebastian, a little farther south, is Pelican Island (not open to visitors but visible from a boat), the nation's oldest wildlife sanctuary (1905), and the McLarty State Museum (W.–Sun., 9–5) with exhibits and dioramas recalling the fleet of Spanish galleons, and the treasures they carried, that sank in the area in 1715. Vero Beach's most striking structure is an eccentric pile representing what might be called "Art Vero" architecture—the Driftwood Inn (407-231-9292), which Waldo Sexton started to assemble in the 1930s from stray pieces of wood and timbers salvaged from an old bar. The hostelry halls house an eclectic collection of old Spanish ship cannons, bells, rust-encrusted chains and other such relics. Meals at the unusual establishment are available at Waldo's Restaurant, while the Sexton-owned Ocean Grill a short stroll up the beach serves dinner. The new (July 1989) Treasure Museum at Fort Pierce houses gold coins, silver ingots and other booty recovered from a fleet that sank in 1715. Near Stuart, south of St. Lucie County—named for a third-century martyr in Sicily—lies the Elliott Museum (1–5), a touch of flinty New England in sandy, sunny Florida, with a dozen Early American-vintage shops transferred there from Salem, Massachusetts, as well as such sterling Sterling Elliott inventions as a knot-tying machine, a quadracycle, and the first addressing device. The 1875 Gilbert's Bar House of Refuge (1–5) on nearby Hutchinson Island survives as the only remaining example of the original dozen or so such facilities built along the coast to rescue shipwrecked sailors. Early life-saving equipment recalls the days when floundering seamen were rescued and brought to the dormitory there.

Just south of Stuart stretches nine-mile long Jupiter Island, a strip of land that contains Hobe Sound, one of the nation's most reclusive and exclusive communities. It's well worth taking highway 707, which bisects the half-mile wide barrier island, but don't tarry as roadside sensors detect traffic that stops, a nonmoving violation of the town ordinance, which prohibits vehicles from pausing on the roadside. Clumps of vegetation shield many of the mansions from view, but enough of Hobe Sound houses are visible for you to realize that you won't be retiring there on Social Security. At the south end of Jupiter Island rises a red brick lighthouse, one of Florida's oldest (1860), which offers a view of the Gulf Stream, clearly apparent out in the Atlantic, while nearby Harpoon Louie's is a popular eating place where the local boatfolk are clearly apparent. For ten years the town of Jupiter boasted the Burt Reynolds Dinner Theater (closed in August 1989), named after the now-famous hometown boy who operates there the Burt Reynolds Ranch, Tack and Feed Store (10–5), with cowboy items, dog food and other sundry wares on sale. North of Jupiter, off U.S. highway 1, the Jonathan Dickinson State Park (8–sunset, free) preserves southeast Florida's only remaining undeveloped river area and also contains so-called Hobe Mountain, a kind of overgrown sand dune topped by an observation tower which offers panoramas of the sea and surrounding wooded terrain. You'll find a bed and breakfast booking agency—B and B of the Palm Beaches (407-746-2545)—in Jupiter, once a terminal town for the Celestial Railroad, an eight-mile line that took its name from such stations as Juno, Neptune, Mars and Venus, as well as Jupiter. A monument in Jupiter recalls the abandoned Celestial line. A new version of Florida's rail network will soon begin when the state awards a franchise in 1991 for a 300-mile high-speed train system, for completion in 1995, to link Miami, Orlando and Tampa.

Roads, both rail and auto, stimulated much of eastern Florida's development. Back in the early 1920s a man named W. J. Connors—called "Fingy" as a result of injuries to his fingers he suffered as a scrappy dockhand—built a toll road from West Palm Beach, just south of Jupiter, out to Lake Okeechobee to the west. "Fingy" fancied the simple life, hunting and fishing, while his wife favored furs, jewels and parties, a contrast which so amused cartoonist George McManus that after meeting the couple he immediately created the soon popular "Bringing Up Father" comic strip. Connors spent nearly two million dollars to build the road, which took only eight months to complete, but six years later, in 1930, he sold the highway, for some years the best route between Florida's east and west coasts, for six hundred thousand dollars to Palm Beach County. Highway 710 now takes you west out to Okeechobee ("big water"), which perches at the north edge of the nation's second-largest lake (after Lake Michigan) totally within U.S. borders. Fish abound in the lake's waters—anglers, both commercial and sport, catch more than three and a half million pounds a year—which are so shallow that in many places wading birds can walk on the bottom. After the 1928 hurricane wreaked extensive damage and caused nearly two thousand deaths, the U.S. Corps of Engineers constructed levees on three sides of the formerly flood-prone lake, while a system of dikes, pumping stations, canals and spillways serve to control the flow to the surrounding fields where vegetables and sugar cane thrive. Belle Glade at the south end of the lake boasts what's said to be the world's largest sugar mill, while a mill in nearby Clewiston conducts tours from November to April. The U.S. Sugar Corporation headquarters is at Clewiston, where you'll also find the comfortable Clewiston Inn, decorated within by a mural of Everglades wildlife. Around to the west at Moore Haven stands the lock that affords access to the lake, and then onward via the St. Lucie Canal to the Atlantic, to ships sailing up the Caloosahatchee from Fort Myers on the Gulf of Mexico. Beyond Moore Haven—which in early March hosts the Chalo Nitka ("big bass" in Seminole) Festival, featuring Seminole Indian entertainment, food and crafts (for information: 813-946-0440)—runs highway 27 which will take you north via two old-time tourist attractions that beguiled early travelers, Gatorland and Cypress Knee Museum, up to Sebring, an avocado-producing town designed in the pattern of the mythical Greek City of the Sun, Heliopolis, with a central park symbolizing the sun and radiating streets. In March, Sebring—site of Highlands Hammock, Florida's first State Park (1935), a nature and animal area—hosts the International Grand Prix Sports Car Endurance race.

Back on the coast the road south from the Jupiter area will take you to Palm Beach, the palms originating from coconuts brought there by Spanish sailors in 1878 and planted by the islanders, the beach from the sands of time, and the up-scale resort from promoter Henry Flagler. "The Rambler," Flagler's yellow-hued private railroad car, stands at Whitehall, the tycoon's turn-of-the-century mansion, now the Henry Morrison Flagler Museum (Tu.–Sat., 10–5; Sun., 12–5, adm.), the car recalling the train line he built along Florida's east coast. After the railroad arrived in 1894 Flagler constructed the Royal Poinciana Hotel, the world's largest wooden building, with thirteen-hundred doors and as many windows. Some of the guests arrived at the posh resort (no longer standing) not simply in private railroad cars but in private trains. The current version of that showplace is The Breakers, an old-fashioned and genteel, if ponderous, pile which will give you an idea of the Palm Beach way of life as it used to be. The Breakers, which may be named as much for its budget-breaking prices as the breaking waves just offshore, is more for looking than for staying unless you want to cash in your IRA to pay the tab, but less expensive accommodations can be found at bed and breakfast establishments like Brazilian Court Hotel, 300 Brazilian Avenue (407-655-7740) and through a booking agency, Open House B and B Registry, P.O. Box 3025, Palm Beach, FL

33480. Around town stand any number of other showplaces, such as the pink Palm Court Hotel, listed on the National Register; Marjorie Meriweather Post's Mar-a-Lago estate, the town's largest private property, complete with its own golf course (nine holes); the house Beatle John Lennon owned at 702 South Ocean Boulevard; the Addison Mizner-designed hacienda-like estate Joseph P. Kennedy purchased in 1933, just beyond 1073 North Ocean Boulevard, where President John Kennedy and other clan members vacationed.

Palm Beach's version of a shopping center is the Esplanade on boutique-rich Worth Avenue, the town's famous shopping—or window-shopping—street. But true bargains reside at the thrift shop (Oct.–May, M.–Sat., 10–5; June–Sept., W., 10–5), 231 S. County Rd.; you'll find penthouse-quality clothes at bargain basement prices. More up-scale are the polo matches held at the Palm Beach Polo and Country Club in West Palm Beach, where you'll also find the Norton Gallery of Art (Tu.–Sat., 10–5; Sun., 1–5, free), with an excellent collection of French and American paintings, while down at Delray Beach to the south—below Lantana, home of the tabloid *National Enquirer* and, along with adjacent Lake Worth, a town settled half a century ago by Finns—is the Morikami Park, Museum and Gardens (Tu.–Sat., 10–5, free), an enclave of Japanese culture donated by a pineapple farmer.

"Rat's Mouth" would seem to be an unpromising name for a plush resort, but so Boca Raton is called, the Spanish version perhaps lending the phrase an exotic touch. In the 1920s architect Addison Mizner orchestrated the building of The Cloisters, an opulent hotel that opened in February 1926 and lasted all of one season before closing, but the showplace survives as the centerpiece of the Boca Raton Hotel and Club whose historic exhibit in the hotel's lobby is worth a look. At the Royal Palm Polo Sports Club in Boca Raton polo matches take place on weekends from December to April, while off Lighthouse Point, just south of town, hides

Cap's Place, an island restaurant serviced by the "S.S. Dram-amine" from Cap's dock reached via North East 24th Street. Rum-runner Cap Knight, a Spanish-American War veteran, opened the colorful ramshackle eatery's forerunner in the 1920s as a gambling den and Prohibition-defying booze joint. Inland at Coconut Creek lies the unusual Butterfly World (M.–Sat., 9–5; Sun., 1–5, adm.) featuring three areas where thousands of butterflies flit through the air in re-creations of their native habitats. At Pompano Beach you'll find installed in two old cottages the town's Historical Museum (M. and W., 12–3; Sat., 1–5, free), while the Pompano Beach Air Park serves as winter home (Nov. through May) of the "Enterprise," a Goodyear blimp whose history the new visitor center traces in a series of displays. Florida Lifestyles B and B, 445 S.W. Second Street, #30 (305-941-7717) in Pompano Beach offers bed and breakfast, as does Oceanside Inn, 1180 Seabreeze Boulevard (305-525-8115) in nearby Fort Lauderdale.

Although Daytona Beach to the north now vies with Fort Lauderdale as the preferred college spring-fling resort, Lauderdale will forevermore be known—thanks to the 1960 movie and song—as "Where the Boys Are." The annual student migration began in 1935 with the Collegiate Aquatic Forum, and soon after word spread across campuses that Lauderdale was the place to go over spring break. One of the nation's few cities with water taxi service, the well-watered town, called "Venice of America," boasts some six miles of beach as well as more than two hundred and fifty miles of canals, inlets, rivers, bays and waterways. Under one such stream, New River, runs Florida's only vehicle tunnel, opened in 1960. To see the canals of this "Venice" you can rent a motorized gondola at the Bahia Mar Yacht Basin, a thirty-five-acre marina said to berth more pleasure craft than any other place in Florida. Novelist John D. MacDonald's Travis McGee character kept his houseboat,

"The Busted Flush," at Bahia Mar's Slip F-18. In this area once stood the wooden fort, named for Major William Lauderdale, built during the Seminole wars and, later, a House of Refuge (another, described above, still stands at Hutchinson Island) for shipwrecked sailors. The nearby Yankee Clipper Hotel, which resembles a cruise ship, carries out the nautical theme, while actual cruise craft use Port Everglades, the deepest harbor between Norfolk and New Orleans, from where the ships of more than twenty lines set sail. At the Swimming Hall of Fame (M.–Sat., 10–5; Sun., 11–4) you'll find aquatic exhibits from around the world, including a life-size likeness of Johnny "Tarzan" Weissmuller. Other Lauderdale attractions include the mid-nineteenth-century antique-filled King-Cromartie House (open winter weekends) at the Himmarshee Village historic restoration area; the adjacent Discovery Center, a hands-on museum in turn-of-the-century New River Inn, the area's first hotel (Tu.–Sat., 10–5; Sun., 1–5); the Stranahan House (W., F., Sat., 10–4; Sun., 1–4), a restored 1890s home and store, Broward County's oldest structure, which sold supplies to the Seminole Indians; the relatively new Museum of Art (Tu., 11–9; W.–Sat., 10–5; Sun., 12–5), featuring ethnological displays on Indian and overseas cultures; Flamingo Gardens (9–5:30, adm.), which claims Florida's largest tree, a fig more than a hundred feet tall and half that in circumference; and Hugh Taylor Birch State Park (8–sunset, adm.) on the beach, with a three-mile mini-train line. Dane-founded Dania, just south of Lauderdale, is known for its antique shops, while to the west lies Florida's "wild West" town of Davie, a cowboy settlement with Grifs Western Store, a Rodeo Arena (for information on performances: 305-434-7062), hitching posts for your horse and other ranch, range and wrangler touches.

By now the magnetic pull of Miami—of "Vice," "Beach," "Moon Over" and other pop culture connotations—exerts itself. But not always was Miami such a draw, for as recently as a century ago the settlement remained remote and isolated, accessible only by boat or by an overland trail. After a series of freezes chilled northern Florida in the mid-1890s, damaging the orange crop, Henry Flagler decided to make Miami his railroad's southern terminus, and in 1896 the town of Fort Dallas, named for a military outpost built in 1835, became the incorporated city of Miami. These days nearly half of Dade County's two million residents are Hispanic, three-quarters of them Cuban in origin, so the greater Miami area is the nation's most international region, with a flavor to match. The neighborhood around Calle Ocho (Eighth Street), center of the Cuban section, includes not only Little Havana but also a Little Bogota, a Little Quito, a Little Caracas, other such "little" foreign enclaves and more than a little local color and atmosphere. Ethnic restaurants abound, religious shrines lend pious touches and picturesque street scenes animate the area.

The Cuban Memorial Park contains a monument to the unsuccessful Bay of Pigs invasion, while Antonio Maceo Park, where locals gather to gossip and play dominoes, and the Cuban Museum of Art and Culture (M.–F., 10–5; Sat. and Sun., 1–5, free) presents pictures—real life in the parks, still-life in the gallery—of Cuban culture. An even more lively carry-over from pre-Castro Cuba is the bombastic floor show at Les Violins, 1751 Biscayne Boulevard, reminiscent of the costumed (or uncostumed) showgirl extravaganzas common in old Havana. More exotic touches enliven Miami's Mideast district along Southwest 3rd Avenue near the Rickenbacker Causeway exit from I-95, where Lebanese, Syrian, Greek and Palestine bakeries, shops, cafes and churches cluster; while the onion-shaped dome of Assumption Ukranian Church, 58 Northwest 57th Avenue, also lends the city a foreign flavor. Other lesser known areas in Miami include the Fashion District, second-largest in the country, where shops along Northwest 5th Avenue between Northwest 24th and 30th Streets offer discounted designer clothes, while factory outlet stores along Northwest 20th Street between 17th and 27th Avenues feature even lower prices. More toney and pricey is Decorator's Row, a ten-block area around Northeast 40th Street between North Miami and Northeast 2nd Avenues, with a group of furniture and accessory establishments.

Period architecture scarcely survives in modern Miami, but the city does boast the Western Hemisphere's oldest building, an immigrant to the area like so much else in the foreign-filled Florida metropolis. Newspaper magnate William Randolph Hearst bought the 1141 St. Bernard Monastery (M.–Sat., 10–5; Sun., 12–5, free) and imported the building in nearly eleven thousand crates, later sold to a group which reassembled the monastery. Other old—though hardly twelfth-century vintage—buildings embellish Miami Beach, whose Art Deco Historic District includes the nation's largest group of Art Deco-style structures, the first twentieth-century buildings listed on the National Register (walking tours of the area leave at 10:30 Saturday morning from the Design Preservation League at 1201 Washington Avenue in the District). Civic structures at the now-decayed town of Opa Locka to the northwest present a fantastical Arabian Nights appearance, while back in the center of Miami the ceiling in the ornate lobby at the 1938 Dupont Building, 169 East Flagler, bears painted scenes of Florida history. Tucked away on skyscraper-filled Brickell Avenue, at number 1500, stands a fourteen-room stone residence modeled after the fourteenth-century St. Julienne priory in Duoy, France; while out at 3115 Brickell is Villa Serena, home of three-time Presidential candidate William Jennings Bryan, next to which rises the imposing seventy-room structure known as Vizcaya (9:30–5, adm.), an Italian Renaissance-style villa built in 1916 by International Harvester tycoon James Deering. Vizcaya houses the Dade County Art Museum, while across the road is the Museum of Science (Sun.–Th., 10–6; F. and Sat., 10–10), and down in town you'll find the Bacardi Art Gallery; at the Metro-Dade Cultural Center is the Historical Museum of South Florida (M.–F., 10–6; Th. to 9; Sat., 10–5; Sun., 12–5); the University of Miami houses the Lowe Art Museum, with selections from the Kress Collection; and Miami Beach offers the Bass Museum of Art (Tu.–Sat., 10–5; Sun., 1–5). History haunts some of Miami's landmarks: the Orange Bowl served temporarily as a holding area for detainees rounded up by the FBI when war broke out in 1941, while in Bayfront Park Giuseppe Zangara fatally wounded Chicago mayor Anton J. Cermak on February 15, 1933, in an unsuccessful attempt to assassinate President-elect Franklin Roosevelt. Dinner Key, site of City Hall, served as the Pan American Clipper air base in the days when Pan Am was flying high, a truly pan-American line with an extensive Latin American route system.

Near Dinner Key lies Coconut Grove, Miami's oldest area, an attractive Greenwich Village-like neighborhood of galleries, boutiques and nineteenth-century buildings, including Bahamian-style frill-trimmed houses on Charles Avenue; 1897 Plymouth Congregation Church, built to resemble a Spanish mission, near which lies the area's first schoolhouse, constructed from wood salvaged from wrecked ships; and the Barnacle State Historical Site (tours, W.–Sun., 9, 10:30, 1, 2:30, adm.), also built, in 1880, of materials salvaged from shipwrecks by Ralph Munroe, a Coconut Grove pioneer, who in 1895 jacked up the jerry-built residence and inserted beneath it a new first floor. Many of the Grove's pioneer residents repose in the historic Charlotte Jane Stirrup Memorial Cemetery. Near Coconut Grove is poinciana-garnished Coral Gables, a plush residential district filled with foreign-style architecture and boasting the newly reopened

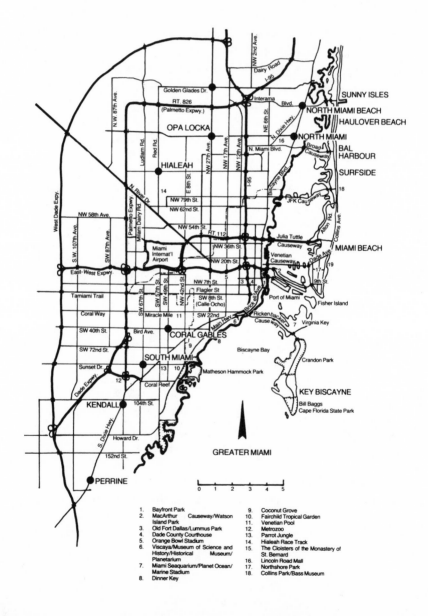

GREATER MIAMI

0   1   2   3   4   5

1. Bayfront Park
2. MacArthur   Causeway/Watson
    Island Park
3. Old Fort Dallas/Lummus Park
4. Dade County Courthouse
5. Orange Bowl Stadium
6. Viscaya/Museum of Science and
    History/Historical   Museum/
    Planetarium
7. Miami Seaquarium/Planet Ocean/
    Marine Stadium
8. Dinner Key

9. Coconut Grove
10. Fairchild Tropical Garden
11. Venetian Pool
12. Metrozoo
13. Parrot Jungle
14. Hialeah Race Track
15. The Cloisters of the Monastery of
    St. Bernard
16. Lincoln Road Mall
17. Northshore Park
18. Collins Park/Bass Museum

Biltmore, built in the mid-1920s by town promoter George Merrick, a magnificently restored hotel that, among other amenities, claims the nation's largest swimming pool. Offshore lies another Miami enclave, Key Biscayne, where an 1825 lighthouse, Dade County's oldest structure, rises in Bill Baggs Cape Florida State Recreation Area (8–sunset, adm.). At the lighthouse—open for climbing and the view— the restored five-room keeper's house recalls the era of a century and a half ago. In the water off the beach rise the propped-up shacks of Stiltsville, a well-irrigated community of fishermen's huts and homes out in the water. Key Biscayne offers bed and breakfast at Tropical Isles B and B (305-361-2937), as does the Bed and Breakfast Company, 1205 Mariposa Avenue, #233 (305-661-3270) in Miami and the European-style Hotel Place St. Michel, 162 Alcazar Avenue (305-444-1666) in Coral Gables, while at the high end of the scale little-known and untouristed Fisher Island, a private club on a spur that once formed the south end of Miami Beach, offers villas at the former Vanderbilt estate, accessible only by boat, for $400–600 a day, a price that includes a sweet placed on your pillow every night (for reservations: 305-535-6020).

Nearby Dodge Island serves as the Port of Miami, the world's leading cruise ship facility, while opposite the northwest edge of the island is the seaplane base for Chalk's Flying Service, the world's oldest airline, whose amphibious planes fly to the Bahamas. Back on the mainland, across from Bayside Park, stands the Everglades Hotel, with a rooftop sundeck that affords a splendid view of the city. The nearby *Miami Herald* Building (for tours of the newspaper: 305-350-2491) is a local landmark, as is flamingo-filled Hialeah Park racetrack out on the west side of town. South of town, not far from Goulds, is the Monkey Jungle (9:30–5, adm.) where visitors remain in cages while the animals run free, and nearby rises the eccentric Coral Castle (9–5, adm.), assembled out of coral rock by a Latvian immigrant jilted by his fiancee. Around Homestead—from where glass-bottom boats depart on tours for Biscayne National Park reefs (Th.–Tu., at 10, free)—stretch fields of vegetables, a reminder that Dade, although highly urbanized in the Miami area, is one of the country's top one hundred agricultural counties. Two well-garnished places near Homestead are the Fruit and Spice Park (9–5, free), a twenty-acre garden lush with fruit, nut and spice plants from around the globe, and Knaus Berry Farm (8–5:30 in the winter), a bakery and vegetable stand run by Dunkers—so called as they're baptized by triple immersion—a tradition-possessed German Baptist sect whose men wear beards and black hats and women bonnets and shawls. Nearby Florida City offers accommodations at Grandma Newton's Bed and Breakfast, 40 Northwest Fifth Avenue (305-247-4413).

The visitor center near the main Everglades National Park entrance, just west of Florida City, offers a film, brochures, talks, activity schedules and other information which will help you get the most out of your visit to the Everglades, a fifty to seventy-mile-wide, six-inch-deep sawgrass-filled river. The facility, second-largest National Park in the continental United States, after Yellowstone, occupies 2,200 of the Everglades' 10,200 square miles. Back in 1898 Hugh L. Willoughby observed in *Across the Everglades:* "It may seem strange, in our days of Arctic and African exploration, for the general public to learn that in our very midst, as it were, on one of our Atlantic coast states, we have a tract of land one hundred and thirty miles long and seventy miles wide that is as much unknown to the white man as the heart of Africa." It is somehow enthralling to realize that still today, a century later, Willoughby's comment remains true, for some remote corners of the Everglades remain unexplored—"enthralling" in the sense that even now, in this mechanized, computerized, televised age, there survives in

America a primeval area untouched by human hands. From the highway between the main visitor center and Flamingo, forty miles southwest, run half a dozen spur roads that take you to trails, boardwalks and observation areas that enable you to get an idea of the Everglades ecosystem. The visitor center at Flamingo can provide information on canoe excursions and boat trips along the hundred-mile Wilderness Waterway to Everglades City in the west. Accommodations are available in Flamingo at the Flamingo Inn (813-695-3101) and at campgrounds. Another entrance point into the Everglades—best visited from January to March, when the weather is cool and dry (the wet period begins in May or June, a season that brings 80 percent of the region's average annual rainfall)—lies at the park's north edge where tram tours along a fifteen-mile loop road (you can also walk or bike) take you through Shark Valley, the Everglades' largest slough (pronounced "slew": a freshwater channel). Near the entrance to Shark Valley the Miccosukee Indian headquarters, where some six hundred tribespeople reside, offers a museum, crafts and a typical village (9–5:30).

The Florida Keys—detached from the rest of the state and scattered a hundred and eighty miles from Miami's Biscayne Bay to the Dry Tortugas, eighty-six miles north of Havana— are, like the Everglades, a world unto themselves. The thirty-two islands you'll cross on the famous Overseas Highway— more than a hundred miles of road and forty-three bridges down to Key West—represent only a fraction of the eight hundred and eighty-two keys large enough to appear on official hydrographic maps of the area. The Upper Keys, those closest to the mainland, extending from Key Largo to Long Key, are the remains of an ancient coral reef, while the Middle and Lower Keys, from beyond Long Key to Key West, consist mainly of oolite, a lime-based rock.

Key Largo, made famous by the Humphrey Bogart-Lauren Bacall-Edward G. Robinson movie named after it,

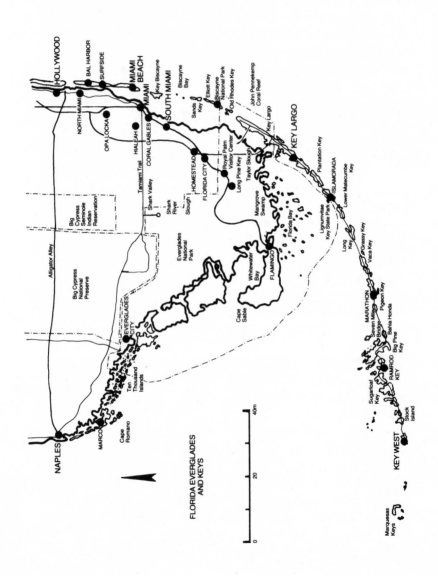

FLORIDA EVERGLADES
AND KEYS

retains a Bogartian touch at the Caribbean Club Bar, a hangout with stills from the film on the walls and colorful characters at the bar, and at the Holiday Inn where the creaky
old "African Queen" river freighter featured in the 1951
Bogart-Katherine Hepburn film recalls that screen classic.
Off the Key Largo coast lies the John Pennekamp Coral
Reef State Park, an underwater enclave protecting coral clus-
ters teeming with fish. Depending on your interests and
skills, you can visit the liquid park three different ways: the
"M/V Discovery," a glass-bottom boat, offers three tours
a day (9, 12, 3) of Molasses Reef; "Dive Master" runs two
trips daily (9:30 and 1:30) for certified scuba divers; and "El
Capitan" departs three times a day for those who want to
snorkel. For information on the park and these trips you
can call or stop at the visitor center off U.S. highway 1
(8–5, 305-451-1202). For those who acquire at the park in
the briny a taste for the underwater way of life Key Largo
offers what is perhaps the nation's most unusual hotel—Jules'
Undersea Lodge, located thirty feet below the surface. The
capsule originally served as a sea lab off Puerto Rico before
being converted into an underwater hotel with two bedrooms and a living room area. Guests don bathing suits,
a diving mask and fins for the descent from a platform to
the hotel, furnished with picture windows that afford views
of the outside underworld. A stay at Jules' Undersea Lodge
is truly a visit to the Deep South. The Key Largo Undersea
Park, an enclosed lagoon with a "living sea" section, a marine
research facility and a snorkeling area, opened in the fall
of 1989.

Beyond Tavernier, once home port of an eighteenth-century wrecking fleet that salvaged goods from ships grounded
by the treacherous coral reefs, lies Islamorada, a major sea
fishing center, where the attractive but expensive Cheeca
Lodge claims one of the Keys' rare beaches. In town is the
Theater of the Sea marine aquarium (9:30–4. adm.) and the

Spanish Mission House, an art gallery, where a monument to the deadly 1935 hurricane, which killed nearly six hundred people, stands. During the tempest the barometer dropped to 26.35, the lowest pressure ever recorded in the Western Hemisphere. Farther south, out to sea, lie Indian and Lignumvitae Keys, both accessible only by boat. In 1832 John James Audubon visited Indian, Dade County's first seat, where he found a wealth of bird life, including the solemn-looking pelicans he called "Reverend Sirs." Indian Key offers remarkable tropical foliage and memories of Indian settlements and attacks and of the nineteenth-century town Jacob Housman established there. On Lignumvitae, named for the hardwood tree that grows there, you'll find unusual vegetation (one species with peeling red skin is called the "tourist tree"), rusting cannons, the 1919 Matheson House, and a mysterious stone wall—no one knows when, why or by whom it was built—three thousand feet long. On Long Key, the last of the Upper Keys, a creek named for Zane Grey recalls the fishing visits made there by the famous author of Westerns, while the Shark Institute, next to the attractive Lime Tree Bay Resort, functions as a training academy for fish that perform at Sea World in Orlando. At another fish college, Flippers Sea School (10–5, adm.) on adjacent Grassy Key, named for the famous finny TV star, dolphins learn show-business routines, while at the nearby fancy Hawk's Cay Resort guests can frolic in the water with the hotel's resident dolphins. You can also swim with dolphins at Theater of the Sea at Islamorada and Dolphins Plus at Key Largo, although the National Marine Fisheries Service, which monitors the attractions, may opt to close them for ecological reasons. Marathon down the way offers bed and breakfast at 5 Man-o-War Drive (305-743-4118), while in mid-January the town mounts a Renaissance Faire, featuring medieval jousting, madrigals and other such old-tyme activities.

Beyond Marathon, an un-Key-like community which more resembles main-line mainland suburbia than a tropical island, begins Seven Mile Bridge, the most challenging stretch along the route of Henry Flagler's Overseas Railroad, the famous line, completed in 1912, which operated until the devastating 1935 hurricane. On Big Pine Key, second in size only to Key Largo, roam mini-deer the size of large dogs, once hunted but now protected in the National Wildlife Refuge, and on Sugarloaf Key down the road rises the curious Perky Bat Tower, listed on the National Register, not especially perky but named after its builder, a local businessman who erected the structure around 1920 to house bats imported to devour huge mosquitos which, some locals claim, ate the bats, leaving as the state's largest bevy of bats the ones used in the Grapefruit League spring training baseball games.

Key West, which lies at road's end, finds itself in an unusual position: the southernmost point of the continental United States (Hawaii extends farther south), a full six hundred miles below Los Angeles. The town presents an unusual admixture of run-of-the-mill American life, complete with fast-food eateries, chain motels and shopping centers, and Cuban, Bahamian and West Indian influences combined with Yankee and Southern cultures. This makes for a vibrant, colorful town populated by a confusion of eccentrics, artists, writers, hippies, yuppies, flakies, retirees, gays, straights, pleasure-bents (some of these categories may overlap) who lend Key West an exotic air. The Conch Train (9–4, adm.), which takes you on a tour through town, furnishes a good introduction to Key West, as does the twilight gathering at Mallory Square where locals of all types show up to celebrate the sunset, after which the crowd disperses to such watering holes—"water" is never far away in Key West—as Captain Tony's Saloon, believed to be the state's oldest bar, which was the original Sloppy Joe's, and to the present

Sloppy Joe's, originally the Midget Bar, where photos and memorabilia recall visits by Ernest Hemingway.

Hemingway's Key West house (9–5, adm.), a lovely old place where the novelist lived and wrote for about ten years, is both a delightful relic in its own right and a kind of Hemingway museum that evokes the great writer's presence there. Other venerable structures include Audubon House (9–11:25, 1–4:25, adm.), a restored 1830 residence containing original works by the famous naturalist-artist; The Oldest House (10–4, adm.), an 1830s home (actually two houses) which contains the Wrecker's Museum, recalling when a century and a half ago salvaging shipwreck debris made Key West the nation's wealthiest town on a per capita basis; the East Martello Art Gallery and Historical Museum (9:30–5), with a special section devoted to local authors, such as Hemingway and Tennessee Williams; the Lighthouse and Military Museum (9:30–5); Fort Zachary Taylor (8–sunset), also a military museum; the Little White House, at the former Navy Station (closed in 1974), visited eleven times by President Harry Truman; plus the large stock of tin-roofed, veranda-fronted houses, many restored, that embellish the area between Caroline and Southard Streets in the heart of the old town. At the end of Fleming the Zero Milestone indicates the termination of U.S. highway 1 that begins in Kent, Maine, and the Southernmost Point and House at the bottom of Duval Street mark the continent's end. Monuments in the City Cemetery to those killed in 1898 on the "U.S.S. Maine" in Havana—deaths that touched off the Spanish-American War—and to other defunct beings, one a Key Deer, a mourned pet, mark another sort of end. More on the bright side are the glittering objects salvaged from wrecked Spanish galleons by Mel Fisher, a treasure trove on display at his Gold Exhibit (10–6, adm.), while two commercial establishments which offer special attractions are Key West Aloe Perfume Factory (9:30–5:30, free), where you can tour the cosmetic laboratory, and Key West Handprint Fabrics (M.–Sat., 9:30–5:30; Sun., 11-4, free), with cloth printers working at sixty-yard-long tables on silk-screen designs. Between mid-January and late March Key West celebrates Old Island Days with a series of art shows, theater performances, food festivals and other events that enliven the town, while in mid-July the city hosts a Hemingway Days Festival, and the weekend closest to Halloween the rather raucous Fantasy Fest, featuring costumed revelers, takes place.

Key West is the end of the road but not the end of the line for travelers, as out at the scattered bits of land called the Dry Tortugas some seventy miles west of the city and reached only by air or by private boat lies massive Fort Jefferson, a redoubt built in the mid-nineteenth century. Federal troops occupied the fort during the Civil War, after which it housed prisoners, including Dr. Samuel Mudd, whose crime was to set the broken leg of John Wilkes Booth, Lincoln's assassin. Florida continues on even farther, out to Loggerhead Key, to the west, where a still functioning 1850s lighthouse stands watch over the remote waters. And here the state and the American South finally end at that dot of land far from the mainland and the mainstream, lost in the great and desolate sea.

Florida Practical Information

For tourist information: Florida Department of Commerce, Division of Tourism, Collins Building, Tallahassee, FL 32399, 904-487-1462. The state of Florida operates five Welcome Centers: at the state Capitol building in Tallahassee and, to the west, on Interstate 10 near Pensacola; to the north: entering from Alabama, highway 231, entering from Georgia Interstate 75 and Interstate 95. For information on Florida's hundred and five state parks: Department of Natural Resources, 3900 Commonwealth Boulevard, Tallahassee, FL 32399, 904-488-7326. For information on historical sites, Department of State, Division of Historical Resources, Gray Building, 500 South Bronough Street, Tallahassee, FL 32399, 904-487-2333.

For information on some of the main tourist areas: Pensacola, 904-434-1234; Tallahassee, 904-224-8116; Jacksonville, 904-353-0300; St. Augustine, 904-829-5681; Daytona, 904-255-0981; Orlando, 407-345-8882; Sarasota, 813-957-1877; Tampa, 813-228-7777; St. Petersburg, 813-821-4069; Fort Myers, 813-334-1133; Palm Beach, 407-655-3282; Miami, 305-573-4300; Key West, 305-294-2587; Walt Disney World, 407-824-4321.

Eighteen of the twenty-six major league baseball teams train in Florida every spring. On the west coast: the Chicago White Sox in Sarasota, the Toronto Blue Jays in Dunedin, the Philadelphia Phillies in Clearwater, the Pittsburgh Pirates in Bradenton, the St. Louis Cardinals in St. Petersburg, the Texas Rangers in Port Charlotte. In or near Orlando: the Boston Red Sox in Winter Haven, the Cincinnati Reds in Plant City, the Detroit Tigers in Lakeland, the Houston Astros in Kissimmee, the Minnesota Twins and the Kansas City Royals in Orlando. On the east coast: the Montreal Expos and the Atlanta Braves in West Palm Beach, the New York Mets in Port St. Lucie, the New York Yankees in Fort Lauderdale, the Baltimore Orioles in Miami, the Los Angeles Dodgers in Vero Beach.

IV

The Civil War South

6. Civil War Sites in the Atlantic South

Walt Whitman called the conflict "a strange sad war," and the Southerners labeled it the War Between the States and "The Lost Cause." By whatever name, the Civil War—in which more Americans lost their lives (620,000 dead, plus nearly 1.1 million casualties) than during the two World Wars combined—was no doubt the nation's most traumatic, tragic and fascinating episode. Hundreds of reminders of the great conflict, which included an estimated 10,000 military encounters, survive—battlefields, historic buildings, displays, monuments, cemeteries, geographic features and other places which recall the bloody war. The following compilation lists the main Civil War sites in the Atlantic South, and also includes some of the lesser known or more unusual such attractions.

Virginia

Alexandria

Boyhood Home of Robert E. Lee. In 1812 Lee's father, "Light Horse Harry" Lee, brought five year old Robert to this 1795 Federal-style town house where the young man lived until 1825 when he enrolled at West Point.

Christ Church. A silver plaque marks the pew where Lee worshiped. A marker also indicates the communion rail where he was confirmed. In the yard of the church, completed in 1773, Lee was asked to take command of the Army of Northern Virginia.

Fort Ward Museum and Historic Site. At the outbreak of the War, Washington found itself virtually defenseless. The Union began to build a series of earthwork forts known as the Defenses of Washington, and by 1865 a total of one hundred and sixty-two installations guarded the capital, by then one of the Western Hemisphere's most heavily fortified places. Fort Ward—armed with thirty-six guns mounted in five bastions—ranked as the fifth largest of the sixty-eight major Union forts which formed the Defenses network. The museum features a Civil War collection.

Alexandria National Cemetery. The burial ground includes the graves of more than 3,500 Union Soldiers.

Appomattox

Appomattox Court House National Historic Park. At the village the "Lost Cause" was finally lost by the South in April 1865 when Lee surrendered to Ulysses S. Grant. Among the buildings, restored to their 1865 appearance, are the Meeks General Store, the 1819 Clover Hill Tavern, and residences. The surrender took place at the now reconstructed house (the original residence was dismantled in 1893) owned by Wilmer McLean. During the first battle at Manassas—the War's initial major confrontation—a shell dropped down McLean's nearby farmhouse chimney, prompting him to vacate the property and move to Appomattox Court House. The War eventually caught up with McLean there, as Grant and Lee met in his living room for the surrender. According to tradition, McLean commented that "the war began in my front yard and ended in my parlor."

Arlington

Arlington House. For thirty years Lee occupied this magnificent mansion, built by his father-in-law between 1802 and 1818. In his second floor bedroom, on the night of April 19, 1861, Lee pondered his allegiances: for thirty-two years he had served as an officer of the United States Army, but for six generations his family had belonged to Virginia's landed gentry. The next day Lee resigned from the army. Two days later Lee left Arlington House to take command of Virginia's military forces, and never again did the Virginian return to his beloved mansion where he had lived for three decades.

Arlington National Cemetery. The Union army seized Lee's house and land, and in 1864 the North established on the residence grounds a cemetery for Union dead. The burial ground expanded to become the nation's largest national cemetery, with more than 100,000 graves.

Berkeley Plantation

Union general George McClellan headquartered here in the summer of 1862 during his Peninsular Campaign. President Lincoln visited the estate (where future President William Henry Harrison was born) to confer with McClellan. While stationed at Berkeley in 1862, General Daniel Butterfield composed the later famous bugle call "Taps."

Brandy

The Battle of Brandy Station, the largest cavalry battle in United States history, unfolded at a site now near U.S. highway 15 east of Culpeper. On June 9, 1863, Jeb Stuart's forces—protecting Lee's advance toward Gettysburg—engaged Union troops, an encounter during which Rooney Lee, General Lee's son, suffered wounds.

Buckingham

A mile east of town Lee occupied a tent on the night of April 12, 1865, after his surrender at Appomattox.

Charles City

Evelynton Plantation. In 1847 Edmund Ruffin, Jr., whose father fired the first shot of the War at Fort Sumter, South Carolina, bought the land where he built Evelynton Plantation. Skirmishes took place on the property during the 1862 Peninsular Campaign. Ruffin descendants own the current Georgian Revival-style manor house, built in the 1930s of 250 year old brick.

Charlottesville

A statue in Jackson Park depicts Confederate general Thomas "Stonewall" Jackson mounted on his horse, Little Sorrel, while a monument in Lee Park recalls Lee. The Confederate army established a military hospital in the University of Virginia Rotunda building.

Cumberland Gap

Cumberland Gap National Historic Park includes the famous mountain pass crossed by the Wilderness Road, the main route for westward migration. At the outbreak of the War, the South controlled the strategic Gap, then Union troops captured the pass but evacuated the area three months later. Northern forces later retook the Gap, which they controlled until the end of the War.

Danville

Danville Museum of Fine Arts and History. The museum occupies the Sutherlin House, an 1857 Italian-style villa where for one week, from April 3-10, 1865, Jefferson Davis and the Confederate government made their headquarters. The South's last cabinet meeting took place here on April 4. After the surrender at Appomattox, Davis left Danville and fled farther south.

Fredericksburg

The Fredericksburg and Spotsylvania National Military Park encompasses 8,000 acres where four major battles took place. The South lost some 35,000 men and the North twice as many during the encounters at Fredericksburg, Chancellorsville, the Wilderness and Spotsylvania Court House. The park includes a national cemetery and the house where "Stonewall" Jackson died after accidentally being shot by his own men at Chancellorsville.

Brompton. Now the residence of the president of Mary Washington College, the house perches above the city on Marye's Heights, a Confederate stronghold. The residence still bears signs of damage from two battles. Built in 1740, Brompton stands on land surveyed by George Washington, whose only sister was married to Fielding Lewis, owner of the property.

The National Bank of Fredericksburg. During the War banking operations were removed and the building served as Union headquarters. From the front steps Lincoln addressed soldiers and citizens in 1862. The 1820 structure, restored to its pre-War appearance, is perhaps the nation's oldest building continuously occupied by a bank.

Confederate Cemetery. Nearly 1,500 Southern troops repose at the burial ground.

Front Royal

Warren Rifles Confederate Museum. Items on display include Jackson, Lee and Davis memorabilia.

Warren Heritage Society. The house of Belle Boyd—

a Confederate spy who gathered information that helped
Jackson win the Battle of Fort Royal—contains a museum
which depicts life in the area during the War.

Gordonsville

The Exchange Hotel. Confederates used the Greek
Revival-style 1860 railroad hotel as a military hospital.
The restored building contains exhibits and antiques.

Hampton

Fort Monroe. Lee was assigned to the fort in 1831 to
serve as second in command of the detachment building
the facility, which was completed in 1834. Lee's personal
knowledge of the fort's strength deterred the Confederacy
from attacking the redoubt, which the Union occupied
during the War. The Casement Museum includes the cell
which held Jefferson Davis after the War. Displays recount
the fort's role in the War.

Fort Wood. The fort, started in 1819, occupies an
artificial island off the coast near Fort Monroe. Nearby,
the ironclad "Monitor" and "Merrimac" clashed on March
9, 1862, in the famous naval battle. Built on Long Island
and launched on January 30, 1862, the "Monitor" arrived
at Hampton Roads on March 8. When the "Merrimac"—
raised in June 1861 after being sunk, then rebuilt as an
ironclad vessel—advanced to attack the Union's "Minnesota," the "Monitor" tried to block the assault. This was
the first encounter between ironclad warships. After the
Confederates evacuated Norfolk on May 9, the "Merrimac's"
skipper sunk the ship; the "Monitor" was lost in a gale off
the coast of Cape Hatteras, North Carolina, on December
31, 1862. Lincoln observed an attempt to capture Norfolk
from an observation point at Fort Wood. Cruise boats
(804-727-1102) visit the area.

Harrisonburg

Warren-Sipe Museum. The museum houses a twelve foot high electronic relief map, occupying an entire wall and containing more than three hundred lights. Computer operated sequences indicate how Jackson's Valley Campaign unfolded. With less than 17,000 men, the Southern general kept 60,000 Union troops pinned down for twelve weeks.

Lincoln Family Cemetery. Four miles north of town the great-grandparents of Abraham Lincoln repose in the burial ground.

Hopewell

City Point. The peninsula lies at the confluence of the James and the Appomattox Rivers. A cabin built on the grounds of Appomattox Manor, the 1763 home of Dr. Richard Eppes, served as headquarters for Grant, where the general met with Lincoln. Grant's staff used the manor house from June 1864 to March 1865. A number of other surviving structures on the Point also figured in Civil War activities.

Leesburg

Ball's Bluff Civil War Battlefield. At the fourth armed engagement of the War, Confederate soldiers ambushed and killed forty-nine Federal troops. The area includes the nation's smallest national cemetery.

Lexington

Virginia Military Institute. Jackson served as a professor at the school from 1851 to 1861, when he entered the War. The VMI museum includes exhibits on military history from the Mexican War to the Vietnam conflict, with the Civil War featured. One relic is the bullet riddled raincoat Jackson wore when his men shot him by mistake at Chancellorsville.

Jackson House. The only residence Jackson ever owned, which he purchased in 1858, contains a large collection of his personal possessions.

Jackson Grave. Edward Valentine's statue depicts a solemn faced, bearded Jackson, left hand on a sword and right hand holding binoculars.

Washington and Lee University. After the War, Lee became president of Washington College, renamed Washington and Lee following his death in 1870. The Lee Chapel includes his office, the Valentine recumbent statue of the general, and Lee's tomb.

Lynchburg

Fort Early. On June 18, 1864, Confederate general Jubal A. Early repulsed a Union advance in the area. Union general David Hunter's staff included two future presidents: Rutherford B. Hayes and William McKinley. Early reposes at Spring Hill Cemetery in Lynchburg.

City Cemetery. A stone archway in the burial ground leads to the Confederate Cemetery, with 2,000 graves.

Monument Terrace. In the center of downtown a rise honoring soldiers of all wars includes a Confederate soldier bronze statue at the top of the terrace.

Riverside Park. In the park survives the hull of the packet boat "Marshall," the vessel which carried Jackson's body home to Lexington.

Manassas

Manassas National Battlefield Park. The War's first major battle unfolded here in mid-July 1861, while in late August 1862 Lee's victory at the Second Battle of Manassas opened the way for his invasion of the North. At the dedication of the red sandstone obelisk-like monument in the Confederate Cemetery, where 250 Southern soldiers repose, Lee's son, General W.H.F. Lee, delivered an address. The 5,000 acre park includes trails, viewpoints, explanatory signs and period buildings.

Manassas City Museum. The museum contains Civil War displays, artifacts, weapons and period photos.

Liberia. The 1825 Federal-style plantation manor east of town served from July to September 1861 as Confederate general P.G.T. Beauregard's headquarters. After the First Battle, Jefferson Davis visited the house and here the decision was made not to attack Washington. Liberia later served as headquarters for Union generals McDowell and Sickles, and Lincoln visited the estate. The mansion was perhaps the only house used as headquarters by both armies and visited by both presidents.

Manassas. Through the center of town ran the world's first military railroad, built by the Confederates in the winter of 1861. The track ran from the main line of the Orange and Alexandria (now Norfolk-Southern) to Centreville, six miles northeast, following in general the route of today's highway 28.

Middleburg

Red Fox Inn. Established in 1728 and now believed to be the nation's second oldest operating inn, the Red Fox contains equestrian sculpture and paintings. The building's horse history began during the War when Confederate general Jeb Stuart's cavalry detachment was based at the inn.

Middletown

Belle Grove. James Madison's brother-in-law, Isaac Hite, built this 1794 Federal-style limestone mansion, based in part on a design by Thomas Jefferson. Since 1783 the property has functioned as a working cattle and grain plantation. In the area unfolded the Battle of Cedar Creek, an October 1864 encounter begun when Jubal Early's forces attacked sleeping Union soldiers encamped around Belle Grove. Early's troops routed the Northerners in this early attack, but in the late afternoon General Philip Sheridan— who rode from Winchester through Middletown to the scene of the battle—rallied his men, and the Union forces proceeded to defeat the Confederates. This ensured Union control of the Shenandoah Valley, which remained under Northern domination for the rest of the War. On the attic walls of the house appear the names of Union soldiers.

McDowell

Sitlington's Hill. At the rise on the eastern edge of town occurred the Battle of McDowell, the first engagement of Jackson's Valley Campaign. The house where Jackson spent the night still survives.

Mount Jackson

Confederate Cemetery. This is supposedly the only burial ground in Virginia where solely Southern soldiers, and no Yankees, repose.

New Market Battlefield Historic Park

During the Battle of New Market on May 15, 1864, 247 teenage cadets from the Virginia Military Institute at Lexington fought under Confederate general John C. Breckinridge, former vice president of the United States. The Hall of Valor Museum, which presents two films and military exhibits, recalls the campaign and the War.

New Market Battlefield Military Museum. The museum contains displays on all American wars, from the Revolutionary era to the present. Included among the some 1,500 artifacts housed in the building, modeled after Lee's Arlington House, are Civil War items.

Newport News

War Memorial Museum of Virginia. A collection of more than 60,000 military history items includes Civil War displays.

Mariners Museum. Exhibits include Civil War nautical items and material on the famous battle between the ironclads "Monitor" and "Merrimac" in nearby waters. (See the entry for Fort Wood under Hampton.)

Newport News Park. Union trenches, Confederate gun positions and one of the three fortified dams built to create lakes on the Warwick River to block the Northern advance survive in the park.

Orange

St. Thomas Church. The church houses the original pew which Lee used during the winter of 1863. The only surviving example of Thomas Jefferson's church architecture, the 1830s sanctuary includes two Tiffany stained glass windows. While in the area, Lee's army camped on the grounds of Montebello, a mansion where the general and his staff were entertained.

Petersburg

Petersburg National Battlefield. Five rail lines radiated from Petersburg, making the city a key transportation nexus for the Confederacy. From June 1864 to April 1865 Grant mounted a siege which finally brought Petersburg under Union control, followed a week later by Lee's surrender at Appomattox. The siege was the War's longest and involved the conflict's largest battlefield, some 170 square miles. A crater 170 feet by 60 feet, created when Union troops exploded four tons of powder under Confederate positions, remains.

Siege Museum. The attractively proportioned Greek

Revival-style Exchange Building houses displays on the ten month siege, with an emphasis on the human side of the War.

Centre Hill Mansion. The house served as Union headquarters after the siege, and—more recently—as the setting for the film *Lincoln* by Gore Vidal.

Farmers Bank. The 1817 building contains a display of Civil War bank notes and the press that printed them.

Old Blandford Church. The 1735 sanctuary was restored in 1901 as a Confederate memorial to honor the 30,000 Southern soldiers buried on the grounds. The church, with fifteen Tiffany stained glass windows, is one of the world's five buildings in which every window was designed by Louis Comfort Tiffany.

Richmond

Museum and White House of the Confederacy. Jefferson Davis and his family occupied the 1818 classic style house from 1861 to 1865. The adjacent museum contains what is believed to be the largest collection of Confederate memorabilia in existence.

Capitol. The Virginia state house, designed by Jefferson, served as the capitol of the Confederacy. Statues and busts of Lee, Jackson and other Southern military heroes decorate the building.

Richmond National Battlefield Park. A nearly 100 mile route takes visitors to ten park units scattered around the city, featuring McClellan's 1862 Peninsular Campaign and Grant's 1864 attacks at Cold Harbor.

St. Paul's Church. Attending services at the church, Davis received word that Federal forces were preparing to invade Richmond.

Monument Avenue. Statues of Confederate leaders stand along the thoroughfare.

American Historical Foundation Museum. Artifacts

belonging to Confederate general Jeb Stuart are on display.

Valentine Museum. The studio of sculptor Edward Valentine contains statutes of Civil War figures.

Virginia Historical Society. The Battle Abbey facility contains extensive records, portraits, archives and artifacts relating to the War. The United Daughters of the Confederacy headquarters is located nearby.

Hollywood Cemetery. Davis, Stuart and other Southern leaders—as well as Presidents James Monroe and John Tyler—repose at the burial ground.

Leight Street Baptist Church. The 1854 Greek Revival-style sanctuary, a building of impressive simplicity, served as a Confederate hospital during the War.

Sailor's (also spelled Saylor's) Creek Battlefield Historical State Park

At the swampy bottomland along Sailor's Creek Lee's army suffered a crushing defeat on April 6, 1865, after fleeing from Petersburg and from Richmond, thirty-five miles northeast. Within three days of this encounter—the War's last major battle—Lee surrendered at Appomattox.

Staunton

The Oaks. Jed Hotchkiss, aide and mapmaker to Lee and Jackson, lived in this house, whose angular three story addition to the front he added in 1888. The Library of Congress contains Hotchkiss's Virginia campaign maps.

Virginia School for the Deaf and Blind. The 1846 Greek Revival-style structure, fronted by six thick columns, served as a hospital during the War.

Strasburg

Strasburg Museum. The former Southern Railway depot houses Civil War relics from area battlefields. During the War era the Manassas Gap Railroad, a spur of the Orange and Alexandria line, passed through Strasburg. When Federal forces blocked or destroyed the main line, Southern soldiers hauled locomotives cross country, then put them on the spur line at Strasburg so the equipment could be sent out to help the Confederate cause elsewhere.

Burnt Mills. Near where U.S. highway 11 crosses Cedar Creek north of town remain the ruins of two mills, the larger of them (nearest the road) destroyed by Sheridan during his devastating march through the Shenandoah Valley in 1864.

Fisher's Hill. On U.S. 11 two miles south of town rises the hill where Sheridan defeated Early on September 22, 1864.

Banks' Fort. The water tower on a hill west of the town center occupies the site of the fort built, starting May 1862, by Union general Nathaniel P. Banks to house his some 10,000 troops.

Stratford

Stratford Hall. Four generations of Lees lived at the 1730s Potomac River plantation, birthplace of Robert E. Lee (1807).

Warrenton

Warren Green Hotel. At the well preserved nineteenth century hostelry, now a county office building, McClellan delivered from the upper porch of the two story arcade his farewell address to officers when the general was relieved of the command of the Army of the Potomac.

Presbyterian and Baptist Churches. The churches on Main Street served as hospitals after both battles of Manassas.

Mosby House. At 173 Main stands the c. 1850 house

of Colonel John S. Mosby, who led raids on Warrenton when Federal troops occupied the town.

Williamsburg

College of William and Mary. At the College—90 per cent of whose student body joined the Confederate army—occurred some minor skirmishes. In September 1862 the Wren building suffered fire damage. The same month, Southerners captured thirty-three Union troops as they slept on the college lawn.

Winchester

"Stonewall" Jackson Headquarters Museum. The Confederate general lived in the 1854 Gothic Revival-style house the winter and spring of 1861-2 when he was planning the Shenandoah Valley campaign. The residence—built by Lieutenant Colonel Lewis T. Moore, great-grandfather of actress Mary Tyler Moore —contains a collection of Jackson items and his office, preserved as it appeared during the War.

National Cemetery. At the cemetery repose some 4,500 Union soldiers, killed during the five battles fought in and around Winchester, which changed hands more than seventy times during the War, once four times in a single day. A nearby Confederate cemetery contains the remains of 3,000 Southern troops.

Woodbridge

Leesylvania State Park, opened in 1989, includes remains of gun emplacements on the bluffs overlooking the Potomac. At the site "Light Horse Harry" Lee, father of Robert E. Lee, was born in 1756.

Yorktown

Confederate general J. Bankhead Magruder enlarged the area's 1781 Revolutionary War defenses to block McClellan's thrust up the peninsula toward Richmond. Near Jones Mill Pond survive remains from the 1862 Battle of Williamsburg, while along the James River remain several installations built to prevent the Union navy from advancing up the waterway.

North Carolina

Aberdeen

Bethesda Church. The 1790 sanctuary, near the Malcolm Blue Historical Farm, bears bullet holes from a War battle.

Atlantic Beach

Fort Macon State Park. The 365 acre park includes the fortress, begun in 1826 and completed eight years later, which North Carolina seized from the Federal government at the beginning of the War in 1861. A year later, on April 25, 1862, Union forces heavily bombarded the redoubt, which surrendered the next morning. With the fort's fall, Federal forces controlled the North Carolina coast from Beaufort north to the Virginia line. The North used the installation as a coaling station. After the War it served as a federal prison, and later remained abandoned from 1900 until transferred to North Carolina in 1924, when the area became a state park.

Averasboro

Averasboro Battlefield. At the battleground, near the

town of Dunn, occurred on March 16-17, 1865 the first organized resistance to Sherman's thrust into North Carolina. After his "march to the sea" through Georgia, Sherman sent his army of 60,000 men to invade the Carolinas in mid-January 1865. The battle at Averasboro was the prelude to the larger encounter, which took place March 19-25, at Bentonville (see below). Markers and maps around the Averasboro site recall the battle, whose dead repose in Chicora Cemetery. Lebanon, a plantation mansion on the field of battle, served as a hospital. Members of the same family have occupied Lebanon since the picturesque house—topped by a red tin roof and fronted with a two story gallery—was built in the 1840s.

Bentonville Battleground State Historic Site

Union trenches, a Confederate cemetery and the Harper House—furnished as a field hospital—recall the March 1865 battle between Sherman's army and General Joseph E. Johnston's forces, numbering less than half the Union's 60,000 men. The encounter proved to be the last full-scale Confederate offensive action of the War, as well as the only major attempt to defeat Sherman after his "march to the sea." Although the Confederates initially dominated the action, Union reinforcements eventually forced a retreat, followed on April 26 by Johnston's surrender to Sherman at Bennett Place near Durham (see the Durham entry).

Brunswick Town

In March 1862 the South built Fort Anderson (originally called Fort St. Philips), an activity which revived a settlement moribund for almost a century since the British burned the original town in 1776. Stone and brick salvaged from the burnt town served to build the barracks chimneys of the new fort, constructed to guard the river

route leading to Wilmington, an important Southern supply point. After heavy shelling the fort fell to Northern
forces on February 19, 1865, a month after nearby Fort
Fisher succumbed to Union troops.

Burlington

The **Southern General Bed and Breakfast** house
(919-226-9909) contains antiques and also portraits, books
and memorabilia pertaining to Jefferson Davis and Confederate generals. Each of the four guest rooms is based on
a theme connected with a Southern general.

Cape Hatteras

The Lighthouse. The present Cape Hatteras lighthouse, which dates from 1869-70, replaced the original
1803 tower located 600 feet north. After the Federal government established the Lighthouse Board in 1852, the
Board decided to raise the half-century old tower and to
install a newly invented Fresnel lens. Named for its French
inventor, the lens used a web of triangular prisms and
magnifying glasses to intensify the small oil wick flame
into a powerful beacon. During the War, Confederate forces
targeted the facility to deprive Union ships of the navigation aide. Union forces successfully defended the tower
during a series of skirmishes in 1861, but the Confederates
managed to capture and remove the Fresnel lens. The North
reactivated the beacon in 1862. After the War, authorities
decided it was cheaper to build a new facility than to
repair the damaged old lighthouse, which was eventually
dynamited and destroyed.

The "Monitor." The ironclad Union warship survived
its famous encounter with the "Merrimac" at Hampton Roads,
Virginia, in March 1862, only to succumb to a gale sixteen miles off the coast of Cape Hatteras where the "Monitor"
sank on December 31, 1862.

Cashiers

High Hampton Inn resort occupies property used as a summer home for nearly a century by the Hamptons, a prominent South Carolina family. Wade Hampton III served as a Confederate general and as the first governor of South Carolina after Reconstruction.

Chapel Hill

Presbyterian Manse. At the end of the War the house's occupant, Charles Phillips, professor of engineering and mathematics at the University of North Carolina, persuaded Federal troops to spare the school's buildings. The residence, 513 East Franklin Street, was built c.1850 by the Reverend William Mercer Green, who ranked number two in the class of 1818, second only to James K. Polk, future president of the United States.

Lloyd-Wiley House. Cotton mill owner Thomas Lloyd, who served with Lee at Appomattox, lived in the c.1850 house, 412 West Cameron.

Charlotte

Jackson House. "Stonewall" Jackson's wife lived at a house located at 834 West 5th Street during the War.

Mint Museum. The facility, which opened in 1837 as the nation's first branch mint, served during the War as Confederate headquarters and as a hospital.

Durham

Bennett Place State Historic Site. After the battles at Averasboro and Bentonville failed to stop Sherman's advance, Confederate general Joseph E. Johnston began on April 17, 1865, a series of three meetings with his adversary at the house of James and Nancy Bennitt (as the family spelled the name). At the first meeting Sherman showed Johnston a newly arrived telegram telling of Lincoln's assassination. The generals met again on April 18 and on April 26, when Johnston surrendered nearly 90,000 men in the Carolinas, Georgia and Florida, the largest single troop surrender of the War. In the 1960s the state constructed the present buildings based on the originals, which burned in 1924.

Duke Homestead. During the War soldiers stationed in the Durham area acquired a taste for the bright leaf tobacco cigarettes, a habit which inspired the post-War development of the North Carolina tobacco industry. About the same time as the Confederate surrender at Bennett Place, Washington Duke was released from a Union prison. Penniless, the farmer walked 135 miles to his property, which Federal troops had looted. Duke, then 45, started anew, growing tobacco and then processing it in a log cabin on the farm. So began what became the world's largest tobacco company—an outgrowth of the War—whose origins are recalled by the Duke Homestead.

Fayetteville

Arsenal House. In the closing days of the War Sherman marched into Fayetteville to destroy the Confederate Arsenal. Supposedly as a personal favor for one of his friends, Sherman spared the one story frame house (now the Arts Council office and gallery) across the street.

Cross Creek Cemetery. A Confederate monument commemorates soldiers buried in the graveyard.

Flat Rock

St. John Chapel. Buried at the sanctuary is C.C. Memminger, a banker from Charleston, South Carolina, who from 1861-4 served as the Confederacy's first Secretary of the Treasury. Lincoln biographer Carl Sandburg later occupied Memminger's nearby c.1838 summer house,

Connemara. George A. Trenholm, Confederate Treasury Secretary in the last year of the War, also owned a summer house in the area.

Forest City

A house built by James McArthur burned in the mid-1850s, leaving two standing chimneys which inspired the name of the village—Burnt Chimney. During the War the area around the chimneys served as the muster ground for the Burnt Chimney Volunteers, a unit of 125 men which entered the conflict on May 1, 1861. In the 1880s the town changed its name to Forest City.

Guilford College Station

Near the town was born in 1789 Levi Coffin, a leading figure in the Underground Railroad, the network of way-stations escaped slaves used to travel north to free territory.

High Point

Oakwood Cemetery. Confederate soldiers repose in the burial ground.

Jamestown

Mendenhall Plantation. An avidly anti-slavery Pennsylvania Quaker family arrived in the area in the early 1760s, and in 1811 the Mendenhalls started to build the plantation house. Family members served as leaders in the Manumission Society, which favored freeing of the slaves. Under restoration, the property recalls that not all Southern plantation owners supported slavery and the Confederate cause.

Kenansville

"The Liberty Cart." The historical pageant, held from mid-July to late August, includes Civil War scenes. On July 4, 1863, Federal forces destroyed a weapons factory near town which turned out Bowie knives, bayonets and other small arms.

Kinston

The Confederate States Ship "Neuse." In the fall of 1862 the Confederacy began construction on the Neuse River of the gunboat 'Neuse," one of the twenty-two ironclad ramming vessels built by the South. In March 1863 the ship arrived at Kinston for fitting with engines and other equipment. Low water prevented the craft's entry into the War, so the "Neuse" remained in Kinston. When Union forces advanced along the Neuse River toward Kinston in mid-March 1865 the Confederate commander scuttled the ship to keep it out of Northern hands. The "Neuse" remained under water for nearly a century until completion in 1963 of a local project to raise the relic. A visitor center, built to resemble the top of an ironclad, recounts the story of the C.S.S. "Neuse," now on display near where the ship was completed in 1864. The "Neuse" is one of only three recovered Civil War ironclads, the others being the C.S.S. "Jackson" at Columbus, Georgia, and the U.S.S. 'Cairo" at Vicksburg, Mississippi.

Kure Beach

Fort Fisher State Historic Site. As many as a thousand men labored to build this imposing fortress by the Cape Fear River. Until the last few months of the War, the redoubt served to keep the port of Wilmington open for blockade runners who brought supplies in for the Confederate forces. After the heaviest naval bombardment of the nineteenth century—some say to that time—Fort Fisher finally fell to Union forces on January 15, 1865. This severed the South's last supply line, followed about a month later by the evacuation of Wilmington, a key supply point. Displays at the visitor center relate the fort's story, while old earthwork fortifications recall the original installation.

Mocksville

On U.S. highway 64 two miles west of town lies the farm once owned by Daniel Boone. Hinton Rowan Helper grew up at the farm house on the property. Helper lived there until shortly before publishing *The Impending Crisis*, an anti-slavery book which inflamed Southern passions.

Murfreesboro

Rose Bower. Here lived Charles Henry Foster, who in 1859 arrived from Maine to become editor of *The Citizen*, a Union-sympathizing newspaper which so irritated locals that they forced the Yankee to leave town under the threat of lynching. Foster returned to Murfreesboro in 1863 as a Union Officer.

Wesleyan Female College. The original cornerstone of the 1853 building marks the site of the school, which Federal troops ransacked, destroying the library and many of the furnishings.

Harrell House. Tristram Capehart—member of the family which for many years occupied the early nineteenth century residence—advocated an African colony for blacks. Capehart freed sixty slaves so they could emigrate to Liberia.

Yeates-Vaughn House and Law Office. The office was supposedly built by Jesse Jackson Yeates, a Confederate army officer, three term United States Congressman, and grandson of Sarah Boone, Daniel Boone's sister.

New Bern

Charles Slover House. During the War General Ambrose Burnside occupied the brick 1847 townhouse. In 1908 the house was bought by C.D. Bradham, who invented "Brad's Drink," later renamed Pepsi Cola.

Attmore-Oliver House. The New Bern Historical Society occupies the c.1790 residence, which houses a Civil War Museum Room.

Cedar Grove Cemetery. A Confederate monument marks a mass grave in the venerable burial ground, established by Christ Church in 1800 and transferred to the city in 1853.

National Cemetery. The burial ground includes the graves of more than 3,500 Federal troops.

Pettigrew State Park

Near the park—named for area plantation owners—and Lake Phelps lies the Pettigrew family cemetery, where three generations of the clan repose. One family member, serving as a general in the Southern army, led the Confederate charge at Gettysburg.

Somerset Place. Located in the park and by Lake Phelps, the plantation house and out-buildings present a picture of the antebellum way of life. Three hundred slaves maintained the farm, which grew rice and, later, corn. In addition to the surviving structures, archeological work has unearthed the remains of a hospital, chapel and overseer's house.

Plymouth

Federal forces strung a chain across the Roanoke River to defend the city, captured by the Confederates in April 1864 after their armed ship "Albemarle" managed to float over the barrier. Wood from the pews and gallery of Grace

Episcopal Church in town served to make coffins for Confederate soldiers.

Raleigh

Mordecai Historic Park. In 1975 the city moved to the park the birthhouse of Andrew Johnson (1808), Lincoln's successor.

North Carolina Museum of History. The museum's more than 100,000 artifacts include War items.

Dorothea Dix Hospital. Opened in 1856 as an insane asylum, the hospital stands on wooded, rolling terrain once part of Theophilus Hunter, Sr.'s eighteenth century plantation. During the Union occupation of Raleigh, Federal troops frequented the grounds.

Oberlin Village. Former slaves established the area after the War. In 1868 the residents of the neighborhood organized a schools which pre-dated the advent of Raleigh public grade schools by seven years.

Century Post Office. The 1878 building was the first federal project in North Carolina after the War.

Oakwood Cemetery. After Union authorities confiscated the Rock Quarry Cemetery—now the National Cemetery—it became necessary to remove the remains of Southern troops from the burial ground. The Wake County Memorial Association supervised the transfer of 538 bodies to the new Confederate Cemetery, where more than 2,800 Southern soldiers now repose. The seven acre National Cemetery, established in 1866, includes the graves of 1,161 Union soldiers.

Reidsville

In the area Martha D. Martin married in 1847 Stephen A. Douglas, Lincoln's opponent and political adversary in Illinois. She reposes at the Settle family cemetery at Reidsville.

Salisbury

Confederate Monument. The monument dominates the entrance to the downtown area on West Innes Street.

Hall House. The 1820 residence belonged to Dr. Josephus Hall, who served as chief physician at Salisbury's Confederate prison. Stately oaks and boxwoods garnish the grounds of the house, which General George Stoneman, the Union commander, used as his headquarters after the War. Stoneman liberated Salisbury in April 1865, finding miserable conditions at the infamous prison, whose site remains.

Smithfield

Hastings House. The 1854 residence built by William Hastings, a landowner, farmer and merchant, served as a Confederate headquarters for General Joseph E. Johnston.

Boyette Slave House. This relic of the pre-War era is northeast of Smithfield, south of highway 222.

Near Smithfield, on April 12, 1865, Sherman's army celebrated Lee's surrender at Appomattox.

Tarboro

Town Commons. Boston, Massachusetts, and Tarboro boast the nation's only two remaining original town commons. At the six acre public ground, set aside by the town in 1760, stands a monument to Edgecomb County Confederate soldiers.

Topsail Island

Confederates used the area on the coast, south of present-day Marine Corps Camp Lejeune, as a salt source, processing the mineral from ocean waters. Union forces carried out frequent raids on the operation, destroying many of the salt works. During one raid in 1862 the gunboat

"Ellis" ran aground in the New River Inlet, at the north end of the island. Confederate forces attacked the ship, which the crew burned before fleeing.

Vance Birthplace

Fifteen miles northeast of Ashville lies the reconstructed birthhouse of Zebulon B. Vance, known as the "War Governor of the South." Vance served as governor of North Carolina and as United States Senator for three terms each. The five room log house and six log out-buildings recall the era when Vance rallied the people of North Carolina to the Southern cause. The state provided 125,000 men, one sixth of all Confederate soldiers, and lost more citizens in battle and from disease (a total of 40,000) than any other Southern state.

Warrenton

Bragg House. At the house lived three illustrious Bragg brothers—Confederate general Braxton B., for whom Fort Bragg, near Fayetteville, was named; Thomas B., from 1855-59 governor of North Carolina; and John, a United States Congressman. Their father built Emmanuel Episcopal Church, where on July 5, 1836, *New York Tribune* editor Horace Greeley married.

John White House. White served during the War as North Carolina commissioner to buy ships and supplies in England for the Confederacy. In 1870 Lee stayed at the house while visiting the grave of his daughter, Annie Carter Lee, who spent the early War years at an area resort and died in 1862 at age twenty-three.

Weaverville

Dry Ridge Inn. The facility, built in 1849 as the parsonage for the Salem Campground, a religious revival camping area established in 1832, served during the War as a hospital for Confederate soldiers suffering from pneumonia.

Wilmington

Orton Plantation. Established in 1725 as a rice plantation, the property includes Orton House, used by the Union in 1865 as a hospital. Although the house does not receive visitors, it can be seen from the adjacent gardens which are open to the public.

Poplar Grove Historic Plantation. The 1795 peanut plantation recalls the antebellum era and the way of life the South fought to preserve.

MacRae House. Henry Bacon, a one time Wilmington resident who designed the Lincoln Memorial, also designed this 1901 shingle-style residence, 15 South Third Street.

Oakdale Cemetery. Bacon reposes in the burial ground, which also contains the grave of Rose O'Neill Greenhow, who spied for the Confederacy and whose information supposedly prevented Southern forces from being surprised at the First Battle of Manassas in Virginia. The 1852 foliage-filled cemetery also contains a number of other Confederate graves.

Wilmington, the last Confederate Atlantic coast port to remain open to blockade runners, finally surrendered on February 22, 1865, after the fall of Fort Fisher (see Kure Beach). Federal forces spared the town, which thus retains its antebellum flavor.

Williamsboro

In the area of the town, seven miles north of Henderson, lived Varina Howell, Jefferson Davis's second wife.

South Carolina

Abbeville

Burt-Stark House. On May 2, 1865, Jefferson Davis presided at the South's War Council meeting, held at the house, at which the decision was made to disband the Confederate Army. The South thus ended its military effort in the so called "Birthplace of the Confederacy," the name given to Abbeville because the town hosted the first public gathering to consider secession. The assembly voted unanimously on November 22, 1860, that South Carolina should leave the Union.

Trinity Episcopal Church. The sanctuary served as a hospital during the War's final days. In the cemetery repose unknown soldiers killed in the conflict. John Alfred Calhoun, a signer of the Secession Ordinance, is buried here.

Beaufort

John Mark Verdier House. Union forces used the house as headquarters. Beaufort's surrender early in the War—in December 1861—prevented the town's destruction and preserved it as an antebellum enclave. From the front porch of the house the Marquis de Lafayette addressed the townspeople during his 1825 visit.

Maxey House. Also known as the Secession House, the 1813 residence served as the site where South Carolina's Secession Ordinance was written. South Carolina became the first state to secede from the Union, on December 20, 1860.

St. Helena Episcopal Church. The 1724 sanctuary served as a hospital during the War. Surgeons used tombstones, brought inside, as operating tables. Civil War figures repose in the church cemetery.

National Cemetery. The burial ground, established in 1863, includes the graves of 9,000 Union soldiers and 122 Confederates.

Beaufort College. The school, housed in an 1852 building at 800 Carteret, was plundered in 1861 by Union troops, who removed the institution's books and sent them north for sale at auction. Treasury Secretary Salmon P. Chase blocked the sale and the books ended up at the Smithsonian Institution, where most of them burned in a 1868 fire.

Bennetsville

Courthouse. On March 6, 1863 Sherman's forces occupied the Marlboro County courthouse.

Jennings-Brown House. The residence supposedly served as Union headquarters when Federal forces occupied the city.

Bluffton

Secession Oak. The site is where, in 1844, Congressman Robert Barnwell Rhett called for South Carolina to secede.

Boykin's Mill

At the area, nine miles south of Camden, General Edward R. Potter, commanding 2,700 Union troops assigned to destroy the railroad between Sumter and Camden, encountered a small Confederate force on April 19, 1865, in one of the War's last engagements.

Calhoun Mill

The village near Mt. Carmel took its name from the family of Southern statesman John C. Calhoun, born here in 1782. Located seven miles south of Abbeville, the property was settled in the 1750s by Calhoun's father, Patrick.

Camden

Confederate Generals Monument. The fountain includes six columns commemorating the six Southern generals from Camden.

Mulberry Plantation. Here grew up James Chestnut, Jr., a Confederate leader who served as a general and as an assistant to Jefferson Davis. His wife, Mary Boykin Chestnut, wrote a later famous Civil War diary.

Charleston

Fort Sumter National Monument. The War began April 12, 1861, with a Confederate artillery barrage on the outpost, located on a man-made island just off shore from Charleston.

Aiken-Rhett House. Governor William Aiken hosted Jefferson Davis at the 1817 house in 1863. The following year Confederate general P.G.T. Beauregard occupied the house as his headquarters.

Confederate Museum. The museum, established in 1898 by the Daughters of the Confederacy, is housed in the 1841 Market Hall, the main building of the old city market.

St. Philip's Episcopal Church. During the War the congregation donated the church bells—replaced only in 1976—to make cannons. John C. Calhoun is buried in the churchyard.

St. Michael's Episcopal Church. The church bells were melted during the War and sent to England for recasting.

First Scots Presbyterian Church. In 1863 the congregation voted to donate to the Confederacy the sanctuary's bells, never replaced.

Military Museum. The museum includes Civil War exhibits.

The Charleston Museum. The nation's oldest museum, established in 1773, houses Civil War displays.

Magnolia Cemetery. Many Confederate soldiers and South Carolina politicians repose in the graveyard.

Moultrie Tavern. The establishment serves plantation-style cuisine in a War-era ambiance which includes memorabilia of the time.

East Side. After the War more than 3,000 freed slaves, many of them craftsmen and artisans, settled in this neighborhood.

Drayton Hall. The only Ashley River plantation house to survive the War escaped destruction, supposedly because a Confederate officer brought in smallpox-infected slaves whose disease deterred enemy soldier from entering.

Middleton Place. Sherman's army ransacked and burned the 1755 mansion, but the nation's oldest landscaped garden (1741) survived. In the 1870s and the 1920s the family restored the south wing of the house.

Cheraw

St. David's Episcopal Church. The cemetery contains what is supposedly the nation's oldest monument to Confederate dead. It could not originally refer to Southern troops, as Union forces occupied the area at the time.

Merchant's Bank. The largest bank outside Charleston before the War was the last one to honor Confederate currency. The organization still operates as a bank, but now accepts no Dixie notes—only U.S. greenbacks.

The Lyceum. The 1825 building served as a telegraph and quartermaster's office during the war. It now houses a town museum.

Inglis-McIver Law Office. J.A. Inglis helped draft South Carolina's Ordinance of Secession.

Chesterfield

In 1865 Union forces burned the seat of Chesterfield County, the state's first county to call for secession. Citizens of the rebuilt town, now an attractive village, assert that the first secession meeting took place at the courthouse, an honor also claimed by Abbeville.

Clemson

Clemson University. The school occupies land given by Thomas G. Clemson, son-in-law of United States senator and vice president John C. Calhoun. On the campus stands the c.1807 Fort Hill, the mansion occupied by Calhoun and by Clemson, who bequeathed his plantation to the state for an agricultural college. The house contains antiques and family mementos.

Columbia

State House. The c. 1855 building bears on the outer western wall six bronze stars marking where Union cannons scored direct hits. The State House grounds contain Confederate monuments, while the interior houses portraits, plaques and statues, some relating to the War era.

Governor's Mansion. Union troops burned all buildings of the Arsenal Academy except the 1855 officers' quarters, later used as a residence for the governor.

University of South Carolina. The World War Memorial Building on the campus houses the Confederate Relic Room, a display of weapons, uniforms, flags and other War items. Federal troops used the area in front of Thomas Cooper Library as a parade ground during the North's military occupation of North Carolina. The soldiers' barracks occupied this and nearby squares. During the War, facilities of South Carolina College (as the school was then called) served as a Confederate hospital and as living quarters for Union soldiers.

Carolina Town House. Sherman established his headquarters here when Federal forces took control of Columbia February 17-19, 1865.

Hampton-Preston Mansion. Wade Hampton III, United States Senator, Confederate general and South Carolina's first post-War governor (1876-9), died at the house in 1902. He reposes in Trinity Episcopal Church, along with two other Wade Hamptons and War-era figures. During the War, one of Sherman's generals occupied the house.

Chestnut Cottage. Mary Boykin Chestnut, author of a later famous War-era diary, lived at the house, where on October 5, 1864, Jefferson Davis and his staff were entertained. From the steps the Confederate president addressed the townspeople.

First Baptist Church. The site of the December 1860 First Secession Convention survived, as Federal troops burned the original 1811 frame church on February 17, 1865, under the mistaken belief that it was there, rather than at the 1859 sanctuary, where the meeting had taken place.

South Carolina State Museum. The museum, which occupies a former textile mill, includes War exhibits.

South Carolina Department of Archives and History. Records as far back as 1731 include War documents. On sale is a facsimile of the state's Ordinance of Secession.

Millwood Plantation. Wade Hampton II built the mansion (before 1820) where Wade Hampton III grew up. Ruins of the historic property, burned by Union troops in 1865, can be seen only on tours offered the last Sunday of the month from March to November (803-252-7742).

West Columbia. On the Salude River stood a four story granite building, burned by Sherman on February 17, 1865, which housed the state's largest cotton factory, operated by slaves. On February 16, the day before entering Columbia, Sherman shelled the capital from batteries in the area of the Congaree River Bridge. The original wooden bridge was burned to delay Sherman's advance.

Darlington

St. James Church. Freedmen established the church in 1866.

Edgefield

Brooks House. In 1856 United States Congressman Preston Brooks—son of Whitfield Brooks, who built the house in 1815—attacked Senator Charles Sumner of Massachusetts with a cane after he had insulted Senator Andrew P. Butler, Brook's uncle. The incident inflamed public opinion and contributed to events which led to the War.

Holmewood. At the c.1820 house lived Francis Hugh Wardlaw, an author of the December 20, 1860, Ordinance of Secession, by which South Carolina became the first state to secede.

Willowbrook Cemetery. The burial ground includes the graves of 150 Confederate soldiers and the tombs of Preston Brooks and Francis Wardlaw.

Oakley Park. From the balcony of the 1835 mansion speakers incited "Red Shirts" to intimidate blacks from voting, so ensuring the election in 1876 of Wade Hampton III as governor. His victory ended the power of the Reconstructionists.

Mims Corner Store. Confederate general M.C. Butler established the store just after the War. Still in business, the emporium retains the flavor of the era.

Florence

Timrod Park. The memorial to Henry Timrod commemorates the so called Confederate poet laureate, who in 1859 taught at a one room schoolhouse in the area.

Florence was named by William Wallace Harllee, later a Confederate general, for his daughter. During the War, Confederates operated a disease-plagued prison camp in town.

Folly Beach

In 1862 the Confederate army, moving an arms depot from the area, loaded weapons on the steamer "Planter" for shipment elsewhere. Robert Smalls, one of the slave crew, navigated the ship into the hands of Federal forces. Smalls later served as a general and a United States Congressman. At Folly Beach, in the summer of 1934, lived George Gershwin and Dubose Hayward while collaborating on *Porgy and Bess*, the folk opera based on Hayward's novel *Porgy*.

Georgetown

Morgan-Ginsler House. The c.1825 residence served as a hospital for Union officers.

Rainey-Camlin House. Joseph H. Rainey, the first black elected to the United States House (1870), lived in the c.1760 residence.

Prince George Winyah Church. The cemetery includes graves of Confederate soldiers.

Graniteville

At the town operated the South's first cotton mill (1847), considered the place where the region's vast textile business began. Here, then, originated the industry based on the South's antebellum cotton culture and agriculture.

Hartsville

Jacob Kelley House. For two days in 1865 Sherman occupied the c.1820 residence west of town as his headquarters.

Hilton Head

About 13,000 Federal troops—supported by eighteen Union warships and some fifty-five smaller vessels—carried out the nation's largest naval invasion prior to World War II in a November 7, 1861 attack on Fort Walker. On the island the North established the main Atlantic south coast blockade base.

Lancaster

Lancaster Presbyterian Church. When Sherman's army occupied the town his troops stabled their horses in the church, the second oldest brick building in Lancaster County. At the cemetery reposes Dr. Robert Lafayette Crawford, a delegate to the secession convention and Confederate surgeon twice wounded in the War and then killed on April 20, 1863.

Laurens

Andrew Johnson, Lincoln's successor operated in the town a tailor shop with his brother, William.
Laurens City Cemetery. The burial ground contains graves of local War era figures.

Mount Pleasant

Christ Church. East of town stands the brick sanctuary whose interior Union troops destroyed in 1865.
Confederate Cemetery.

Orangeburg

A park now occupies the site of Orangeburg County's third courthouse, built in 1826 and destroyed by Union forces on February 12-13, 1865.

Edtido Gardens. Some 600 soldiers temporarily halted Sherman's advance at the Edisto River Bridge in February 1865. The defenders finally withdrew and retreated to Columbia.

Presbyterian Church. Union soldiers stabled horses in the church basement.

Pendleton

St. Paul's Church. In the churchyard reposes Bernard Elliott Bee, a West Point graduate and Confederate general who on July 21, 1861, at Manassas, Virginia, gave Thomas J. Jackson the nickname " Stonewall." Bee, who commanded a brigade of the Army of the Shenandoah, was mortally wounded the next day. Also buried here is Thomas Green Clemson (died 1888), a native of Philadelphia and one time United States Superintendent of Agriculture, who married John C. Calhoun's daughter, Anna, and later bought the Calhoun home, Fort Hill, at Clemson (see Clemson). The graves of Anna Calhoun Clemson and Mrs. John C. Calhoun are also here.

Pee Dee

Near the bridge over the Great Pee Dee River, about eight miles west of Marion, the Confederates operated a navy yard where in 1863 they built the wooden gunboat C.S.S. "Pee Dee."

Ridgeland

Pratt Memorial Library. The library includes a collection of Civil War items, as well as other artifacts and books.

Ridgeway

Century House. Confederate general P.G.T. Beauregard

made his headquarters at the house on February 17-19, 1865, while he waited to determine Sherman's line of March following the evacuation of Columbia. While here, Beauregard telegraphed Lee telling him that Columbia had been evacuated. Union troops arrived in Ridgeway on February 21.

Rivers Bridge State Park

In 1865 a Georgia Confederate colonel claimed he could defend his position at Rivers Bridge "until next Christmas." With fewer than 1,500 men he managed to delay 22,000 of Sherman's men for two days in early February. Union forces than crossed the Salkehatchie River and continued on to Columbia. Confederate breastwork fortifications remain to recall the encounter.

Rose Hill State Park

The park includes the restored 1832 plantation mansion of William Henry Gist, an ardent secessionist known as "the Secession Governor." His cousin, States Rights Gist, perished in the War.

Rock Hill

White House. The one time plantation house was used to care for Confederate soldiers during the War. A Confederate monument, removed to Laurelwood Cemetery, once stood in Confederate Park.

Stateburg

Church of the Holy Cross. At the 1850 church near town reposes Revolutionary War hero Thomas Sumter (died 1855), elected to the first United States Congress, whose name designates the Charleston fort where the War began. His name also designates a city and a county.

St. Helena

Penn Normal, Industrial and Agricultural School. The South's first school for freed slaves, established in 1862, occupied St. Helena Baptist Church.

Tombee. The oldest remaining house on the island belonged to Thomas B. Chaplin, whose War-era journal was published under the title *Tombee: Portrait of a Cotton Planter.*

The rather isolated island remains a self-contained enclave somewhat reminiscent of the post-War era. Descendants of rice plantation slaves continue the black culture which stems from the nineteenth century.

Sullivan's Island

Fort Moultrie. Before the War Sherman served as commanding officer at the fort, a federal military facility from the Revolutionary War until 1947. The present fort—completed in 1809 as the third on the site—now contains a museum relating to seacoast defenses.

Sumter

Battle of Dingle's Mill. At a site 1½ miles south of town on April 9, 1865—the day of Lee's surrender—occurred one of the War's last battles as 158 Southern soldiers managed to block for a few hours the advance of 2,700 Northern troops engaged in destroying area railroads. Sumter native George E. Haynesworth, a cadet at the Citadel in Charleston, fired the first shot on January 9, 1861, at the "Star of the West" in Charleston Harbor.

Winnsboro

Ebenezer A.R. Presbyterian Church. "The Old Brick Church," built in 1788 with bricks hand-molded by congregation members, suffered damage when Federal troops tore out the floors and pews to use rebuilding a bridge across the nearby Little River. On an inside wall of the church a Union soldier wrote an apology for the destruction.

York

Bratton House. At 8 Congress Street stood the 1820s house of Confederate army surgeon Dr. James Rufus Bratton, who bought the property in 1847. On the night of April 27, 1865, Jefferson Davis stayed at the house as he fled south to avoid capture by Federal troops following the fall of Richmond.

Thomas Dixon set his novel *The Clansman*, made into the movie *The Birth of a Nation*, in the York area, where the South Carolina Ku Klux Klan was supposedly founded.

Georgia

Andersonville National Historic Site

The 475 acre park recalls the largest Confederate prison, established in early 1864 after authorities decided to move captured Union soldiers from Richmond to a more secure location with better food supplies. During the camp's fourteen months of operation nearly 13,000 of the 55,000 Union captives there died. The visitors center houses exhibits on the War. The National Cemetery, established in July 1865, contains the graves of 13,669 Union troops, some reinterred there after removal from Confederate burial grounds elsewhere in Georgia.

Andersonville

Drummer Boy Civil War Museum. The museum in

town includes a collection of War memorabilia from the North and the South.

The village of Andersonville retains its nineteenth century flavor which recalls when the town served as a prisoner receiving point and as a supply center for the prison.

Athens

City Hall. On the grounds stands the 1862 double-barreled cannon designed to sweep a chain across the battlefield. The Athens Foundry, which cast the cannon, also fabricated the 1859 main gateway arch to the University of Georgia.

University of Georgia. Union soldiers camped on the grounds of the chapel, whose columns they used for target practice. The Ilah Dunlap Little Memorial Library collection includes whiskers snipped off Jefferson Davis's chin.

Taylor-Grady House. Henry Grady lived at the residence when he attended the University. A well known Southern moderate who helped heal the wounds of the War, Grady—known as the voice of the New South—edited the *Atlantic Constitution* from 1879 to 1889.

Atlanta

Cyclorama. The 1885 cylindrical canvas forms part of a multimedia show depicting the July 22, 1864, Battle of Atlanta. Sherman burned the city, a key Confederate rail center, destroying two-thirds of its houses and all of its commercial establishments. The state of Georgia lost three-quarters of its material wealth during the War.

Capitol. Flanking the plaza leading to the main entrance of the state house are metal markers, installed by the United Daughters of the Confederacy, recounting the "Siege of Atlanta," the "Evacuation of Atlanta," the "Battle of Ezra Church," and "The Transfer of Command." During the occupation of Atlanta in 1864, Federal troops camped on the Washington Street side of the capitol grounds, where on September 6, 1864, Union authorities ordered citizens to assemble for registration and eviction from the city.

Atlanta Historical Society. Walter McElreath Hall houses the exhibit "Atlanta and the War: 1861-65."

Georgia Department of Archives and History. The boxy windowless marble building houses a hand-carved mahogany staircase backed by glass windows depicting the rise and fall of the Confederacy. These originally embellished the 1903 castle-like Amos Rhodes residence, now headquarters of the Georgia Trust for Historic Preservation.

Fulton County Library. The downtown facility includes memorabilia of Margaret Mitchell, author of the 1936 War-era saga *Gone with the Wind*.

Oakland Cemetery. Mitchell reposes at the monument-filled Victorian-era cemetery, which also contains the graves of Confederate generals.

McPherson and Monument Avenues. A cannon monument marks the site where Union general James McPherson—who captured Decatur and led the fighting on the eastern side of Atlanta—was killed on July 22, 1864.

Augusta

Confederate Powderworks. The 1862 factory, supposedly the world's largest munitions plant, manufactured more than two million pounds of gunpowder. A 176 foot high obelisk-like chimney survives as what is supposedly the nation's only remaining Confederate-commissioned construction.

Confederate Monument. The 72 foot high marble shaft bears four lifesize statues of Southern generals, but above them stands the likeness of a lowly private, Berry

Greenwood Benson, a daring Southern sharpshooter. Local women raised nearly $20,000 for the monument, dedicated in 1878.

Old Slave Market Column. Only the pillar survives at the market, destroyed in 1878 by a cyclone—supposedly as the result of a curse put on the facility by an itinerant preacher.

St. Paul's Church. In the crypt beneath the altar lies the tomb of Leonidas K. Polk, known as the "fighting bishop of the Confederacy."

First Presbyterian Church. The sanctuary was used as a hospital during the War. In 1861 the General Assembly of the Presbyterian Church of the United States held its organizational meeting at the church, designed by Robert Mills, who also designed the Washington Monument.

Blakely

Courthouse Square. On the square stands the last remaining Confederate flagpole, erected in 1861.

Brunswick.

Hofwyl-Broadfield Plantation. This estate, north of town, remains as one of the few surviving pre-War coastal rice farms. The property, a typical "low-country plantation," recalls the antebellum agricultural way of life which the South fought to preserve.

Calhoun

Confederate Cemetery. The burial ground includes the graves of some 400 soldiers killed in the 1864 Battle of Resaca.

Cartersville

Cooper's Iron Works. A furnace survives as remnant

of the factory which supplied iron to the Confederacy. Sherman destroyed the facility in May 1864.

Stilesboro Academy. The 1859 building housed a sewing center where workers tailored items worn by Confederate soldiers. Students from the Academy served in the Southern army.

Depot. In May 1864 Southern soldiers barricaded themselves inside the building, then opened gunports by removing some of the depot's building blocks.

Roselawn Museum and Etowah Historic Museum. Exhibits at both collections include War items.

Etowah River Bridge. East of town, on the way to Allatoona Pass, survive pillars of the bridge burned by Confederate forces as they retreated on October 5, 1864.

Cassville

Confederate Cemetery. Among the 400 Southern soldiers buried here is General William T. Wofford.

Cave Spring

Baptist Church. The 1851 sanctuary includes a balcony where slaves sat during services.

Chickamauga and Chattanooga National Military Park

The Park, the nation's first (1895) and the largest such facility, includes in the Georgia portion a visitor center with a weapons collection, and a seven mile driving tour through the battlefield. A total of 34,000 Union and Confederate soldiers died during the late 1863 clashes. Sherman's victory opened the way for his devastating advance through Georgia on to the sea.

Gordon-Lee Mansion. The 1847 house served as a Union hospital in 1863.

Clinton

Battles swirled in and around the hamlet, where in November 1864 a unit of Sherman's forces, including 20,000 soldiers and 4,000 head of cattle, camped on the way to Savannah. About a dozen early nineteenth century houses which survived Sherman's destruction recall a pre-War Georgia rural county seat. Union cavalry general Judson Kilpatrick made his headquarters at the 1810 Parrish-Billue House. At the Iverson-Edge House lived the Iverson family, whose father and son both served as Confederate brigadier generals.

Columbus

Naval Museum. The museum houses hulls of the gunboats "Chattahoochee" and "Muscogee," raised from the Chattahoochee River a century after Southerners sank the vessels to prevent their capture.

Columbus Iron Works. Along the river stands the large former foundry, established in 1853, where the South manufactured cannons.

Fort Benning. The base was named in the late 1920s for the Columbus native Henry L. Benning, a Confederate general.

Dalton

Dug Gap Battle Park. The 2½ acre park includes some 1,200 feet of Confederate breastworks which helped Southerners successfully defend against Union forces ten times as numerous.

Blunt House. The 1848 residence served as a Union hospital in 1864.

Western and Atlantic Depot. The 1850 terminal housed a Confederate ordnance depot.

Confederate Cemetery. The burial ground has 421

Confederate and four Union graves.

Decatur

Decatur Cemetery. One grave belongs to Mary Gay, heroine of the Battle of Decatur and author of *Life in Dixie During the War.* An obelisk of Italian marble—imported during the War by Southern blockade runners—marks the grave of Charles Murphey, delegate to the Secession Convention. Murphey often stated he hoped he would not live to see Georgia secede. He died before the convention began, so Murphey's wish was granted.

Mason's Corner. Opposite Decatur Square to the northwest stood the house of Ezekiel Mason, where women gathered during the War to tailor uniforms for the Dekalb Light Infantry.

Depot. Although dating from 1891, the depot recalls that Decatur served as a way-station to Terminus, Atlanta's original name. The rail line, attracting Federal troops to the area to destroy the tracks, led to the Battle of Decatur.

High House. According to tradition, Sherman watered his horse from a well in the corner of the lot, where the residence stood on a slightly elevated point.

Eatonton

Uncle Remus Museum. The museum, which occupies a log cabin made from old slave houses, recalls the Southern stories and characters native son Joel Chandler Harris created. Exhibits give the flavor of the antebellum plantation way of life.

Fayetteville

Fife House. Believed to be the nation's only unaltered antebellum residence, the facility housed faculty and students of Fayetteville Academy, attended by Scarlett O'Hara of *Gone with the Wind.* The library in town named for the author Margaret Mitchell contains memorabilia relating to the novel as well as one of the South's largest collections of books on the War. The novelist did research for her famous War-era saga at the courthouse in nearby Jonesboro.

Fitzgerald

Blue and Grey Museum. The museum houses both Union and Confederate War memorabilia. This unusual mixture of displays from both sides originated because Union veterans established the Deep South town, settling here just after the War. At Fitzgerald lived General Jordan Bush, the last Georgia Confederate veteran, who died in 1952 at age 107.

Hinesville

Military Museum. The museum at Fort Stewart includes displays from the War.

Irwinville

Jefferson Davis Memorial Park. Federal troops captured the Confederate president here in May 1865.

Kingston

Confederate Cemetery. At the graveyard took place the first Confederate Memorial Day celebration, held April 1864. The burial ground includes the graves of 250 Confederate and four Union soldiers.

La Fayette

John B. Gordon Hall. In September 1863 Confederate general Braxton Bragg established his headquarters at the 1863 building, where he planned for the Chickamauga campaign.

Macon

Old Cannonball House. The name originated for the 1853 residence after a cannonball fired by General George Stoneman's forces bounced off a column, smashed through a window and landed in the main hallway. The servants quarters behind the house contains a Confederate Museum.

Woodruff House. At the 1830s mansion a ball was held for Winnie Davis, daughter of the Confederate president.

Madison

The antebellum city became known as "the town Sherman refused to burn," for the Northern commander spared the settlement on his march to the sea. Local residents and U.S. Senator Joshua Hill—who opposed Georgia's secession and had known Sherman in Washington—persuaded the Union forces not to burn Madison.

Marietta

Kennesaw Mountain National Battlefield Park. Cannons and earthworks recall the attempt to block Sherman's march to Atlanta in June 1864.

Big Shanty Museum. An old cotton gin houses "The General," a vintage steam engine stolen by Northerners in April 1862. They intended to head north and destroy Confederate supply lines, but the plan failed. The participants, however, received the first Congressional Medals of Honor awarded. Walt Disney's movie, *The Great Locomotive Chase*, featured the episode.

Confederate Cemetery. More than 3,000 Southern soldiers repose at the burial ground, established in 1863 for fatalities from a train wreck at Allatoona Pass.

National Cemetery. Established in 1866, the graveyard includes the tombs of 10,000 Union soldiers.

Battle of Gilgal Church. Original trenches at the twenty acre park recall the June 15-16, 1864, encounter.

Fair Oaks. Confederate general Johnston occupied the 1852 house as his headquarters during the Battle of Kennesaw Mountain.

Kennesaw House. The gang which stole "The General" met at the house the night before the escapade. On July 3, 1864, Sherman made his headquarters at the house.

Milledgeville

Old State Capitol. Now the administration building for the Georgia Military College, the facility recalls that the town served as the state capitol during the War years. The capital remained at Milledgeville from 1803 until 1868, when Atlanta became Georgia's seat of government. The reconstructed Old Governor's Mansion served as the residence for ten Georgia chief executives.

St. Stephen's Church. Union troops stabled horses in the sanctuary.

Newnan

Male Academy Museum. The museum, which occupies the 1833 boys' school building, includes War artifacts. During the conflict Newnan served as a medical center, with seven hospitals—which treated wounded of both sides—installed in churches and other buildings. Because of the town's medical facilities, Sherman spared Newnan, which contains a number of antebellum houses.

Oxford

The town has a Confederate cemetery.

Resaca

Confederate Cemetery. The burial ground originated when two young girls and two former slaves interred two dead soldiers in a flower garden. The girls' father, Colonel John Green, later donated the land for burial of Confederate troops.

Ringgold

Whitman House. During the 1863 Battle of Ringgold Gap, Grant occupied the house. He offered to pay for his stay in Yankee dollars, but the Whitman family refused the U.S. money. At Ringgold Gap, on May 7, 1864, Sherman began his campaign to take Atlanta.

Rome

Noble Machine Shop Lathe. The huge antique (1847) machine, installed by the train depot, bears scars inflicted by sledge hammers Union troops used to smash the equipment when they destroyed the Noble Iron Works, located by the Etowah River, in November 1864.

Myrtle Hill Cemetery. The enclave includes a monument to Confederate women who cared for the wounded, as well as a statue of General Nathan Bedford Forrest, who successfully defended Rome.

Oak Hill. During the May 1864 military encounters in the Rome area Union troops camped on the grounds of the plantation.

First Presbyterian Church. The 1849 sanctuary served as a hospital during the War.

St. Paul African-Methodist-Episcopal Church. Union troops stabled horses in the 1852 sanctuary.

Rosewell

Rosewell Manufacturing Company Mill. On Vickery

Creek remain ruins of the 1838 mill, burned by Sherman's forces in July 1864.

Rosewell Presbyterian Church. Union troops used the town's first church, built c.1840, as a hospital during the occupation in July 1864.

Bulloch Hall. The 1840 Greek Revival-style home where Theodore Roosevelt's mother and grandfather lived includes a room with War displays.

Chattahoochee River Bridge. Confederates burned the original covered bridge as they fled from General Garrard's advancing cavalry.

Sandersville

The last official business of the Confederate States Treasury was transacted in the town.

Savannah

Central of Georgia Depot. The War-era terminal, now housing the visitor center, includes displays of historic artifacts.

Green Meldrim House. The 1826 residence served in December 1864 as Sherman's headquarters at the end of his "march to the sea."

Fort Jackson. The installation, on the south bank of the Savannah River, saw service in the War of 1812 and the Civil War. Historical displays relate to Savannah and the coast.

Fort McAllister. The well preserved War redoubt twenty-two miles south of town defended against several naval attacks but finally fell to Sherman in December 1864. The museum contains artifacts.

Fort Pulaski. The installation, fifteen miles east of town, took eighteen years to build. Lee worked for a time as one of the engineers for the construction. On April 11, 1862, the newly developed rifled cannon for the first time defeated a masonry fortress, making such an installation obsolete.

Sea Island

At Hampton Plantation on the island lived in 1838-39 English actress Fanny Kemble, whose *Journal of a Residence on a Georgia Plantation*, published during the War, inspired anti-slavery sentiment in the North and in England.

Sparta

Hotel Lafayette. War refugees took shelter at the hottel in Sparta, a village east of Eatonton.

Christ Church. While occupying the church at Frederica, Union troops nearly destroyed the sanctuary, rebuilt in the 1880s.

Lighthouse. Confederate soldiers built Fort Brown at the site in 1861. The following year they evacuated the area, destroying the fort and the 75 foot high 1810 lighthouse. The present lighthouse was begun two years after the end of the War.

Stone Mountain

Lee, "Stonewall" Jackson and Jefferson Davis are depicted by huge relief carvings—made between 1923 and 1964—on the world's largest single granite mass. The images comprise the world's largest bas relief sculptures. The 3200 acre park also includes a Civil War museum.

Thomson

Depot. A statue of a female in front of the old depot honors Southern women who supported the Confederate cause.

Thomasville

Confederate Prison. A park now occupies the area which included the prison, recalled by a few ditches that formed part of the facility.

Varnell

Prater's Mill. In February 1864 six hundred Union soldiers camped at the 1855 three story grist mill, and two months later some 2,500 Confederate troops set up camp at the site, located east of the Chickamauga battlefield. To the southwest lies Tunnel Hill, a village with an 1849 railroad tunnel controlled by Union forces in February-March 1864 when Sherman headquartered nearby.

Washington

Robert Toombs House. At the residence lived the radical Confederate supporter known as the "Unreconstructed Rebel." Toombs, Confederate Secretary of State and rival of President Jefferson Davis, resigned and returned to his Washington house where he sulked and criticized Davis's conduct of the War. After hostilities ceased, Toombs refused to take an oath of allegiance to the United States, declaring: "I am not loyal to the existing government of the United States and do not wish to be suspected of loyalty."

Washington-Wilkes Historical Museum. Displays installed in the 1830s dwelling include Confederate memorabilia and a Confederate gun collection.

On May 5, 1865, a remnant of the Confederate cabinet met in Washington before dispersing.

Florida

Amelia Island

Fort Clinch State Park. At Florida's northernmost point, the tip of 13½ mile-long Amelia Island, stands Fort Clinch, built of French military-type brickwork. Both Southern and Northern troops occupied the fort during the War. On the first weekend of the month, costumed performers reenact War-era history.

Fernandina Beach. The area served as a slave smuggling point after the United States banned the importation of slaves. Union forces took control of the area in March 1862.

Apalachicola

Trinity Church. The bell of the 1830s church—one of the state's oldest—was melted to make Confederate cannon.

Cedar Key

Island Hotel. The hostelry—seemingly little changed from the War era—housed both Confederate and Union troops during the conflict.

De Funiak Springs

Confederate Monument. The 1871 monument on the courthouse lawn was Florida's first memorial commemorating Confederate soldiers.

Fort Jefferson

Out in the Dry Tortugas, some 70 miles west of Key West, lies the massive outpost, started in 1846 and built over the next thirty years. The government never completed the fort, intended to control navigation in the Gulf of Mexico, as the new rifled cannon—introduced during the War—made this type of installation obsolete (see the entry for Fort Pulaski under the Savannah, Georgia, listing). During the War Federal troops occupied the moat-surrounded, six sided fort, whose 40 million hand-made bricks form fifty foot high walls. The fortress, used as a prison for captured deserters, also held Dr. Samuel Mudd, who set the broken leg of Lincoln assassin John Wilkes Booth. Sentenced to lifetime hard labor, Mudd arrived in 1865 but was pardoned four years later for his work in treating yellow fever victims at the prison during the 1867 epidemic.

Gamble Plantation State Historic Site

The mid-1840s mansion, on the sixteen acre site, survives as the oldest house on Florida's west coast. Major Robert Gamble, Jr., built the residence, centerpiece of a 3,500 acre plantation which extended along the Manatee River and produced sugar, molasses, citrus, olives and wild grapes. In 1925 the mansion was designated the Judah P. Benjamin Confederate Memorial to commemorate the episode when the Confederate Secretary of State hid at the house as he fled from the country. As Benjamin escaped from Richmond on April 2, 1865, and headed south, Federal troops mounted a search for the Confederate cabinet member, who had also served as Attorney General and Secretary of War. On May 15 he crossed the Suwannee River in northern Florida, then arrived in the Gamble mansion area on the 20th. A $40,000 price on Benjamin's head brought searchers to the plantation, where he hid while friends chartered a boat for him. On May 23 Benjamin sailed from Sarasota Bay and made his way via Bimini, Nassau, Havana and St. Thomas to London, where he arrived on August 30.

Jacksonville

Kingsley Plantation State Historic Site. On Fort George Island survives the 1792 plantation house, furnished in pre-War style, and rows of dilapidated slave quarters which recall Zephariah Kingsley's business of importing, training and then re-selling slaves. Troops from both sides used Yellow Bluff Fort on Fort George Island, an earthwork on the north bank of the St. Johns River built by Confederates to supplement the batteries at St. Johns Bluff across the river, used by blockade runners during the War.

Mandarin. In 1867 Harriet Beecher Stowe, author of *Uncle Tom's Cabin*, moved to a winter cottage (12447 Mandarin Road) by the St. Johns River. The steamboat company, which ran vessels on the waterway, paid the writer a stipend to sit on her veranda as a tourist attraction when ships passed by.

Key West

Fort Zachery Taylor State Park. Union troops occupied the fort during the War. What is supposedly the nation's largest group of War cannons, as well as a small museum with artifacts and photos, recall the conflict. During the War Key West—supposedly the only Southern city which never flew the Confederate flag—prospered, as cargoes from nearly three hundred captured Confederate blockade-runners were auctioned in the city.

Lake City

Live Oak Cemetery. The burial ground includes the graves of one hundred fifty-one Confederate soldiers killed at the Battle of Olustee.

Madison

Confederate Memorial Park. The enclave which commemorates the Confederacy serves to remind locals that John C. Breckenridge, the Confederate War Secretary, spent a night in the town in 1865 as he fled from the country after Lee's surrender.

Marianna

Confederate Park. A monument commemorates the September 27, 1864,Battle of Marianna.

At Sylvania, north of town, lived War governor John Milton, a descendant of the English poet of that name. He committed suicide on April Fools Day 1865 shortly after stating in his last message to the legislature that "death would be preferable to reunion."

Torreya State Park. Located south of town, the park includes Confederate gun pits.

Natural Bridge Battlefield State Historic Site

On March 6, 1865,Confederate forces carried out a surprise attack and blocked Union troops—who wore hats labeled "To Tallahassee or Hell"—from advancing to the state capital. Southern soldiers included the "Cradle and Grave Company," so called as the unit consisted of young cadets from the West Florida Seminary (later Florida State University) and oldsters of the Gadsden County Grays, a home guards group.

Olustee Battlefield State Historic Site

On February 20, 1864, a Confederate victory blocked Federal troops from advancing into Florida, thus preventing the North from severing interior supply lines and confining Union forces to the coast. A museum recalls the War's biggest Florida battle, in which 10,000 soldiers participated.

Pensacola

Lee Square. In 1891 the town changed the name from Florida Square to honor the Confederate general. A fifty foot high monument contains a duplicate of the figure at an Alexandria, Virginia, monument.

Pensacola Historical Museum. The museum occupies Old Christ Church, the state's oldest remaining church building (1832), used by Union soldiers as a hospital, barracks, prison and military chapel.

Dorr House. Descendants of Maine native Eben Dorr built the house. Dorr branded the hand of a man named Jonathan Walker for stealing slaves, an incident John Greenleaf Whittier recounted in his poem, "The Branded Hand."

St. Michael's Cemetery. Dorr (died 1846) reposes in the burial ground, as does Stephen R. Mallory (died 1873), U.S. Senator and Secretary of the Navy for the Confederacy, who promoted the development of the ironside warship "Merrimac."

Lee House. A Confederate officer named William Franklin Lee, who lost an arm at the Battle of Chancellorsville, built the house in 1866. It was moved to its present site and restored by the Pensacola board of realtors for its office.

Tivoli High House. The reconstructed structure recalls the 1805 original, occupied by Union forces during the War.

Seville Square. The area was a popular riding place for Union soldiers.

Fort Pickens. Outside town are the remains of the 1834 installation, now part of the Gulf Islands National Seashore. In the opening days of the War the fort, on Santa Rosa Island, exchanged fire with the Confederate stronghold of Fort Barracas on the nearby mainland. According to some sources, the first shots of the War occurred here and not at Fort Sumter at Charleston, South Carolina. By May 1862 Southern forces were forced to evacuate the Pensacola area, which the Northerners then occupied. Fort Pickens was one of four forts in the South to remain under Union control throughout the War (the others in Florida were Fort Taylor at Key West and Fort Jefferson in the Gulf west of Key West).

San Marcos de Apalache State Museum

The 1679 Spanish-built fort was used by Spaniards and then British and French forces before the Confederates occupied the facility during the War. Exhibits at the museum recall the history of the fort, and a trail leads through Confederate earthworks.

St. Augustine

Castillo de San Marcos National Monument. Union forces controlled the fortress.

On June 2, 1865, St. Augustine native Edmund Kirby Smith surrendered at Galveston, Texas, the last Confederate force of the War. When Smith, a West Point graduate, died in 1893 he was the last surviving full general of either side.

Suwannee River State Park

This park contains the remains of a Confederate defensive installation.

Tallahassee

The Grove. From the front steps of the 1836 residence, built by two-time territorial governor Richard Keith Call, the moderate politician delivered a warning in January 1861, just after Florida had seceded, to Southern sympathizers gathered there: "Well, gentlemen, all I wish to say to you is that you have just opened the gates of hell."

White Springs

Stephen Foster Culture Center. A diorama and displays—including memorabilia and manuscripts of the composer—recall the War-era Southern-theme songs written by Foster.

Yulee Sugar Mill State Historic Site

In 1864 Union troops destroyed the sugar plantation, established in 1851 by David Levy Yulee, Florida's first U.S. Senator. Ruins of the operation—which supplied sugar to the Confederate army—remain.

Index